Machiavelli to Marx

Modern Western Political Thought

Machiavelli to Marx

Modern Western Political Thought

Dante Germino

The University of Chicago Press
Chicago and London

Originally published under the title *Modern
Western Political Thought: Machiavelli to
Marx*

The University of Chicago Press, Chicago 60637
The University of Chicago Press, Ltd., London

© 1972 by Dante Germino
All rights reserved. Published 1972
Phoenix Edition 1979
Printed in the United States of America

86 85 84 83 82 81 80   5432

ISBN: 0-226-28850-1
LCN: 77-181415

To
Helen
Ruskin
Laura
Renata
Monica

PREFACE

This book is about a few of the political thinkers who lived and wrote during what has come to be called the "modern" period of Western history. I have found these men worthy of study, and I believe that the light they cast on the human condition well repays the effort required to master their texts. That light, given the nature of things, can at best clarify only a part of our condition, for as Nicolai Hartmann once observed, being has only one side turned toward man. Nonetheless, one is grateful for what he receives; in the country of the blind, even the one-eyed man is king.

In sixteen years of teaching and writing about political theory, I have developed certain priorities in the study of modern political thought. This book reflects those priorities. They are not the only criteria that could be adopted, of course. A number of important writers inevitably must be omitted. But I believe my selection is defensible and I hope that this work will assist at least some students and teachers—or better, some younger and some more experienced students—in their study of modern political thought.

To begin with, I have not attempted to survey all the thought in this area, but have concentrated on those authors who made significant new approaches to the critical understanding of our world. I am quite deliberately omitting major consideration of ideas directly related to the everyday political struggle. This does not mean, of course, that I attach little importance to the study of public opinion and the popular literature of political life. It would be difficult to undervalue the pamphlet and other forms of journalistic literature dealing with current problems as they appear to the people who have to cope with them; we are all profoundly affected by the kinds of questions selected for discussion and by the resolutions of the debates over immediate issues in our time. But the study of political theory and philosophy has other concerns than the examination of literature conceived in the language and style of any particular political struggle. One of the advantages of studying less popular—because more theoretical and systematic—writings is that they help to bring into focus the assumptions and limitations of political journalism, whether of our own time or of an earlier period. Furthermore, it may be that with the spread of higher education and the development of increased political awareness and sophistication among a substantial segment of the rising generations of our own time, the gulf that has tended to separate works of serious political theory from those directly tied to an activist concern with politics may be narrowing significantly. Political philosophy may come to be more "popular" than it used to be, with the result that our political debates may become more self-conscious about basic assumptions—that is, more "theoretical." (There is also the danger that the narrowing of this gulf may corrupt political philosophy and transform it into propaganda.) Today's radical critics must have a theoretical basis for their negative conclusions about existing political and social arrangements if their criticism is to have lasting effect. The crisis of our day is of such proportions as to ensure that we shall continue to have radical critiques for an indefinite time to come. If these critiques are to have the cogency they need, and if liberals and conservatives who answer them are to be well informed about the issues they raise, a historical perspective is essential.

I have considerable sympathy for current demands for greater "relevance" in university and college curricula; if I were not convinced that the history of political theory has enormous relevance for the problems of our time, I would turn to some more rewarding line of inquiry. I have found that the many thoughtful and concerned students who do not at first relish the idea of "taking" a course in political theory also become convinced of the subject's importance after a period of study. The antitheoretical, "pragmatic" bias of our culture—some of which is healthy—at first discourages many students from pursuing philosophical kinds of inquiry. Leo Strauss has written that today Rome is burning; I agree with him, and I have no desire to encourage fiddling while the crisis lasts. This fire, however, must be fought with a serious effort to understand what can be saved, what can be built to replace what we do not save, and the consequences of our choices.

In the pages that follow I have attempted (1) to give substantial accounts of what the intellectual giants of the period from Machiavelli to Marx taught about politics; (2) to allow representatives of diverse political styles to speak for themselves about the advantages of their orientation; and (3) to indicate the degree to which these men were engaging in the perennial conversation of mankind. I have concentrated on relatively few authors, and have dealt mainly with what I take to be their major political works. I have deliberately given little emphasis to the historical contexts of their work, although I have mentioned these

considerations when they help to correct a widely accepted misinterpretation of a writer. In doing so I realize that I open myself to some of
the objections raised by Quentin Skinner in his article "Meaning and
Understanding in the History of Ideas" (*History and Theory*, 8, no. 1
[1969] : 3–53). Skinner asserts (on page 48) that "it must be a mistake
even to try either to write intellectual biographies concentrating on the
works of a given writer, or to write histories of ideas tracing the
morphology of a given concept over time."

Although I grant that Skinner has raised some questions that deserve
pondering, I am not convinced that he has said the last word on the
subject. When we study the history of political thought, are we not
justified in concentrating on the most influential works of political theory?
Is it not more important for the student of political theory to acquire a
sense of that high intellectual adventure which only a Hobbes or a
Rousseau can convey than to lose oneself in details of the author's career,
his personal relationships, the vicissitudes of his daily life, and so on? I
believe it is. We study the thought of the political giants, and I hope we
shall continue to study them, for their insight into the human condition.
Without the perceptions they can add to our intellectual imagination and
vision, our work in the history of political theory would be an arid thing,
especially difficult to justify when Rome is burning.

Inevitably, a historian of political thought is himself a political
thinker, and I am not so naive as to pretend that my own evaluations and
predilections do not reveal themselves here. Every reader is urged to
treat my evaluations critically. In the last analysis, one thinks as one
dies—alone. A man educates himself. No one can presume to make
evaluations for anyone else. The best I can do is to show others how one
finite being groping for meaning in existence came to evaluate a flow of
events within time, and to issue an invitation to join in the search. What
rescues us from an unbearable solipsism is the knowledge of our membership in a community of inquirers.

ACKNOWLEDGMENTS

In writing a book of this kind, one incurs extensive intellectual indebtedness. It is impossible to mention all of those from whom I have learned much and who have assisted me in various ways, but in particular I wish to thank Carl J. Friedrich, my former teacher at Harvard, from whom I have learned more political theory than from anyone else; John H. Hallowell, who introduced me to political theory as an undergraduate at Duke; Kenneth W. Thompson, whose constant interest in my work over the years has been an inspiration; Lucien A. Gregg, M.D., on whose staff in the Rockefeller Foundation's University Development Program in the Philippines it was my privilege to serve, and who did everything possible to forward my research, teaching, and writing; and Edward A. Kolodziej, who as chairman of the Department of Government and Foreign Affairs at the time of my arrival at the University of Virginia offered similar support and friendship.

From 1968 to 1970 I had the good fortune to be a member of the University of Virginia's Center for Advanced Studies. The major portion of the book was written during this period, and I wish to thank W. Dexter Whitehead, the director, and his unfailingly helpful staff, headed by the late Evelyn Beverley, for their support in this enterprise. Frances Lackey typed, retyped, and made numerous corrections in the entire manuscript; her expert eye has made this volume more readable than it would otherwise have been. In the Philippines, where the volume was begun in 1966, Pilar Basilio and Ching Castro of the local Rockefeller Foundation office staff typed an early version of the manuscript, and I am grateful for their faithful assistance.

Two persons at Rand McNally & Company have been particularly helpful: Lawrence J. Malley, manager and editor in chief of the College Department, and Barbara H. Salazar, editor in the same department. Mr. Malley's general supportive role in relation to the entire enterprise over the past five years and Mrs. Salazar's painstaking and informed editing of the final draft of the manuscript are alike deeply appreciated and gratefully acknowledged.

A good portion of the introductory chapter originally appeared in *New Literary History* (February 1970, pages 93–112), and Chapter 13 appeared in the *Journal of Politics* (November 1969, pages 885–912). Both articles, with minor changes, are included here by permission.

Quotations in English from Machiavelli's works are from Allan Gilbert, trans. and ed., *Machiavelli: Chief Works*, 3 volumes (Durham, N.C.: Duke University Press, 1965); quotations from Marx are from the translation by Loyd D. Easton and Kurt H. Guddat, *Writings of the Young Marx on Philosophy and Society* (New York: Doubleday, 1967). Both of these translations are used with the permission of their respective publishers.

I have received extensive comments that have helped to make this a better book from Paul Kress of the University of North Carolina and from my former colleague here at the University of Virginia, Alan Ritter, now of Indiana University. Alpheus Mason read the chapter on Locke and James Childress of the Department of Religious Studies, University of Virginia, reviewed the Reformation chapter. None of these helpful and perceptive reviewers, of course, is responsible for any errors of fact or judgment that may remain; these are mine alone.

Teaching is a reciprocal process, and I have learned much over the years from my students, undergraduate and graduate, at the University of Virginia, the University of the Philippines, and Wellesley College. I wish I could cite here all those students from whose association I have especially profited. They know, I believe, of my gratitude and friendship.

This book is dedicated to my children. In their critical aliveness, they help to point the way toward that newer world for which we hope. Writing this book has inevitably taken time away from our life together, but they have shown their customary understanding and indulgence toward their father's preoccupations. I would give them all the world if I could—and if they didn't seem to have it already. And so, in spite of all its imperfection, I offer them the best I can do.

D. G.

Park Hill
Charlottesville, Virginia
May 1971

CONTENTS

1

Introduction:
"Modernity" in the History of
Western Political Thought

Is it meaningful to speak of "modern political thought," and if so, on what grounds and with what qualifying observations? This is obviously a vast problem, and one can hope at best only to illustrate some of the difficulties involved and to offer some hints at their possible resolution.

The conventional periodization of political history assumes that a profound break in the continuity of Western political speculation occurred around 1500; this date presumably marks the beginning of "modern" as opposed to "premodern" political thought. One possible objection to this conventional periodization—or to any other periodization, for that matter—is that serious, comprehensive political theory is a branch of philosophy, and since philosophy, strictly speaking, is the love of wisdom, it cannot appropriately be compartmentalized into historical periods, like modes of transportation and English drama. The temporal location of a particular thinker is of only peripheral importance; we are interested primarily in whether a political teaching can sustain what it asserts when brought to the bar of reason and experience. From this point of view, political theory, conceived of as the critical inquiry into the first principles of politics, is a seamless web, and to divide it into modern and premodern phases is to act arbitrarily and conceivably to betray a bias for or against one group of writers or the other; and in philosophical inquiry any such bias is of course inadmissible. From this perspective, the decisive distinction is not between early and late political philosophy, but between political philosophy as such and non-philosophical modes of thought about politics.

There is much to be said for the argument that political philosophy is a unity, a continuing conversation about the ends of political existence and the nature of political reality. It is also true, however, that this very

1

concept of self-conscious and critical inquiry into the timeless (or universally "timely") first principles of politics emerged at a particular point in time in a particular civilization, the same civilization that has bequeathed to mankind the consciousness of existence itself as historical (as distinct from mythical and cosmological). A strong case can also be made, then, for Eric Voegelin's contention that "theory is bound by history," and for Hegel's observation that every man (including the philosopher) is a "son of his time."

POLITICAL PHILOSOPHY, POLITICAL THEORY, AND POLITICAL THOUGHT

Thus far I have employed three allied terms without sharply distinguishing them: political philosophy, political theory, and political thought. Political philosophy I shall take to be the most comprehensive, self-conscious mode of reflection developed and articulated by man in his attempt to understand his existence in community with his fellows. Political theory aspires to the same level of understanding and critical awareness as political philosophy, but it typically confines itself to the explicit elaboration of only one segment or dimension of man's political existence, and so only implicitly includes the comprehensive reflection of political philosophy proper. Political thought I take to mean any political discussion that is coherent enough to be seriously considered by serious minds.

In distinguishing these three terms we have moved from the specific and limited to the general: there are few political philosophers, a somewhat greater number of political theorists, and a vast number of political thinkers. All political philosophers are also political theorists in some area, but not all political theorists are political philosophers. Both political philosophers and political theorists are political thinkers, but by no means all political thinkers are either theorists or philosophers. They may be preachers, partisans, publicists, behavioral scientists, institutional analysts, ideologues, utopian dreamers, or wardheelers, but few of these are also political philosophers or theorists.

The Interrelationship of Philosophy and Culture

These distinctions raise the issue of the relationship of political philosophy and theory on the one hand and the general stream of relatively less reflective and self-conscious political thought on the other. Does a periodization that may be adequate to the evolution of political doctrines also apply to the tradition of inquiry known as political philosophy or theory? My own answer is a qualified yes, because political theories and philosophies develop in part as responses to the prevailing symbolizations and self-interpretations of the societies in which they arise. Yet to argue, as some proponents of the sociology of knowledge have done, that political philosophy is simply a reflection of the prevailing climate of opinion would be arbitrarily to ignore the important differences among levels of political thought. One would be on firmer ground to maintain that while political philosophy is inevitably influenced by the prevailing winds of opinion, its very nature—which is to be critical—compels it to be discriminating in its choice of ideas to absorb and transform.

Thus there is some basis for the view that, inasmuch as political philosophy is an inquiry into the perennial questions of political existence, it cannot be appropriately periodized; in this sense there is only political philosophy, and to speak of ancient, modern, seventeenth-century, French, German, or any other kind of political philosophy it to betray confusion. Nonetheless, we must not lose sight of the fact that political philosophy unfolds in time and thus has a history, or that the "timeless" questions with which it is concerned can never be completely free of temporal influences, since all men and their concerns are inevitably bound by the times in which they exist. Political philosophy develops in interreaction with nonphilosophical elements in the political culture. One of the tasks of the political philosopher is to examine critically the prevailing political ideas of the world in which he finds himself. Any examination of this sort would benefit from a periodization valid for political thought in general, since such a periodization would also cast light on the development of political philosophy as a particular mode of inquiry.

I trust I have made it clear that I dissociate myself both from an extreme historicism that leaves no room for the *philosophia perennis* and from an abstract rationalism that views philosophy as an activity conducted by some strangely disembodied creature occupying an Archimedean point outside history and the drama of existence.

PROBLEMS OF PERIODIZATION

All attempts at periodization must deal with two interrelated problems: (1) the boundaries of the period and (2) its unifying characteristics. Any periodization is open to the objection that it arbitrarily segmentalizes the historical process, which is in reality a continuous flow of events in time. If a particular periodization is to be justifiable, the historians who utilize it must be able to offer reasonable explanations for their choice of particular points in time to designate the "beginning" and "end" of an era, and to make clear in what respects the events between these points constitute a unity.

In defense of periodization as such, we must acknowledge that it is difficult to see how the historian could keep his subject manageable without it. In defining a period, the historian engages in an activity that Hegel described as *Nachdenken* (literally "thinking after," or "recollection"). He imposes an interpretive pattern upon the events he describes which those who had a hand in shaping them could not wholly have perceived at the time. In principle, there is nothing wrong with writing history in this way; in fact, as Michael Oakeshott has observed, history is precisely the attempt to "understand past conduct and happening in a manner in which they were never understood at the time."[1] In a similar vein, Oakeshott has also noted that history

> is "made" by nobody save the historian: to write history is the only way of making it. . . . The course of events is, then, the result not the material of history; or rather, it is at once material and result. And the course of events is not a mere series of successive events, but a world of co-existent events—events which co-exist in the mind of the historian.[2]

The Boundary Problem

Why accept the prevailing interpretation of modernity as beginning with the Renaissance and the Reformation? Conceivably this particular periodization could be nothing more than a historiographic cliché that has long since outlived its usefulness and deserves to be scrapped. It is certainly not for the lack of alternative suggestions that I opt for retaining what has come to be the conventional periodization. One eminent contemporary political theorist, Eric Voegelin, has suggested that a "suitable date" for the "formal beginning" of modernity "would be the activation of ancient gnosticism through Scotus Erigena in the ninth century, because his works . . . were a continuous influence in the underground gnostic sects before they came to the surface in the twelfth and thirteenth centuries."[3] Voegelin comes to this remarkable

---

1. Michael Oakeshott, "The Activity of Being an Historian," in *Historical Studies: Proceedings of the Second Irish Conference of Historians* (Dublin, 1958), p. 17.

2. Oakeshott, *Experience and Its Modes* (Cambridge: At the University Press, 1933, 1966), pp. 99–100.

3. Eric Voegelin, *The New Science of Politics: An Introduction* (Chicago: University of Chicago Press, 1952), p. 128. See also p. 133: "Conventionally, Western history is divided into periods with a formal incision around 1500, the later period being the modern phase of Western Society. If, however, modernity is defined as the growth of gnosticism, beginning perhaps as early as the ninth

conclusion as a result of his theory that "gnosticism"—a particular style of thought that he finds to be spiritually diseased—is the "essence of modernity." Other writers of note would have modernity's boundaries moved forward in time. J. B. Bury, the historian of the idea of progress, insists that "in the realm of knowledge and thought, modern history begins in the seventeenth century."[4] In his famous study of the perils of abstract ideological thinking, *The Rebel*, Albert Camus called the French Revolution the true beginning of modern times, at least as far as political thought is concerned, for he held that the French Revolution launched the radical secularization of the Christian rectilinear concept of history which constituted the basis for a cast of mind that he called "political messianism."[5] Although J. L. Talmon does not equate this intellectual orientation with modernity, his own studies of the phenomenon of political messianism, conducted independently, systematically reinforce Camus's interpretation.[6] When we take into account earlier political writers preoccupied with periodization, such as Giuseppe Mazzini and Auguste Comte, we see the boundaries of modernity shift even farther forward in time. Both of these writers held that it was only in the nineteenth century (conveniently coinciding with their own appearance on the scene) that modernity truly began. Comte and Mazzini maintained that the French Revolution closed out premodern times; a new era of progress, order, association, and science had begun in their day.[7] In fact, in surveying the literature of modern political thought one encounters a multiplicity of opinions regarding the bounda-

---

century, it becomes a process within Western Society extending deeply into its medieval period." Voegelin's position is discussed in further detail later in this chapter.

4. J. B. Bury, *The Idea of Progress* (New York: Dover Publications, 1955), p. 64. "Ubiquitous rebellion against tradition, a new standard of clear and precise thought ... a flow of mathematical and physical discoveries so rapid that ten years added more to the sum of knowledge than all that had been added since the days of Archimedes, the introduction of organized co-operation to increase knowledge ... characterise the opening of a new era" (ibid.).

5. See the interesting discussion in Richard H. Cox, "Ideology, History, and Political Philosophy: Camus' *L'homme révolté*," *Social Research*, 2, no. 1 (Spring 1965): 71–97, especially pp. 78–79.

6. J. L. Talmon, *Political Messianism: The Romantic Phase* (London: Secker & Warburg, 1960).

7. See Mazzini's essay "Thoughts on the French Revolution of 1789," in *The Duties of Man and Other Essays* (London: Everyman's, 1907), p. 265. Comte thought in terms of the three historical stages (theological, metaphysical, and scientific). For him the French Revolution represented the last gasp of individualistic, destructive "metaphysical" speculation and was to be followed by a new "organic," "positive," and "scientific" age in which Comtean "positivism" would be the reigning intellectual orthodoxy.

ries of modernity. It is worth noting, however, that Hegel, the most gifted and profound philosopher of history to appear in the nineteenth century, did consider that modern times began with Luther and the Protestant Reformation.

Faced with this kind of evidence, then, the contemporary historian conceivably might prefer to avoid the concept of modernity altogether, and limit himself to discussing periods more easily delineated and defined, such as the Renaissance, the Reformation, the age of the baroque, the Enlightenment, the romantic reaction, the age of ideology.

Diversity of opinion need not lead us to abandon the search for modernity, however. One argument in favor of the conventional periodization, which dates the inception of modernity from the Renaissance, is that the idea of a modern age, as opposed to ancient and medieval ages, originated in the Italian Renaissance itself. It was the historian Flavio Biondo (1392–1463) who first described the millennium from the fall of Rome in 410 to the year 1410 as a "closed age of the past."[8]

The Boundary Problem in Relation to the Unity Problem

Biondo's conception of his own period as the beginning of a new historical epoch raises the question of how much weight the contemporary historian should give to men's interpretations of the times in which they live as he attempts to arrive at his own interpretation of the period. Perhaps Oakeshott's characterization of the historian's task should be amended, at least with respect to intellectual history. The historian of political thought deals with the writings of men who possessed an unusual capacity for self-awareness, who reflected in a highly self-conscious fashion on the human predicament as it was manifested in the particular problems of their times. The intellectual historian must not only attempt to understand past events "in a manner in which they were never understood at the time"; he must also be concerned with these events as they appeared to the people who took part in them. Without the perspective of the historian writing after the fact, a period cannot be grasped in its wholeness; but if the historian neglects the perspectives of the participants, he is likely to miss much of the significance of the events he seeks to interpret. Thus, for the interpreters of political thought, the paradigmatic interpretation of a period—rarely if ever fully achieved, but always to be striven for—results from the synthesis of retrospective detachment and concurrent, self-conscious involvement

---

8. On Biondo, see Voegelin, *New Science of Politics*, pp. 133–34, and Denys Hay, "Flavio Biondo and the Middle Ages," *Proceedings of the British Academy*, 45 (1963): 117. Biondo was the author of the *Decades*, a history of the millennium from 410 to 1410, later designated the *medium aevum*.

in the mind of the historian. Only by such an act of conceptual synthesis can the intellectual unity of a period be clearly understood.[9]

With these considerations in mind, we may accept as valid Mircea Eliade's characterization of the "modern world" as a "certain state of mind which has been formed by successive deposits ever since the Renaissance and the Reformation."[10] This succinct formulation has the virtue of emphasizing both the unity and the diversity of the modern period. Instead of assuming the substantive intellectual homogeneity of the period, Eliade represents modernity as an amalgam of elements that are highly diverse yet which nonetheless can be seen to form an intelligible unity from the vantage point of the contemporary historian.

The problem, then, is to find a way of characterizing the unity of outlook that binds a multiplicity of thinkers together. Eliade goes on to define modern societies as "those which have pushed the secularization of life and the Cosmos far enough."[11] If not confused with a militant and narrow "secularism," secularization in the broad sense can be readily accepted as the end product of modernity; but when we remember the need for dual perspectives in the mind of the historian, we can immediately observe that by no means all those who have engaged in the shaping of modern consciousness intended any such result as secularization, even broadly defined. The secularization of life and the cosmos was certainly far from the minds of the Reformation thinkers, although this great religious movement of the sixteenth century indirectly contributed a great deal to the process.

The modern age in political thought, then, tends to base its interpretations of political life primarily on man's temporal or personal needs and concerns. In terms of categories I have employed elsewhere,[12] this period is characterized by the increasing dominance of anthropocentric forms of political speculation, as opposed to theocentric modes. Questions related to man's relationship to a transcendent divine being are set aside or relegated to the private, "nonpolitical" sphere by an ever increasing number of significant political thinkers. This does not necessarily mean that the experience of transcendence or the authenticity of religious experience as such is explicitly denied, or if it is denied, as

9. Hegel's dialectical concept of the concept (*Begriff*) has some utility, even though his dialectic as such is obscure and unusable as a method of coming to grips with intellectual history.

10. Mircea Eliade, *Myths, Dreams, and Mysteries: The Encounter Between Contemporary Faiths and Archaic Realities* (New York: Harper & Row, 1960), p. 25n.

11. Ibid., p. 28.

12. See my *Beyond Ideology: The Revival of Political Theory* (New York: Harper & Row, 1967), chap. 2.

it was by Bakunin and Marx, that it is truly repressed. I am myself convinced that the spirit of openness essential to a valid humanism is capable of asserting itself in religious, nonreligious, and even anti-religious modes of thought.

Clearly there is a shift of emphasis in modern political thought from the transcendent to the immanent, from the divine to the human, from being to becoming, from eternity to time. Even if we maintain the validity of explicitly theocentric speculative forms, this shift can scarcely be condemned as a derailment of political philosophy. Being and transcendence need not disappear as a result of the process of secularization, but may appear in different forms. Anthropocentric and metastatic forms of humanism contain rich and valuable insights, and constitute an enduring part of man's continuing attempt to discover meaning in his existence. Yet if theocentric orientations and philosophies explicitly grounded in the experience of transcendence do not simply disappear as modern political thought develops, they do assume minority status, despite the fact that the West is still rather widely assumed to be "Christian."

From the viewpoint of the leading participants in the events with which modern political thought is concerned, rather than from our own perspective as we look back over the period, are there any traits that unite these participants, giving all of them, despite the real diversity among them, a common outlook that can be designated as modern? I believe there are two such unifying characteristics: a sense of existing in a new historical era and a heightened appreciation of the seriousness of the world's business. For purposes of brevity, let us designate these shared thought patterns as (1) a consciousness of novelty and (2) a predilection for active involvement in the world.

NOVELTY AND ACTIVISM

The leading thinkers of the period repeatedly professed an awareness that they were living in a new age, which required the development of new symbols and concepts for its comprehension and illumination. Thus Machiavelli wrote of charting a "new way not yet traveled by anyone"; both Luther and Bodin propounded concepts related to temporal government which they claimed could be found nowhere in the political thought of the past; Hobbes modestly insisted that "civil philosophy" was "no older" than his book *De cive;* Vico entitled his major work *The New Science;* and a long line of writers—Condorcet, Comte, Mazzini, Marx—presented themselves as harbingers of a new age of enlightenment and progress about to dawn for mankind. The conscious quest for novelty—for new political symbols, styles, and orientations—comprises a large part of the story of modern political thought. This basic restlessness accounts for much of the creativity and intellectual vitality of the period. Since serious political thought influences events as well as being influenced by them, this intellectual restlessness also helps to account for the period's numerous institutional upheavals and crises, which have occurred on a scale and with a frequency hitherto unknown.

The awareness of participating in a new era in the development of the human spirit did not necessarily carry with it a belief in the idea of inevitable and illimitable progress in history. The idea of progress in this sense does not appear and gain wide acceptance until the French Enlightenment of the eighteenth century. But when the awareness of living in a new age was coupled with a heightened appreciation of personal fulfillment in the world—in contrast to the cloistered life of the observantine monastic orders or the secluded, "self-sufficient" existence of the contemplative philosopher—the ground was prepared for the later emergence of the conception of history as progress. While Renaissance humanists such as Petrarch, Lorenzo Valla, and Erasmus sought to purify the life of the spirit, other humanists such as Coluccio Salutati and Leonardo Bruni were turning their classical learning to the service of their city-states; and while Luther and Calvin insisted repeatedly that worldly activity was meaningless or vicious unless it were engaged in for the greater glory of God and in hope of eternal salvation by God's grace, they were at the same time involving themselves and their followers in the political affairs on which their very existence depended. Thus thinkers of both the Renaissance and the Reformation were calling Western man to a sense of responsibility for himself and his world, and thereby paving the way for an activist, dynamic, and secularized society. As Ernst Troeltsch points out in *Protestantism and Progress*, there were tendencies in Protestantism "drawing it toward the modern world," and these tendencies originated in the thought of Luther and Calvin themselves.[13] Philipp Melanchthon, Luther's most able lieutenant, praised the "worldly works" of God, such as service in "government, courts, and wars," as superior to the "glamour of ceremonies and monkery," provided that knowledge of the gospel and faith in Christ were present in the minds and hearts of those who engaged in them.[14]

In stressing the activist predilection of modern political thought,

---

13. Ernst Troeltsch, *Protestantism and Progress* (Boston: Beacon Press, 1958), p. 92.

14. Philipp Melanchthon, *On Christian Doctrine* (*Loci communes,* 1555), trans, and ed. Clyde L. Manschreck (New York: Oxford University Press, 1965), p. 331. God requires not sacrifices and "soft works," but "improvement in living, justice in the courts, and protection of widows and orphans" (ibid.).

I do not mean to contend, as some critics do, that modern political thinkers have assured the triumph of a civilization based on vulgar materialism, absolute temporalism, and opposition to the life of the spirit. Concern for the quality and style of an authentically human existence persists in all but the most philistine of the period's political writers. We are dealing for the most part with men of sensitivity, breadth of vision, and compassion. If we read his books with care, we find that even so "worldly" a writer as Machiavelli, who clearly ranks as one of the initiators of the modern period, was concerned with the life of the spirit. In his little-known *Exhortation to Repentance* he echoes a theme of other humanists more noted for religious concern: that when man repents of his sins, the genuineness of his repentance is more evident in concrete acts of service to his fellows than in fasting and mortification of the flesh. In his *Discourses* Machiavelli explicitly condemns those who have interpreted Christianity "according to sloth rather than to vigor."

Opposition to any other-worldly interpretation of the life of the spirit is characteristic of all leading political thinkers in the modern period. For all their differences, Hobbes, Locke, Rousseau, Hegel, Marx, and Nietzsche, as well as a host of writers of the second rank, share the conviction that the spirit properly manifests itself in activity directed toward the concerns of this world.

We may therefore conclude that when the consciousness of novelty is combined with a pronounced shift of orientation toward activity in the world—that is, with the *vita activa* as opposed to the *vita contemplativa* given priority in classical and Christian political philosophy—the result is a distinctive intellectual and spiritual phenomenon identifiable as the modern spirit or political consciousness.

MONISTIC INTERPRETATIONS OF MODERNITY

Although the evidence clearly permits and even requires us to speak of a modern period in the history of political thought, I see no virtue in adopting any of the monistic substantive interpretations of that period which have been offered either recently or in the more distant past. Modernity as such is to be neither extolled nor condemned by the historian of political thought. At the substantive level—the level of experiences of order and of the meaning of an authentically human existence—the modern age displays a rich diversity of insights that together make a formidable contribution to man's self-knowledge. At the same time, modernity also reveals unresolved tensions and contradictions that require clarification if we are to understand and cope with the problems it has brought to us. Aside from the broad tendencies toward activism in public and private concerns, it is doubtful that any discernible spiritual or intellectual homogeneity characterizes the history of political thought from the sixteenth century—or any of the later benchmarks—until today. The nature of the period is distorted when any one strand of modern political thought is given such emphasis that it is permitted to define the whole.

Monistic interpretations of modernity may be either negative or affirmative. Affirmative monistic interpretations typically see the period as one of continual advance for the human spirit; in other words, they tend to adopt one or another version of the idea of progress. Most negative monistic interpretations arose as reactions to the easy victory of fascism in Italy, the horrors of nazism in Germany, and the degeneration of the October Revolution into Stalinism in Russia. In thus rejecting the idea of progress, however, those who have taken the negative path may have erred in the opposite direction and embraced an unnecessarily pessimistic—and equally monistic—interpretation of the modern period. Three leading contemporary political philosophers who portray modernity in such unflattering relief are Bertrand de Jouvenel, Leo Strauss, and Eric Voegelin.

Bertrand de Jouvenel

According to Jouvenel, Western political thought has been dominated since 1500 by a "hedonist and productivist" outlook that has profoundly antihumanistic implications. The contemporary historian can discern that Western consciousness has been moving toward the creation of a civilization today identifiable as the "modern world, which is the apotheosis of the *libido* in all its forms," a world that "takes pride in its capacity to satisfy ever more fully all desires . . . and where political systems aspire only to achieve the same objective: to dispense satisfactions more fully."[15]

Leo Strauss

Leo Strauss is also convinced that political thought in the modern era displays a particular kind of substantive intellectual unity. He unfailingly opposes "ancient" to "modern" philosophy, attributing to modern political philosophers a consistent line of attack against the "Great

---

15. Bertrand de Jouvenel, "Essai sur la politique de Rousseau," in his edition of Rousseau, *Du contrat social* (Geneva: Cheval Ailé, 1947), pp. 25–26. Martin Heidegger makes essentially the same point when, in his "Letter on Humanism," he describes contemporary "Russia and America" as "the same."

Tradition" of premodern thought. Strauss labels this attack, mounted by Machiavelli, Hobbes, Locke, Rousseau, Hegel, Marx, Nietzsche, and others, as the "modern project," according to which

> philosophy or science was no longer to be understood as essentially contemplative and proud but as active and charitable; it was to be in the service of the relief of man's estate; it was to be cultivated for the sake of human power; it was to enable man to become the master and owner of nature through the intellectual conquest of nature. Philosophy or science should make possible progress toward ever greater prosperity . . . [which] would thus become, or render possible, the progress toward ever greater freedom and justice.[16]

For Strauss, the contrast between "ancient" and "modern" philosophy, and therefore also political philosophy, is decisive:

> The quarrel between the ancients and the moderns seems to us to be more fundamental than either the quarrel between Plato and Aristotle or that between Kant and Hegel.
> . . . Only in the light of the quarrel between the ancients and the moderns can modernity be understood. By rediscovering the urgency of this quarrel we return to the origins of modernity.[17]

For Strauss, modern political philosophy is a reaction to ancient political philosophy, the result of a direct confrontation with political reality itself. By drawing a sharp distinction between the ancients and the moderns, he clears the way for an attack on the contemporary preference for modern political philosophy. He admits that to seek today simply to imitate classical political philosophy would be neither feasible nor desirable, since new situations call for fresh approaches to things political; but he sees a return to the premodern classics as a necessary precondition of the elaboration of a political philosophy relevant to contemporary problems.

There is no question that for Strauss modernity as such constitutes a retrogression in the history of thought, and that the results of modern civilization, far from being justified by any "idealism," are profoundly inimical to human freedom and dignity. Modern political thought, particularly as it is expounded by its most eminent theorists, virtually eliminates standards of excellence, blurs the distinction between just and unjust regimes so central to premodern thought, and destroys the philosopher's critical perspective vis-à-vis his own society or any other

---

16. Leo Strauss, *The City and Man* (Chicago: Rand McNally, 1964), pp. 3–4.

17. Strauss, "Jerusalem and Athens," *Commentary*, 43 (June 1967): 55, and *What Is Political Philosophy? and Other Studies* (Glencoe, Ill.: Free Press, 1959), p. 172.

that might conceivably replace it. Modern thought makes impossible the Socratic position and any radical questioning based upon it. At the same time it imprudently helps to sweep away religious restraints on unvirtuous conduct among the majority of ordinary people (people who are not philosophers, and thus need such restraints) by either overtly or covertly teaching atheism. Further, modern thought at first weakens (through the subjective "natural rights" doctrines) and later destroys (through "historicism") the premodern teaching that there exists an objective moral order knowable by reason—that is, that there is a "right by nature."

While there is much that is thoughtful and worthy of serious consideration in Strauss's interpretation, it is highly doubtful that modern political philosophers have been so self-consciously and consistently revolutionary as he depicts them, or that they have engaged in a carefully premeditated or willfully blind assault on the basic tenets of premodern teaching. Machiavelli, for example, sought that fresh, immediate contact with reality to which Plato aspired, and was like the Socrates of Plato's dialogues in at least one respect, his belief in questioning everything. While modernity is a distinct and identifiable phase within the "great conversation" of Western political thought, it does not represent so abrupt a break with the speculation of previous ages as Strauss would have us believe. The leading modern thinkers, like their distinguished predecessors, have been questing spirits, and their teachings do not possess that monolithic consistency which Strauss—albeit with great learning and ingenuity—discovers in their works.[18]

Eric Voegelin

Eric Voegelin also finds a fundamental homogeneity in the intellectual substance of modern political thought, despite its apparent diversity. In his *New Science of Politics* he adopted the highly controversial position that "gnosticism" is the "essence of modernity," and he has reiterated this idea in more recent writings.[19] Gnosticism, of course, is a school of thought that was originally held to be a Christian heresy, but more recent scholarship has demonstrated that it originated independently of Christianity and approximately contemporaneously with it. The early gnostics were gripped by a desire to escape from the existing

18. For further discussion of Strauss's works, see Victor Gourevitch, "Philosophy and Politics I," *Review of Metaphysics*, 22 (September 1968), and "Philosophy and Politics II," ibid. (December 1968); Dante Germino, *Beyond Ideology*, chap. 7, and "Second Thoughts on Leo Strauss's Machiavelli," *Journal of Politics*, 28 (August 1966): 794–817.

19. See in particular Voegelin, *Science, Politics, and Gnosticism* (Chicago: Henry Regnery, 1968).

world, which they condemned as the emanation of an evil demiurge. Only by acquiring a privileged kind of knowledge (*gnosis*) could they liberate themselves from the confines of the world of the flesh and become new, "spiritual" ("pneumatic") men. The inherent uncertainty and limitations of the human condition prove too much for some men to bear; all varieties of gnosticism, ancient and modern, are attempts to allay man's existential anxiety by creating a "second reality" or dream world in which he can find release from his fundamental (and in truth irremediable) unease.

Gnostic forms of thought claim to have bridged the chasm between the human and the divine. In place of a valid conception of man's existence in "uncertain truth," such as we find in Greek philosophy, Judaism, and Christianity, the gnostic intellectual offers the "certain untruth" of ideology and a bogus eternity within time. According to Voegelin, following its revival by Johannes Scotus Erigena in the ninth century, the gnostic symbolic form manifested itself in the millennarian movements of the later Middle Ages (Joachim of Fiore is the key figure in this development), the radical sects of the Reformation, and increasingly secular movements in the later modern period. The "system" constructions of Hobbes and Spinoza, Enlightenment progressivism, Hegelian idealism, Marxist communism, Nazi racism, and various types of militant secular ideologies are all related to each other, whatever their apparent contradictions, as more or less perverted types of gnostic speculation. Modern material progress is purchased at the price of the "death of the spirit."[20] Thus, for Voegelin, modern political thought is spiritually diseased at its core. The only hope of avoiding disaster lies in recognizing the gravity of the crisis and elaborating a political philosophy based on the insights of Plato and Aristotle, and on the basic common sense of much of Anglo-American political thought.

A summary as bald as this scarcely does justice to the subtlety of Voegelin's analysis. The detailed critiques of modern political thinkers that he and Strauss have produced from different yet related perspectives are of considerable value in provoking the kind of self-

---

20. "The death of the spirit is the price of progress" (Voegelin, *New Science of Politics*, p. 131). Voegelin's concept of gnosticism is too broad and amorphous to be usable in the analysis of modern political thought. Furthermore, to portray the antihuman and totalitarian Nazi regime as an intellectual and spiritual outgrowth of modernity as such is to overstate the case, since its intellectual content can be much more precisely traced to the pernicious biologism and racist thinking of one specific school of writers, of whom Gobineau and Houston Chamberlain are best known. Nor are all "Third World" symbolizations in modern political thought substantively or functionally equivalent.

examination demanded of a critical science of politics. Although I have no wish to denigrate in any way the impressive achievements of these scholars, I am nonetheless convinced that their judgments of the modern period in the history of political thought are overly sweeping and unsympathetic. Critical reflection on politics did not cease with the advent of modernity, and such thinkers as Hobbes, Locke, Rousseau, Hegel, and Marx have cast so much light on so many aspects of man's existential condition that we must be grateful for their contributions to the continuing conversation begun by the Greek philosophers over two thousand years ago. Since they were men and not gods, they were fallible and limited in their perspectives; but to regard their thought as spiritually diseased and a product of the systematic deflection of the intellect from its proper course runs dangerously close to the kind of dogmatism that Voegelin and Strauss themselves reject as inimical to philosophical inquiry. With due appreciation for their immense learning and insight, we must push beyond the critiques of these gifted interpreters if we are to attain a critical understanding of modern political thought.

THREE TYPES OF HUMANISM

In *Beyond Ideology* I spoke of three types of humanism in the development of Western political thought: theocentric, anthropocentric, and messianic. While I continue to find these distinctions helpful in bringing some conceptual order out of what might otherwise seem a bewildering succession of political ideas, I think now that a few modifications may make them more helpful still.

Theocentric Humanism

By theocentric (literally "God-centered") humanism, I mean the conception of man found in the Western political tradition that extends from Plato ("God is the measure of all things") and Aristotle through Stoicism to Christianity. Of course, there are significant differences among Greek philosophy, Stoicism, and the Judeo-Christian tradition, but all theocentric humanists are in agreement that the divine ground of being is the source of order for men and societies, and that the good man is he whose soul is open to attunement with this world-transcendent source. The highest good (*t'agathon kai to ariston,* or *summum bonum*) is not worldly dominion, but an inward disposition that flows from the right ordering of the inclinations of the psyche. Justice or righteousness, whether for the individual or for society, is more important than power, wealth, glory, or even freedom.

Anthropocentric Humanism

The term anthropocentric humanism, originally suggested by Jacques Maritain, has its origins in the dictum of Protagoras, one of the "great four" among the Greek Sophists, that "man is the measure of all things." Anthropocentric humanism views man's needs and aspirations in this world as primary for any political inquiry. Typical proponents of this position in the modern period are Machiavelli, Hobbes, and Locke. Although anthropocentric humanists seldom explicitly reject the position of theocentric writers, their key concepts are secular and naturalistic by comparison. Modern liberalism, with its stress on human rights, individual liberty, and man's capacity for autonomy, is a prime example of anthropocentric humanistic political thought.

Messianic Humanism

What I have called messianic humanism is that strand of political thought which seeks to transform the quality of man's existence, to transcend the limitations and inequities of the human historical situation as it has hitherto been experienced and make a fundamentally new beginning. Earlier, in common with Eric Voegelin, J. L. Talmon, and Norman Cohn, I tended to see messianic humanism as at least indirectly contributing to the growth of twentieth-century totalitarian regimes. In doing so I have perhaps overstressed the extent to which messianic humanists seek to overthrow any idea of limitation on human action.

I am now convinced that totalitarian government, insofar as it ruthlessly and deliberately seeks to destroy individuals in the interest of the social system—some by forceful subjugation, and others, defined as "undesirable" by the ideology, by administrative massacre—is a product of a number of factors probably quite unrelated to this third type of humanism. It now makes little sense to me to link Marx, Saint-Simon, and Fourier, for example, to twentieth-century totalitarianism, however indirectly.

In *Beyond Ideology* I suggested that whereas theocentric humanists call for a "change of heart" (*metanoia*) or attitude toward existence, messianic humanists envisage the qualitative transformation (*metastasis*) of existence—a goal, I then believed, that lies completely beyond the pale of possibility. I no longer see such a sharp contrast between *metanoia* and *metastasis*. Messianic or metastatic humanists are also concerned with the inner conversion of men; they are simply more optimistic than the theocentric humanists about man's ability to liberate himself and his fellows through planned political reorganization. While

I continue to be disturbed by the possibility that this benevolent impulse toward radical improvement of humanity's lot might be transformed into a kind of manipulation and social engineering that would only make further inroads on individual freedom and dignity, it now seems to me that many of the proponents of messianic humanism were and are also sensible of these dangers, and as determined as I to combat them. I also find it reasonable to conclude that there is much authentic realism in the radical position, and unreasonable to assume that messianic humanists are *ipso facto* extremists or advocates of nihilism and terror. (This is a matter to which I shall return in the last chapter.)

The Betrayal of Humanism

In *Beyond Ideology* I did not bring out so forcefully as I might have the fact that all three types of political thought are varieties of the same current of thought: Western humanism. None of the three has a monopoly of insight and compassion. Each has a perspective on the human condition and a caveat for the supporters of the other positions.

Furthermore, all varieties of humanism are separated from the kind of "hatred for the human in man" which Ernst Nolte found to have consumed Hitler and which was the basis for the National Socialist and Italian Fascist regimes.[21] As Hannah Arendt has indicated, the second great colonial expansion of the western European powers after 1880 was accompanied by the development of a racist consciousness that was a betrayal of the humanism fundamental to the Western intellectual tradition.[22] We shall be dealing in this book with writers who affirm and support, rather than deny and oppose, that which is human in man. Some of them are more helpful than others in answering the haunting question posed by Frantz Fanon in *The Wretched of the Earth:* Why is it that the West speaks so eloquently of man and so often behaves so brutally toward individual men, especially men who differ from its own majority in skin color and physiognomy? (This proclivity is hardly confined to the West, of course, but we all have our blind spots, and Fanon at least has a good excuse for his; and it is with the West that we are concerned.) Yet virtually all of the writers discussed here would agree that in spite of everything, the gulf between aspiration and practice can and must be enormously narrowed.

---

21. Ernst Nolte, *Three Faces of Fascism* (New York: Holt, 1966), pp. 425f. Nolte speaks of a "resistance to transcendence" by fascist leaders and intellectuals. See also Carl J. Friedrich, "The Changing Theory and Practice of Totalitarianism," in *Il Politico* (Pavia, 1968), pp. 59–60.

22. Hannah Arendt, *The Origins of Totalitarianism* (New York: Harcourt, Brace, 1951), especially chap. 7, "Race and Bureaucracy," pp. 184–221.

HAVE WE REACHED THE END OF "MODERNITY"?

Some years ago the German philosopher Romano Guardini published a volume entitled *Das Ende der Neuzeit* (The End of Modernity), in which, after sketching the contours of the ancient, medieval, and modern world views as he saw them, he concluded that the modern world view is today in an advanced state of dissolution. According to Guardini, a new epoch, still unnamed, is emerging, and present indications are that it will be marked by a lack of confidence in the beneficence of nature and the capability of the physical world to fulfill human aspirations. To postmodern man, the winning of the world seems a less attainable or desirable goal than it did to men of the modern period.[23]

Evidence on Guardini's proposition is inconclusive; presumably future historians, who will have the advantage of hindsight on the events in which we are caught up today, will be able to cope with this question better than we can. Nevertheless, serious contemporary writers, and their less intellectual fellows as well, do indeed give indications of a rather profound disenchantment with the two key tenets of modern political thought, that man is living in an age excitingly different from any that existed prior to the Renaissance and that by his own psychic and physical energies he can and should fulfill his human potential in this world. This discontent with the promise and prospect of the world is particularly evident in the radical protest movements within the so-called affluent societies of western Europe and North America; but it is not only here that one sees signs that the political creeds of the immediate past no longer stir the majority of their followers as they once did. Everywhere the inherited labels of "left" and "right" are increasingly irrelevant to the political forces of contemporary modernized societies.

We cannot know whether the current malaise indicates only a temporary flagging of the modern spirit, which can be expected to reassert itself against its time of troubles and recover its enthusiasm for the active life of this world. There are some indications that what F. S. C. Northrop styled rather optimistically the "meeting of East and West," coupled with widespread dissatisfaction with at least some of the fruits of modern industrial society, may eventually produce a new style of thought that places renewed emphasis on the contemplative and aesthetic dimensions of experience, with the goal of attaining some measure of inner serenity in a world of flux. And yet the same encounter of East

---

23. Romano Guardini, *Das Ende der Neuzeit: Ein Versuch zur Orientierung* (Basel: Hess Verlag, 1950).

and West that is belatedly broadening the Western intellectual horizon to include at least some familiarity with the great nonwestern religions and mythical speculations is also confronting the "developed" nations with the responsibility of assisting materially impoverished societies to achieve their own version of modernization. The frequency with which we encounter the terms "modernize" and "modernization" reveals that, in the face of the monumental practical problems of increasing the food supply, improving health services, and facing up to the whole complex of problems brought on by unprecedented population increases, the activist spirit will indefinitely continue to have a *raison d'être*. From the interchange of cultural styles and norms between East and West it is not utopian to foresee the possible emergence of a postmodern age in which both the unity and the diversity of mankind will receive their due recognition in the domain of political thought and life. Over such hopes and possibilities hangs the terrible threat of nuclear and other forms of annihilation, a threat that goes far toward explaining why the celebration of a new world to be won no longer evokes the response it once did.

Can a more decent and humane world arise from the ashes of the twentieth century? I suspect that our best hope for an affirmative answer lies in the present and coming generations of questioning young people, and in those youthful in spirit among the older generations.

2

Machiavelli

"With such a name, there is no need for eulogy." This is the epitaph (in Latin) inscribed upon Niccolò Machiavelli's tomb in the Church of Santa Croce in his native Florence. This recognition was a long time coming, however. In fact, it was only with the achievement of Italian independence and unification in the 1860s that Machiavelli fully came into his own in Italy. Although he acquired some fame as a writer during his lifetime (largely because of his play *Mandragola,* a popular rustic comedy), his posthumously published *The Prince* and *Discourses on the First Ten Books of Titus Livius* earned him at first only a reputation for unparalleled infamy. The legend of "Machiavellianism" began in Italy and France; twenty to thirty years after his death the papacy moved to ban all writings of the "atheist Machiavel." In England, Cardinal Reginald Pole blamed Machiavelli for the church's difficulties with Henry VIII. According to Pole, the successful design of Thomas Cromwell, Henry's principal secretary, to wrest ecclesiastical control from the pope and deliver it to the king was inspired by Machiavelli's "satanic influence." (Actually it was from another Italian, Marsilius of Padua, that Cromwell received his inspiration.) Nor did Machiavelli escape the wrath of the Protestants. Perhaps the most vitriolic of all the attacks upon him was one published in 1576 by Innocent Gentillet, a French Calvinist writer, in which he blamed Machiavelli for the dreadful massacre of St. Bartholomew's night in 1572. Only quite recently, with the publication of Roberto Ridolfi's biography, has an adequate account of his life been made available.[1]

The debate about the character of Machiavelli's teachings—as distinct from the character of the man himself—continues to be waged with some heat. Fairly recently Leo Strauss provided us with a brilliant interpretation of Machiavelli as, for all the "perverted nobility" of his

---

1. Roberto Ridolfi, *The Life of Niccolò Machiavelli* (Chicago: University of Chicago Press, 1963). The original Italian version was published in Rome in 1954.

works, a deliberate "teacher of evil."[2] On the whole, however, the trend of recent scholarly writing has been to rediscover in Machiavelli a political and historical mind of the first rank.[3]

THE TEMPER OF MACHIAVELLI'S MIND

Machiavelli was capable of viewing the events of his time with a remarkable degree of detachment, even events in which he was directly involved—and as a holder of high government office he was involved in many of them. He appears always to have been conscious of the opportunity his position afforded him to study and eventually record the political activities of men. He was burdened with a passion for removing the illusions with which human beings shield themselves from uncomfortable truths, and although he did not regard life as without hope and meaning, he thought its meaning far more difficult to fathom than had the old philosophers. There is a Stoic element in his attitude toward the world, though his Stoicism has no explicit moorings in transcendence. For Machiavelli the cosmos is not an ordered whole, but rather a field of unpredictable forces into which a masterful intelligence can inject some degree of order and purpose. The Stoic virtues that Machiavelli exalts are courage and duty. One should endure unflinchingly the adversities of fortune and wait with patience for the time when one can employ his talents for the public good.

From 1498 until the fall of the Florentine republic in 1512, Machiavelli held the post of second chancellor and secretary of the Council of Ten, an executive body with independent power over war and diplomacy. During these years he reorganized the Florence militia and carried out a number of diplomatic assignments, the most interesting of which took him to the courts of Louis XII of France and Emperor Maximilian and the campaign headquarters of those indefatigable expanders of the Papal States, Cesare Borgia and Pope Julius II. After the overthrow of the republic and the return to power of the Medici family in the fall of 1512, Machiavelli lost his post and was tortured and imprisoned for alleged complicity in an anti-Medici plot. When Giovanni de' Medici was elected to the papacy in 1513, the family released Machiavelli as a gracious gesture, and he left Florence for his small farm outside the city, where he remained for many years in virtual exile. It was this enforced retirement that gave him the occasion to write about politics,

2. Leo Strauss, *Thoughts on Machiavelli* (Glencoe, Ill.: Free Press, 1958).

3. See Eric W. Cochrane's useful bibliographical article "Machiavelli: 1940–1960," *Journal of Modern History*, 33 (June 1961): 113–36. I agree with Cochrane's evaluations only in part, however.

to record the results of his fifteen years of "studying the art of the state." Fortune determined, he wrote to Francesco Vettori, "that since I don't know how to reason about the silk business or the wool business or about profits and losses, I must reason about the state; I must either take a vow of silence or discuss that."[4]

The disgrace of being removed from office and imprisoned undoubtedly had lasting effects on Machiavelli. His letters reveal, however, that although he considered that he had been unjustly dealt with—and still was, since he was not permitted new employment that would put his talents and experience to use—he retained an almost superhuman calm and detachment with regard to the events themselves. He possessed a resignation and patience that we would do well to recall when we come across passages in his works that glorify activism. There are many such tensions to be found in his thought.

In a famous letter to Piero Soderini, gonfaloniere (chief executive) of the overthrown republican regime in Florence, Machiavelli demonstrates his unusual ability to view events dispassionately. There are no recriminations, although we know from his Discourses that he had a low regard for Soderini's performance in the entire matter. He shows understanding of Soderini's position, and recognizes that as gonfaloniere he looked at things through the "mirror" of "prudence." But he goes on to draw a lesson from those turbulent events, a lesson that was to become a major theme of The Prince: Prudence and caution alone are not enough. When the times call for bold action, the statesman must not shrink from it, even if it requires him to break his word, to be cruel and violent. For in politics we cannot always use as our measure the standards of an upright and virtuous man; we must judge policies not by their morality or immorality, but by their results in a world peopled by men who are more prone to evil than to good. "Consequently, I see, not with your mirror, where nothing is seen but prudence, but with that of the many, which is obliged to judge the result [of events] when they are finished, and not the management when they are going on." Statesmen must learn to "understand the times" and "adapt themselves to them." Otherwise, they will be at the mercy of fortune and the tides of human affairs. History alternates between periods in which "humanity, loyalty, and religion" are sufficient for the ordering of human

4. Machiavelli to Vettori, April 9, 1513, in Machiavelli: The Chief Works and Others, 3 vols., ed. and trans. Allan H. Gilbert (Durham, N.C.: Duke University Press, 1965), vol. 2, pp. 900–1. I have altered Gilbert's translation of this passage in two respects: he renders raggionare as "talk" and lo stato as "government." Gilbert's edition, hereafter cited as Gilbert, is the most useful and on the whole the most reliable of all the extant English translations. For the Italian text I have used Antonio Panella, ed., Niccolò Machiavelli: Opere, 2 vols. (Milan and Rome, 1938).

affairs and others in which "cruelty, treachery, and irreligion" dominate.[5]

Machiavelli considered variability to be inherent in human affairs because of the nature of man himself. "As bitter things disturb the taste and sweet ones cloy it, so men get bored with good and complain of ill."[6] The objective of politics must be to accommodate the many temperaments and imaginations among men, rather than hope to eliminate their differences, and to achieve such order as is possible by human contrivance.

Machiavelli was himself a profoundly complex man who was fascinated by the world as a profoundly complex place. He saw human experience as encompassing a rich diversity of activities and inclinations. With his characteristic ability to view himself and his situation with ironic detachment, he wrote to Vettori:

> Anybody who saw our letters, honored friend, and saw their diversity, would wonder greatly, because he would suppose now that we were grave men, wholly concerned with important matters, and that into our breasts no thought could fall that did not have in itself honor and greatness. But then, turning the page, he would judge that we, the very same persons, were lightminded, inconstant, lascivious, concerned with empty things. And this way of proceeding, if to some it may appear censurable, to me seems praiseworthy because we are imitating Nature, who is variable; and he who imitates her cannot be rebuked.[7]

In one of his letters to the great historian Francesco Guicciardini, Machiavelli styled himself a "historian, comic writer, and tragic writer." He could have added poet and sermonizer to this list. His writings reveal a man of many interests and robust pride of life as well as a serious student of politics and history. But of all his many activities and interests, reasoning about politics occupied first place. It was impossible for him not to think about the state.

As we have noted, however, Machiavelli was not only a political theorist: he was also a poet, a playwright, a historian, a biographer of sorts, and a writer of short stories, brilliant reports, and remarkable letters. Even if he had never written The Prince or the Discourses he would have earned a measure of literary fame. The Art of War is a classic work on military tactics; it also reveals the importance that Machiavelli attached to the citizen militia. His comedy Mandragola (although at a

5. Machiavelli to Soderini, n.d. (presumably January 1513), in Gilbert, vol. 2, p. 895.

6. Ibid., p. 897.

7. Machiavelli to Vettori, January 31, 1514 or 1515, in ibid., p. 961.

deeper level it is much too bitter to be considered "merely" a comedy) mercilessly exposes the moral corruption of contemporary Italian society, with particular emphasis upon the venality of the clergy. His *History of Florence* occupied the last years of his life, when, having regained a measure of favor, he was commissioned by the Medicis to write a history of their city-state. Though it was still incomplete at his death in 1527, it is a valuable contribution to European historiography in its pragmatic use of historical analysis to provide instruction in his overriding concern, the securing of the state against onslaughts from without and dissolution within. As a historian of his time and place, Machiavelli ranks second only to Francesco Guicciardini. Any mention of his works should also include such lesser pieces as his *Discourse on Reforming the Government of Florence,* his *Life of Castruccio Castracani,* and the remarkable lay sermon, *Exhortation to Repentance.*[8]

THE PRINCE

No work in the history of political thought has aroused greater controversy than *The Prince.* Machiavelli's full intention in writing the work remains obscure. What does come through clearly is his ironic quality of mind. Irony, as a perceptive Filipino scholar has observed, can be used in two ways: (1) to express a quality of mind and (2) to sharpen the contrast between fact and fancy, or between events as they were anticipated and as they actually turned out to be. The latter sort of irony is "dependent upon chance occurrence of events or on the appearance of unexpected effects." As a quality of mind, irony

> recognizes experience as an intricate tissue of lies and truths and facts and fancies, a specimen that reveals new complexities yet after one layer has been explained and labelled. The ironic temper is therefore a mental set that urges the intellect to probe corners darkened by fear or ignorance and drag their secrets into the light.[9]

8. All of Machiavelli's writings are ably translated in full by Gilbert, with the exception of the *Legations,* or diplomatic reports, of which excerpts are included. For other outstanding English translations see Machiavelli, *The History of Florence,* Torchbook ed. (New York: Harper & Row, 1961); Machiavelli, *The Art of War,* ed. Neal Wood, trans. Ellis Farneworth, rev. ed. (Indianapolis: Bobbs-Merrill, 1965); and J. R. Hale, ed. and trans., *The Literary Works of Machiavelli* (New York: Oxford University Press, 1961). For a discussion of Machiavelli's sermon, see my article "Second Thoughts on Leo Strauss's Machiavelli," *Journal of Politics,* 28 (August 1966): 794–817.

9. Bienvenido Lumbera, "Literary Notes on the Filipino Personality," *Symposium on the Filipino Personality* (Manila: Psychological Association of the Philippines, 1963), pp. 2–3.

Purpose and Meaning

In his dedicatory epistle to the new ruler of Florence, Lorenzo de' Medici (grandson of Lorenzo the Magnificent), Machiavelli states that his intention in writing *The Prince* is to present in short compass "everything that [he] has learned and everything that [he] understands" from his "long experience" in political life, so that Lorenzo may learn the same "in a very short time." Contrasts have often been noted between the Dedication of *The Prince* and the Dedication of his other great political work, the *Discourses*. Machiavelli dedicated the *Discourses* to his friends, whereas *The Prince* was dedicated to the very ruler who turned him out of office and was the cause of all his subsequent misfortunes. If we take Machiavelli literally, we must believe that he wrote *The Prince* in an attempt to ingratiate himself with the new authorities and to show that his knowledge and experience could be of use to them; he wanted to get his old job back and was willing to use any amount of flattery to do it. Doubtless he did want his job back; but to say that Machiavelli wrote *The Prince* with no other end than to say what he thought would be pleasing to Lorenzo, as some interpreters claim, seems vastly to oversimplify the workings of an extraordinarily complicated mind.

There can be no question that Machiavelli's situation was exceptionally precarious during the time he wrote *The Prince*. If we can take seriously his remarks in the *Discourses*, he did not believe it possible for a person who had been deeply involved in affairs simply to withdraw and find satisfaction in tranquillity. Such a person will not be believed if he says that he no longer has any ambition for office and wishes only to be left in peace. "It is not enough to say: 'I do not care about anything, I do not desire either honors or profits, I wish to live in retirement without trouble.'" Rather, one must "play the fool like Brutus" and pretend to be a madman, "praising, speaking, seeing, and doing things contrary to your purpose, to please the prince."[10] We can scarcely overlook the fact that in the Dedication of the *Discourses*, Machiavelli condemns those who "always address their works to some prince" and, "blinded by ambition and avarice, praise him for all the worthy traits, when they ought to blame him for every quality that can be censured."[11]

---

10. Machiavelli, *Discourses on the First Ten Books of Titus Livius*, bk. 3, chap. 2, in Gilbert, vol. 1, p. 424. When the passage *contro allo animo tuo* is translated literally, as "contrary to your own soul," it has an even deeper significance. I am grateful to Professor Roger Masters of Yale for pointing out to me the probable relationship between this passage in the *Discourses* and Machiavelli's intention in writing *The Prince*.

11. Ibid., Dedication, p. 188.

Whatever we may say about *The Prince*, it is clear that its meaning can be fathomed only with extreme difficulty. What its author appears to say is not necessarily what he really means. As he himself said in a letter to Guicciardini, "For a long time I have not said what I believed, nor do I ever believe what I say, and if indeed I happen to tell the truth, I hide it among so many lies that it is hard to find."[12]

Machiavelli's situation—so absurd it would have been comic if it had not contained a real threat that his life might again be put in jeopardy at any time—demanded that he do something pleasing to the new ruler of Florence. It may be assumed, then, that one of the purposes of *The Prince*, which was the finest gift Machiavelli could give, was precisely to please Lorenzo and the house of Medici. We may also assume, however, that Machiavelli knew what he was doing—not being "blinded by ambition and avarice"—and that he wrote *The Prince* both to please his hoped-for benefactors and to accomplish a larger purpose: to teach his views on politics. It is also quite possible that he entertained a third objective: by the use of irony and shocking examples to expose the failures and senseless brutalities of contemporary princes, both foreign and Italian. If this latter objective was indeed part of his purpose, *The Prince* represents a call for a "new politics" of honesty and openness. In its Dedication he declares that he is presenting "everything" that he knows and understands; he makes the same claim in the Dedication of the *Discourses*, a work addressed not to princes but to his friends, and intended for circulation among them. Apparently Machiavelli did not consider that his need to please the Medicis required him to suppress his true meaning in *The Prince*. All the same, we shall have to dig for it.

The Argument of *The Prince*

The Prince abounds in sweeping statements; "all" and "none," "always" and "never" appear again and again. Consider the opening sentence: "All the states, all the dominions that have had or now have authority over men have been and now are either republics or principalities."

Principalities are of two types: hereditary and newly created. There are also "mixed principalities," which are essentially cities or territories newly conquered by an established principality. It is with the new principality and the new prince that Machiavelli intends to concern himself.

Machiavelli draws attention to the particularly vexing problems of these new principalities and new states. They are not buttressed by the authority of tradition, and so are preserved from overthrow only with

---

12. Machiavelli to Guicciardini, May 17, 1521, in Gilbert, vol. 2, p. 973.

difficulty. This is true of mixed principalities as well. Exceptional tactics are required to hold conquered territories, because the ruler has incurred the enmity of those he has dispossessed, and even those who gladly supported a change of regime will soon turn against him when they discover that their condition has not been bettered.

Violence. Wolin has written that Machiavelli was an advocate of the "economy of violence," and that his originality consists in having created a "new science" of politics which makes "brutality and cruelty unnecessary" for those who will but follow it. It is certainly true that Machiavelli did not glorify violence (as his detractors allege), and I fully agree with Wolin that Machiavelli's outlook is not at all congenial to romantic talk of "purification by the holy flame of violence," if in fact this is an accurate rendition of the teaching he attributed to Georges Sorel.[13] Nonetheless, Wolin goes too far in maintaining that Machiavelli's "new science" will make "brutality and cruelty unnecessary." On the contrary, Machiavelli goes out of his way *not* to disguise the fact that politics as it has been practiced may require cold-blooded and brutal actions, and that the political leader must not shrink from committing evil deeds if "necessity" requires them. Machiavelli gives numerous examples of the most shocking cruelty and brutality in both *The Prince* and the *Discourses,* claiming that such deeds are "necessary" in view of the fact that ambitious men will always struggle for power and glory in a world of scarce resources. Wolin notwithstanding, then, what Machiavelli emphasizes is not the economy but the ubiquity of violence. Whether there is also another dimension of his political vision which points toward a new politics or new way out of the quagmire of blood and violence is a matter to which we shall return at the conclusion of this chapter.

The Prince, then, begins as a manual purporting to teach the art of war and conquest, both by drawing on recent—or "modern"[14]—examples and by drawing lessons from the history of ancient Rome. The analysis proceeds logically: certain ends follow from certain means; if one's goal is conquest, one uses the means that will lead to it. Tactics must vary with the situation and the times, however. There are occasions for peace and occasions for war. Force and violence attend the founding

---

13. Sheldon S. Wolin, *Politics and Vision* (Boston: Little, Brown, 1960), pp. 223–24.

14. Machiavelli frequently uses the term "modern" to designate the recent or contemporary as distinct from the earlier or old ("In this connection, I bring up a modern example [*un esemplo moderno*]" [*Prince,* chap. 23]; "in accordance with knowledge of ancient and modern affairs [*secundo le cognizione delle antique e moderne cose*]" [*Discourses,* bk. 1, Preface]. He is one of the first major political writers to use this precise term.

of a new political order, for "all armed prophets win, and unarmed ones fall."[15]

The Privileged and the People. Chapter 9 of *The Prince* considers the regime based on popular support, a theme that was to become especially prominent in the *Discourses.* In speaking of the "civil principality" —that is, the regime of a man who has gained princely power not by unjust usurpation but through the aid of his fellow citizens—Machiavelli distinguishes between two elements or "humors" (*umori*): the privileged class (*li grandi*) and the people. The people desire "not to be oppressed or dominated by the *grandi* and the *grandi* desire to oppress and dominate the people." Since both of these desires cannot be satisfied at the same time, "one of three effects appears in the city: princely rule or liberty or license." Princely rule can be set up either by the *grandi* or by the people. Machiavelli's own preference can be detected in the very juxtaposition of the two social elements. The people's aim is held to be more "honest," because they desire simply to be free of oppression. But he continues to view the matter in its relation to power as well: the support of the people is a more secure foundation for princely rule than the support of the *grandi.* One can secure oneself against the enmity of the few, but not of the many.

As we shall see when we consider the *Discourses,* Machiavelli is well aware of the novel nature of his favorable estimate of the people. And even in *The Prince* he defends himself against anticipated criticism:

> Let no one oppose this belief of mine with that well-worn proverb: "He who builds on the people builds on mud"; it is indeed true when a private citizen lays his foundation on the people and allows himself to suppose that they will free him when he is beset by his enemies or by public officials. In this case he often does find himself deceived, as in Rome the Gracchi, and in Florence Messer Giorgio Scali. But when he who builds on them is a prince who can command, is a stout-hearted man who does not waver in adverse times, does not lack other preparations, and through his courage and his management keeps up the spirits of the masses, he never is deceived by them, but receives assurance that he has made his foundations strong.[16]

The Militia and Other Matters. Beginning with Chapter 10 of *The Prince,* Machiavelli considers a number of topics not strictly related to one another: the ability of a society to defend itself unaided, the special case of the Papal States ("ecclesiastical principalities," discussed with

---

15. *Prince,* chap. 6, in Gilbert, vol. 1, p. 26.
16. Ibid., chap. 9, p. 41.

heavy sarcasm), and the dangers of employing mercenary troops instead of a citizen army. The citizen army is one of Machiavelli's favorite subjects, and if we were not aware of the ease with which one can blunder from the path of his argument by taking his most sweeping statements literally and by failing to consider the context in which they occur, we would have to accuse him of disingenuousness on the matter of mercenaries. Who could conceivably agree with his statement that "the present ruin of Italy is the result of nothing else than her reliance upon mercenaries for a stretch of many years,"[17] or that "the chief cause for the fall of the Roman Empire" was "solely that she took to hiring Gothic mercenaries"?[18] It was statements such as these that led Guicciardini, in his *Considerations of Machiavelli's Discourses*, to pronounce Machiavelli naive and unrealistic in some of his judgments—hardly the image that later generations have formed of him. It seems more reasonable to conclude that this complicated man wished to convey some more subtle idea than these simplistic statements suggest at first glance: possibly that a well-ordered society based on excellence brings forth a citizen army, and that the absence of such an army is a sign that all those ideas and institutions that support a society are decayed or decaying. Certainly in the *Discourses* he qualified the oversimplification that "good laws rest on good arms," but even if he had not done so there, he could still be shown to have denied the idea, since it is contradicted by the whole of *The Prince*. For the authentic prince was to be a leader who would bring about the political reeducation of the Italian people.

Conquest as the Summum Bonum. The exaggerations and sweeping statements continue in Chapter 14, which opens with the statement that a prince "has no other object and no other interest and takes as his profession nothing else than war and its laws and discipline," and goes on to contend that a wise prince "never withdraws his thought from training for war; in peace he trains himself for it more than in time of war."[19]

We now begin to see some method in Machiavelli's seeming madness, and to glimpse the secret of his greatness as a political theorist. *The Prince* takes on a ruthless consistency, a certain juggernaut quality, in its single-minded insistence on military conquest as the sole end of political activity. Once military conquest is accepted as the *summum bonum* of political life, certain policies and tactics consistently follow.

---

17. Ibid., chap. 12, p. 47.
18. Ibid., chap. 13, p. 54.
19. Ibid., chap. 14, p. 55.

The *summum bonum* of life itself, as the classical and Christian philosophers conceived it, is simply set aside (not rejected) as irrelevant to his immediate purpose of analyzing an arbitrary good: conquest for human ends and "worldly glory."

If Machiavelli's political teaching were no more than this, it would have all the rigidities of an ideological tract. But it is an *inquiry*, and retains at least some of the playful quality that has been observed in Plato's dialogues. "It is well to reason about everything," our theorist observes in the *Discourses* (Book I, Chapter 18), and it is in this spirit that he devises a kind of reverse paradigm in which all political reality is measured in terms of war and its demands.

The clarity with which Machiavelli analyzes the subject is exceedingly helpful in illuminating the consequences and implications of such a world view. As a picture of the world of practice it is admittedly unbalanced and out of focus. In a sense, all theoretical constructs based on a coherent theory of the *summum bonum* are out of focus; the clarity of such analysis is not fully appropriate to the foggy world of practice. The analysis itself, however, may aid us all by thinning the fog, or even by lifting it for a single glorious hour. Machiavelli, let us remember, is writing political theory, a discipline that gives him the freedom to pursue the implications of a particular view of the *summum bonum* to the farthest reaches of the intellect. He need not remain within the mental fog of practical experience, where ends are not perceived with maximal clarity and pursued with relentless single-mindedness. His analysis in *The Prince*, although this may not have been his deliberate intention, actually demonstrates the theoretical insufficiency of worldly glory as the *summum bonum*. Such glory is surely a sham and a deception if it is deliberately sought as the highest good. But perhaps, as the *Discourses* would seem to indicate,[20] he was more aware of this than most of his detractors believed him to be.

Virtues and Vices. Chapter 15 of *The Prince* is generally recognized as a new departure in the argument. Some of the harsh conclusions to which we have been previously introduced are further elaborated and refined, all with the stated objective of elucidating *la verità effetuale della cosa* (the real truth of the matter). The crux of the argument is that many qualities that are considered highly praiseworthy by "all men" turn out to be destructive of the prince's objectives if they are followed unfailingly and unquestioningly. Machiavelli names a few of the qualities that bring men, "and especially princes," praise or blame:

---

20. "Our religion" has shown us the "true way" by rejecting "worldly honor" as the "highest good" (*Discourses*, bk. 2, chap. 2).

To wit, one is considered liberal, one stingy (I use a Tuscan word, for the avaricious man in our dialect is still one who tries to get property through violence; stingy we call him who holds back too much from using his own goods); one is considered a giver, one grasping; one cruel, one merciful; one a promise-breaker, the other truthful; one effeminate and cowardly, the other bold and spirited; one kindly, the other proud; one lascivious, the other chaste; one reliable, the other tricky; one hard, the other tolerant; one serious, the other light-minded; one religious, the other unbelieving; and the like.[21]

Chapter 15 ends with the observation that if we "carefully examine the whole matter, we find that some qualities that look like virtues" will lead to the prince's ruin if he cultivates them, while "other qualities that look like vices" will lead to his "safety and well-being."

The Exercise of Power. Chapters 17 and 18 contain some of Machiavelli's more important general pronouncements on man as a creature more prone to evil than to good, and on the statesman's need to consider the consequences of his actions in the light of the manner in which men actually tend to behave. It is in this context that we may evaluate his famous remark in Chapter 18 (sometimes misconstrued to mean that "the end justifies the means") that "in the actions of all men, and especially those of princes ... one looks at the result" (*nelle azioni di tutti gli uomini ... si guarda al fine*). If a certain policy has a successful result, most men will not condemn the man who put it into practice, even if he has been ruthless in his manner of implementing it. This is the way of the world. If the ruler attempts to practice justice and charity in a world where "many are not good," he will only come to grief. This is the hard side to Machiavelli's teaching.

Machiavelli's cynicism appears to reach its height in the celebrated passage on the lion and the fox in Chapter 18:

Since, then, a prince is necessitated to play the animal well, he chooses among the beasts the fox and the lion, because the lion does not protect himself from traps; the fox does not protect himself from the wolves. The prince must be a fox, therefore, to recognize the traps and a lion to frighten the wolves. Those who rely on the lion alone are not perceptive.... The one who knows best how to play the fox comes out best, but he must understand well how to disguise the animal's nature and must be a great simulator and dissimulator. So simple-minded are men and so controlled by immediate necessities that a prince who deceives always finds men who let themselves be deceived.[22]

---

21. *Prince,* chap. 15, in Gilbert, vol. 1, p. 58.
22. Ibid., chap. 18, p. 65.

When we encounter a passage like this, we wonder whether the author has not abandoned all normative standards and given himself over wholly to the uncritical exaltation of power as an end in itself. But we must remind ourselves again that *The Prince* is a *tour de force* based on the premise that power is the *summum bonum* of political life, and that here everything is viewed from this single perspective. That Machiavelli is aware of other perspectives is apparent not only in his other works, but in *The Prince* itself. In Chapter 8 he distinguishes between mere dominion (*imperio*) and true glory (*gloria*), so it is clear that he recognizes other dimensions of politics than the mere technical feat of conquering and maintaining a state. Furthermore, the problem of conscience is not dismissed out of hand, although it may appear to be as the *tour de force* unfolds. Machiavelli never attempts to conceal the fact that the means by which dominion is obtained are frequently evil, and that among these evil means there are some that completely transgress the bounds of humanity. Finally, we are occasionally permitted glimpses of some of the nobler objectives of politics, as in Chapter 19, where Machiavelli contends that "well-ordered states" (*li stati bene ordinati*) take care to deal justly with both the common people and the privileged classes.

The Prince is a concise statement of Machiavelli's belief that classical and Christian political theory is unworkable in a world that defines politics as the exercise of power and the struggle for power. It is also implicitly a rejection of a nihilistic counterethic, that only power and brute force matter. The rejection presumably has to be largely implicit, because the work is addressed to a prince for whom we may safely assume Machiavelli had only contempt, but whom he nevertheless wished to please. The nihilism of much of the argument in *The Prince* is attuned to the mentality of a Medici prince as Machiavelli had good reason to believe it to be. Whatever else he attempted to do, he wanted to revive the high esteem in which political activity was held in pagan Rome. He sought to educate a new ruling elite possessed of *grandezza dell'animo* (nobility of purpose).

Machiavelli urges that all rulers must squarely face the fact that politics and evil frequently go hand in hand. Especially at the establishment of a regime, circumstances may compel harsh and painful measures. Yet despite Machiavelli's contempt for rulers who shrink from violence out of sentimentality and feckless compassion, he also shows abhorrence of thoughtless, needless inhumanity, and deep concern that it be brought under control. Force alone, cruelty alone will not found and maintain a regime. When he must, especially in founding the state, the prince should look to Severus (a "very savage lion and a very tricky fox") as an exemplar; but whenever he can, he should model himself on Marcus Aurelius, noted for his justice and compassion.

Chapters 20 through 24 are brief, almost perfunctory, and purport to advise the prince on alliances, on the planning of "great enterprises," and—most importantly—on the kind of advice he should take. The prince should carefully choose only a limited number of advisers and then ask for their views only on such subjects as he is willing to discuss openly. If he is himself not wise, then "he cannot be advised well." He should above all avoid flatterers. If a prince fails, it is his own ineptitude, lack of preparation, and laziness that bring him down, rather than adverse fortune.

Fortune. Chapter 25, on fortune, is one of the most famous in the entire work. It discusses, in a tone more in keeping with the *Discourses* than with the rest of *The Prince,* an old question: whether men can control their own fate, or whether the outcome of their efforts is determined by forces beyond their power and comprehension. Machiavelli begins by saying that he has often been inclined to agree with those who argue that human affairs are inherently unpredictable. However, "in order not to annul our free will, I judge it true that Fortune may be mistress of one half our actions but that even she leaves the other half, or almost, under our control."[23] As in virtually all his discussions of fortune, however, Machiavelli alternates between optimism and pessimism in regard to men's capacity to control the contingent and the unpredictable in human affairs. If men were supremely adaptable, and could shift from boldness to caution as the times demand, then they could master fortune. But no man is wise enough to know how to accommodate himself to the variability of affairs, both because "nature" disposes an individual to act in a certain way and because he cannot be induced to depart from methods that have worked for him in the past. To be successful, then, one needs to shift with the times; some times require boldness, others caution. Yet if one had to choose one or the other, "it is better to be impetuous than cautious, because Fortune is a woman and . . . the friend of young men, because they are less cautious, more spirited, and with more boldness master her."[24]

The Redemption of Italy. The final chapter of *The Prince,* entitled "An Exhortation to Seize Italy and Free Her from the Barbarians," has been the occasion for vast controversy. Some hold it to be just what it appears to be: the climax of the book, giving meaning to all that has gone before. Others, pointing to its rhetorical style (quite uncharacter-

---

23. Ibid., chap. 25, p. 90.
24. Ibid., p. 92.

istic of Machiavelli's usual manner of writing), view the final chapter
as an appendix designed to bring the work to an end with a literary
flourish, but not to be taken literally. There are difficulties with both
interpretations. In defense of the latter view, it may be observed that
Machiavelli is constantly reminding us of the difference between appearance and reality, and of the need to look beneath the surface of
words and actions to find their meaning. Furthermore:

> This work of mine I have not adorned or loaded down with swelling
> phrases and magnificent words or any kind of meretricious charm
> or extrinsic ornament, with which many writers dress up their
> products, because I desire either that nothing shall beautify it, or
> that merely its unusual matter and the weight of its subject shall
> make it pleasing.[25]

However, the material of the final chapter is sufficiently related to the
preceding text to permit us to conclude that it is an integral part of
the work. The problem is to distinguish the kernel of meaning from the
shell of rhetoric.

The rhetoric and bombast presumably have the function of pleasing
and flattering the particular prince to whom the work is addressed.
Though Machiavelli has already warned that a prince should not be
deceived by flattery, what else can we make of passages such as these:

> There is not, at present, anyone in whom she [Italy] can have
> more hope than in your glorious family, which, through its fortune
> and its wisdom and strength, favored by God and by the Church—of
> which it is now head—can make itself the leader of this redemp-
> tion. . . . We see marvelous unexampled signs that God is directing
> you: the sea is divided; a cloud shows you the road; the rock pours
> out water; manna rains down; everything unites for your greatness.[26]

But interspersed with this gross flattery we find this:

> That [the freeing of Italy from its "barbarian" invaders] will
> not be very hard if you bring before you the actions and the lives of
> those named above. And though these men were exceptional and
> marvelous, nevertheless they were men; and every one of them had a
> poorer chance than the present one, because their undertaking was
> not more just than this, nor easier, nor was God more friendly to
> them than to you. Here justice is great, "for a war is just for those to
> whom it is necessary, and arms are sacred when there is no hope
> except in arms." Now your opportunity is very great, and when there
> is great opportunity, there cannot be great difficulty, if only your

25. Ibid., Dedication, p. 10.
26. Ibid., chap. 25, pp. 93–94.

family will use the methods of those whom I have set up as your aim. . . . God is directing you. . . . The rest you must do yourself. God does not do everything, so as not to take from us free will and part of the glory that pertains to us.[27]

During the second half of the fifteenth century the peace of Italy had depended upon a delicate balance of power among its major city-states, and their increasing rivalry had opened the way for invasion by Charles VIII of France in 1494. Since then Italy had been invaded repeatedly by the French, Spaniards, and Germans, and had suffered frequent incursions by the Ottoman Turks to the east. Clearly Machiavelli believed that Italy's only hope was a messianic leader who could, by an understanding of the times and the exercise of *virtù*, unify the people of the peninsula and lead them in a drive to expel their foreign invaders.

Although Machiavelli's writing is often sober and even pessimistic, there is no mistaking the chiliastic strain in his thinking. Much of this final chapter reminds one of Dante's political messianism, of his longing for a *dux* (in the *Divine Comedy* he employs the symbol of the *veltro*, or greyhound) who would lead "servile Italy" to a new age of secular salvation. But in *The Prince* Machiavelli sounds a nationalistic note that is altogether new. Dante's redeemer was to be the Holy Roman emperor, that "high Henry who shall come to set Italy straight" and restore the authority of the universal empire in Italy. But by that time the Holy Roman Empire had become in fact, if not yet in name, a German political institution, and Henry VII was a German prince elected to his high office by other German princes. Machiavelli's "new prince" was to be a native son, who would expel "this barbarian domination" that "stinks in our nostrils"—a domination in which the current Holy Roman emperor played a large part.

The chapter's closing words resound with a fervor typical of nationalist oratory in many newly independent lands in our own time:

By no means, then, should this opportunity be neglected, in order that Italy, after so long a time, may see her redeemer come. I cannot express with what love he will be received in all the provinces that have suffered from these alien floods, with what thirst for vengeance, with what firm loyalty, with what gratitude, with what tears! What gates will be shut against him? What people will refuse him obedience? What envy will oppose him? What Italian will refuse him homage? For everyone this barbarian tyranny stinks. Let your glorious family, then, undertake this charge with that spirit and that hope with which men undertake just labors, in order that beneath

27. Ibid.

her ensign this native land of ours may be ennobled and, with her guidance, we may realize the truth of Petrarch's words:

> Valor against wild rage
> Will take up arms, and the combat will be short,
> Because ancestral courage
> In our Italian hearts is not yet dead.[28]

When we view *The Prince* as a whole, we must be skeptical of the simple fervor of much of its concluding chapter. Surely Machiavelli cannot have believed so strongly that "so many things now join together for the advantage of a new prince" that he literally could not think that any "time could ever be more fit for such a prince to act."[29] Machiavelli's teaching is characterized not by simplicity but by tension. There is tension between his optimism and his pessimism, but he never overlooks the formidable obstacles to far-reaching political renovation. He was apparently convinced that the opportunity was present for a new beginning for Italian politics, for a rebirth of the "ancient valor" of the Romans. A new prince, capable of mobilizing the people and founding a new political order, might create the conditions in which republican rule would flourish again in Italy. The superiority of republican institutions is the major theme of the *Discourses*.

THE *DISCOURSES*

Machiavelli's *Discourses on the First Ten Books of Titus Livius* ranks along with *The Prince* in importance for political theory. In some respects the *Discourses* is a more significant work than the more celebrated and widely read *Prince*. Using the device of a commentary on Livy's history of Rome, Machiavelli is able to discuss at leisure and at greater length the topics that were introduced in the shorter, more hastily composed treatise. The chapters are truly "discourses"—discussions, reflective essays, debates—on the political problems uppermost in his mind. The work is divided into three books, with Book 1 supposedly dealing with Rome's internal affairs, Book 2 with its policies of external expansion, and Book 3 with the actions of individual leaders of the Roman republic. The author announces his conviction that a sound knowledge of ancient affairs will aid men to understand their present political situation.

---

28. Ibid., p. 96. (The closing lines are from Petrarch's *Canzone*, no. 16, lines 13–16.)

29. Ibid., p. 93.

Forms of Government

Machiavelli begins, logically enough, with the beginnings of political communities. Without explicitly indicating his source, he draws on Polybius' *History* in discussing the origin and cycle of governmental forms. The three simple forms (monarchy, aristocracy, democracy or "popular government") easily degenerate into their corresponding corruptions (tyranny, oligarchy, and mob rule). Alternation between the orderly and corrupt forms would continue indefinitely if it were not for the fact that the resulting instability weakens the society and makes it easy prey for a society with a more stable regime. The only hope of breaking the vicious cycle of instability and avoiding eventual conquest lies in establishing a mixed form of government, in which monarchical, aristocratic, and democratic elements are combined in such a way that each serves as a restraint on the others:

> All the said types are pestiferous, by reason of the short life of the three good and the viciousness of the three bad. Hence, since those who have been prudent in establishing laws have recognized this defect, they have avoided each one of these kinds by itself alone and chosen one that partakes of them all, judging it more solid and more stable, because one keeps watch over the other, if in the same city there are princedom, aristocracy, and popular government.[30]

The leading examples of the mixed form of government were Sparta and Rome. Sparta was blessed with a brilliant founder, Lycurgus, who gave it a constitution that endured for eight centuries with no need for substantial revision. Rome was founded as a monarchy, and then, with the aid of chance, gradually evolved into a republic with a mixture of monarchical, aristocratic, and popular elements in the institutions of the consuls, the senate, and the tribunes.

Internal Political Struggles

According to Machiavelli, political struggles within a society are inevitable, but under the proper circumstances they can have markedly beneficial results. In fact, the Romans under the republic enjoyed liberty precisely because of the struggle between the *grandi* and the common people. Instead of repressing the desires of either the common people or the privileged classes, republican Rome permitted both interest groups to express their demands and aspirations freely. Their continuing debate kept the society vigorous and kept the claims of both groups

---

30. *Discourses*, bk. 1, chap. 2, in Gilbert, p. 199.

from growing excessive. It is particularly important that the people were afforded the means "to express their ambition." The common people, who aspire not to oppress the minority, but rather to keep the minority from oppressing them, are the best guardians of liberty.

Republicanism and Expansion

Machiavelli distinguishes between two types of republics: expansionist and nonexpansionist. If a republic, by choice or necessity, commits itself to expansion beyond its own narrow limits (that is, the confines of a city-state), it must, as Rome did, provide for and encourage the participation of the many. Such participation will inevitably lead to tension and conflict between the popular and privileged elements of the society, but good laws and institutions can generally keep the disturbances within bounds. Constitutions that restrict popular participation are suited only for societies—like ancient Sparta or modern Venice—that are content not to expand, and seek only to enjoy their independence. When and if this type of republic embarks on expansion, it will certainly come to ruin, because its institutions are not suited to the enterprise.

After weighing the various advantages and dangers involved both in expanding and in attempting to maintain a healthy state without growth, Machiavelli comes down decisively in favor of expansion and the Roman example.

Machiavelli does not explicitly discuss the question of whether Rome's transformation from a republic into an empire was inevitable once its dominion had been extended beyond a certain scope. Were republican institutions capable of managing territories far removed from their base? As a passionate advocate of republicanism, Machiavelli was faced with a dilemma when he had to consider whether Rome's indefinite expansion was compatible with his republican principles. Much of the *Discourses* is written as if republicanism and expansion go well together; yet it is clear that the Roman republic came to an end with Caesar. It is also clear that Rome itself subjugated many republics in the course of its expansion, a fact upon which the author comments in Book 2, Chapter 2 of the *Discourses*. After first blaming defective "education" (a result of "false interpretations" of Christianity) for the fact that the number of republics in the world had declined since ancient times, with the result that people had come to place a lesser value on freedom than before, he says:

> Still I believe that the cause of this is rather that the Roman Empire with her arms and her greatness wiped out all the republics and all the self-governing communities. And though later that Empire was

liquidated, the cities have not yet united themselves or reorganized themselves for government according to law, except in a very few places in that Empire.[31]

It may be that this remark was only a prudent attempt to disarm the inevitable critics of the preceding paragraph, which does lay the blame for the decline of republican institutions and the love of liberty on "our religion." As the *Discourses* abundantly shows, there is nothing more central to Machiavelli's political teaching than his republicanism. Republican institutions are paradigmatic for Machiavelli; they go together with a quality and style of life that he regards as inherently noble and praiseworthy. Republicanism for him is certainly more than a means to the end of military expansion. And yet military expansion was ultimately not conducive to the survival of the Roman republic, the greatest, most glorious, most "perfect" example of a republic in the annals of recorded history.

In confronting Machiavelli's dilemma, we would do well to recall the dynamism of his thinking. Machiavelli retained the view of the majority of classical writers, that history was cyclical in nature and that no regime lasted forever. Whether a republic would expand or not was in good measure the result of *necessità*—a key concept in his thinking. The Swiss republics of his day, geographically isolated and protected by the authority of the Holy Roman emperor, were exempt from the need to expand. Rome was not. Rome therefore expanded, and used its democratic republicanism to good advantage in doing so. Since history has apparently decreed that all societies that rise must eventually decline, Rome could not escape forever the fall of its republican institutions. Its task was to preserve those institutions, through intelligence and *virtù*, as long as possible, and this it did.

Republicanism in Theory and in Fact

We are reminded in all this how thoroughly Machiavelli appears to have translated his paradigm of the best regime from the theoretical sphere to the historical world. In Chapter 15 of *The Prince* Machiavelli says that "many have fancied for themselves republics and principalities that have never been seen or known to exist in reality [*in vero*]," but that he will concentrate on the real truth as it emerges from the stream of historical events themselves. Although this rejection of "imaginary" models such as Plato's (in the *Republic*) and Aristotle's (in Books 7 and 8 of the *Politics*) is a gain for "realism" in one sense, it also heightens the dangers of parochialism and the loss of critical perspective. Machia-

31. Ibid., bk. 2, chap. 2, p. 332.

velli's model, like Cicero's, is historical Rome of the republic. This is the best regime; we do not need to search our imagination for a model. Machiavelli thus exposes himself to the charge that he is more of an apologist for a specific regime than a seeker after truth.

Although there is something to this accusation, it does not do justice to Machiavelli's overall teaching. That teaching, insofar as it falls within the sphere of political theory, definitely reflects his republican —and specifically Roman republican—bias. And yet he did produce a kind of incipient general theory of man and society, which itself led to the endorsement of a republic styled on that of ancient Rome (but not identical with it).

We must recall here Machiavelli's claim to novelty in the opening paragraph of the Preface to Book 1 of the *Discourses*. This passage appears to make unmistakably clear that he intended to chart a "new way" in politics, and not simply to imitate the modes and orders of ancient Rome:

> On account of the envious nature of men, it has always been no less dangerous to find ways and methods that are new than it has been to hunt for seas and lands unknown, since men are more prone to blame than to praise the doings of others. Nevertheless, driven by the natural eagerness I have always felt for doing without any hesitation the things that I believe will bring benefit common to everybody, I have determined to enter upon a path not yet trodden by anyone; though it may bring me trouble and difficulty, it can also bring me reward, by means of those who kindly consider the purpose of these my labors. And if my poor talents, my slight experience of present affairs, and my feeble knowledge of ancient ones make this my attempt defective and not of much use, they will at least show the way to someone who, with more vigor, more prudence and judgment, can carry out this intention of mine, which, though it may not gain me praise, ought not to bring me blame.[32]

Machiavelli, then, is more theoretical than Cicero, and his thinking is more oriented to universal questions. For him, republicanism is only a part—though an exceedingly important part—of a general theory of politics.

The Founder of a Political Community

Like Augustine before him and Hobbes and Freud after him, Machiavelli emphasizes the antagonistic element in man's natural endowment. Men are prone to violence and combat; they are antisocial by

---

32. Ibid., bk. 1, Preface, p. 190.

nature. However, necessity (chiefly the demands of survival) impels men to associate with each other, to constitute themselves into a series of rival groups. Within these groups, which evolve into complex and interdependent societies, men learn to cooperate, to restrain their demands, to solve by speech and law issues that formerly had been settled by brute strength and the sword. In a word, they become "civilized"— that is, accustomed to living with their fellow men in a *civitas*. They are taught the meaning of justice and to distinguish between their particular good and the common good. But this is not an easy lesson to learn, and only an extraordinary man can teach it.

Machiavelli nowhere more clearly reveals his affinities with classical political thought (affinities that remain even while he revolts against many of its premises) than in his emphasis on the founders of political communities. These men, particularly those who founded republics— Machiavelli cites Moses, Solon, Lycurgus, and Cleomenes—occupy the center of his stage[33] (although it should be noted that in Book 1, Chapter 10 of the *Discourses* he ranks founders of religions ahead of them).[34] An ordered society must have its origin in the work of one superior man, since men are rivals by nature, and no two or more men can have the same clear vision of the public good. It is this necessity— the need for the foundation of the state to be the work of one man only— that leads to the awesome crimes and bloodshed that characterize the beginnings of societies. That Romulus slew his brother Remus was morally a great crime but politically a harsh necessity:

> Therefore a prudent organizer of a republic and one whose intention is to advance not his own interests but the general good, not his own posterity but the common fatherland, ought to strive to have authority all to himself. Nor will a prudent intellect ever censure anyone for any unlawful action used in organizing a kingdom or setting up a republic. It is at any rate fitting that though the deed accuses him, the result should excuse him; and when it is good, like that of Romulus, it will always excuse him, because he who is violent to destroy, not he who is violent to restore, ought to be censured.[35]

---

33. It is puzzling that Wolin should assert that in the *Discourses* "the political hero largely disappears" (*Politics and Vision*, p. 229). I agree, however, that Machiavelli "showed greater insight into the nature of the political mass than any other thinker before the nineteenth century" (ibid.).

34. In descending order of those "praised," he lists founders of religions, founders of republics or kingdoms, captains of armies, and men of letters.

35. *Discourses*, bk. 1, chap. 9, in Gilbert, vol. 1, p. 218. This is another passage that is sometimes taken to mean that "the end justifies the means." But Machiavelli does not say that the result is justified; he says the man is excused. A result that is justified is one that has such moral or legal warrant that no guilt

He who "reads the Bible intelligently" will see that Moses likewise had to employ violence to eliminate rivals to his authority; he was "forced to kill countless men who, moved by nothing else than envy, were opposed to his plans."[36]

The founder of a well-ordered community is an extraordinary man who is capable of resisting the temptation to employ his absolute power so as to set up a tyranny. Tyranny is condemned in numerous places and at length in the *Discourses*. The founder should be

> so prudent and high-minded that he will not leave to another as a heritage the authority he has seized, because, since men are more prone to evil than to good, his successor might use ambitiously what he had used nobly. Besides this, though one alone is suited for organizing, the government organized is not going to last long if resting on the shoulders of only one; but it is indeed lasting when it is left to the care of many, and when its maintenance rests upon many.[37]

In these and other passages we have the resolution of the seeming contradiction between Machiavelli's stated preference for republicanism and his espousal of one-man rule. One-man rule is essential to the creation of a well-ordered society and as a temporary measure for its survival during periods of extreme crisis (the Romans had the "constitutional dictatorship" for this purpose); but the best regime for normal times was a republic, in which power was shared by the chief magistrate (or magistrates) with the "many." The aim of the ruler, if he was true to his great mission, was not to glorify his own power, but to use that power for a larger end—the construction of an institutional order along republican lines. If he could do this, he could ensure himself not temporary fame, but a glory as lasting as human affairs permit.

Founding and the need for periodic refounding are recurrent themes in Machiavelli. Even the best order becomes corrupt over time and needs to be recalled to its origin. If it is not, it will degenerate into tyranny and ultimately collapse or succumb to external conquest. Caesar could have taken a corrupt city and given it a new beginning; instead he chose, to his eternal infamy, to inaugurate a tyranny.

Politics and Religion

Machiavelli frequently refers to the political utility of religion. Almost always the discussion is concerned with the efficacy of religion in eliciting

---

attaches to it; a man excused is exempted from retaliation because of extenuating circumstances, but his guilt is still acknowledged. See my article "Second Thoughts on Leo Strauss's Machiavelli," pp. 803–7, for a further discussion.

36. *Discourses*, bk. 3, chap. 30, in Gilbert, vol. 1, p. 496.

37. Ibid., bk. 1, chap. 9, pp. 218–19.

obedience to the laws and a spirit of self-sacrifice, rather than with the truth or falsehood of religious teachings. Some have concluded from this that he was an atheist. Even after scrutinizing all his works, including his pious *Exhortation to Repentance,* we are still unable to form a clear picture of the nature of his religious belief or lack of it. That he was in general profoundly skeptical of the claims of revealed religion, Christianity included, seems evident; on the other hand, he preserved a formal allegiance to Christianity and a general awareness of the demands of Christian morality. Although much of his writing is inconsistent with a serious commitment to Christianity, he does not always show that he is aware of the inconsistency, or, if he is, that he regards the claims of such a commitment and the implications of his naturalistic world view as irreconcilable.

Machiavelli does not overtly or by implication call for the overthrow of Christianity and its replacement with a neopagan cult of the state. He appears to have thought that Christianity could be adapted to the needs of the modern polity. At the most he seeks to supplement the morality of the gospel with the martial vigor of ancient Rome. His animus is directed not against Christianity in general, or even against the corruption of the Renaissance papacy, but against the specific temporal power of the Roman Catholic church, which he, like Marsilius of Padua, found to be the chief cause of Italy's tragic disunity:

> We Italians, then, have as our first debt to the Church and to the priests that we have become without religion and wicked. But we have one still greater, which is the second reason for our ruin: this is that the Church has kept and still keeps this region divided. And truly no region is ever united or happy if all of it is not under the sway of one republic or one prince, as happened to France and to Spain. The reason why Italy is not in that same condition and why she too does not have one republic or one prince to govern her is the Church alone; because, though she has dwelt there and possessed temporal power, she has not been so strong or of such ability that she could grasp sole authority in Italy and make herself ruler of the country. Yet on the other hand she has not been so weak that, when she feared to lose dominion over her temporal possessions, she could not summon a powerful man to defend her against anyone who in Italy had become too powerful.[38]

Nationalism

In this highly significant passage we have another indication that Machiavelli was a nationalist before the emergence of nationalism. Furthermore, he was not only a nationalist, but a political nationalist.

38. Ibid., chap. 12, p. 228.

Not only did he possess a strong consciousness of his *italianità,* but he considered it essential that this *italianità* be concretely realized in the form of the nation-state. He does not use the terms "nation," "province," and "country" with precision, nor does he have an explicit and coherent theory of sovereignty. Such a theory had to wait for Bodin and Hobbes. He sometimes employs the term "state" (*lo stato*) in something close to its modern secular sense, but on other occasions he uses it in a more archaic fashion, to mean simply the prince's "estate" or "realm." In view of the path-breaking nature of his thinking in this area, it is scarcely remarkable that we should find these confusions in his writing. With Machiavelli we have decisively crossed the threshold into modernity, into a world where "new modes and orders" are to prevail. The medieval *respublica christiana,* with its double articulation of a multiplicity of peoples into a political community whose boundaries were religious and civilizational rather than national, has vanished almost without a trace in his teaching.

Machiavelli seeks to go back to Rome in order to go forward to new modes and orders—to a world in which Italy will take its place with France and Spain as a major power. In his glorification of the Roman republic it sometimes appears that he continues to think in imperial rather than national terms, and that he envisages the resurrection of the ancient Roman dominion—of a Europe ruled from Italy. As G. A. Borgese has shown, the "call of Rome" plagued Italian thought until it reached its apogee in the Fascist regime.[39] It is more probable, however, in view of Machiavelli's frequent stress on the importance of placing limitations on men's aspirations, that he envisaged a more modest role for a modern Italy as one among several powerful continental nation-states, ranged against each other in uneasy confrontation and constantly shifting alliances.

The "cult of antiquity" in Machiavelli is therefore only one side of his political teaching. In the Preface to Book 2 of the *Discourses* he warns against "always praising ancient times and finding fault with the present." The achievements of the ancients are overrated, because the historians of the epoch "concealed" matters that "would bring those times into bad repute." It is in this context that we need to understand the following striking passages:

> He who considers present affairs and ancient ones readily understands that all cities and all peoples have the same desires and the same traits and that they always have had them. He who diligently

39. G. A. Borgese, *Goliath: The March of Fascism* (New York: Viking Press, 1937).

examines past events easily foresees future ones in every country and can apply to them the remedies used by the ancients or, not finding any that have been used, can devise new ones because of the similarity of the events. But because these considerations are neglected or are not understood by those who read or, if they are understood, are not known to rulers, the same dissensions appear in every age.[40]

I do not know, then, whether I deserve to be numbered with those who deceive themselves if in these Discourses of mine I overpraise ancient Roman times and find fault with our own. And truly, if the excellence that then prevailed and the corruption that now prevails were not clearer than the sun, I would keep my speech more cautious, fearing to bring upon myself the very deception of which I accuse others. But since the thing is so clear that everybody sees it, I shall be bold in saying clearly what I learn about Roman times and in the present, in order that the minds of the young men who read these writings of mine may reject the present and be prepared to imitate the past, whenever Fortune gives them opportunity. For it is the duty of a good man to teach others anything of value that through the malice of the times and of Fortune you have been unable to put into effect, in order that since many will know of it, some of them more loved by Heaven may be prepared to put it into effect.[41]

Fortune

Machiavelli clearly saw the unification of Italy as a present possibility. New modes and orders could be established if the value of the classical Roman conception of politics were recognized, adapted, and applied to the contemporary situation. In any such enterprise, however, the role of fortune in human affairs would have to be carefully assessed and taken into account.

Machiavelli's discussion of fortune is as labyrinthine in the *Discourses* as it is in *The Prince*. He appears to make contradictory statements about the power of fortune over men, but to incline to the view that a man of sufficient knowledge and *virtù* can conquer the vicissitudes of fortune and succeed in a bold and difficult enterprise.

In Book 2 of the *Discourses* Machiavelli emphatically challenges Plutarch and Livy (although he asserts merely that Livy "seems" to share Plutarch's position) on the question of whether the Romans conquered their empire through ability (*virtù*) or fortune:

---

40. *Discourses,* bk. 1, chap. 39, in Gilbert, vol. 1, p. 278.
41. Ibid., bk. 2, Preface, p. 324.

Many hold the opinion, among them Plutarch, a very weighty writer, that the Roman people in gaining their empire were more favored by Fortune than by ability. Among the reasons he brings forward, he proves by the Romans' admission that they attributed all their victories to Fortune, since they built more temples to Fortune than to any other god. Livy seems to embrace the same opinion, because he seldom has any Roman make a speech in which he refers to ability without adding Fortune. But I am not willing to grant this in any way nor do I believe it can be supported. Because if no republic ever produced such results as Rome, there has never been another republic so organized that she could gain as Rome did. The efficiency of her armies caused her to conquer her empire, and the order of her proceedings and her method, which was her very own and discovered by her first lawgiver, caused her to keep it when conquered. . . .[42]

Machiavelli thus aligns himself with the view that the Romans' "ability was much more effective than their fortune" in gaining them their empire. Later, however, he quotes with approval Livy's opinion that fortune blinds men's intellects "when she does not wish them to check her gathering might," and he adds that "nothing can be more true than this conclusion."

Hence men who commonly live amid great troubles or successes deserve less praise or less blame, because most of the time we see that they have been pushed into a destructive or an elevated action by some great advantage that the Heavens have bestowed on them, giving them opportunity—or taking it from them—to work effectively. Skillfully Fortune does this, since she chooses a man, when she plans to bring to pass great things, who is of so much perception and so much ability that he recognizes the opportunities she puts before him. So in the same way when she intends to bring to pass great failures, she puts there men to promote such failure. And if somebody there is able to oppose her, she either kills him or deprives him of all means for doing anything good.[43]

In the concluding portion of Chapter 29 he appears to take a median position:

I assert, indeed, once more that it is very true, according to what we see in all the histories, that men are able to assist Fortune but not to thwart her. They can weave her designs but cannot destroy them. They ought, then, never to give up as beaten, because, since they do not know her purpose and she goes through crooked and

---

42. Ibid., chap. 1, pp. 324–25.
43. Ibid., chap. 29, pp. 407–8.

unknown roads, they can always hope, and hoping are not to give up, in whatever fortune and whatever affliction they may be."

The final sentence of Chapter 30, however, brings Machiavelli back to a resounding affirmation of the power of extraordinary men of *virtù* to control fortune:

> Because, where men have little ability, Fortune shows her power much, and because she is variable, republics and states often vary, and vary they always will until someone arises who is so great a lover of antiquity that he will rule Fortune in such a way that she will not have cause to show in every revolution of the sun how much she can do.⁴⁵

The relative strengths of *virtù* and fortune constitute one of Machiavelli's principal themes. We find the subject discussed in his famous letter to Piero Soderini and in his later biography of Castruccio Castracani.⁴⁶ His conclusion is always the same: fortune can be an ally or an adversary, depending on the circumstances. If the tide of events is running against one, there is small chance to escape being overwhelmed, but still there is hope that a rare man of exceptional intelligence and foresight can build dikes against adversity and stem that tide when it comes. Machiavelli's last word on the subject is one of cautious optimism: given an exceptional man and the right circumstances, boldness can, at least for a time, master fortune.

Always closely allied with this optimism, however, is a certain wry detachment and thinly veiled irony, products of a mind that can never quite help looking at even its own enthusiasms with suspicion and more than a touch of contempt. Thus, the buoyancy of Book 2, Chapter 30 of the *Discourses* is immediately followed by a chapter entitled "It Is Dangerous to Believe Banished Men," in which Machiavelli, himself an erstwhile banished man, informs his readers:

> It should be observed . . . how vain are the pledges and promises of those who are excluded from their native city. For as to their loyalty, it must be reckoned that whenever through other means than yours they can enter again into their native city, they will leave you and ally themselves with others, notwithstanding any promises they have made. And as to vain promises and hopes, so violent is their desire to return home that they naturally believe many things that are false, and to these they artfully join many others. Hence, between what they believe and what they tell you they believe,

---

44. Ibid., p. 408.
45. Ibid., chap. 30, p. 412.
46. *The Life of Castruccio of Luca*, in Gilbert, vol. 2, pp. 533f.

they fill you with such hope that, if you rely on it, you either enter into useless expense or go into an enterprise in which you are ruined.[47]

The Republic

Machiavelli was following one of the great traditions in Western political thought when he espoused the mixed regime as the most stable and equitable of governmental forms. We find the mixed regime endorsed as the most practicable form of government in Plato's *Laws*, Aristotle's *Politics* (the concept of "polity"), Polybius' *History*, Cicero's *De republica*, and Aquinas' *Summa theologica*. It is only with Bodin and Hobbes, with their theories of indivisible sovereignty, that we see the concept of the mixed regime decisively challenged and overthrown, only to reemerge in the new garb of modern constitutionalism.

In a sense, then, nothing could be more conventional than Machiavelli's defense of the mixed regime, which combines elements of three simple forms of lawful government: monarchy (government of one man), aristocracy (government of the few), and democracy (government of the many). In Machiavelli's scheme the mixed regime is unavoidably a republic; there is no question that the republic takes precedence over one-man rule (the principality) in his political teaching. When he espouses concentration of power in the hands of one man, it is for the purpose of either founding a republic where one has not existed before or temporarily weathering a crisis in the life of an established republic (as in the case of the Roman constitutional dictatorship, which could be instituted only to cope with a serious emergency, only after debate in the senate, and only for a maximum period of six months). Otherwise, the best that Machiavelli can find to say for absolute monarchy is that it is the only form of government suitable for a populace so corrupt that it has no present hope of profiting from a reformation of its institutions and the establishment of republican rule.

Having noted the traditional aspect of his republicanism, we must also consider the novel side of his teaching. Machiavelli has warned us that he is charting a new course, and his republicanism is novel in at least two respects: its frank advocacy of democratic governmental forms and its equally frank defense of struggle between opposing interest groups as inevitable and, if properly channeled, beneficial.

Machiavelli clearly saw himself as blazing new trails in the defense of the claims, interests, and political competence of ordinary citizens. He considered all previous political thought excessively oligarchical. In the

---

47. *Discourses*, bk. 2, chap. 31, in ibid., vol. 1, p. 412.

first book of the *Discourses* he presents himself as spokesman of the many in answer to charges against them, charges made down through the centuries by "all the writers" about politics. One reason the people are attacked as inconstant and unreliable is that writers are free to attack them "without fear and freely, even while they are in power. Of princes everybody speaks with a thousand fears and a thousand cautions."[48] A corrupt people will err in the same way as a tyrannical prince; but the government of ordinary people who have had the benefits of good education and good laws will be superior to the government of any prince, even one who abides by the law:

> I conclude, then, against the common opinion, which says that the people, when they are rulers, are variable, changeable and ungrateful, for I affirm that in those sins they do not differ from individual princes. And anybody who accuses both the people and the princes surely tells the truth, but in excepting the princes he deceives himself, because a people that commands and is well organized will be just as stable, prudent, and grateful as a prince, or will be more so than a prince, even though he is thought wise. And on the other hand, a prince set loose from the laws will be more ungrateful, variable and imprudent than a people. And the variation in their actions comes not from a different nature—because that is the same in all men, and if there is any superiority, it is with the people —but from having more or less respect for the laws under which both of them live.[49]

One of the characteristics of the republican form that most appealed to Machiavelli is its flexibility: a well-ordered republic is capable of producing leaders of various sorts to meet the requirements of various circumstances. Machiavelli always stressed the importance of a leader's ability to change his tactics quickly in response to changing conditions; yet most leaders, he believed, have one characteristic way of responding to all circumstances, and find it exceedingly difficult to shift from boldness to caution or the reverse. A republic, however, can draw on a number of able leaders, and can follow the counsel of those whose temperaments best meet the demands of the times; it is not saddled for a lifetime with the rule of one man, on whom the fate of the society rests. Thus republican Rome could avail itself of the abilities of both Fabius and Scipio, as circumstances required:

> If Fabius had been king of Rome, he could easily have lost that war, because he would not have known how to vary his policy as

---

48. Ibid., bk. 1, chap. 58, p. 318.
49. Ibid., pp. 315–16.

times varied; but he was born in a republic where there were different citizens and different opinions; hence, just as Rome had
Fabius, who was the best in times requiring that the war be endured, so later she had Scipio, in times fit for winning it.

Thence it comes that a republic, being able to adapt herself,
by means of the diversity among her body of citizens, to a diversity
of temporal conditions better than a prince can, is of greater dura-
tion than a princedom and has good fortune longer. Because a man
accustomed to acting in one way never changes, as I have said. So
of necessity when the times as they change get out of harmony with
that way of his, he falls.[50]

But beyond this technical explanation—of a kind so congenial to
Machiavelli's spirit—his preference for a republic is based on his sympathy for the relative justice of popular aspirations and his corresponding
antipathy to the abuse and exploitation of common people by the
privileged classes. Machiavelli is not a blind partisan. As we have seen,
he distinguishes between popular government, which he praises, and
mob rule, which he condemns. And he did not think it either possible or
desirable to abolish all distinctions of class and rank; he viewed the
struggle between the small upper class and the mass of common people
as an inevitable and perpetual contradiction within societies. If kept
within bounds, the struggle between the few and the many could lead to
results that would further the interests of both groups.

Nonetheless, his sympathies were not evenly distributed; he thought,
as we have seen, that the cause of the common people was more just
because these people aspired not to dominate but to avoid being
dominated. They were not ambitious in the narrow, individual sense.
They constituted the mass of industrious and productive citizens upon
which a state's greatness is based. And Machiavelli did not conceal his
scorn for the idle rich. The *gentiluomini* (gentry) who lived in parasitic
luxury on their estates were "dangerous to any republic." Even more
dangerous, however, were "they who, besides the aforesaid fortunes,
command castles and have subjects who obey them." These feudal lords
"crowd the Kingdom of Naples, the City of Rome, the Romagna, and
Lombardy. From this it comes that in those lands there never has risen
any republic or well-ordered government," because such men are
"altogether hostile to all free government."[51] This is the voice of
Machiavelli the modernizer, Machiavelli the implacable enemy of
feudalism and the medieval social structure with its loosely articulated

---

50. Ibid., bk. 3, chap. 9, pp. 452–53.
51. Ibid., bk. 1, chap. 55, pp. 308–9.

network of semiprivate governments in the hands of the landed aristocracy. Like Hobbes, Machiavelli saw a strong central government as the
key to a thoroughgoing social reform and the liberation of individual
energies from the burdens of unjust restrictions and unmerited privileges.
Unlike Hobbes, however, he rejected monarchy as the form of government most likely to bring about these reforms.

So far as I am aware, Leo Strauss is the only author to lay appropriate stress on the novel nature of Machiavelli's use of the venerable
concept of the "common good."[52] To Machiavelli the common good was
virtually identical with the good of the common people. The rich and
wellborn naturally tended to pursue their own private interests, while the
common people, unless they had been hopelessly corrupted, naturally
tended to work to strengthen the fabric of the entire body politic in their
efforts to avoid being oppressed. Republics were superior to monarchies
and aristocracies because they afforded opportunities for popular participation in governmental processes and thereby advanced the common
good, the good of the commoners.

We have noted that Machiavelli regarded the struggle between the
patricians and the plebeians in republican Rome as an advantage rather
than a misfortune. He is perhaps the first major Western political thinker
to praise political competitiveness on principle. The seeds of the modern
liberal idea of competitive democracy are present in his teaching. Also
present is the notion of relatively free public speech, although the
desirability of freedom of private conscience is not articulated. Yet
Machiavelli did not view internal political struggle as an unqualified
good; particularly in his *History of Florence* he indicated that it could
lead to excess and anarchy if it were not restrained by cohesive traditions, laws, and institutions, and he described the Florentine factional
struggles in unflattering terms.[53]

Conflicts between competing interests were expressed in debates in
Rome, but in Florence they resulted in pitched battles, with the survivors
among the losers subject to exile or execution. Whereas political divisions
benefited Rome, they harmed Florence, because in Florence these divisions led to the growth of factionalism. The major parties—the Guelphs,
commoners who supported the papacy in its struggle for political power
over the Holy Roman Empire, and the Ghibellines, aristocratic supporters of the emperor—broke into a number of competing factions, until
they were fighting as bitterly among themselves as they were against
each other.

52. Strauss, *Thoughts on Machiavelli*, pp. 127f. and *passim*.
53. *History of Florence*, bk. 7, chap. 1, in Gilbert, vol. 3, pp. 1336–37.

Under such conditions Florence could never rise to the heights of republican Rome; and though from our perspective the Florence of the Renaissance achieved a glory of its own, Machiavelli's distaste for everything medieval—a typical Renaissance attitude—caused him to see his city as falling into decline.

Machiavelli's fascination with the Roman political experience kept him from conceptualizing the representative principle. Logically he should have gone on to advocate the establishment of a national republic in Italy, with a legislature representative of its various regional, political, and socioeconomic interests. But the Roman republic had had no such representative institutions; its conception of citizenship remained limited, and though it extended its control over outlying territories, only "citizens" immediately present in Rome experienced anything like effective political participation. And this was the model on which Machiavelli formed his political conceptualizations.

MACHIAVELLI'S VISION OF MAN

Machiavelli's teaching is notorious for its tensions and seeming contradictions. Benedetto Croce has called him an "enigma." One can find in his works attitudes of gentleness and cruelty, selflessness and self-seeking, nobility and baseness, passion and detachment, high-mindedness and vulgarity, piety and blasphemy. It is possible to view these tensions as indications of a confused mind or of a hopelessly unclear writer. It is surely more profitable, however, to see the contradictions as resulting from a passionate search for clarity. Machiavelli appears always to have been intent on describing reality as he found it, both in himself and in his observations of others; the ambiguity and tensions in his thought flow from his vision of the existential situation itself. Existence to him is itself an enigma. His entire effort may be seen as an attempt to describe as clearly as possible the enigmatic character of the human condition.

Machiavelli is the silent partner of many modern political thinkers. Although his thought is linked with the ideas of classical antiquity, he has more in common with those who came after him than with those who went before. In his views of man we see a definite shift from theocentric to anthropocentric humanism. Man is seen as a union of craftiness and passion; reason is the faculty by which man recognizes the means for efficiently implementing his desires. In Machiavelli the traditional priorities of Greek philosophy, Stoicism, and Christianity, of the contemplative over the active life, are overthrown. Although he takes obvious delight in the contemplation of political matters as an end in itself, his explicit teaching is in harmony with Bacon's dictum that knowledge is power.

It is said that Machiavelli was a pessimist about human nature, and in many respects this is true. Yet in his faith in the capacity of favorable institutions to channel human ambition for the public good he seems irrepressibly optimistic. The faith of much of modern political thought in the power of institutions to produce constructive effects from destructive impulses in man, to sublimate and transform human drives, is very much present in Machiavelli. He cannot quite say with Rousseau that human nature is transformed by social institutions, but he comes close to this idea in his belief that man can acquire a second nature through civil society.

Nevertheless, Machiavelli retains his capacity for irony and detachment to the last. He seldom gives himself over wholly to optimism, and in his conclusion that "an everlasting commonwealth" (*una repubblica perpetua*) is impossible to create, he reminds himself as well as his readers of the mutability of everything human. Yet he did not despair, for it was this very mutability that permitted him to hope that his own actions and writings might further human freedom and renewal.

The "New Way"

In his great work *Les deux sources de la morale et de la religion* of 1932, Henri Bergson distinguishes between the "closed morality" and the "open morality." The closed morality is formed in accord with the "pressure of nature"; it is grounded on the sentiment of "love of country" and is preoccupied with individual and social preservation. By an ineluctable logic Bergson shows us that the closed morality leads to violence, war, and "murder." The open morality, on the other hand, expressed by the great philosophic mystics and religious seers of mankind, is animated by the "love of mankind" and is formed in response to man's "supra-rational" aspiration for moral liberation.

For the most part, Machiavelli appears to give us a luminous exposition of the character of politics within the context of the closed morality. Yet is it not possible that, side by side with this teaching, we also find in Machiavelli veiled intimations of a new politics and morality of humanistic openness? For Machiavelli not only wrote of violence and the morality of the *patria;* he also wrote, among other things, Chapter 26 of Book 1 of the *Discourses*, and a lay sermon entitled *An Exhortation to Repentance*. In these pages and elsewhere we find strong evidence that for all his realism and sardonic bitterness, Machiavelli felt very acutely indeed the tension between the demands of conscience and the requirements of power politics. Is it not conceivable that the "new way" of which he spoke at the beginning of the *Discourses* was that which led in the direction of the politics and morality of the open soul? After all, it was none other than Machiavelli himself who, in Book 1, Chapter 10 of the *Discourses*, listed "founders of religion" ahead of founders of republics and generals of armies, and men of letters as "most praised" among men. But the religion he appears to have had in mind was to be expressed in the symbolism of man's worldly concerns, and therefore remains very much in the framework of anthropocentric humanism.

3

Reformation Political Thought: Luther, Calvin, Hooker

As Robert McAfee Brown has observed, the "sixteenth-century movements usually referred to as 'the Protestant Reformation' are not easy to assess. Few historical periods have been subjected to such diverse interpretations."[1] Evaluations of the theological and ecclesiological implications of the Reformation continue in our own age—the age of the Christian ecumenical movement. A detailed discussion of the issues debated with such learning and passion in the sixteenth century—justification by faith, the nature of the sacraments, the form of the liturgy, the role of the priesthood, the significance of apostolic succession, rival claims of papal, episcopalian, and congregational church structures, and so on—would take us far from the area of our concern. These issues were—and are—by no means unimportant. Indeed, it seems reasonable to assume that if such controversies had not raged, there would have been no Reformation as we know it. Whatever its implications for social, political, and economic history, the Reformation was first and foremost a momentous upheaval in the *religious* history of Western man. Our concern, however, is with the principal political tendencies, implications, and influences of the movements collectively known as the Reformation.

THE LAUNCHING OF THE REFORMATION

The chief catalyst of the Reformation was an Augustinian monk named Martin Luther, who was ordained into the priesthood in 1507 and ten years later posted ninety-five theses on the door of the Castle Church in the Saxon city of Wittenberg, attacking the sale of indulgences to raise funds for the building of St. Peter's Cathedral in Rome and questioning their validity. This action triggered an immense controversy

---

1. Robert McAfee Brown, *The Spirit of Protestantism* (New York: Oxford University Press, 1965), p. 13.

over the condition and practices of the church, and Luther went on to assault the "three walls of the Romanists": the arguments that only the pope was competent to interpret the Bible, that no one but the pope could summon a church council, and that secular powers had no jurisdiction over the clergy and members of monastic orders. In the debates that followed, Luther was denounced by the Dominicans (ancient rivals of the Augustinians) and papal spokesmen, and was eventually excommunicated by Pope Leo X and placed under a ban by the Holy Roman emperor. The most dramatic episode in his confrontation with the power structure of his day came in 1521 at a diet of empire convened in the city of Worms, to which Luther was summoned to answer charges of heresy. Before the emperor and the assembled princes of church and state he acknowledged that all the books and pamphlets on display were indeed his, and when he was asked if he would retract them he replied with these fateful words:

> Unless I am convinced by the testimony of the Scriptures or by clear reason (for I do not trust either in the pope or in councils alone, since it is well known that they have often erred and contradicted themselves), I am bound by the Scriptures I have quoted and my conscience is captive to the word of God. I cannot and will not retract anything, since it is neither safe nor right to go against conscience.
>
> I cannot do otherwise. Here I stand. May God help me. Amen.[2]

What began as Luther's personal revolt quickly became the Lutheran revolt. Germany became a battleground for defenders of the Roman Catholic church and supporters of the former priest. Far to Luther's left, as we shall see, appeared other groups demanding more radical changes in church structure and worship, and above all radical economic and social transformations. In time, Zwingli in Zurich and Calvin in Geneva launched the movements that were to merge in the Reformed church organizations, and in England a national church independent of Rome was proclaimed.

The map of Europe would never be the same again. By 1600 what had been the Western Catholic *respublica christiana* (Christian commonwealth) was irretrievably fragmented. The heart of Germany, Prussia, and the Scandinavian countries became predominantly Lutheran; Calvinism spread from Geneva to the Netherlands, Scotland, and parts of France, Germany, England, and eastern Europe; Anglicanism became

---

2. Cited in Lewis W. Spitz, *The Renaissance and the Reformation Movements* (Chicago: Rand McNally, 1971), pp. 328–29.

the established religion of England; and the Anabaptists formed substantial minorities everywhere east of France. Only in Italy, France, Spain, Bavaria, the Tyrol, Austria, eastern Europe, and Ireland (which was officially Anglican) did Catholicism hold its own. Ignatius Loyola founded the Jesuit order to serve the pope and defend the faith, and a "Catholic Reformation" (sometimes referred to as the Counterreformation) was inaugurated under Pope Paul III. Other religious orders dedicated to renewal of the Catholic church developed and received papal approval. Finally the Council of Trent (1545–1563) clarified and restated Catholic dogma.

The Rise of Nationalism

Clearly the West had entered a new historical epoch. Religious unity on the basis of common allegiance to the pope was dead, and with it the papacy's claim to preeminence over secular powers and to ultimate jurisdiction over political legitimacy. With the snapping of the religious bonds that had held Europe together, the rise and consolidation of the nation-state as the effective unit of political representation and power were greatly hastened. In some territories (Scandinavia, England, and parts of Germany) national churches were established, so that the medieval principle of the "ecclesiastical polity" was at least formally maintained, although these churches were no longer permitted the large measure of independence from secular control that the Roman Catholic church had enjoyed in medieval times. Elsewhere (the Netherlands, parts of France) and especially in England, society was so deeply divided on religious matters that the solution of a nonecclesiastical polity presented itself as the only viable alternative to perpetual chaos and civil war. Jean Bodin, the French theorist of sovereignty, concluded that governmental institutions should be grounded in a secular body politic if the society was deeply divided in its ecclesiastical allegiances. It is in his work that we find the first clear articulation of the idea of the modern sovereign nation-state. Other writers were to defend religious toleration on grounds of freedom of conscience as well as for reasons of political expediency. The liberal principle of the separation of church and state was the logical end product of movements begun in the Reformation of the sixteenth century.

One could endlessly debate the precise relationship between the Reformation and the development of the modern political world. As I suggested in Chapter 1, Luther, Calvin, Melanchthon, and other great figures of the Protestant Reformation never advocated secularism or nationalism. Indeed, a world dominated by the cares and concerns of this life to the neglect of man's eternal salvation would have been anathema to them; nationalism interested them only to the extent that it advanced the universal Christian renewal they championed.

Capitalism and the Protestant Ethic

Max Weber's brilliant and provocative thesis that the capitalist economic system (really finance capitalism) was a consequence of the Protestant (really Calvinist) ethic of thrift, hard work, and the accumulation of worldly rewards as visible signs of God's favor[3] raises numerous problems for the interpreter of the period. Calvin did not define usury so strictly as the medieval church had done, but he did condemn speculative operations, the charging of interest on money loaned without security, and the accumulation of wealth as an end in itself. Weber is on stronger ground when he refers to certain later Calvinists, such as Richard Baxter, who extolled moneymaking as a sacred calling; but were these Calvinists instrumental in shaping the modern capitalist consciousness, or can we more properly say that they themselves were influenced by the ethos rooted in an openly secular attitude that arose during the Renaissance and developed outside the religious context? Other writers have argued that Calvinism was the seedbed of modern constitutional democracy. Whatever the weaknesses of these political and economic arguments, it does seem clear that the Protestant Reformation was congenial to the development of new political forms and of a changed political consciousness in a way in which Catholicism was not.

Church and State

The Reformation encouraged the eventual emergence of a secular as distinct from a church-oriented civilization. In the medieval period Thomas Aquinas, despite his general recognition of the legitimate autonomy of the temporal realm, had assumed that the church would exercise a *vis directiva* (as opposed to a *vis coactiva*) over society at large. The medieval Catholic church was in a position to exert powerful pressure against the development of a society dominated by secular concerns. In practice—and this was one of the principal contentions of the reformers—the church was so deeply involved in temporal affairs that its spiritual mission was often in jeopardy. In its doctrines and certain of its institutions, however, the church did hinder the development of institutional forms that could support the emerging humanist ethos. Its commitment in principle to the "two swords" concept of Pope Gelasius I

---

3. Max Weber, *The Protestant Ethic and the Spirit of Capitalism*, trans. Talcott Parsons (New York: Scribner, 1950).

(the idea that the authority of the priesthood is much greater than the power of kings, since the priest is responsible for the welfare of the king's soul) meant that the church assumed a strong and even occasionally militant role in challenging what it held to be the excessive pretensions of the temporal power structure. Similarly, the church's commitment to the monastic ideal was inherently inimical to any view that saw value in activism and involvement in worldly affairs outside the official structure of the church, as Joan of Arc learned to her sorrow.

The reformers repudiated the monastic ideal and the authority of the papacy. Luther and Richard Hooker in effect supported the temporal power as the ultimate authority over the ordering of the church visible, although neither man advocated the complete subordination of the church to the state. As Ernst Troeltsch observes, Lutheranism "let itself be erected by the modern State into a Church with an elaborately complicated legal position, hovering between dependence and independence."[4] Calvinism, on the other hand, favored in principle the establishment of a new kind of political community, in which Scripture was sovereign. Although Calvin's Geneva may outwardly have resembled a theocracy, with its morals police and its powerful Company of Pastors, the Holy Commonwealth was intended to function as a "bibliocracy," governed through the "harmonious combination of spiritual and secular authorities."[5] Since the Calvinists were in the minority nearly everywhere, they were never able to establish their Holy Commonwealth; but their attempt to create such a society in England under Cromwell was a strong indication of the zeal to make over the world that came to permeate Calvinism.[6] Taking an overall view of the situation, however, Troeltsch concludes that the "inner ecclesiastical structure of the Protestant Churches, and especially of Lutheranism, is considerably weaker than that of Catholicism, and therefore when confronted with the modern world of ideas, has less resisting power than Catholicism."[7]

In assessing the relationship of the Reformation to the modern political consciousness, we must do more than indicate its indirect and unintended effects. Protestantism, as Troeltsch points out, has been able to "amalgamate" with the modern world "much more solidly than

---

4. Ernst Troeltsch, *Protestantism and Progress* (Boston: Beacon Press, 1958), p. 74.

5. Ibid., p. 70.

6. For an acute if controversial analysis of the political thought and style of the seventeenth-century Calvinist revolutionaries, see Michael Waltzer, *The Revolution of the Saints: A Study in the Origins of Radical Politics* (Cambridge: Harvard University Press, 1965).

7. Troeltsch, *Protestantism and Progress,* pp. 90–91.

Catholicism ... has been able to do." There are, he concludes, "tendencies" in Protestantism "drawing it toward the modern world."[8] Perhaps the most important of these tendencies is the higher value placed on worldly activity by both Luther and Calvin. Both men condemned the pursuit of worldly success as an end in itself; yet in urging men on to the busy life of active involvement, and in repudiating the idea that contemplation and withdrawal from the world are essential for the fullest life of the spirit, they contributed more than they knew to the victory of what might be called the modernizing ethos.

MARTIN LUTHER

More than any other single individual, Luther symbolizes the Reformation. His courage in indicting the "Christian estate" of his time for having buried the Christian message under an accretion of practices nowhere to be found in the Gospels cannot in any way be challenged or discounted. His indignation against widespread corruption among hierarchy and clergy had its source in a profound conception of authentic Christian existence. The passion and depth of his religious thought, his brilliant exposition of the doctrine of justification by faith (or grace) alone, his commitment to the proposition that all men within the church, regardless of rank or station, are equal before God, and that all members are called to the full profession of the Christian life (the celebrated "priesthood of all believers")—these concepts comprise his imperishable legacy to mankind. In appearing before the Diet of Worms and challenging in the name of freedom of conscience the greatest array of temporal and spiritual power that could be assembled against him, Martin Luther demonstrated once again that man, the existing human person, is capable of transcending any system. Luther, then, was a religious genius of the first rank. Whatever came after, Luther at Worms joined the company of Socrates and Jan Hus.

At the same time, however, there were also profound differences between Luther and these predecessors. After Worms, Luther was not content only to take a stand for his own beliefs. He wished to create a new mass movement, to overthrow the prevailing religious institutional structure, to transform the universities, and to change the world through direct action.

Luther as Innovator

Most of the works in which Luther deals significantly with political and social life are in one way or another calls to action or polemics against

---

8. Ibid., p. 92.

some position set forth by the "enemy" or the forces of "darkness." In this respect, at least, he prefigures the age of ideologies, of direct mass appeals couched in programmatic terms and designed to effect sweeping, rapid institutional change.[9] There is something very modern in all this, and it is another reason that Luther has come to be portrayed as one of the principal shapers of the modern consciousness.

Psychological Interpretations. Working within the psychoanalytic tradition, Erik H. Erikson and Norman O. Brown have contributed in their own ways to our understanding of Luther and his historical significance. Erikson credits Luther with anticipating Marx's insights into the importance of work for man's full development as a human being and for rediscovering, at least "when he was not in acute conflict," a joyful attitude toward the world and its pleasures. Luther's experience of justification by faith was one of enormous relief and liberation from the oppressive burden of guilt he had felt as a result of his perceived inadequacy to cope with the temptations of the devil.

Erikson's general assessment of Luther's relation to modernity is of particular interest to our concerns here:

> Luther was the herald of the age which was in the making and is—or was—still our age: the age of literacy and enlightenment, of constitutional representation and the freely chosen contract; the age of the printed word which tried to say what it meant and to mean what it said, and provided identity through its own effort.[10]

Luther was not only a revolutionary, however. As Erikson's study shows, his development may be traced through various phases or "identity crises," of which the role of reformer was only one. Indeed, there is also a reactionary side to his thought. Nonetheless, by his initial revolt against established authority he helped unleash a process of criticism and reform that has remained with us throughout the modern period.

Brown, in a much bolder reinterpretation of Luther, has pointed out the relevance of some of Luther's insights to contemporary radical Christian and neo-Freudian attempts to lay the groundwork for a non-alienated existence for man. Luther saw man's condition as sick or evil, and his "eschatology challenges psychoanalysis to formulate the conditions under which the dominion of death and anality could be abolished."[11] And Brown concludes that "Luther's ethic, like the ethic of

---

9. See Sheldon S. Wolin, *Politics and Vision* (Boston: Little, Brown, 1960), for emphasis on the way in which Luther anticipated the rise of ideologies and mass movements.

10. Erik H. Erikson, *Young Man Luther* (New York: Norton, 1958), p. 224.

11. Norman O. Brown, *Life Against Death: The Psychoanalytical Meaning of History* (Middletown, Conn.: Wesleyan University Press, 1959), pp. 232–33.

primitive Christianity," is an interim one, "looking forward to the speedy abolition of its own premises."[12] Clearly, with Luther we are in the presence of a man who, whatever his faults, provided Western man with new vision and insight.

Institutional Change. The first important tract in which Luther confronted social problems, "An Open Letter to the Christian Nobility of the German Nation Concerning the Reform of the Christian Estate" (1520), dealt with the practical problem of achieving prompt and sweeping institutional change. Profoundly hostile to tradition, the work sought to arouse the German-speaking world to resentment of foreign domination. The parallels with Machiavelli are striking. For whatever their differences in temperament and religious awareness, both Luther and Machiavelli condemned the old *respublica christiana* as an institutional structure based on false principles, and both were determined to replace it with a new type of community.

Like Machiavelli, Luther strenuously advocated new modes and orders. Although initially he had called only for the reform of the papacy, he soon was demanding its abolition. "Nothing good has ever come out of the papacy and its laws, nor ever will,"[13] he sweepingly concluded. The characterization of the pope as Antichrist ("O Pope, not most holy, but most sinful ... O that God from heaven would soon destroy thy throne and sink it in the abyss of hell!")[14] is frequently encountered in Luther's writings. His view of history was strongly affected by apocalyptic thinking. He believed that the end of the world was approaching; before Christ would come in his glory to preside over the Last Judgment, the world would be rocked by a series of profound crises in which the children of light would oppose the forces of darkness and the devil. The transformation of institutions was necessary to secure victory over the diabolical forces and prepare for the final triumph of the Lord.

Luther also placed great emphasis upon the need for a thorough reform of the universities, which he described as "places for training youths in Greek glory, in which loose living prevails, the Holy Scriptures and the Christian faith are little taught, and the blind, heathen master Aristotle rules alone."[15]

---

12. Ibid., p. 218. "If ... Christianity cannot foresee the kingdom of Christ on earth, it consigns this earth to the eternal dominion of Satan [ibid]."

13. "An Open Letter to the Christian Nobility of the German Nation Concerning the Reform of the Christian Estate," in Martin Luther, *Three Treatises,* trans. C. M. Jacobs, A. T. W. Steinhaeuser, and W. A. Lambert (Philadelphia: Muhlenberg Press, 1943), p. 68.

14. Ibid., p. 85.

15. Ibid., p. 93.

Aristotle emerges as a prime *bête noire* for Luther:

Aristotle's *Physics, Metaphysics, On the Soul, Ethics* . . . should be altogether discarded. . . . Nothing can be learned from them either of the things of nature or the things of the Spirit. . . . It grieves me to the heart that this damned, conceited, rascally heathen has with his false words deluded and made fools of so many of the best Christians. God has sent him as a plague upon us for our sins.[16]

Luther concludes that the devil himself has introduced the study of Aristotle. He is not impressed by the fact that such scholars as Thomas Aquinas viewed the Aristotelian corpus as a treasure of immense value:

I care not that so many great minds have wearied themselves over him for so many hundred years. Such objections do not disturb me as once they did; for it is plain as day that other errors have remained for even more centuries in the world and in the universities.[17]

Luther's university reform also called for the removal of the study of canon law from the curriculum. "It were well," he observes, "if the canon law, from the first letter to the last . . . were utterly blotted out. The Bible contains more than enough directions for all our living."[18] Nor does the study of civil or "temporal" law escape Luther's denunciation: "although much better, wiser, and more rational" than the canon law, "there is far too much of it."[19]

In the "Open Letter to the Christian Nobility of the German Nation" Luther emerges as the impatient innovator who calls for thorough institutional changes to be effected at once. He possessed the inner certainty and outward charisma necessary to play the role of the founder-legislator of the new order. Machiavelli and Rousseau theorized about the need for a founder of new modes and orders. Luther did not need to do so, for he filled the role himself and was highly conscious of doing so.

The Problem of Luther's "Conservatism"

Despite Luther's bold challenge to established authority, he is sometimes categorized as conservative.[20] This judgment is based on his

---

16. Ibid.

17. Ibid., p. 94.

18. Ibid., p. 95.

19. Ibid.

20. "More was a conservative, Luther was a conservative, and Burke was a conservative. They were three of the great conservatives of history" (R. H. Murray, *The Political Consequences of the Reformation* [New York: Russell, 1960], p. 77).

studied exaltation of the temporal power, his dark view of human nature (the Augustinians traditionally stressed original sin), and his opposition to the egalitarian political ideas being put forward by the Anabaptists and the followers of Thomas Müntzer.

Temporal Power and Christian Conscience. Luther was convinced that his principal contribution in the area of political thought, strictly conceived, was his sharp distinction between the spiritual and temporal lives of man. He did not conceive of the problem as in any sense a part of the traditional *regnum-sacerdotium* dichotomy. As far as political power and jurisdiction were concerned, to Luther the *regnum* was all. The church had no moral or legal right to contravene decisions of the temporal authorities, to depose rulers, or to claim special legal jurisdiction over its clergy. There were no limits to the scope of temporal power over the external lives and actions of men. Men were duty-bound to obey the secular rulers because of the state's divine institution (Romans 13 was heavily stressed in this connection) and the necessities of social life (which he sometimes referred to as the "natural law"). Luther did conceive of the possibility of passive disobedience in extreme cases; if a subject were required by his prince to renounce his most deeply held religious convictions, he could not be obliged to obey. No one could be compelled to believe; liberty of conscience was essential. The inner citadel of the heart and conscience, then, was inviolable to Luther. Still he held that even wicked rulers were sent by God, and if a Christian suffered persecution because of his faith, it was his duty to endure it. Suffering was an important part of the Christian life.

Luther held that, although true Christians do not need to be coerced into right action by temporal law or government because they are spontaneously guided by a spirit of love, compassion, and sacrifice for their neighbors, the great majority of men, burdened with original sin, are inclined to viciousness and evil, and must be governed by force.[21] His view is in some ways an echo of Augustine and a premonition of Hobbes: anarchy would surely result if the ruler, with his power of the sword, were to be removed and men permitted to act as they pleased. But unlike Hobbes, Luther rejected as "Turkish" any attempt at absolute monarchy, in which a ruler arrogated all power to himself and refused to permit lesser magistrates any share of authority. Nonetheless, the effect of his teaching is greatly to strengthen the power of the prince.

---

21. F. Edward Cranz, in his *Essay on the Development of Luther's Thought on Justice, Law, and Society* (Cambridge: Harvard University Press, 1964), argues that Luther later "drops the emphasis of *Von weltlicher Obrigkeit* on the division of mankind into two exclusive groups" (p. 169), thereby recognizing temporal government as a "divine ordinance" rather than simply a negative restraint on the wicked. While I agree that there is a shift of emphasis in Luther's writings, I am not persuaded that this indicates any basic change in his views.

Luther accepted the traditional status differences in the feudal social order as necessary and salutary. Those in the lower ranks of the social hierarchy should submit to the demands of their superiors; even if these orders were unjust, resistance was evil. Only in matters of religious belief was one free to refuse obedience to higher authority.

The Christian was indifferent to material possessions beyond his immediate needs, but would accept the state's protection for any property he did own. He did not need the state's law courts, but would support the system for the sake of those in the community who lacked his self-discipline.

Yet within the "Christian estate," or the organized community of men who were at least outwardly Christian, Luther, as we know, had proposed sweeping changes. He abolished on principle the distinction between priest and laity, and declared that all who in faith and goodwill labored at an honest calling, no matter how humble, were equal members of the church. All members were priests in essence, even if only a few among them would have to be designated to preach the gospel and administer the sacraments. In performing these priestly functions the clergyman acted in behalf of the community, not as one initiated into sacred mysteries that set him apart from the laity. The community of the faithful was governed by persuasion and consent, not by priestly dictates. Indeed, the willing consent of congregations to follow pastors of their own choice in all matters of the life of the faith, including the interpretation of the Scriptures, was essential to Luther.

Luther's preoccupation with theological questions and the fact that most of his writings on man and society were occasional pieces might lead us to underestimate his importance in the history of political thought. His own view of his role as a political thinker was anything but modest; he claimed to have been the first man in Christendom to understand the nature and function of civil government.[22] His assertion that his political thought was wholly novel is characteristically modern, as I suggested in Chapter 1.

Civil Authority and Natural Law. Luther held that the Christian ruler was restrained by the divine or "natural" law. This law did not reveal itself in any automatic or easy fashion, however; the ruler came to grasp it only through a personal encounter with God as he struggled

---

22. "This was the state of things at that time [1520]: no one had taught, no one had heard, and no one knew anything about temporal government, whence it came, what its office and works were, or how it ought to serve God. The most learned men (I shall not name them) regarded temporal government as a heathen, human, ungodly thing, as though it jeopardized salvation to be among the ranks of rulers" ("On War Against the Turk" [1529], in *Luther's Works*, 55 vols., Helmut T. Lehman: vol. 45, *The Christian in Society II*, ed. Walther I. Brandt [Philadelphia: Muhlenberg Press, 1962], p. 163).

with his conscience. Luther made little reference to the role of the visible church or the traditional idea that the prince was guided by the law of God in making his decisions. Here we have an instance of the untraditional handling of a traditional concept (natural law). As Luther wrote:

> A prince ... must depend neither upon dead books nor living heads, but cling solely to God, and be at him constantly, praying for a right understanding, beyond that of all books and teachers, to rule his subjects wisely.[23]

> Of this I am certain, that God's word will neither turn nor bend for princes, but princes must bend themselves to God's word.[24]

> Therefore, we should keep written laws subject to reason, from which they originally welled forth as from the spring of justice. We should not make the spring dependent on its rivulets, or make reason a captive of letters.[25]

Moderation vs. Extremism.   Contrary to the impression conveyed by some of his most impassioned pamphlets, Luther was not a man who reveled in violence or who opposed moderation and restraint. In his work on temporal authority he argued that the ruler should use the punishing power with extreme care, and if he errs at all it should be on the side of punishing too little.[26] Wars of aggression should not be undertaken. When a prince must defend his realm against foreign invaders, destruction of life and property should be kept to a minimum, and he should be magnanimous to his enemies after he has vanquished them.[27]

These passages and others[28] reveal Luther as an opponent of extremism and excess. In other works, however, Luther abandons his moderate position and advocates the most cruel punishment for those whom he regards as the representatives of evil and disorder. The occasional violence of his language and his almost bloodthirsty demands for death and destruction for those in rebellion are still capable of producing a sense of shock. The most famous example is his treatise "Against the Robbing and Murdering Hordes of Peasants," in which he offers to "instruct the rulers" as to "how they are to conduct themselves in these circumstances."

---

23. Luther, "Temporal Authority: To What Extent It Should Be Obeyed," in ibid., p. 119.

24. Ibid., p. 121.

25. Ibid., p. 129.

26. Ibid., p. 105.

27. Ibid., pp. 124–25.

28. See, for example, Luther's judicious comments in his treatise "On Christian Liberty": It is not a mark of true liberty simply to find fault with "ceremonies, traditions, and human laws"; on such questions as fasting, use of familiar rituals in the church, and so on, it is best to "take a middle course" (*Three Treatises,* p. 234).

The most memorable sentence of this lamentable document (which Luther later defended and refused to qualify) enjoined "everyone who can, smite, slay and stab, secretly or openly, remembering that nothing can be more poisonous, hurtful, or devilish than a rebel."[29]

Luther and the Sectarian Revolutionary Movements

The advocacy of violent repression of social protest movements in the name of law and order can hardly be considered a contribution to the development of a justly ordered society in any age; but we may be able to see Luther's savage attack on the "robbing and murdering hordes of peasants" in better perspective if we consider the nature of the peasant revolts that racked Germany from 1524 to 1526, and in particular the part played in them by Thomas Müntzer.

Groups of peasants, interpreting Luther's Christian liberty as social freedom, made a series of demands on their feudal overlords. Some of the demands were moderate enough—the abolition of the death tax, the restoration of hunting, fishing, and forest rights preempted by the nobles —but when they were not promptly met, the peasants rampaged through the countryside, burning, looting, killing. In central Germany alone over forty castles and monasteries were destroyed. All of the defenders of the castle at Weinsberg were killed after they had surrendered; the count of Helfenstein was stabbed to death before the eyes of his wife and child.

Some of the wildest assaults were made by the followers of the fanatical Thomas Müntzer. Originally a follower of Luther, Müntzer abandoned him around 1520 to take up the cause of a "militant and bloodthirsty chiliasm."[30] Müntzer is a tragic example of the messianic revolutionary who wholly surrenders himself to terrorism and violence.

Müntzer taught that mankind was divided into two camps, the Elect and the ungodly. The Elect were privileged to have direct communication with the Almighty, for they had become new "spiritual" (or "pneumatic") men. In fact, the pneumatic man took on the aspect of divinity itself; he was entrusted by God with the mission of exterminating the forces of evil. The final victory, however, would take place only after a dreadful (but brief) interval of warfare, suffering, and upheaval, dur-

---

29. Luther, "Against the Robbing and Murdering Hordes of Peasants," in *Luther's Works*, vol. 46: *The Christian in Society III*, ed. Robert C. Schultz (Philadelphia: Fortress Press, 1967), p. 50. See also his "Open Letter" on this work in ibid., pp. 63–85, especially pp. 65, 73, and 81, where he repeatedly uses the violent language of the earlier tract, calling for rulers and obedient subjects to "stab, hew, beat, cut," and so on. This was the will of God, and anyone slain in a war waged to protect the authority of the state "would go straight to heaven" (p. 81).

30. Norman Cohn, *The Pursuit of the Millennium*, 2nd ed. (New York: Harper & Row, 1961), p. 252. The following discussion of Müntzer is based on Cohn's penetrating study, pp. 251–71.

ing which the forces of Antichrist, represented by the pope and the Turks, would prevail. But the sufferings of the Elect would only help to strengthen them for the final apocalyptic struggle.

Müntzer's thought went through a number of permutations. For a time he apparently hoped to enlist some of the princes on his side, princes who would begin the salutary enterprise of assassinating all "priests, monks, and godless rulers." The ungodly, he declared, "have no right to live, save what the Elect choose to allow them."[31] In order to attract men of power to his side, he counseled his followers to obey their overlords in temporal matters and not to press for the immediate overthrow of prevailing social and economic institutions. Material abundance and the abolition of status distinctions would come after the messianic revolution as a matter of course; the prime objective was to increase the strength of the Elect and to win converts.

When princes and lords failed to respond to his call, however, Müntzer turned on them with a vengeance, declaring that the hour had come for the overthrow of all "tyrants" and the commencement of the messianic millennium. It was at this point that Luther began to take up the cudgels against Müntzer and to warn the princes how dangerous his erstwhile follower had become.

Luther's attack called forth from Müntzer the pamphlet colorfully entitled "The Most Amply Called-for Defense and Answer to the Unspiritual Soft-Living Flesh at Wittenberg." Müntzer castigated Luther as an unstinting flatterer of princes and a defender of the unjust social order. Luther was silent, he sneered, about the "origin of all theft"— the expropriation by "our lords and princes" of land that rightfully belonged to all. The law was used by the princes to protect their own stolen bounty.

Müntzer was beheaded in 1525 after leading a virtually defenseless peasant army against the princes' forces, which cut them down in one of the bloodiest episodes of the revolts. The cause of violent egalitarian revolution was then taken up by others, culminating in the establishment of a dictatorship under Jan Bockelson, known as John of Leyden, in the town of Münster in 1534.

The revolutionaries of the Reformation are frequently lumped together under the heading of Anabaptists. Actually there were many groups that called themselves Anabaptists, and many of them had little in common with each other beyond their rejection of infant baptism. The original Anabaptists, former members of Zwingli's reform movement, were totally committed to pacifism, and the great majority re-

---

31. Ibid., p. 257.

mained nonviolent even after their religious concern was extended to the social sphere. A minority, however, spurred to indignation by the senseless slaughter of as many as 100,000 people in the peasants' revolts, turned to unlimited violence, and the reign of Bockelson at Münster was one of almost unbelievable terror and insane destructiveness. Yet to place the blame for violence exclusively on sectarian extremists is wholly unjustified, for the established rulers refused to listen to reasonable requests for correction of economic and social injustices and engaged in savagely bloody repression of dissidents. There is quite possibly some contemporary relevance in all this.

CALVIN AND THE HISTORY OF POLITICAL THOUGHT

In considering the relationship of Luther and John Calvin, one must bear in mind that, although Luther was the initiator and foremost figure of the Reformation, Calvin was no mere disciple or follower, but an independent thinker. In some respects their relationship is comparable to that of Plato and Aristotle, except that Calvin was never a student of Luther. He emerged as a leader in his own right around 1536, when the Lutheran revolt had already taken root and spread. Luther (1483–1546) and Calvin (1509–1564) were separated by a generation. More than that, they were men of profoundly different temperaments. Calvin was austere and sober; his writings are models of lucidity and organization. He was more practical than Luther in his handling of political questions, and he often showed more balanced judgment.

Calvin was more "radical" than Luther on questions of church ceremonial and organization. His teachings, together with those of Zwingli, the leading Protestant reformer in the German-speaking part of Switzerland, formed the nucleus of the Reformed church movement. The name Reformed was chosen in part to signify that the Lutheran (and later also the Anglican) church was not reformed enough. Vestments, images of Christ, Mary, and the saints, and elaborate stained-glass windows were ruled out as distracting from a properly spiritual worship of God. The episcopal structure of church organization, retained by the Lutherans, was abolished in favor of the congregational principle. Traditional practices such as the veneration of Mary, the keeping of saints' days, fasting during Lent, and so on were abolished in the Reformed communities.

Predestination

In his theology Calvin stressed the absolute sovereignty of God; the doctrine of predestination of the elect to heavenly bliss and of the damned to eternal perdition was a central tenet of Calvinism. In this doctrine Calvin was essentially at one with Luther, but he expressed it in ways that made for a different style of behavior on the part of his followers. Although Luther accepted the doctrine of predestination, as Augustine and Aquinas had done, he did not stress it and in fact did not seem to be entirely comfortable with it. Men were necessarily lost, Luther held, through some fault of their own under God's permissive or secondary will. Calvin found this position paradoxical and illogical. He carried the tenet of God's omniscience to its bitter conclusion in that "horrible decree," as he himself termed it, which his later followers turned into an unshakable conviction of their own righteousness, despite Calvin's denial that anyone could know who was saved and who was not.

Civil Government

Calvin was more realistic than Luther in his assessment of political matters. Again, the difference is one of emphasis and degree, but it is quite pronounced. If Calvin was more "revolutionary" with regard to changes in the form of worship, he was somewhat more traditional in his general political ideas. There is greater continuity between Calvin and classical or medieval political thought than between this tradition and Luther's political beliefs.

Whereas Luther, like Augustine, tended to view temporal government in negative terms (as the "kingdom of sin to restrain sin"), Calvin defended the Aristotelian and Thomistic thesis that man was by nature intended to live in a political community. Reason and natural law, shared by all men, he argued, demonstrate the necessity for secular law and government:

> Since man is by nature a social animal (*homo animal est natura sociale*), he is also inclined by a natural instinct to cherish and preserve society. Accordingly, we see that there are some general precepts of honesty and civil order impressed on the understanding of all men. For this reason there is no one who does not recognize that all human associations ought to be ruled by laws, and there is no one who does not possess the principle of these laws in his own understanding. For this reason there is a universal agreement among nations and individuals to accept laws, and there is a seed planted in us by nature rather than by a teacher or legislator.[32]

---

32. John Calvin, *Institutes of the Christian Religion,* trans. John Allen, 2 vols., 4th American ed., rev. (Philadelphia: Presbyterian Board of Education, 1843), vol. 1, bk. 2, chap. 2, sec. 13. Luther also declared man to be *naturaliter constitutus ad civilitatem et societatem* in his *Commentary on Galations* in 1531. Such expressions may be attributed in part to his eagerness to combat radical sectarianism and its rejection of worldly government. Luther's general position is that worldly government is necessary, but that this necessity is unfortunate. The gulf between Luther and Calvin

Calvin's emphasis on natural law and on the capacity of human reason to arrive at political judgments in conformity with this "higher law" points up another difference between his teaching and Luther's. While it is true that Luther did not explicitly repudiate the concept of natural law, and even used the term on occasion,[33] and while it is also true that the prominence of the sovereign will of God in Calvin's theology is in some degree uncongenial to traditional thinking on natural law,[34] Calvin did nonetheless restore a good part of the scholastic political theory thrown out as "pagan" by Luther. In fact, Calvin had much greater respect than Luther for premodern political thought in general and for Aristotle in particular.

Although Calvin agreed with Luther on the need to make a sharp distinction between the spiritual and the temporal spheres, he thought

on the benefit of worldly social existence can be measured by comparing this passage from the *Institutes* with Luther's statement in *De servo arbitrio* that "there is no middle kingdom between the kingdoms of God and of Satan, which fight together perpetually. This shows that the highest virtues in the heathen, the best things in the philosophers, appear to be honourable before the world, but before God they are in truth flesh, and they serve the Kingdom of Satan."

33. In his *Commentary on Psalm 101*, for example, he refers to natural law as "healthy law" and "positive" law as "sick law." It appears, however, that Luther believed that reliable interpreters of natural law are very rare and exceptional "heroes" or "miracle workers" (*Wunderleute*). These extraordinary men are in effect not bound by law as ordinary mortals understand it. Such a doctrine, of course, fundamentally distorts the basic concept of natural law as it had been understood—that is, a law that is knowable in principle by all men through right reason. To Aquinas, participation in eternal reason through natural reason is the fundamental characteristic of man's humanity. We have indeed come far from this idea in Luther. See *Luther's Works*, vol. 13: *Selected Psalms II*, ed. Jaroslav Pelikan, trans. Martin H. Bertram et al. (Philadelphia: Muhlenberg Press, 1956), pp. 163–65, and Cranz, *Luther's Thought*, p. 109.

34. The significance of natural law in Calvin's theology and his estimation of man's rational capacities continue to be debated to this day. Karl Barth and his followers minimize the place of natural law in Calvin's thought, while Calvinists such as Emil Brunner give it central importance. See John Baillie, ed., *Natural Theology* (London, 1946). A little light may be thrown on the problem by a consideration of the ways in which his views differed from Aquinas'. For Calvin, the fall of man was of such significance as to mar and deform (although not to blot out) man's natural understanding; nature was always *fallen* nature in a way in which it was not for Aquinas. Similarly, government for Calvin was "natural," but only because man's fall from grace made it necessary. He did not agree with Aquinas that government was needed even in the state of innocence before the fall. As Calvin expressed the matter in his *Commentary on James* (3:9): "Were anyone to say that the image of God in human nature had been blotted out by the sin of Adam, we must indeed confess that it has been miserably deformed, but in such a way that some of its lineaments still appear. Righteousness and rectitude and the freedom of choosing what is good have been lost; but many excellent endowments, by which we excel the brutes, still remain." I am indebted to James Childress of the Department of Religious Studies of the University of Virginia for pointing out this passage, as well as for generally helpful comments on this chapter.

it crucial to point out that "this distinction does not lead us to consider the whole system of civil government as a polluted theory which has nothing to do with Christian men."[35] For him "civil magistracy" was not only a "holy and legitimate" calling, but "by far the most sacred and honorable in human life."[36] While Luther always affirmed the necessity of civil government, he did not in principle confer so exalted a status upon it.

In spite of Max Weber's brilliantly argued thesis that Calvinism was a key motive force in the development of modern capitalism,[37] Calvin himself did not break abruptly from the teachings of Aquinas and other medieval writers on the question of usury and the hazards to the soul of valuing wealth as an end in itself;[38] and even though his ideas about church government were completely opposed to the Catholic papal-monarchical principle, his concept of an ecclesiastical polity as the normative social order wherever it could be achieved was more medieval than modern. Nevertheless, one can detect in Calvin's thought a certain potentiality and even propensity for secularization, particularly in his doctrine of vocation or "calling"; Calvin was even more emphatic than Luther in rejecting monasticism and in stressing that all worthy occupations in the world were "holy." The Calvinist ethic was strenuously activist.

It is not surprising that numerous commentators have detected a close relationship between Calvinism and the growth of modern constitutional government. The seeds for this development are in Calvin's own writings; he unambiguously opposed absolute monarchy and favored a polity that combined democratic and aristocratic elements.[39] Furthermore, his references to the salutary effects of the ephorate (the collective body of magistrates) of ancient Sparta in checking the excesses of the kings and his explicit exhortation to contemporary magistrates to exer-

---

35. "The spiritual kingdom of Christ and civil government are things very different and remote from each other" (Calvin, *On God and Political Duty*, ed. John T. McNeill [New York: Liberal Arts Press, 1958], p. 45).

36. Ibid., p. 49.

37. Weber, *Protestant Ethic.*

38. See, for example, André Bieler, *The Social Humanism of Calvin*, trans. Paul T. Fuhrmann (Richmond, Va.: John Knox Press), especially pp. 28–63.

39. Calvin, *On God and Political Duty*, p. 53: "I shall by no means deny that either aristocracy or a mixture of aristocracy and democracy far excels all others" (i.e., all other forms of government). He goes on to observe that it is rare that kings can "regulate themselves" so that they always rule justly. "The vice or imperfection of men therefore renders it safer and more tolerable for government to be in the hands of many, that they may afford each other mutual assistance and admonition, and that if anyone arrogate to himself more than is right, the many may act as censors and masters to restrain his ambition."

cise a similar function whenever possible influenced the development of a "duty to resist" doctrine in French Huguenot, Dutch, and Scottish Reformed political thought.[40] The key passage, which was the subject of numerous commentaries and explications by Calvinists in the sixteenth and seventeenth centuries, may be found in his *Institutes of the Christian Religion:*

> For though the correction of tyrannical domination is the vengeance of God, we are not, therefore, to conclude that it is committed to us, who have received no other command than to obey and suffer. This observation I always apply to private persons. For if there be, in the present day, any magistrates appointed for the protection of the people and the moderation of the power of kings, such as were, in ancient times, the Ephori, who were a check upon the Lacedaemonians [Spartans], or the popular tribunes upon the consuls among the Romans, or the Demarchi upon the Senate among the Athenians; or with power such as is perhaps now possessed by the three estates in every kingdom when they are assembled; I am so far from prohibiting them, in the discharge of their duty, to oppose the violence or cruelty of kings, that I affirm that if they connive at kings in their oppression of their people, such forbearance involves the most nefarious perfidy, because they fraudulently betray the liberty of the people, of which they know that they have been appointed protectors by the ordination of God.[41]

Undoubtedly, Calvinists such as John Knox (who invoked the authority of this passage in demanding the deposition of Mary of Guise as queen regent) and George Buchanan in Scotland, François Hotman and Theodore Beza in France (exiled to Geneva), the anonymous Huguenot author of the *Vindiciae contra tyrannos,* and Johannes Althusius in the Netherlands went beyond Calvin in preaching the right of resistance; for Calvin, this right belonged exclusively to the "magistrates"—men legally empowered to take action. Calvin "confessed" that "rulers owe mutual duties to their subjects," but since he stated explicitly and at length that subjects owed obedience to the ruler whether he treated them justly or not, this "confession" can hardly be considered the equivalent of a social contract theory. Nonetheless, in these passages from the *Institutes* and in others of Calvin's writings we can detect sign-

---

40. See the excellent discussion in Wolin, *Politics and Vision,* p. 188.

41. Calvin, *Institutes,* bk. 4, chap. 20, sec. 31. For a discussion of Calvin's endorsement of government "by common consent," see the informative article by H. D. Foster, "The Political Theories of Calvinists Before the Puritan Exodus to America," *American Historical Review,* 21 (1916): 481–503, especially p. 484. "Even when men become kings by hereditary right, this does not seem consistent with liberty," Calvin wrote in his *Commentary on Micah.*

posts pointing the way toward these doctrines. It would be more difficult to deduce them from Luther, whose denial that anyone at all had the right to challenge the authority of the prince leads more logically to a form of absolutism than to constitutionalism.

Like Luther, Calvin was always eager to combat millennarian interpretations of the New Testament, such as those espoused by the radical sectarians. In the final chapter of the *Institutes* (Book 4, Chapter 20) he proclaims civil government to be "equally as necessary to mankind as bread and water, light and air, and far more excellent." Those who argue that temporal government can be done away with and that the church can take the place of all laws "foolishly imagine a perfection which can never be found in any community of men." To "entertain a thought of its extermination" is "inhuman barbarism," Calvin concludes.

Important as is the civil polity for our sojourn on earth, the redeemed man's true government is the kingdom of God within him. Christ is at once prophet, priest, and king. The kingdom over which he presides is spiritual and "not of this world." All those who would seek to create a perfect community of the saints without government or private property have completely misunderstood Christ, who himself refused all external worldly dominion. "It ought to be known," proclaims the great Geneva reformer, that

> whatever felicity is promised in Christ, consists not in external accommodations, such as a life of joy and tranquility, abundant wealth, security from every injury, and numerous delights suited to our carnal desires, but in that which is peculiar to the heavenly state. ... Christ enriches his people with every thing necessary to the eternal salvation of their souls, and arms them with strength to enable them to stand invincible against all the assaults of their spiritual foes. Whence we infer that he reigns rather for us than for himself. ... Here we are briefly taught what advantage results to us from the kingdom of Christ. For since it is not terrestrial or carnal ... but spiritual, it elevates us even to eternal life, that we may patiently pass through this life in afflictions, hunger, cold, contempt, reproaches, and other disagreeable circumstances, contented with this single assurance: that our King will never desert us. ...[42]

RICHARD HOOKER AND THE ANGLICAN *VIA MEDIA*

By the Act of Supremacy of 1534, the English parliament had proclaimed King Henry VIII "Head of the Church of England," thereby abolishing the papal jurisdiction in the realm. This left England with a national

---

42. Calvin, *Institutes*, bk. 2, chap. 15.

church that claimed to be both Catholic and reformed: Catholic because episcopal government was maintained, the apostolic succession of bishops was continued unbroken, and much of the ceremony and ritual of Catholicism was retained; reformed because increased emphasis was placed upon Scripture, certain medieval accretions in ecclesiastical practice and dogma were discarded, and the claim of the pope (regarded by Anglicans as having jurisdiction only over the see of Rome) to ultimate spiritual authority over all Christians was rejected.

After Henry's death in 1547, many Protestant reforms were effected in liturgy and doctrine during the reign of Edward VI. Two editions of the Book of Common Prayer were issued, one in 1549 and a more radically Protestant one in 1551. After Edward there was a brief movement back to Rome under Mary, who was succeeded by Elizabeth I in 1558.

It was the new queen who brought about what became known as the Elizabethan Settlement, which gave Anglicanism the form in which it continues today. A new Act of Supremacy was passed by parliament and a new edition of the Book of Common Prayer was issued, with many of the Protestant features of the second Edwardian edition removed. The Act of Supremacy claimed to base the monarch's position as head of the church on ancient statutes; thus the Church of England was "no new thing," but rather a continuation of the church as it had been established in England centuries earlier.

Church Organization and Practices

When the learned Anglican priest Richard Hooker started writing his multivolumed work *Of the Laws of Ecclesiastical Polity* in 1593, his purpose was to justify and defend the Elizabethan Settlement against the Puritans, or English Calvinist dissenters. Hooker (widely known as "the judicious Hooker," thanks to John Locke's repeated references to Sir William Cooper's epithet) argued that the specific form of church order was a matter for human reason to devise, and that Scripture contained no specific blueprint of ecclesiastical organization. So long as the "essentials" of Christian faith and practice were maintained—and Hooker accepted as authoritative the creeds and pronouncements of the first four church councils, held prior to the schism between East and West in the eleventh century—it was of no importance which specific practices and patterns of organization were adopted.

Although it would be a mistake to consider Hooker an unreflective mossback who ritualistically defended all ancient and venerable usages, he did possess a far greater respect for tradition than Luther, and he did not, like Calvin, accept as valid only those religious practices specifically mentioned in the Scriptures. He took a relaxed view of what he regarded as "things indifferent," preferring to follow "reason" *and* "tradition" than to risk "turning the world upside down." He admitted that no specific warrant could be found in the Bible for many practices of the Church of England, as the Puritans charged, but he contended that these practices were allowable so long as they were not specifically prohibited by Scripture. Traditions evolved over the centuries by organized communities of Christians should not be summarily overthrown, he held, since these communities too were authoritative sources of Christian practice.

Philosophy and Theology

As Hooker worked on his *Laws of Ecclesiastical Polity* he became increasingly absorbed in the larger philosophical and theological questions raised by his subject. He was so far from being a mere polemicist writing in defense of an immediate practical interest that he never even concluded the final book of the *Laws,* in which he was to provide the clinching arguments for the type of church government worked out in the Elizabethan Settlement. His main interest was clearly in broader questions of political philosophy (the nature of law and authority, the relationship of reason and tradition, the source of moral and political knowledge). Book 1 is a masterful exposition of the nature of law, rivaling that of Thomas Aquinas in depth, conceptual sophistication, and lucidity. As Christopher Morris has written, it is "remarkable how often Hooker's argument transcends the purely ephemeral purposes of his own day. Much that he wrote was written ... 'for all time' and has seemed valid ... to men of other generations."[43] In an age of ferocious controversy, Hooker was widely admired for his courtesy and equanimity even by many of his most vehement opponents and critics, and, if we are to believe the account in Izaak Walton's *Life of Mr. Richard Hooker,* was hailed by Pope Clement VIII as a man who "indeed deserves the name of an author" and whose "books will get reverence by age."

Reason and Revelation. Richard Hooker was learned in Greek, and his pages are sprinkled with references to the Greek philosophers, especially Aristotle, whom he hailed as the "archphilosopher." His evaluation of both classical and medieval scholastic philosophy was basically positive. He rejected any attempt by radical Protestants to repudiate the Western philosophical tradition and its high valuation of reason.

Hooker's intellectual affinity with Thomas Aquinas (both men were

---

43. Richard Hooker, *Of the Laws of Ecclesiastical Polity,* 2 vols. (London: Everyman's Library, 1907), vol. 1, Introduction, p. xii.

temperamentally judicious and both attempted to reconcile reason with
revelation and Greek philosophy with Christian theology) has led at least
one scholar to conclude that he was basically a "Thomist and an Aristotelian."[44] Although this conclusion seems unnecessarily sweeping, particularly when the same author finds Hooker's teaching diametrically
opposed to Calvin's,[45] it would appear far closer to the mark than another interpretation that holds Hooker to have been a "Calvinist" and
"Calvinistic in doctrine."[46] As the leading intellect of sixteenth-century
Anglicanism and as a principal defender of the Elizabethan Settlement,
Richard Hooker was a proponent of moderation and the *via media*.
He could and did draw from both Calvin and Aquinas in his own work,
although he roundly opposed those Calvinists who he concluded went
far beyond Calvin in disparaging reason, and disagreed with Aquinas
on the question of church government and its relation to temporal authority, without ever furnishing a clear solution to this problem himself.

Hooker rejected on principle the doctrine that fallible man could
attain to a perfect and infallible knowledge of God. "Here below we
see through a glass darkly"—these words from 1 Corinthians 13 summarize
Hooker's general position on the interpretation of biblical revelation.
Through reason man can know God only by analogy with finite experi-
ence. In his use of the doctrine of the analogy of being (*analogia entis*),
Hooker was following in the footsteps of Aquinas—and ultimately of
Heraclitus.

> Dangerous it were for the feeble brain of man to wade far into
> the doings of the Most High; whom although to know be life . . .
> yet our soundest knowledge is to know that we know him not as
> indeed he is, neither can know him: and our safest eloquence con-
> cerning him is our silence, when we confess without confession
> that his glory is inexplicable, his greatness above our capacity and
> reach. He is above and we upon earth; therefore it behooveth our
> words to be wary and few.[47]

We cannot grasp God as we grasp intellectually an object of sense
experience: with "religious ignorance" we can only "humbly and meekly
adore" him.

---

44. Peter Munz, *The Place of Hooker in the History of Thought* (London:
Routledge & Kegan Paul, 1952), p. ix.

45. Ibid., p. 145.

46. H. D. Foster, "International Calvinism Through Locke and the Revolution
of 1688," *American Historical Review*, 32 (1927): 476. One cannot help wondering
whether Foster has confused Richard Hooker with the later Puritan Thomas Hooker,
who emigrated to America in 1633 and in 1636 founded the colony of Connecticut.

47. Hooker, *Laws of Ecclesiastical Polity*, vol. 1, pp. 150–51.

"Think ye are men, deem it not impossible for you to err"—this is the key to Hooker's spirit and style of thought. The quiet sobriety of his treatises and sermons contrasts markedly with the hysterical outbursts of lesser writers in this period of passionate controversy. Quite obviously he had little taste for polemical exchanges:

> Far more comfort it were for us (so small is the joy we take in these strifes . . .) to be joined with you [the Puritans] in bonds of indissoluble love and amity . . . rather than in such dismembered sort to spend our few and wretched days in a tedious persecuting of wearisome contentions. . . .[48]

Hooker vigorously denied that he wrote to "serve the time," and his denial appears credible when we consider the work as a whole. In his view, the mind of man, "being by nature speculative and delighted in contemplation in itself," could desire to know things for no other reason than "for mere knowledge and understanding's sake."[49] It may be that Hooker left the *Laws of Ecclesiastical Polity* unfinished because he was never able to reconcile his belief in the church's fundamental freedom of inquiry with its subjection to a temporal head.

The Nature of Law

But if the *Laws of Ecclesiastical Polity* is incomplete and insufficient as an apology for Anglicanism, as a work of political theory it ranks very high indeed. As I have said, Book 1, dealing with the nature of law, is on a par with Aquinas' magisterial discussion of law in the *Summa theologica*.

Aquinas formulated a fourfold division of law: eternal law, natural law, divine law, and human law. (1) Eternal law is the reason of God, known fully only to himself. All law that is truly law participates in the eternal law, though this participation may vary in mode and degree. Man participates in the eternal law not only instinctually, as animals do, but consciously and deliberately, through his reason. (2) This "participation of the rational creature in the eternal law" is called the natural law (*lex naturalis*). It is by virtue of the natural law that man becomes aware of those moral principles essential to human existence, as distinct from merely animal existence. The first principle of the natural law is that the good is actively to be sought and evil avoided. From this it follows that man should recognize his obligation to honor God, respect the lives and possessions of his fellow human beings, and fulfill his duties as a member of the family and organized society. The natural law is capable of varied application, but its general principles remain un-

---

48. Ibid., p. 144.
49. Ibid., p. 178.

alterable; it is immutable and universal, morally binding on all men everywhere. (3) Divine law is that part of the eternal law made known to man by revelation; to the Christian this means specifically the revelation contained in the Bible. Divine law can be subdivided into the old and the new laws of the Old and New Testaments. Divine law does not annul or contradict human law, just as revelation does not annul reason: "Grace does not annul nature but perfects it." Divine law supplements natural law by indicating a perfection beyond nature; it also confirms men in the knowledge of natural law by adding divine sanction to the teachings of the natural law arrived at by reason, independently of revelation. Thus many of the Ten Commandments also form part of the natural law. (4) Human law for Aquinas is law only insofar as it conforms to natural law. An unjust law is not a true law and the man of conscience is not obliged to obey it, although he may choose to obey it if an even greater evil would result from an act of disobedience. Tyrannical rule is characterized by a willful and persistent disregard of the natural law.

The Law of Nature

Hooker appropriates Aquinas' formulations in substance and in much of their detail. He does not merely restate the Thomistic teachings, however; he elaborates on them even more eloquently than Aquinas did, particularly in regard to the natural law. Here Hooker makes a distinction that Aquinas does not, cutting through the ambiguity in the term "nature." The Roman jurisconsult Ulpian wrote that the natural law is what nature has "taught all animals"; this law is concerned with the biological preservation of all creatures. This raises a problem for man, who is a compound of two natures: the "lower," which he shares with all animals, and the "higher," which concerns the sphere of reason and the intellect. Aquinas includes under natural law both the "lower" and "higher" aspects of nature. Hooker, on the other hand, distinguishes between the "law of nature" and the "law of reason." It is the law of reason that governs man as a rational being and moral agent, whereas the law of nature rules his physical existence and biological impulses (hunger, sex), as it rules those of "all animals." Insofar as he is a "natural agent," man is subject to the law of nature; but insofar as he is a "voluntary agent," capable of rational choice, he is responsible to the law of reason.

The Law of Reason

Man, Hooker declares, possesses in addition to "sensible knowledge which is common unto us with beasts the ability of rising higher than unto sensible things." He can "attain unto knowledge of . . . things unsensible" by virtue of the faculty of reason. Here Hooker recalls Plato's teaching that the philosopher inwardly "sees" the Good by means of his intellect (*nous*) and reason (*logos*). Man "sees" goodness, writes Hooker, "with the eye of the understanding"; and the "light of that eye is reason." It is by the "light of reason" that "good may be known from evil." Hooker's distinction of reason, will, and appetite[50] preserves the essentials of Platonic psychology, with its tripartite division of the soul into reason, spirit and appetite.

Hooker defines the law of reason, or that "which men commonly used to call the law of nature," as "the law which human nature itself is in reason universally bound unto." This law "comprehendeth all those things which men by the light of their natural understanding evidently know, or at leastwise may know, to be beseeming or unbeseeming, virtuous or vicious, good or evil for them to do." As its name suggests, this law is "investigable by the light of natural understanding" and not dependent on God's revelation to man at a particular point in space and time. The world "has always been acquainted" with the immutable and binding principles of natural law, Hooker says, and he cites the famous reference to "unwritten" higher laws in the *Antigone* of Sophocles as supporting evidence.[51]

The Fall of Man. The law of reason is accessible to all men who will consult it. Many men "smother their natural understanding," however, and out of slavishness to appetite and intellectual laziness distort its meaning and fail to follow its precepts. Hooker is closer to Calvin than to Aquinas in his views of the depravity of fallen man. For Aquinas, the fall of man as told in Genesis impaired but did not invalidate the operation of reason. While neither Calvin nor Hooker fundamentally disagrees with this conclusion[52] (otherwise it would have been impossible for them to embrace any meaningful doctrine of natural law), both of them stress the deleterious consequences of the fall far more than Aquinas did, and consequently may be regarded as more pessimistic than he about men's probable behavior. ("Laws politic," Hooker says, "are never formed as they should be, unless presuming... man to be in regard of his depraved mind little better than a wild beast."[53]) Aquinas was not blind to man's enormous potential for evil, however. He, Calvin, and Hooker all sought to express within the Christian tradition a funda-

---

50. Ibid., p. 172.

51. Ibid., p. 182.

52. See n. 34 on contemporary disagreements on the place of natural law in Calvin's theology. See also Jacques Ellul, *Theological Foundation of Law,* trans. Marguerite Weiser (New York: Seabury Press, 1969).

53. Hooker, *Laws of Ecclesiastical Polity,* vol. 1, p. 188.

mental truth of human existence: that human development always falls short of its potential, and man cannot escape the tension between his life as it is and as it might be. Some men "fall" further and more consistently than others from the maximal expression of their humanity, but even among the fallen, the light of natural reason has not been extinguished. For Hooker, men are essentially equal in their potentiality to conform to the "sacred law of their nature," but empirically unequal in their ability to fulfill the task. Any theory of human nature must take its bearings from the highest character type, however, not from the lowest.

Hooker regarded intellectual sloth as one of the factors that prevented many men from consciously grasping the law of reason implicit in their being. "The search for knowledge is a thing painful," he observed, "and the painfulness of knowledge is that which maketh the will so hardly inclinable thereunto."[54] The soundest means to discover the law of reason is through "causes," or by philosophical inquiry into first principles. Those unwilling or unable to master the intellectual discipline necessary for that enterprise can learn what the law is from "signs." Signs of the law of reason are practices that have the approval of "the general and perpetual voice of men"—practices that men have at all times regarded as just and good. The law of reason itself is not the product of human agreement, however; even if some collective absence of mind were to cause this universal approbation to cease, the law of reason would still remain as the objective measure of right action. Making explicit the philosophical basis for the law of reason is therefore an essential and enduring task of the philosopher.

Supernatural Law and the *Summum Bonum*

Hooker's doctrine of the law of reason clearly contains a philosophical anthropology or critical inquiry into the nature of man. This anthropology is completed with his discussion of "supernatural law" (the equivalent of Aquinas' "divine law"), in which Hooker takes up the topic of the highest good (*summum bonum*) for man in the absolute sense. Here he reminds one of Augustine's analysis in Book 19 of *The City of God*. Hooker argues that even if a man led the life of reason to its fullest possible perfection, he would yearn for an even greater perfection. Even contemplation is an instrumental rather than an absolute end. Aristotle took the contemplative life (*bios theorētikos*) to be the highest kind of life; for Hooker philosophic contemplation is not an end in itself, but the means by which we come more fully to behold the order fashioned by God. "No good is infinite but only God."

---

54. Ibid., p. 173.

Therefore not even the joys of the life of reason can fulfill man; beyond this perfection of his natural powers there is a supernatural perfection for which he yearns. The eternal enjoyment of God beyond time and the world is the true *summum bonum* for man. Supernatural law—the law of the gospel—guides man to this ultimate end.[55]

Human Law

In analyzing human or "positive" laws, Hooker takes up the question of the foundation of government as such. It is primarily from this section that Locke later quoted in order to lend Hooker's authority to his own ideas on civil government, particularly his notions of the state of nature and the social contract.[56] Although it would be idle to deny that there are traces of both of these ideas in Hooker, he and Locke differ decisively in the weight and importance they give them. The state of nature and the social contract are central to Locke but only peripheral to Hooker.

The State of Nature. Hooker is far closer to Aristotle than to Locke in his analysis of the origin and end of the body politic. Indeed, in the passage from Hooker that Locke cites to support his own view of the state of nature,[57] Hooker is actually citing Aristotle as his authority for the contention that there is a right by nature, or universal justice, binding on all men, whether they are members of the same body politic or not. Hooker here passes over the whole question of a so-called state of nature to make a very Aristotelian point: that men are "naturally induced to seek communion and fellowship with others." For him, as for Aristotle, society is man's natural condition (man is "by nature" a "political animal"); by declaring that man's natural state is presocial and that society is artificial and conventional, Hobbes and Locke basically transform the Aristotelian teaching, echoed in Aquinas, on the natural sociability of mankind. Hooker continues and reaffirms that teaching. Here we have the measure of the distance between Hooker on the one hand and Hobbes and Locke on the other, although traces of the idea of natural sociability can still be discerned in Locke's often rather inconsistent account of the state of nature.

What Hooker actually says on this subject is that inasmuch as

---

55. Ibid., pp. 202–3.

56. "But I thought Hooker alone might be enough to satisfie those Men, who relying on him for their Ecclesiastical Polity, are by strange fate carried to deny those principles upon which he builds it" (John Locke, *Two Treatises of Civil Government*, ed. Peter Laslett [New York: Mentor Books, 1965], p. 239). Locke here uses Hooker to appeal to his more "conservative" readers, especially among the Anglican clergy. As Laslett points out, Locke decided to add quotations from Hooker after completing the work.

57. Ibid., p. 15.

we are not by ourselves sufficient to furnish ourselves with competent store of things needful for such a life as our nature doth desire, a life fit for the dignity of man; therefore to supply these defects and imperfections which are in us living singly and solely by ourselves, we are naturally induced to seek communion and fellowship with others.[58]

It was by natural inclination, then, that men united themselves in "politic Societies, which societies could not be without Government." Following Aristotle, who had discovered the *polis* to exist by nature with the assistance of art or human contrivance, Hooker finds that "two foundations there are which bear up public societies; the one, a natural inclination, whereby all men desire sociable life and fellowship; the other, an order expressly or secretly agreed upon touching the manner of their union in living together." This "order" Hooker refers to not as a contract, but as the "law of a Commonweal, the very soul of a politic body, the parts whereof are by law animated, held together, and set on work in such actions as the common good requireth."[59]

When Hooker does refer specifically to the presocial condition, it is to compare it unfavorably with that of civil society. There is no idealization of the state of nature as a state of peace and liberty, as we find in parts of Locke's work.

We all make complaint of the iniquity of our times: not unjustly, for the days are evil. But compare them with those times wherein there were no civil societies, with those times wherein there was as yet no manner of public regiment established . . . and we have surely good cause to think that God hath blessed us exceedingly, and hath made us behold most happy days.[60]

The presocial state was one to which man was reduced by catastrophe; it was a condition of limitation, not a fulfillment of his "nature."

The Social Contract. Following Aquinas, Hooker held that human laws, or those "laws which men impose upon themselves," were applications of the principles of the law of reason to particular situations. Although the principles remained the same, their applications varied with circumstances; hence the variety of positive laws among men. Positive laws carry with them the ultimate sanction of coercion; they can affect only the outward actions of men, however, and are not truly

58. Hooker, *Laws of Ecclesiastical Polity,* vol. 1, pp. 187–88. The reference in Hooker's footnote (given in Greek) from Aristotle's *Rhetoric* reads: "For there really is, as everyone to some extent divines, a natural justice and injustice that is binding on all men, even on those who have no association or covenant with each other."

59. Ibid., p. 188.
60. Ibid., p. 190.

laws unless they conform to right reason. Hooker contends that the legitimacy of laws depends on consent; but for all practical purposes this consent is tacit, not explicitly stated in any way that could be interpreted as a contract. If specific laws and institutions have existed for many generations without being challenged, we may assume that they have "public approbation." A respect for tradition, however, need not restrain government from ordaining "that which never was," or generally from rectifying abuses, if in so doing it obtains the "public approbation" of the current generation. Men may be presumed to consent to the "public regiment" under which they live "when that society whereof we are part hath at any time before consented, without revoking the same after universal agreement."[61]

Though Hooker does not actually use the term "social contract," he does refer to men "growing into composition and agreement amongst themselves by ordaining some kind of government public."[62] But this idea, like the concept of the state of nature, is touched upon only tangentially in Hooker's writing. It is in no sense at the center of his political theory, unless we define "consent" in the broad sense in which it was often understood in the Middle Ages. By invoking consent he does not mean to endorse any specific constitutional mechanism, although, as we would expect, he does employ the language of consent to indicate his hostility to tyrannical and arbitrary government. A government's laws must be measured by the law of reason, and basic constitutional principles and practices are to be modified only after suitable deliberation. Unless positive laws reveal "manifest iniquity" and are clearly against the law of reason, however, men are obliged to obey them.

Nor does he mean by "consent" the sovereignty of contemporary public opinion. For Hooker, consent is ordinarily implicit in a society's quiet acceptance of established institutions and practices. Acceptance does not necessarily require complete approval. Men cannot expect or demand that social arrangements will suit their private preferences in any precise fashion, for these arrangements can be determined in a variety of ways that meet the minimal condition of legitimacy by not violating the law of reason. Therefore, they may be regarded as "indifferent." We are obliged by the law of reason to accept indifferent arrangements long established, for it is a precept of the law of reason that the public takes precedence over private preference; for "except our own private but probable resolutions be by the law of public determinations

<hr />

61. Ibid., p. 194.
62. Ibid., p. 190.

overruled, we take away all possibility of sociable life in the world."[63]
By "following the law of private reason, where the law of public should
take place," we "breed disturbance."[64]

The Law of Nations

In addition to the universal law of reason, binding on all men, and the
positive or "municipal" laws of each society, Hooker cites a "third kind
of law which toucheth all such several bodies politic, so far forth as one
of them hath public commerce with another." This is the "law of nations,"
or what today we would call international law. Hooker follows the Stoics
in holding that there is a universal community of men, for all men by
nature "covet (if it might be) to have a kind of society and fellowship
even with all mankind." Hooker does not dwell on the law of nations:

> Primary laws of nations are such as concern embassage, such as be-
> long to the courteous entertainment of foreigners and strangers,
> such as serve for commodious traffick, and the like. Secondary laws
> in the same kind are such as this present unquiet world is most
> familiarly acquainted with; I mean laws of arms, which yet are
> much better known than kept. But what matter the Law of Nations
> doth contain I omit search.[65]

Hooker has such a lively and immediate sense of the community of
nations that he is led to draw an analogy between the law of nations and
the civil law of a particular society. Just as no individual subject can
"overrule" municipal or civil law, so no individual nation can rightfully
"annihilate that whereupon the whole world hath agreed."[66] Hooker
assumes that both the law of nations and the civil laws of particular
societies are forms of positive human law, and therefore enforceable on
men by governmental authority. He does not specifically discuss the
difficulties of enforcing the law of nations when there is no world
government to undertake the task, but it is clear that he is aware of
these difficulties when he observes that the "laws of arms" are "much
better known than kept." It is probable that he believes the universal
community of mankind (what the Stoics called the *cosmopolis*) to be an
existential reality even if it is not represented by a power structure.

It is around the existential situation, with its tensions between order
and freedom, the potential and the actual, that Hooker's analysis is

---

63. Ibid., p. 228.
64. Ibid., p. 229.
65. Ibid., p. 199.
66. Ibid.

structured. The breakdown of order and the violation of justice are not the whole of political reality to Hooker; man's imperfect but constant striving for right order and his consciousness of his failure to conform to a pattern knowable by reason are also dimensions of political reality. Since he stresses man's capacity for fellowship and community at least as much as his propensity for antagonism and violence, Hooker doubtless may be categorized as a normative rather than an empirical theorist by those who have become fond of this distinction. Yet he may well be more fully empirical than many writers who are called empiricists.

Church Polity

It is only after the lengthy philosophical discussion of the nature and kinds of law in Book 1 that Hooker actually turns his attention to the Anglican-Puritan controversy over the form of church polity. Even after he changes his focus, however, he is never merely partisan, and he never abandons the discussion of theoretical issues. And although he argues vigorously, he retains his good manners to the end. Again and again he defends human reason against the denigrations of some Puritan spokesmen, counseling intellectual modesty and a recognition of the inherent limits and fallibility of all human knowledge in the face of claims by some authors to possess infallible "spiritual" knowledge through revelation. All of man's knowledge of the invisible divine order is "darkly apprehended," and yet such as it is, it is still knowledge. Recognition of both the range and the limits of knowledge is characteristic of Hooker.

Hooker cites Aristotle and Aquinas in rejecting the view that Athens and Jerusalem, reason and revelation, philosophy and Scripture are antithetical. Predictably, this reliance on philosophy drew the ire of some neo-Calvinist writers, although it is not certain how much it would have disturbed Calvin himself. "If Aristotle and the Schoolmen be such perilous creatures," Hooker wryly noted, his opponents, "whom God hath so fairly blest from too much knowledge in them," must indeed be happy men. As for the authority of Scripture, he wrote, "I think of the Scripture of God as reverently as the best of the purified crew in the world. I except not any, no not the founders themselves and captaines of that faction."[67]

Supremacy vs. Sovereignty. Since Hooker experienced the universe as an ordered whole in which each part was governed by laws that participated in God's eternal law, it is scarcely surprising that he could not accept the ideas of political absolutism that were to be so congenial

---

67. Ibid., p. 318n.

to Hobbes. Although Hooker does use the phrase "uncommanded commander" (in Book 8) to describe the king, there actually is no monistic view of sovereignty in his writings. Within the English commonwealth the king has "supremacy," but this term is not the equivalent of Hobbes's absolute and unrestrained "sovereignty." Hooker ascribes too much importance to law to place any ruler beyond its requirements. The king possesses supremacy, but supremacy is not unlimited power, "simply without exception of anything." "What man is so brainsick" as to believe the ruler above the law of God and the fundamental laws of the commonwealth? "The best established dominion . . . is where law doth most rule the King."

Hooker, then, is a proponent of constitutional monarchy, although the restraints he envisages are as medieval as they are modern. He is a transitional figure in the history of political thought. Although he is aware of parliament's potential as a counterforce to the power of the king, he relies primarily upon the restraints of the "higher law" and the fundamental "laws of the land" to prevent arbitrary government rather than on a "social contract" or bill of rights. Certainly Hooker makes no mention of the right to revolution, of parliamentary supremacy, or of natural rights as claims against the government.

Temporal Power and the Church. If legitimate rule was identical with rule under law in temporal affairs, the same was true in church polity. As a defender of the Elizabethan Settlement, Hooker could hardly have been expected to plead either for the separation of church and state or for church control of the government. Even so, he did not seek to hand over the English church, lock, stock, and barrel, to the temporal authorities. Over the centuries the English church had developed a complicated set of laws and procedures appropriate to its life and its work; changes in these laws, he contended, could not be rightfully made by the monarch without the consent of the clergy "in convocation assembled." As one subdivision of the larger unity of Western Christendom, the Church of England was also subject to the decisions of the first four church councils, the only ones that could truly be called ecumenical. (Admittedly, there was more than a small amount of unresolved tension between Christian universalism and the idea of a national church.)

As head of the church, then, the king was legally empowered to appoint its prelates and to give final approval to changes in its ritual and dogma. The monarch's powers were severely limited, however, and his rule of the church was no more absolute than his rule of the temporal realm. It would be a "thing very scandalous and offensive . . . if either kings or laws should dispose of the law of God, without any respect had unto that which of old hath been reverently thought of throughout the world,"[68] Hooker declared. Although he invoked some of the arguments of Marsilius of Padua in his argument against papal authority, Hooker, as one scholar has pointed out, was closer in spirit to Thomas Aquinas than to Marsilius.[69]

The Dissolution of the Christian Polity

In his reformulation of the medieval concept of the ecclesiastical polity, with its two distinct yet interrelated realms of church and common-wealth, Hooker was affirming an institutional complex that was already in its death throes. The form of the "established church" would remain in England and on the continent, but the substance of the medieval *respublica christiana* had vanished. Just as Aristotle chose to ignore the advancing crush of empire while he sang a hymn of praise to the *polis,* so Hooker chose to ignore the signs of dissolution at the very foundations of the Western ecclesiastical polity, a society in which every citizen was assumed to be a Christian and as such to participate simultaneously in two institutional realms, the temporal and the sacred. (Nonchristian minorities such as Jews and Moslems were tolerated out of expediency or necessity but were not considered part of the social fabric; atheists were tolerated only so long as they did nothing to disturb the illusion that they did not exist.)

Yet Hooker was aware that the old order changeth, as we can see from the opening sentence of the Preface to the *Laws of Ecclesiastical Polity:*

> Though for no other cause, yet for this: that posterity may know we have not loosely through silence permitted things to pass away as in a dream, there shall be for men's information extant thus much con-cerning the present state of the Church of God established amongst us, and their careful endeavor which would have upheld the same.[70]

The general institutional pattern supported by Hooker was defective from its inception in its denial of political participation to all people who did not share the religious beliefs of the majority. This pattern is viable in small, closely knit, and comparatively isolated societies, but the people of Europe have been a heterogeneous lot since long before the Christian era. Whatever Hooker may have believed, no amount of "careful en-

---

68. Ibid. (London: R. Scott, T. Basset, J. Wright, and R. Chiswel, 1682), bk. 8, pp. 437–70.

69. Munz, *Place of Hooker,* pp. 110–11.

70. Hooker, *Laws of Ecclesiastical Polity* (Everyman's ed.), vol. 1, p. 77.

deavor" could have preserved it. Yet we must recognize that secular political processes have been unable to recover the concern for the full range of human aspiration that was lost when Western society relegated religious and spiritual concern to the private, nonpolitical sphere. Hooker agreed with Aristotle that the aim of political association was not mere life, but the good life. "Human societies are much more to care for that which tendeth properly to the soul's estate than for such temporal things which the life hath need of," he wrote, and it is a "gross error" to believe "that the regal power ought to serve for the good of the body and not of the soul, for men's temporal peace and not for their eternal safety; as if God had ordained kings for no other end and purpose but only to fat up men like hogs and to see that they have their mast."[71]

Reason and Reality

In Richard Hooker's teaching one encounters a particularly eloquent expression of the central insight of theocentric humanism: that man's freedom and nobility lie in his attunement to a transcendent order of being. As creature he is subject to the Creator. Reality does not bend to his will; he is obligated to bend his will to conform to reality. This reality is not a compound of surface facts and the irrational; it is the essential pattern of the world, derived from the eternal law of God and within the reach of human reason, if not wholly within its grasp. Hooker therefore could not follow those who "instead of framing their wills to maintain that which reason taught ... bent their wits to find how reason might seem to teach that which their wills were set to maintain."[72] He felt that man's essential nature consisted in his capacity to participate consciously in the world-transcendent reason through the exercise of his own reason. Man discovered himself to be not autonomous but theonomous; he was not, except in a very restricted sense, his own lawgiver. The source of all law is the eternal law of God, which "hath been the pattern to make and ... the card to guide the world by."[73]

Richard Hooker was a compassionate man who was tolerant of the failings of ordinary mortals. If his opponents could with justice accuse him of complacency and insufficient zeal to correct injustice, he could in fairness reply, in words that cut through all ideological differences and still have significance for us today: "Think ye are men, deem it not impossible for you to err."

---

71. Ibid (1682 ed.), bk. 8, p. 462.
72. Ibid. (Everyman's ed.), bk. 3, p. 314.
73. Ibid., bk. 1, p. 53.

4

Hobbes

Thomas Hobbes was born in 1588 on the eve of the sighting of the Spanish armada off the coast of England. His mother was supposedly so frightened by the threatened invasion that she gave birth prematurely. He later said that fear and he were twins. It has sometimes been maintained that Hobbes placed such great emphasis on man's fear of violent death because of the circumstances surrounding his birth. But he lived through fearful times, and we need not resort to dubious psychologizing to discover why he was so preoccupied with danger and disorder. His great masterpiece, *Leviathan*, was published in 1651, and was "occasioned by the disorders of the present time." Those disorders resulted from the civil wars that had ravaged England during the preceding decade, culminating in the execution of Charles I and the establishment of Oliver Cromwell as lord protector.

Hobbes is rightfully considered one of the great political thinkers of all time. When he is wrong he is splendidly wrong, and we learn even from his errors and distortions. He has never been a popular thinker, and we may assume that the only reason more opprobrium has not been heaped upon him is that Machiavelli has overshadowed him as the villain of modern political thought.

Hobbes is generally described as a pessimist regarding human nature and a proponent of political absolutism. While these labels may with some accuracy be attached to him, they need to be qualified. He was optimistic about the possibility of easing the human predicament by improving man's understanding of it. He was liberal in many of his assumptions and goals. Utilitarian liberalism later bore close affinities to many of his ideas.

PHILOSOPHY AND POLITICAL THOUGHT

Hobbes divided philosophy into two parts, natural and civil, and was equally interested in both. He took great delight in philosophical speculation for its own sake, holding that "voluptuous men" neglect philosophy "only because they know not how great a pleasure it is to the mind of man to be ravished in the vigorous and perpetual embraces of the most beauteous world."[1] His original plan, conceived in 1634, called for the completion of the philosophical studies *De corpore* and *De homine* before he began work on his political writings. From the fact that he later revised this plan we need not assume that he simply reacted to political events and took his stand on the basis of his own narrow interest or class position. Hobbes's political thought was born of a spirit of inquiry and cannot be reduced to special-interest pleading. His fierce determination to think for himself and to base his political conclusions on his philosophical analysis of man and society, without regard for those who might be offended by them, earned him the suspicion of both royalists and republicans in England, and the outright enmity of some. With the Restoration of 1660, powerful clergymen and other royalist supporters demanded that he be tried and burned at the stake as a heretic. Preparations for his trial were halted by the intervention of Charles II himself, so we may conclude that the only reason Hobbes was "spared the hemlock" was that his "friends were more powerful than were those of Socrates."[2]

Hobbes's earliest publication (in 1629) was his translation of Thucydides' *History of the Peloponnesian War*. In the Introduction to this work he already gives some indication of the way his political thought was subsequently to be developed in the *Elements of Law* (1640), *De cive* (1642), *Leviathan* (1651), parts of *De homine* (1658), and—more discursively, interspersed with his historical account of the English civil wars—*Behemoth* (1668). Thus Hobbes's political thought, although inevitably influenced by the profound crisis through which he lived, cannot be reduced to the level of an ideological response to that crisis. The "disorders of the present time" made Hobbes acutely conscious of the need to give priority to political considerations, contrary to his original plan of 1634, and led him to write at greater length on political matters than he otherwise would have done. Like all political thinkers of the first rank, however, he viewed political matters from a dual perspective, at once speculative and practical; as he focused his attention on the immediate demands of his time, he never lost his awareness of the broad philosophical background against which the

---

1. Sir William Molesworth, ed., *The English Works of Thomas Hobbes,* 11 vols. (London, 1839–1845), vol. 1, "Epistle to the Reader." Hereafter cited as *Works of Hobbes.*

2. Peter J. Opitz, "Thomas Hobbes," in *Zwischen Revolution und Restauration,* ed. Eric Voegelin (Munich: List Verlag, 1968), p. 75.

current scene was played and the overall human condition that gave
meaning to the actions of the players. Hobbes saw philosophy—and
particularly political philosophy—as useful in relieving man's predicament. Yet the recognition of philosophy's potential practical value did
not diminish his joy in contemplation for its own sake, or lead him to
take such a narrow view of relevance and practicality that future ages
would find his teaching hopelessly dated. In his political studies, he
sought the universal in the particular; his intention was theoretical:
"not to show what is law here and there, but what is law."[3]

Civil and Natural Philosophy

Any interpretation of Hobbes must consider the relationship between
his "civil philosophy" (political science) and his "natural philosophy"
(natural science). Hobbes was understandably impressed by the advances made in the natural sciences during his age, which was also the
age of Galileo, Kepler, and Harvey. From these scientists he learned
the importance of method in any branch of study, and he attempted to
make use of some of the procedures found valuable in the natural sciences in his study of political matters. His political science, however,
was by no means modeled wholly on natural science. On the contrary,
he carefully distinguished between the two types of inquiry. He held
the subject of philosophy to be "every body of which we can conceive
any generation, and which we may, by any consideration thereof, compare with other bodies." Philosophy's task is to "search out the properties
of bodies from their generation, or their generation from their properties;
and, therefore, where there is no generation or property, there is no
philosophy." On the basis of this definition, Hobbes excluded theology
("I mean the doctrine of God, eternal, ingenerable, incomprehensible,
and in whom there is nothing neither to divide nor compound, nor any
generation to be conceived") as a proper domain for philosophical inquiry. There are, then, "two chief kinds of bodies, and very different
from one another," which "offer themselves to such as search after their
generation and properties; one . . . is called a *natural body*, the other is
called a commonwealth. . . ."[4]

Although both natural and civil philosophy are branches of a
single mode of inquiry (philosophy), they investigate different sorts
of subject matter. Men are not the authors of natural bodies, but they
are the makers of commonwealths. Because the commonwealth is "made

---

3. *Works of Hobbes,* vol. 3, *Elements of Law,* p. 251.
4. Ibid., vol. 1, pp. 10–11. "Generation" means here origin or source.

by the wills and agreement of men" and because man has the capacity for reflection and self-knowledge, the knowledge that can be acquired through civil philosophy is of a different order from that obtained through natural philosophy.

The Resolutive-Compositive Method

Hobbes nevertheless recommended and sought to apply the same general method to both lines of inquiry. This was the "resolutive-compositive" method of Galileo. Perhaps the most succinct description of the way Hobbes applied this method to his civil philosophy is found in the Preface of his *De cive:*

> Concerning my method . . . I took my beginning from the very matter of civil government, and then proceeded to its generation, and form, and the first beginning of justice; for everything is best understood by its constitutive causes. For as in a watch, or some such small engine, the matter, figure, and motion of the wheels cannot well be known, except it be taken in sunder, and viewed in parts. . . .[5]

Hobbes's resolutive-compositive method led him to employ the "state of nature" construct as a heuristic device in the study of politics. Whether or not the "state of nature" had ever actually existed was irrelevant to philosophical inquiry as he understood it. He simply considered that

> to make a more curious search into the rights of states, it is necessary (I say not to take them in sunder, but yet that) they be so considered, *as if they were dissolved,* that is, that we rightly understand what the quality of human nature is, in what matters it is, in what not, fit to make a civil government, and how men must be agreed amongst themselves, that intend to grow up into a well-grounded state.[6]

Leo Strauss has argued that Hobbes's political philosophy is not dependent on his natural science.[7] This is true, for Hobbes did conceive of the two types of inquiry as distinct, and he developed his main political insights very early, before he had studied the works of the leading natural scientists of his day. And yet the method he derived

---

5. Hobbes, *De cive; or, The Citizen,* ed. Sterling P. Lamprecht (New York: Appleton-Century-Crofts, 1949), pp. 10–11.

6. Ibid., p. 11 (italics added).

7. Leo Strauss, *The Political Philosophy of Hobbes,* trans. Elsa M. Sinclair, new ed. (Chicago: University of Chicago Press, 1952), p. 6.

from these works unquestionably contributed to the form in which he cast his political teaching, and it was this method that enabled him to avoid the ambiguity that burdened Locke when he confronted the question of the historical existence of a state of nature. For Hobbes the state of nature was simply a logical construct or methodological hypothesis.[8]

Hobbes was always fascinated by geometry, and it has often been said that he applied its method to politics. At least as frequently, he is said to have extended the mechanistic model of the natural sciences to political analysis. Alternatively or additionally, he is called a nominalist, a materialist, and a sensationalist in his metaphysics and epistemology. With varying degrees of accuracy, all of these labels fit him; yet we would wholly fail to understand his greatness as a political philosopher if we thought of him as a servant of any rigid and simplistic method or system claiming to be "scientific." Throughout his writings, and especially his political writings, a basic openness of mind and spirit triumphs over the rigidities of the abstract and rationalistic models he often purports to emulate. As Michael Oakeshott has observed:

> When we come to consider the technicalities of his philosophy we shall observe a moderation that, for example, allowed him to escape an atomic philosophy, and an absence of rigidity that allowed him to modify his philosophical method when dealing with politics; here, when we are considering informally the quality of his mind, this ability appears as resilience, the energy to be perpetually freeing himself from the formation of his system.[9]

As any reader of the *Leviathan* must know, Hobbes's subject is man, not the machine. For all his borrowings from the methods and material of the natural sciences, Hobbes does not treat man in nonhuman terms. Although his political teaching takes a new theoretical path, it continues the tradition of inquiry begun by Plato and Aristotle.

HOBBES'S ANTHROPOLOGY

Hobbes's masterpiece, *Leviathan*, is divided into four parts: "Of Man," "Of Commonwealth," "Of a Christian Commonwealth," and "Of the Kingdom of Darkness." A little less than half the work is devoted to

---

8. This point is well made in Opitz, "Thomas Hobbes," pp. 57–61.

9. Hobbes, *Leviathan: or the Matter, Form, and Power of a Commonwealth Ecclesiastical and Civil*, ed. Michael Oakeshott (Oxford: Blackwell, 1946), Editor's Introduction, pp. xv–xvi.

political problems and theory within the specifically Christian universe of discourse. That the sage of Malmesbury could have placed so much emphasis on Christian theology has occasioned much comment and controversy.

It is immediately apparent that Hobbes's approach to political theory is very much in the Platonic tradition. He adopts the macroanthropological principle; that is, he assumes that before we can arrive at an adequate understanding of society, we must first inquire into the nature of man. Political theory rests on philosophical anthropology, or a theory of human nature. Hobbes assumes that human nature is constant. Men have so much in common that they can discover the nature of mankind by learning to know themselves. This is not the same as knowing men's specific motives and designs; as far as these are concerned, we may not even accurately understand our own, much less those of others. We may deceive ourselves and others and be deceived by them in turn. All men seek goals, but these goals are infinitely variable. Man is a desiring animal. Although the objects of human passions differ, the passions themselves are the same in us all.

When Socrates consulted the Delphic oracle, the answer he received took the form of a command: "Know thyself." For Hobbes, this command signifies that knowledge of oneself yields knowledge of man in general and makes political theory (or knowledge) possible. If man properly "reads" himself and records his observations about human nature, other men can verify or reject the conclusions he reaches on the basis of their own experience. The experience of each man as an existent being is the point of reference for the principles of what Hobbes calls "civil philosophy."

Thus, because of the "similitude of the thoughts and passions of one man" with the "thoughts and passions of another, whosoever looketh into himself, and considereth what he doth, when he does *think, opine, reason, hope, fear,* etc. and upon what grounds," will thereby be able to "read and know, what are the passions and thoughts of all other men upon the like occasions."[10]

Although Hobbes thus continues the tradition of political theory begun by the Greek philosophers, he is at the same time bent upon making a radical departure from that tradition. His *Leviathan* is dotted with references to propositions he considers dubious in Plato, Aristotle, and the Schoolmen. His purpose is to begin afresh, without any reliance on textual authority or tradition, and fashion a new understanding of the

---

10. Ibid., Introduction, p. 6. Hobbes insists it is the passions and not the objects of the passions that are similar and therefore intelligible.

human predicament on the basis of evidence accessible to human reason alone.

Terms and Definitions

Hobbes quickly makes it clear that he rejects the theory of universals inherited from classical philosophy. His antecedents on this issue are the medieval nominalists, men like Ockham and Duns Scotus. Man, through his gift of speech, is capable of assigning names to things. Universals are only names that men agree to assign to categories of things; the only realities are the individual things themselves.

> Of names, some are proper, and singular to one only thing, as Peter, John, this man, this tree; and some are common to many things, man, horse, tree; every of which, though but one name, is nevertheless the name of divers particular things; in respect of all which together, it is called an universal; there being nothing in the world universal but names; for the things named are every one of them individual and singular.[11]

Man's capacity for speech makes reasoning possible. Reasoning consists of summing up the consequences of propositions, so as to understand their relation to each other. Speech and understanding are both properties "peculiar to man." Reason Hobbes defines as "nothing but *reckoning*, that is adding and subtracting, of the consequences of general names agreed upon for the marking and signifying of our thoughts."[12]

The root of error in man's thinking is lack of clear and careful definition of terms at each step in the process. Or the names may not be appropriate to the phenomenon discussed. There is general lack of method in philosophical speculation as it has hitherto been carried on which must be remedied if absurd and contradictory conclusions are to be avoided. Geometry is the model for all scientific discourse. The adoption of the right method will lead to valid scientific generalizations, and this increase in scientific precision will redound to the benefit of mankind.

Human Passions and Desires

Man not only receives sense impressions, but is moved to action by his passions or desires. The desires and appetites of men are exceedingly variable. Good and evil are names given by men to things and conditions they desire or seek to avoid. The words "good" and "evil"

---

11. Ibid., chap. 4, p. 19.
12. Ibid., chap. 5, pp. 25–26.

are ever used with relation to the person that useth them: there being nothing simply and absolutely so; nor any common rule of good and evil, to be taken from the nature of the objects themselves; but from the person of the man, where there is no commonwealth; or, in a commonwealth, from the person that representeth it; or from an arbitrator or judge, whom men disagreeing shall by consent set up, and make his sentence the rule thereof.[13]

Hobbes provides a lengthy list of the passions that animate men and bring them either pleasure or displeasure of mind and body, ranging from cruelty to carnal lust to benevolence, from intellectual curiosity to religious feeling. He is sometimes said to take a narrow view of man, but in parts of the *Leviathan* he displays a profound awareness of the complexity and multiplicity of human motives and inclinations. Human nature is a rich texture of impulses to Hobbes, at least before he begins to sort out and rank these impulses in an attempt to bring some order to human existence and rescue man from his natural predicament.

Particularly noteworthy as a reflection of the theoretic spirit—the appreciation of knowledge for its own sake and the joys of the *vita contemplativa*—is Hobbes's passage on the desire to know:

Desire to know why, and how, Curiosity; such as is in no living creature but man: so that man is distinguished, not only by his reason, but also by this singular passion from other animals; in whom the appetite of food, and other pleasures of sense, by predominance, take away the care of knowing causes; which is a lust of the mind, that by a perseverance of delight in the continual and indefatigable generation of knowledge, exceedeth the short vehemence of any carnal pleasure.[14]

Man, then, is a creature who seeks felicity. Felicity is no narrow and pedestrian pleasure. It is not a state of contentment that, once attained, leaves nothing further to be desired. Felicity is Hobbes's term for personal happiness—the happiness that comes to man when he gains or sees the possibility of gaining the objects of his many and varied desires.

Continual success in obtaining those things that a man from time to time desireth, that is to say, continual prospering, is that men call Felicity; I mean the felicity *of this life*. For there is no such thing as perpetual tranquility of mind, while we live here; because life itself is but motion, and can never be without desire, nor without fear, no more than without sense. What kind of felicity God hath

13. Ibid., chap. 6, pp. 32–33.
14. Ibid., p. 35.

ordained to them that devoutly honour Him, a man shall no sooner
know, than enjoy; being joys, that now are as incomprehensible, as
the word of Schoolmen *beatifical vision* is unintelligible.[15]

Power and Religion

Hobbes is nowhere more clearly representative of the tradition of anthropocentric humanism than in his discussion of man's urge to power.
Natural man, the man with whom the lawmakers must deal, is not a
God-seeker, but a power-seeker, and he can find no lasting contentment
because no one can ever be secure in the enjoyment of power. The *summum bonum* does not exist within the life of this world:

> The felicity of this life, consisteth not in the repose of a mind
> satisfied. For there is no such *finis ultimus*, utmost aim, nor *summum
> bonum*, greatest good, as is spoken of in the books of the old moral
> philosophers. Nor can a man any more live, whose desires are at an
> end, than he, whose senses and imaginations are at a stand. Felicity
> is a continual progress of the desire, from one object to another;
> the attaining of the former, being still but the way to the latter.[16]

These reflections lead Hobbes to the famous conclusion that man
is caught up in the ceaseless pursuit of power:

> So that in the first place, I put for a general inclination of all man-
> kind, a perpetual and restless desire of power after power, that
> ceaseth only in death. And the cause of this, is not always that a
> man hopes for a more intensive delight, than he has already attained
> to; or that he cannot be content with a moderate power: but be-
> cause he cannot assure the power and means to live well, which he
> hath present, without the acquisition of more. And from hence
> it is, that kings, whose power is greatest, turn their endeavours to
> the assuring it at home by laws, or abroad by wars: and when that
> is done, there succeedeth a new desire; in some, of fame from new
> conquest; in others, of ease and sensual pleasure; in others, of ad-
> miration, or being flattered for excellence in some art, or other ability
> of the mind.[17]

Hobbes is often compared with St. Augustine as a pessimist in regard to man. There are of course similarities between the two thinkers;
both stress man's pride and utter absorption with self. Yet their views
are drastically different. There is no reference to original sin in Hobbes's
political teaching. Augustine regards man as a creature weighed down

---

15. Ibid., p. 39.
16. Ibid., chap. 11, p. 63.
17. Ibid.

by sin and in need of deliverance through divine grace; Hobbes sees him as possessed by inclinations that are not evil in themselves, but which can lead to evil results if they are not controlled. Hobbes has much more sympathy for natural man than Augustine ever did. It is not man's passions that Hobbes deplores, but man's ignorance of the results to which they can lead if he makes no effort to check them. Like Machiavelli, Hobbes has a certain affection for natural man and sympathy for his predicament, and again like Machiavelli, he masks these feelings with an argument that leaves him open to the charge that he lacks compassion.

Yet if man's unchecked passions lead him to an endless pursuit of power, his desire for understanding leads him to a belief in a prime cause, a creator. For Hobbes, religious sentiment is natural to man. Belief in the existence of a deity and of "powers invisible and supernatural" can "never be so abolished out of human nature."[18]

Like reason and speech, religion is peculiar to man. It wells up out of anxiety and fear for the future. As man's untutored mind speculates on the causes of events, many occurrences leave him baffled, and he ascribes them to invisible agencies and powers. Fear may be said to be the mother of religious superstitions and the gods of ancient mythology; but acknowledgment of "one God eternal, infinite and omnipotent" is the result not of fear, but of the desire to know. Man's rational search for causes and antecedents ultimately leads him to postulate the existence of a first cause or prime mover.

THE NATURAL CONDITION OF MANKIND

Every man's ceaseless striving after power creates a predicament. Men are ineluctably drawn into competition with each other for riches, honor, and power to command. This competition leads to enmity and war, for the surest way for one competitor to obtain power over another is to "kill, subdue, supplant, or repell the other."[19] Hobbes suggests that the commonwealth emerges as a remedy of sorts, since although it will not eliminate insecurity altogether, it will reduce it to a bearable level.

Hobbes is emphatic in his assertion of the natural equality of men. His radical egalitarianism has not always been noted. Equality is the fundamental characteristic of the so-called state of nature. Although some differences in physical strength and mental ability exist among men, they are not so considerable as to confer exceptional benefit or ad-

---

18. Ibid., chap. 12, p. 77. Note the use of "never"; there can be no equation of Hobbes and Marx.

19. Ibid., p. 64.

vantage on any man. Hobbes explicitly takes issue with Aristotle's dictum that some are born to rule and others to serve. There is natural equality among men, and such inequalities of status, wealth, and power as come to be established are the result of contrivance, not of nature.

Thucydides had named wealth, security, and honor as the "three great things" for which men battled. Without explicitly citing the Greek historian (whose work he had translated), Hobbes closely approximates his conclusion by describing the "three principal causes of quarrel among men" as "competition, diffidence, and glory."[20]

In the absence of a common power "able to over-awe them all," men "have no pleasure, but on the contrary a great deal of grief, in keeping company" with each other.[21] Thus in a condition of "mere nature," men are not drawn together, but rather are driven apart. In their search for felicity and the fulfillment of their passions, they are driven into conflict and war.

Hobbes's description of the natural condition of mankind (usually referred to as the state of nature, although he himself does not use this term) is deservedly famous. For Hobbes, the state of nature, or anarchy, is analogous to a state of war among organized societies:

> In such condition, there is no place for industry; because the fruit thereof is uncertain: and consequently no culture of the earth; no navigation, nor use of the commodities that may be imported by sea; no commodious buildings; no instruments of moving, and removing, such things as require much force; no knowledge of the face of the earth; no account of time; no arts; no letters; no society; and which is worst of all, continual fear, and danger of violent death; and the life of man, solitary, poor, nasty, brutish, and short.[22]

Man, then, is in sore need of deliverance. It is through the creation of a body politic that the competitive struggle can be regulated and sublimated. In this work of creation to avoid mutual destruction, passion and reason cooperate. The passion that most moves men to leave the state of conflict and establish peace is the fear of violent death, to which may be added the "desire of such things as are necessary to commodious living" and "a hope by their industry to obtain them." Reason, here conceived as the efficient ordering of means to ends, does its part by suggesting "convenient articles of peace upon which men may be drawn to agreement."[23] These are otherwise known as laws of nature.

---

20. Ibid., chap. 13, p. 81.
21. Ibid.
22. Ibid., pp. 82–84.
23. Ibid., p. 84.

THE LAWS OF NATURE

Hobbes distinguishes between the right of nature and the law of nature. The right of nature is the liberty of every man to use his power to preserve his life in any way he chooses. Liberty is the absence of external impediment. A law of nature, on the other hand, is a "precept or general rule, found out by reason, by which a man is forbidden to do that, which is destructive of his life, or taketh away the means of preserving the same; and to omit that, by which he thinketh it may best be preserved."[24]

Hobbes enumerates some nineteen laws of nature in Chapters 14 and 15 of the *Leviathan*. The entire discussion is of major importance to an understanding of his work. Hobbes's thinking on natural law differs significantly from the teachings of both the ancient philosophers and the medieval Schoolmen, though he has not completely severed all ties with the earlier tradition. With Hobbes we enter the secular domain where natural laws are maxims of expediency devised for self-preservation, while still retaining their character of ethical imperatives.[25] The groundwork for the "covenant" or social contract of every man with every other man, and for the obligations of the sovereign to his subjects, is laid in these laws.

The Sovereign and the Social Contract

It is not unreasonable to interpret Hobbes's laws of nature, which ostensibly refer to men's relations with each other, as applicable to the sovereign as well. Hobbes was not explicit on this point, probably because, having lived through the civil wars, he was more concerned about the excesses of citizens than about the excesses of rulers. Above all, he wished to refute the Puritan argument as he understood it: that men have a right to pronounce judgment on a political regime and to overthrow it by force if their consciences direct them to do so. If Hobbes is relatively silent on the subject of the sovereign's duties, or speaks of

---

24. Ibid.

25. In recent years a controversy has developed among scholars regarding Hobbes's teaching on natural law and obligation. See, for example, A. E. Taylor, "The Ethical Doctrine of Hobbes," *Philosophy*, October 1938; Howard Warrender, *The Political Philosophy of Hobbes: His Theory of Obligation* (New York: Oxford University Press, 1957); Leo Strauss, *Natural Right and History* (Chicago: University of Chicago Press, 1953), pp. 165–202; and J. W. Watkins, *Hobbes's System of Ideas* (London: Hutchinson University Library, 1965), pp. 85f. Taylor and Warrender contend that Hobbes did have a theory of moral obligation, whereas those who interpret Hobbes in strictly naturalistic terms tend to find his moral counsels based solely on expediency and self-interest. See also Michael Oakeshott's discussion of Warrender's thesis in *Rationalism in Politics* (New York: Basic Books, 1962).

them indirectly while being very explicit about the duties of subjects, we must not assume that he therefore placed little importance on the ruler's obligations. It is more probable that he thought it advisable to treat the obligations of sovereigns with extreme caution, for fear that any statement he made might seem to support the personal opinions of the opponents of some regime, and be seized as an excuse to overthrow it.

Hobbes's political teaching, then, was directed toward both subjects and sovereigns. His intention was to pass "unwounded" between "those that contend on one side for too great liberty" and "on the other side for too much authority."[26]

In return for obedience and the surrender of their natural right to unlimited self-defense, the subjects may legitimately expect the sovereign to establish a milieu in which they can pursue felicity in reasonable tranquility, each in his own way. The task of the sovereign is not to repress men, but to create the conditions under which they can express their individuality. Hobbes is more liberal than has commonly been supposed.

At the same time, Hobbes insists that a powerful sovereign is indispensable if the laws of nature are not to be broken, because most men cannot be trusted to keep any law without fear of punishment by a power stronger than they. Those men who are motivated to keep their word by "glory or pride" are "too rarely found to be presumed on." Hobbes classifies the "greatest part of mankind" as "pursuers of wealth, command, or sensual pleasure." Fear is the only passion strong enough to restrain their natural ambition and covetousness—fear of immediate retribution by a strong visible power (the sovereign) coupled with fear of further punishment by an invisible power (God). The fear of God is not effective by itself; a strong sovereign is necessary.

In abandoning their natural right to universal acquisition in the social state, men are compensated by "propriety" (property—what is their own). The social contract is designed to guarantee that each man recognizes and respects the property and individuality of the other; it is the duty of the sovereign to see that such respect is maintained. For Hobbes the sovereign is a kind of umpire who presides over the social game and sees that its rules and agreements are not broken.

War and Peace. For Hobbes the fundamental law of nature is a "precept or general rule of reason," that "every man ought to endeavor peace, as far as he has hope of obtaining it; and when he cannot obtain it, that he may seek, and use, all helps, and advantages of war."[27]

---

26. Hobbes, *Leviathan,* Dedicatory Epistle to Francis Godolphin, p. 2.
27. Ibid., chap. 14, p. 85.

Liberty. From this

fundamental law of nature, by which men are commanded to endeavor peace, is derived the second law; that a man be willing, when others are so too ... to lay down this right to all things and be contented with so much liberty against other men, as he would allow other men against himself.[28]

The Right to Resist. Hobbes makes clear that while men renounce some of their natural rights when they enter society, *they do not abandon all of them.* (This point needs emphasis because Hobbes is often considered completely opposed to Locke on the surrender of rights.) There are some rights, Hobbes says, "which no man can be understood by any works, or other signs, to have abandoned or transferred." Inasmuch as the

motive and end for which this renouncing and transferring of right is introduced is nothing else but the security of a man's person, in his life, and in the means of so preserving life, as not to be weary of it ... if a man by words, or other signs, seem to despoil himself of the end, for which those signs were intended, he is not to be understood as if he meant it, or that it was his will, but that he was ignorant of how such words and actions were to be interpreted.[29]

The subject can resist anyone (including the sovereign) who comes to take away his life. Man "by nature" chooses "the lesser evil" of resisting at the risk of death rather than submitting to the certainty of death.[30]

Benefits and Obligations. Hobbes's fourth law of nature, dealing with the obligations of subjects to each other, clearly has a bearing on the conduct of the sovereign as well. This law demands that "a man which receiveth benefit from another of mere grace, endeavor that he that giveth it, have no reasonable cause to repent him of his good will. For no man giveth, but with intention of good to himself."[31] Although Hobbes does not specifically say so, we may conclude that by virtue of the social contract, the sovereign receives his power as a gift. Therefore, if he abuses the gift, and harasses and terrorizes his subjects instead of promoting their security and well-being, there will be "no beginning of benevolence, or trust, nor consequently of mutual help; nor of reconciliation of one man to another," and men will revert to the "condition of war."[32]

Punishment. The seventh and tenth laws of nature are also relevant

---

28. Ibid.
29. Ibid., p. 87.
30. Ibid., p. 91.
31. Ibid., chap. 15, p. 99.
32. Ibid.

to the conduct of the sovereign. The seventh forbids men to "inflict punishment with any other design, than for the correction of the offender, or the direction of others." Punishment for mere revenge and to show one's power is "glorying to no end," or "vainglory." Unrestrained action of this sort is cruelty; it is "against reason" and leads to war.[33]

Equal Rights. The tenth law obliges men to recognize the equal rights of others. Hobbes explains:

> As it is necessary for all men that seek peace to lay down certain rights of nature; that is to say, not to have liberty to do all they list: so is it necessary for man's life, to retain some; as right to govern their own bodies; enjoy air, water, motion, ways to go from place to place; and all things else, without which a man cannot live, or not live well.[34]

Here again is a passage that clearly indicates that for Hobbes—as for Locke—there are certain inalienable rights, which are not surrendered to the sovereign. It is "necessary" that he respect them. For Hobbes, necessity and right reinforce each other.[35]

Equal Justice. The eleventh law of nature seems tailored specifically for the sovereign. According to Hobbes, "if a man be trusted to judge between man and man, it is a precept of the law of nature, that he deal equally between them."[36] Inasmuch as the state of nature by definition lacks a judge, and the sovereign acts as judge in controversies between men in society, it seems reasonable to assume that Hobbes is implicitly setting forth a precept for sovereigns.

The Sovereign and the Laws of Nature. In case anyone should be tempted to assume that Hobbes exempts the sovereign from the laws of nature, let us consider the beginning of Chapter 29, where he explicitly states that "sovereigns are all subject to the laws of nature; because such laws be divine, and cannot by man, or commonwealth be abrogated."[37] And in Chapter 30 he says:

> The office of the sovereign, be it a monarch or an assembly, consisteth in the end, for which he was trusted with the sovereign power, namely the procuration of the safety of the people; to which he is obliged by the law of nature, and to render an account

---

33. Ibid., p. 100.

34. Ibid., p. 101.

35. Ibid., p. 99. Every man "not only by right, but also by necessity of nature, is supposed to endeavor all he can, to obtain that which is necessary for his conservation."

36. Ibid., p. 101.

37. Ibid.

thereof to God, the author of that law, and to none but him. But by safety here, is not meant a bare preservation, but also all other contentments of life, which every man by lawful industry, without danger, or hurt to the commonwealth, shall acquire to himself.[38]

Although Hobbes is eager to dissociate himself from those who argue that men have the right to resist or rebel if the sovereign fails to carry out his obligations, it is nonetheless clear that he expects that the sovereign will inevitably fall if he consistently disregards the laws of nature. All men, sovereign and subject alike, are required to observe these laws, not only by moral obligation, but by necessity as well. The sovereign, after all, belongs to the same society as his subjects; he is not in a state of nature. He is obliged to obey the laws of nature not only *in foro interno* (in inner intention), but also *in foro externo* (in external behavior). Only in the state of nature, in which a man has no security against his fellows or they against him, is anyone dispensed from the obligation to obey the laws of nature *in foro externo*. Now subjects have endowed the sovereign not only with their allegiance, but with the sole legitimate authority to use force. He is not only secure against them; he has them at a disadvantage. And "he that having sufficient security, that others shall observe the same laws toward him, observes them not himself, seeketh not peace, but war; and consequently the destruction of his nature by violence."[39]

But the sovereign continues to be in a state of nature vis-à-vis other sovereigns. He is prey to them and they to him. "Kings and persons of sovereign authority" are "in the state and posture of gladiators."[40] Thus, even though the sovereign cannot be physically forced to observe the laws of nature with respect to his subjects, and even though they are obliged not to resist him collectively (although individually they may if he threatens their lives), he will almost certainly fall to the forces of some foreign ruler if he subjects his own people to such harassment that the power of his commonwealth is significantly diminished in the international arena. In sum, Hobbes argues that iniquity in domestic politics does not pay. In foreign politics—theoretically, at least—anything goes, because the participants are bound by no contract and cannot be sure that the laws of nature will be observed. Yet even here sovereigns are morally obligated to observe these laws so far as they can without jeopardizing the safety of their dominions, for otherwise there would be no respite from war.

---

38. Ibid., chap. 30, p. 219.
39. Ibid., chap. 15, p. 103.
40. Ibid., p. 83.

Hobbes concludes his discussion of the laws of nature with an observation that has special significance for the sovereign's jurisdiction:

> The laws of nature are immutable and eternal; for injustice, ingratitude, arrogance, pride, iniquity, acception of persons, and the rest, can never be made lawful. For it can never be that war shall preserve life, and peace destroy it.[41]

The Laws of Nature and Moral Philosophy

Hobbes attached such importance to the laws of nature that he considered the concept to be at the very heart of moral philosophy. "For moral philosophy is nothing else but the science of what is good, and evil, in the conversation and society of mankind." Men have sharply differing ideas of good and bad, right and wrong, but "all men" agree that "peace is good, and there also the way, or means, of peace." The laws of nature instruct us in these means of peace, or virtues, and in their opposites, vices. "Now the science of virtue and vice, is moral philosophy; and therefore the true doctrine of the laws of nature, is the true moral philosophy."[42]

HOBBES'S PARADIGM: THE CONSTRUCTION
OF THE COMMONWEALTH

We have now to consider Hobbes's analysis of the "generation"—or coming into being—of "that great Leviathan ... to which we owe ... our peace and defence."[43] We shall recall that the task of civil philosophy is to trace the generation and properties of the artificial body called the commonwealth. Hobbes's account of the origins of society is essentially hypothetical. His intention is not to describe how commonwealths have actually been founded, but rather how they would be founded if they were consonant with the laws of nature.

Hobbes says quite explicitly that he is constructing a political world in thought—"what I find by speculation, and deduction"[44]—not describing any that ever was. He is therefore not an empiricist in any usual sense of the word. Hobbes is equally explicit, however, in contending that his theory, although admittedly not consonant with the currently observable world, is nevertheless grounded in a realistic analysis of human nature and its possibilities.

---

41. Ibid., p. 104. "Acception of persons" means "favoritism."
42. Ibid.
43. Ibid., chap. 17, p. 112.
44. Ibid., chap. 20, p. 134.

He does not, then, offer his paradigm of the body politic as simply his personal opinion of the way society should be organized and conducted. His "speculations" and "deductions" are based on the "nature, needs, and designs" of men; that is, on a specific anthropology or theory of man. Man is capable of introspection, and of reenacting in thought the experiences basic to his existence. Hobbes assumes that the basic human passions are the same in all men:

> Whosoever looketh into himself, and considereth what he doth, when he does think, opine, reason, hope, fear, etc. and upon what grounds; he shall thereby read and know, what are the thoughts and passions of all other men upon like occasions.[45]

Society and Its Representative

Hobbes's theory of society is bound up with his concept of authority, sovereignty, and the representative. Every society, according to Hobbes, exists by virtue of its representative. Society as such has no essence or unity. "For it is the *unity* of the representer, not the *unity* of the represented, that maketh the person *one*." The sovereign is an artificial person who represents "the words and actions of another." Authority is the "right of doing any action." If the actions of artificial persons are "*owned* by those whom they represent," then the representative is the actor and those he represents are the authors of his words and actions.

If man is to transcend his disordered or "natural condition," self-deception must be eliminated. Man, Hobbes reasons, must face the facts about himself and his impulses squarely, removing the fig leaf of bogus optimism and self-congratulation. It is unpleasant to recognize that we cannot cooperate except under the stern command of the sovereign, that we are inordinately proud, are consumed with a lust for power, and are constantly overestimating our wisdom and capacities.[46] But it is only by recognizing the extent of the predicament to which our unrestrained passion for power reduces us that we can see the way to the remedy that our nature also affords us. Men can freely and self-consciously will their deliverance from disorder and early death through recourse to authority; it is only by establishing a secure political authority that they can enjoy liberty within the limits compatible with the preservation of peace.

> The only way to erect such a common power, as may be able to defend [men] from the invasion of foreigners, and the injuries of one another . . . is to confer all their power and strength upon one

---

45. Ibid., Introduction, p. 6.
46. Ibid., chap. 17, p. 111.

man, or upon one assembly of men . . . which is as much as to say, to appoint one man, or assembly of men, to bear their person; and every one to own, and acknowledge himself to be author of whatsoever he that so beareth their person, shall act, or cause to be acted, in those things which concern the common peace and safety. . . ."[47]

The Social Contract

It is at this point that Hobbes describes the "provisions" of the so-called social contract. Bearing in mind that he is not describing the historical origins of any particular society, but rather setting forth the rational foundations of a hypothetical one—an ordered society consonant with the survival of man as he is, not as he likes to think he is—let us examine the famous passage:

> This is more than consent, or concord; it is a real unity of them all, in one and the same person, made by covenant of every man with every man, in such manner, *as if* every man should say to every man, *I authorize and give up my right of governing myself, to this man, or to this assembly of men, on this condition, that thou give up thy right to him, and authorize all his actions in like manner.* This done, the multitude so united in one person is called a COMMONWEALTH, in Latin CIVITAS. This is the generation of the great LEVIATHAN, or rather, to speak more reverently, of that *mortal god,* to which we owe under the *immortal God,* our peace and defence.[48]

The institution of a commonwealth does not require unanimity; the *majority* has the right to determine the form of government.

> A *commonwealth* is said to be *instituted,* when a *multitude* of men do agree, and *covenant, every one, with every one,* that to whatsoever *man, or assembly of men,* shall be given by the major part, the *right* to *present* the person of them all, that is to say, to be their *representative*; every one, as well he that *voted for it,* as he that *voted against it,* shall *authorize* all the actions and judgments, of that man, or assembly of men, in the same manner, as if they were his own, to the end, to live peaceably amongst themselves, and be protected against other men.[49]

The Rights of the Sovereign

From the original act of institution Hobbes deduces a lengthy catalogue of sovereign rights. These rights, which flow from the original covenant,

---

47. Ibid., p. 112.
48. Ibid. ("As if" is not italicized in the text.)
49. Ibid., chap. 18, p. 113.

are reminiscent of the list of sovereign powers contained in the work of an earlier theorist of sovereignty, Jean Bodin. Bodin does not make clear whether the attributes of sovereignty are descriptive of existing regimes or logically derived from the concept of sovereignty as such; Hobbes's method makes for greater consistency and resolves Bodin's uncertainty. The rights of the sovereign are derived from his obligation to do whatever he must to preserve peace and defend his subjects.[50] Interestingly enough, it is on the basis of this concept that Hobbes excludes certain traditional prerogatives of sovereignty that Bodin had regarded as essential:

> The power to coin money; to dispose of the estate and person of infant heirs; to have praeemption in markets; and all other statute prerogatives, may be transferred by the sovereign; and yet the power to protect his subjects be retained. But if he transfer the *militia*, he retains the judicature in vain, for want of execution of the laws: or if he grant away the power of raising money; the *militia* is in vain; or if he give away the government of doctrines, men will be frightened into rebellion with the fear of spirits."[51]

The Regulation of Doctrine. Hobbes is particularly insistent on the need for the sovereign to regulate the expression of opinions, both in speech and in writing. He emphasizes, not to say exaggerates, the power of publicly propagated doctrines to influence the actions of men, and takes a rather simplistic view of the sovereign's ability to curb the spread of "seditious doctrine." Hobbes seems unaware of the amount of repression and control that such regulation requires. He contemplates no detailed control of specific opinions, only the enactment of certain minimal standards of discourse essential for public order: "And though in matter of doctrine, nothing ought to be regarded but the truth; yet this is not repugnant to regulating the same by peace. For doctrine repugnant to peace, can no more be true, than peace and concord can be against the law of nature."[52]

Hobbes's notion that it is self-evident which doctrines are "repugnant to peace" is disingenuous, to say the least, and he provides no reason for assuming that peace is the *summum bonum*, to which all else must be sacrificed. He is unyieldingly hostile to men who see virtue in fighting for political principles—that is, the promoters of ideal causes. In fact, he is certain that behind the idealism of "men of principle" there

---

50. Ibid., pp. 116–18.
51. Ibid., p. 119.
52. Ibid., p. 116.

often lurks the lust for power. As he rather cynically indicates in his
Behemoth, the Christian clergy is scarcely an exception to this behavioral
rule:

> I confess I know very few controversies amongst Christians, of points
> necessary to salvation. They are the questions of authority and power
> over the Church, or of profit, or of honour to Churchmen, that for
> the most part raise all the controversies. For what man is he, that
> will trouble himself and fall out with his neighbors for the saving of
> my soul, or the soul of any other than himself?[53]

Liberalism, which has been influenced by Hobbes more than is
generally recognized, repudiates his views on censorship and the regulation of speech. Socialism entertains a much more generous view of
man's capacities for disinterested cooperative action. Hobbes must be
given credit for illuminating certain dark sides of man's individual and
collective life; but there is little question that his psychology is out of
focus and that he is blind to men's solidaristic impulses, which coexist
with the agonistic and competitive passions.[54]

Hobbes considers, only to reject, the obvious objection that his
hypothetical subjects have made a bad bargain in contracting among
themselves to confer, at least formally, unlimited power upon one man
or an assembly of men. Willing subjection to the Leviathan, he believes, is far preferable to the anarchy of man's "natural condition," and
there is no *via media:* so-called divided or limited sovereignty only de-
generates into anarchy. If submission is an evil, it is at least a lesser evil
than the only alternative:

> And though of so unlimited a power, men may fancy many evil
> consequences, yet the consequences of the want of it, which is per-
> petual war of every man against his neighbor, are much worse. The
> condition of man in this life shall never be without inconveniences;
> but there happeneth in no commonwealth any great inconvenience,
> but what proceeds from the subjects' disobedience, and breach of
> those covenants from which the commonwealth hath its being.
> And whosoever thinking sovereign power too great, will seek to
> make it less, must subject himself, to the power that can limit it;
> that is to say, to a greater.[55]

---

53. Hobbes, *Behemoth: The History of the Causes of the Civil Wars of England,*
ed. Sir William Molesworth (New York: Bart Franklin, n.d.), p. 81.

54. See my *Beyond Ideology: The Revival of Political Theory* (New York:
Harper & Row, 1967), chap. 6, on Guido Dorso's terminology of the agonistic and
solidaristic passions in men.

55. Hobbes, *Leviathan,* chap. 20, p. 136. See also ibid., chap. 18, p. 120. In this
earlier passage Hobbes sounds almost Calvinistic in his discussion of the vicious
tendencies of "masterless men."

Forms of Government

Those of us who read Hobbes today are conscious of a missing dimension in his concept of freedom: his idea of political freedom is wholly negative (freedom *from* "unnecessary laws") and fails to take into account a human propensity we well recognize—the need to participate. He can scarcely be expected to have anticipated contemporary demands for "participatory democracy," but the English experience of representative government should have given him some awareness of a legitimate impulse in man to feel that he has some say over his destiny. Hobbes's "realistic" psychology seems to have blinded him to an aspect of human behavior that should have been obvious. At the very least, recognition of the participatory impulse would have helped him to view the republican tradition in England more objectively. He equated the desire to participate with the lust for power, but while the participatory impulse may often contain elements of the desire to dominate, they are not the same.

Hobbes's lack of insight into the participatory impulse and his lack of sympathy with the desire for political freedom are revealed both in his discussion of government forms and in his famous chapter on liberty. According to Hobbes, "there can be but three kinds of commonwealth":

> For the representative must needs be one man, or more: and if more, then it is the assembly of all, or but of a part. When the representative is one man, then is the commonwealth a MONARCHY: when an assembly of all that will come together, then it is a DEMOCRACY, or popular commonwealth: when an assembly of a part only, then it is called an ARISTOCRACY. Other kind of commonwealth there can be none: for either one, or more, or all, must have the sovereign power, which I have shown to be indivisible, entire.[56]

Hobbes's typology is reminiscent of Bodin's: theorists on the trail of sovereignty as the distinguishing mark of government cannot be expected to make a distinction between just and unjust regimes, for their definition of justice precludes it. Like Bodin, Hobbes is convinced that tyranny and oligarchy are not different forms of government from monarchy and aristocracy, but are "the same forms misliked."[57]

Inasmuch as Hobbes holds monarchy, democracy, and aristocracy to be equally powerful forms of government and equally legitimate, having been established by consent of the majority, one would expect him to describe them impartially. In fact, however, he comes out decisively for

---

56. Ibid., chap. 19, p. 121.
57. Ibid.

monarchy as the one form most likely "to produce the peace, and security of the people."[58]

Democracy. Throughout his life, Hobbes maintained an extremely negative attitude toward democracy. He was perhaps most hostile in his *Behemoth*, in which he inveighed against those "democratical gentlemen" who wanted the "liberty to govern themselves." Such men, he contended, had an utterly unrealistic view of the political capacities of the common people, who "have been, and always will be, ignorant of their duty to the public, as never meditating anything but their particular interest. . . . If you think the late miseries have made them wiser, that will quickly be forgot, and then we shall be no wiser than we were."[59] In this work, Hobbes appeared more pessimistic than in the earlier *Leviathan* (although he was not noticeably optimistic there) about the prospects of educating the mass of people in his doctrine. Those who had the leisure to study it, he observed, were prevented from doing so by control of the vested interests over the universities, while the rest of the populace lacked the necessary leisure and understanding for sustained reflection on political matters.

Liberty

It was not only his low estimate of the political capacities of the many that led Hobbes to reject democracy. His conception of political liberty, expressed in its definitive form in the famous Chapter 21 of the *Leviathan*, also led him in this direction. Liberty to Hobbes is a negative thing —not being hindered from doing what one has a will to do as a private individual. Political liberty differs from natural liberty in being limited by the civil law; man gives up his unabridged natural liberty when he consents to political rule. Without such a renunciation, peace among men is impossible: "For as amongst masterless men, there is perpetual war, of every man against his neighbor; no inheritance, to transmit to the son, nor to expect from the father; no propriety of goods, or lands; no security; but a full and absolute liberty in every particular man. . . ."[60]

Political liberty, then, is bounded by the civil law; where the laws are silent, man is free:

> The liberty of a subject, lieth therefore only in those things, which
> in regulating their actions, the sovereign hath praetermitted: such as

---

58. Hobbes's preference for one-man rule and his aversion to democracy were evident in his earliest published work dealing with politics; see his introduction ("Of the Life and History of Thucydides") to his translation of Thucydides' *History* in *Works of Hobbes*, vol. 8, pp. xiii–xxxii, especially pp. xvi–xviii.

59. Hobbes, *Behemoth*, in *Works of Hobbes*, vol. 6, p. 2.

60. Hobbes, *Leviathan*, chap. 21, p. 140.

is the liberty to buy, and sell, and otherwise contract with one another; to choose their own abode, their own diet, their own trade
of life, and institute their children as they themselves think fit;
and the like.[61]

Liberty and Obedience. Hobbes's list of liberties of the subject—
which he clearly thought could be expanded—is interesting in the extent
to which it coincides with the later conception of Locke and other proponents of "classical" liberalism. And yet it sits most uneasily with his
absolutist conception of sovereignty. There is a dilemma at the center
of Hobbes's political thought. He clearly does not propose arbitrary and
dictatorial rule, but rather rule by a sovereign who observes the laws of
nature. And yet he also holds that the laws of nature themselves have to
be translated into civil laws in order to be effective; only "when a
commonwealth is once settled . . . are they actually laws, and not before;
as being then the commands of the commonwealth; and therefore also
civil laws: for it is the sovereign power that obliges men to obey them."[62]
The natural law is "a part of the civil law," and, conversely, the civil law
is "a part of the dictates of nature."[63]

We cannot say that Hobbes resolves this problem in any satisfactory way. On the one hand, subjects are obliged both by the (hypothetical) covenant and by the laws of nature themselves (which led them
to the covenant in the first place) to obey the commands of the sovereign.
No right of revolution exists. Subjects cannot substitute their private
ideas of justice for the determinations of the sovereign. On the other
hand, obedience is not blind and unlimited; it is possible to "offend the
Divine Majesty" by "too much civil obedience." Thus subjects owe to
sovereigns "simple obedience, in all things wherein their obedience is not
repugnant to the laws of God."[64]

In his long and at times tortuous treatment of liberty and obligation
in the *Leviathan*, Hobbes appears to be saying that although there is no
legitimate right of resistance to arbitrary government, it is inevitable
that a sovereign will in fact be resisted and overthrown if he flagrantly
and consistently violates the principles of reason or the laws of nature,
which constitute the foundations of civil government. The subjects of
an arbitrary regime, whether it is headed by one man or by an assembly,
will in time desert in droves, and the sovereign will cease to command
the obedience of the remainder of the populace by reason of his inability

---

61. Ibid., p. 139. "Praetermitted" means "permitted."
62. Ibid., chap. 26, p. 174.
63. Ibid.
64. Ibid., chap. 31, p. 232.

to maintain peace and avoid civil war. There is a minimum condition, at once moral and utilitarian, which the law of nature requires of all governments: that they truly protect their subjects rather than systematically exploit them. Anything beyond this minimum condition, however, subjects have no right to expect; they cannot demand that any existing government be abolished simply because they think another would be better. So long as a sovereign is minimally efficient in protecting his subjects and keeping them from each other's throats, they have political liberty. The laws serve as hedges "not to bind the people from all voluntary actions, but to direct and keep them in such a motion, as not to hurt themselves by their own impetuous desires, rashness or indiscretion. . . ."[65] In such a society men will not be burdened by excessive regulations, for "unnecessary laws are not good laws."[66] More than this men have no right to ask. Politics, Hobbes insists, will not afford collective salvation, but only the opportunity for each individual, in the lonely struggle of his separate and private existence, to fashion his own deliverance.[67]

HOBBES'S SECOND PARADIGM: THE "CHRISTIAN COMMONWEALTH"

In effect Hobbes elaborates two paradigms in the Leviathan, one based upon the "principles of nature only" and the other "upon supernatural revelations of the will of God." By the routes of both natural reason and supernatural revelation he purports to arrive at a single truth, for "though there be many things in God's word above reason . . . yet there is nothing contrary to it."[68]

For Hobbes, then, Christian revelation does not contradict the "secular" teaching of the Leviathan, but confirms it. There is no incompatibility between the civil and ecclesiastical aspects of the commonwealth. A reading of the Scriptures in the light of natural reason, he contends, leads to the conclusion that the separation of the church from the control of the civil sovereign is productive of the greatest disorder, and any other interpretation is erroneous. He prefers an Erastian solution to the religious question at the institutional level: the civil sovereign is also "chief pastor" of the church, which is defined as "a company of men professing the Chris-

---

65. Ibid., chap. 30, p. 227.

66. Ibid., pp. 227–28.

67. Hobbes held that, in any event, men's beliefs and "interior cogitations" were "not subject to commands." Man as an individual was ultimately impregnable against even the most power-hungry government. See ibid., chap. 26, p. 187.

68. Ibid., chap. 32, p. 242.

tian religion, united in the person of one sovereign, at whose command they ought to assemble, and without whose authority they ought not to assemble."[69]

Hobbes's "solution" to the problem of church and state in a "Christian commonwealth" was an excessively neat and rationalistic answer to an extremely complicated problem. (The theological and ecclesiastical sections of the *Leviathan* appear quite dated today.) The most that one can say of his position on the church-state question is that it was consistent with the principles of his secular political theory. According to those principles, there could be only one sovereign and he had to possess all power necessary to preserve peace among his subjects. Inasmuch as the outward forms of religious worship had become a matter of controversy, the sovereign had to be empowered to settle that controversy. One such settlement would have been along the lines of religious toleration and the separation of church and state. Hobbes did not advocate this type of settlement.[70] Rather, he assumed, quite traditionally, that a Christian commonwealth would require a single form of public worship—that is, a national church of which the sovereign was head. Religious toleration and the *de jure* secular state were not actually inconsistent with his principles; but as a practical matter, he had every reason to doubt that the separation of church and state would have appealed to any broad segment of his fellow countrymen in the age in which he lived. The idea of religious toleration was slow to take root and spread in the West. Hobbes did not directly assist its development, but indirectly he may have contributed to it more than he knew, for the drift of his political thought was emphatically secular.

---

69. Ibid., chap. 39, p. 305.

70. Hobbes did mention, apparently only to reject, the possibility that the commonwealth might be "of no religion at all." See ibid., chap. 31, p. 240.

5

Locke and the Origins
of Modern Liberalism

John Locke (1632–1704) is one of the major figures in the history of political thought for a number of reasons, not the least of which is the influence that his *Second Treatise of Government* has had on the development of liberalism. The word "liberal" did not come to be employed as a noun until after the French Revolution; the *liberales* in the Spanish cortes were the first to adopt the name, and by it they meant those who held a moderate political position between the conservative right and the "radical" or Jacobin-style left. Liberalism as a doctrine can be traced much further back than this, however; Locke is generally acknowledged to be the first thinker to gather together into a seemingly coherent whole most of the leading themes of liberalism. Locke's achievement was to fashion out of an anthropocentric humanist orientation similar to Hobbes's[1] a political doctrine that appeared more moderate and more conventional than Hobbes's admittedly revolutionary teaching, yet at the same time was more flexible and open to change.

Especially if one dwells on the *Essay Concerning Human Understanding*, Locke's epistemological masterpiece, one can detect numerous resemblances to Hobbes's approach. Some writers make a sharp distinction between the *Essay* and the *Second Treatise*, arguing in effect that there are two Lockes: Locke the philosopher and Locke the political pamphleteer. This distinction seems forced and contrived, for the two works do set forth a coherent vision of man and his world. Certainly there are differences between the *Essay* and the *Two Treatises*, but they

---

1. No assumptions need be made about a direct influence of Hobbes upon Locke. Locke was influenced by numerous predecessors and contemporaries. On the general subject of Hobbes and Locke, see Peter Laslett's introduction to his edition of Locke's *Two Treatises of Government* (New York: Mentor Books, 1965), pp. 80f. (hereafter cited as Laslett). It must now be recognized that Locke was *not* replying to Hobbes in the *Second Treatise*.

are differences of degree rather than kind. Locke shares with Hobbes a general "naturalistic" orientation toward man and his world. Neither Locke nor Hobbes adopts this position rigidly or dogmatically, however. Both men hold that man is the measure, if not of all things, then at least of the "little world of his own understanding." It is to this "little world" close at hand that Locke directs our attention.

LOCKE'S THEORY OF KNOWLEDGE

Dispensing with revelation, theology, and scholastic philosophy, Locke attempts to hammer out a critical theory of knowledge to explain the range, limit, and character of the human mind. In doing so he introduces the famous simile of the mind as a "white paper" on which experience writes. This phrase came to be known in its Latin version, *tabula rasa,* through Leibniz's critique. Some eighteenth-century writers (Helvétius, Holbach) interpreted Locke's teaching to mean that sense experience is the sole source of knowledge and that the mind is a merely passive entity whose content is determined by the sensations impressed upon it. This interpretation would have led to a doctrine of extreme environmentalism.

Actually, Locke did not hold that sense experience was the only source of knowledge. His view was rather that sensation *and reflection* are the twin sources of knowledge. The mind for him was not a passive receptacle of sensations, but an active participant in the selection and ordering of sensations. Although he went after the theory of "innate ideas" with hammer and tongs, he was less thoroughgoing in his rejection of traditional philosophy than is often supposed. The "innate ideas" doctrine that he attacked was not that of Descartes or Leibniz or Plato, but that of third-rate contemporaries who employed a dubious and dogmatic epistemology to shore up their religious opinions. This doctrine held in effect that the first principles of both speculative and practical reason had been "imprinted" directly on the mind by God, enabling man to understand them clearly and with certainty. Locke incorporated most of these principles into his own teaching, not because he thought them innate, but because he believed they were rules discovered by men in their common experience. Reason, common sense, and general consent among men combined to render these rules acceptable and indeed "self-evident."[2]

---

2. See John W. Yolton, *John Locke and the Way of Ideas* (London: Oxford University Press, 1956), for an acute interpretation of Locke's *Essay Concerning Human Understanding* in the context of the contemporary intellectual situation in England.

LOCKE'S POLITICAL THOUGHT

Locke in the *Essay* is a man in search of knowledge, and by his search he contributes significantly to the growth of that critical spirit which is the nourishment of philosophy. In the *Two Treatises of Government* he is a good deal less critical, perhaps because here he is engaged in a polemic against the book *Patriarcha* by Sir Robert Filmer. The *First Treatise*, which virtually no one reads anymore, is a line-by-line refutation of Filmer's tome. Tedious would be perhaps too flattering an adjective for it. The *Second Treatise* is the positive exposition of Locke's own political thought; as such it is inherently interesting because Locke was an interesting man, because he played an important role in the triumph of Whig constitutionalism in England, and finally because of the work's vast influence in modern Western polities, especially in the English-speaking countries. In fact, Louis Hartz has gone so far as to argue that American liberalism rests on a Lockean foundation, and that America has been Locke's "natural" home.[3]

A thoroughgoing theoretical critique of the *Second Treatise* can be devastating, for as William A. Dunning pointed out some decades ago, Locke's political doctrine consisted of a

> theory treating of a state of nature that was not altogether bad and its transformation into a civil state that was not altogether good, by a contract which was not very precise in its terms or clear in its sanction. It embodied, moreover, a conception of sovereignty of the people without too much of either sovereignty or people; of a law of nature that involved no clear definition of either law or nature; of natural rights but not too many of them; and of a separation of powers that was not...a separation. It concluded, finally, with a doctrine as to the right of revolution that left no guarantee whatever for the permanence of the rather loose-jointed structure which the rest of the theory had built up.[4]

Such a critique is of doubtful appropriateness, however. The *Second Treatise* is less an exposition of political theory than of a secular political

---

3. Louis Hartz, *The Liberal Tradition in America: An Interpretation of American Political Thought Since the Revolution* (New York: Harcourt, Brace, 1955), is an eloquent statement of the view that American political thought is Lockean and liberal in form and substance. From the perspective of the 1970s Hartz appears to have greatly exaggerated the extent of political consensus in the United States, but his thesis is nevertheless brilliantly expounded and deserves serious consideration. As Alpheus Mason has pointed out (in a personal communication), however, the political thought of the framers of the Constitution was shaped by a number of intellectual influences in addition to Locke's. Also, the Constitution itself—in its provision for judicial review, for example—goes beyond Locke.

4. William A. Dunning, *A History of Political Theories* (New York: Macmillan, 1923), pp. 367–68.

myth designed to usher in a new "rational" society in accordance with
the principles developed in the *Essay*. (Even rationalism has its myth.)
At least until relatively recently, when Peter Laslett and others began
investigating the matter, the *Second Treatise* was thought to have been
composed immediately after the Glorious Revolution of 1688, with the
objective, as the preface says, to

> establish the Throne of our Great Restorer, our present King William;
> to make good his Title in the Consent of the People, which being
> the only one of all lawful Governments, he has more fully and clearly
> than any Prince in Christendom: and to justifie to the World, the
> People of England, whose love of their Just and Natural Rights,
> with their Resolution to preserve them, saved the Nation when it
> was on the brink of Slavery and Ruin.[5]

Laslett's diligent researches indicate that Locke actually wrote the
Two Treatises in Holland a number of years before the revolution, and
that the work may have been begun as early as 1679. Regardless of the
date of its writing, its objective was primarily practical and only
secondarily theoretical. Locke was not only interested in bringing about
political change in his native England, however; the *Second Treatise* sets
forth a plan for a rational political order of universal applicability.

When Locke's *Second Treatise* is interpreted in the light of the
theory of knowledge set forth in the *Essay*, it is seen to be more provisional and hypothetical than it might otherwise appear. Locke's professed skepticism about the character of political knowledge (which
depends upon "various and unknown interests, humours, and capacities
of men and not upon any settled scheme of things"[6]) should make us
wary of interpreting the treatise too literally. He was writing in a style
designed to convince men and move them to action, and only incidentally
in the language of philosophical speculation. He did not abandon his
philosophy in his attempt to persuade, however; his philosophical presuppositions require men to make their own political world. Man in the
anthropocentric humanist tradition is *homo faber;* he must create his
world of meaning. The *Second Treatise* is a conscious effort at intellectual fabrication.

If we read the *Second Treatise* in this way—that is, as an application
of the epistemology of the *Essay* to the field of politics—then we who
currently live in political cultures that have been importantly influenced
by Locke will gain a new critical freedom in assessing our legacy. If
Locke himself located his political teaching in the "twilight of prob-

---

5. Laslett, p. 171.
6. Cited in Sheldon S. Wolin, *Politics and Vision* (Boston: Little, Brown,
1960), p. 299.

ability" between "skeptical despair" and "proud presumption," it ill behooves us today to regard it as certain and unquestioned dogma. We can respect and admire Locke's humanism and practical common sense even if we question the continued relevance of some of the tenets of his liberalism for our own time.

LOCKE'S ANTHROPOCENTRIC HUMANISM

Before we examine the political ideas of the *Second Treatise* it would be helpful to consider Locke's views on man and his world as he set them forth in the *Essay Concerning Human Understanding*. The plan for the *Essay* itself is said to have been formulated in the early 1670s, and the work was completed while Locke was in exile on the continent, probably in 1687. It was published in 1689 after Locke returned to England in the wake of the revolution of 1688.

In a remarkable "Epistle to the Reader," Locke speaks with eloquence of the joys of philosophical inquiry and extols such speculation as productive of greater delight than any other human "diversion." He employs a hunting simile:

> He that hawks at larks and sparrows, has no less sport, although a much less considerable quarry, than he that flies at nobler game: and he is little acquainted with the subject of this treatise, the UNDERSTANDING, who does not know that as it is the most elevated faculty of the soul, so it is employed with a greater and more constant delight than any of the others. Its searches after truth are a kind of hawking and hunting, wherein the very pursuit makes a great part of the pleasure. Every step the mind takes, in its progress towards knowledge, makes some discovery, which is not only new, but the best too, for the time at least.[7]

Locke reveals in this work the most admirable qualities of mind that come to be associated with the liberal intellectual: delight in free and independent inquiry, recognition of human fallibility, awareness that any perspective gives only a partial view, a yearning for new ideas and modes of expression, and modesty regarding his own contribution. Not the possession but the *pursuit* of truth is the highest reward: those will not "miss the hunter's satisfaction" who will but "let loose their own thoughts and follow them."

Locke was as convinced as Hobbes of the need for a new beginning

---

7. Locke, *An Essay Concerning Human Understanding: In Four Books,* in *The Works of John Locke,* 4 vols. (London: H. Woodfall et al., 1768), vol. 1, p. xxix.

in philosophy and of the sterility of the imitative scholasticism that was passing for philosophy in the universities of his day. Accordingly, the first order of business was to clear away the rubbish blocking the way to knowledge. In an age of great builders of the commonwealth of learning, such as Newton and Boyle, it is

> ambition enough to be employed as an under-labourer in clearing ground a little, and removing some of the rubbish, that lies in the way to knowledge; which certainly had been very much more advanced in the world, if the endeavors of ingenious and industrious men had not been much cumbered with the learned but frivolous use of uncouth, affected or unintelligible terms, introduced into the sciences, and there made an art of, to the degree that philosophy, which is nothing but the true knowledge of things, was thought unfit, or incapable to be brought into well-bred company and polite conversation.[8]

Aristotle began his philosophizing with a sense of wonder and an awareness of his ignorance. Locke does the same, although with the announced intention of restricting his inquiry to what is sufficient to enable man to make his way in the world.

> Our business here is not to know all things, but those which concern our conduct. If we can find out those measures, whereby a rational creature, put in that state which man is in this world, may, and ought to govern his opinions and actions depending thereon, we need not be troubled that some other things escape our knowledge.[9]

Locke's program calls for increased enlightenment on the human condition. For him the essential precondition of such enlightenment is a distinction between the knowable and the unknowable. It will not do to "let loose our thoughts into the vast ocean of being; as if all that boundless extent were the natural and undoubted possession of our understanding." The objective is to discover "the horizon ... which sets the bounds between the enlightened and dark parts of things, between what is, and what is not comprehensible by us."[10] With Locke we are thus continuing Machiavelli's work of narrowing the horizon of inquiry to man's existence in the world without dogmatically excluding the dimension of transcendence. Political and ethical thought continues to focus on man in his worldly concerns.

---

8. Ibid., p. xxxii.

9. Ibid., bk. 1, Introduction, sec. 6, p. 3.

10. Ibid., sec. 7, pp. 3–4.

Innate Ideas and Natural Law

Much of Book 1 is taken up with a rejection of the doctrine that certain basic axioms are innate in the human mind. John W. Yolton has convincingly demonstrated that Locke is here repudiating the dogmatism of many contemporary intellectuals and divines rather than the entire tradition of Greek and medieval philosophy.[11] But Locke makes no attempt to show any continuity between his philosophizing and premodern thought. Rather he is consciously striving to achieve a new departure in epistemology. That this departure did not represent a complete break with the substance of premodern ethical thought, however, seems clear from his retention of the concept of natural law, not only in the *Second Treatise*, but in the *Essay* itself. Early in the *Essay* we find this significant passage in the section dealing with the doctrine of innate ideas:

> I would not here be mistaken, as if, because I deny an innate law, I thought there were none but positive laws. There is a great deal of difference between an innate law, and a law of nature; between something imprinted on our minds in the very original, and something that we being ignorant of may obtain to the knowledge of, by the use and due application of our natural faculties. And I think they equally forsake the truth, who running into the contrary extremes, either affirm an innate law, or deny that there is a law knowable by the light of nature, that is, without the help of positive revelation.[12]

Reason

One of the most important chapters in the *Essay* for an understanding of Locke's philosophical anthropology is Chapter 17 in Book 4, "Of Reason." After examining the argument in this chapter and bearing in mind the general teaching of the *Essay*, the reader will experience no particular difficulty in moving to the *Second Treatise of Government*. The two works are united by Locke's rationalism. As a political creed, rationalism is supportive of policies that active and energetic men will recognize as conducive to a society that maximizes efficiency and productivity and gives the greatest possible scope to entrepreneurial skill. As the word is used in the Lockean liberal tradition, reason is that which accords with dominion and control of the environment by man—but man himself is viewed as a creature bounded by limits; he is creature and not creator, placed in a predicament by nature but afforded the opportunity of over-

---

11. Yolton, *John Locke and the Way of Ideas.*
12. Locke, *Essay Concerning Human Understanding*, chap. 3, sec. 13, p. 23.

coming this predicament through reason, itself the gift of nature. Man's relationship to nature is therefore complex, involving both domination and submission. He does not submit to any arbitrary power, however, but to rules he makes for himself, which he discovers to be consonant with his condition. That condition requires him to recognize that he is a part of nature, but still capable to some extent of understanding its operation.

Locke begins his chapter on reason with this revealing statement:

> The word reason in the English language has different significations: sometimes it is taken for true and clear principles; sometimes for clear and fair deductions from those principles; and sometimes for the cause and particularly the final cause. But the consideration I shall have of it here is in a signification different from all these; and that is, as it stands for a faculty in man, that faculty whereby man is supposed to be distinguished from beasts, and wherein it is evident that he much surpasses them.[13]

Reason and Ideas. Reason's role, we are told in the *Essay,* consists in demonstrating the "agreement or disagreement of our own ideas." Our "knowledge of the existence of all things without us (except only of a God, whose existence every man may certainly know and demonstrate to himself from his own existence)" is derived exclusively from our "senses." The "understanding" itself comprises both "outward sense and inward perception"; reason supplies "sagacity and illation." By sagacity it discovers and takes cognizance of ideas; by illation (or inference) it "orders the intermediate ideas, as to discover what connection there is in each link of the chain, whereby the extremes are held together." The "greatest part of our knowldge" consists of "deductions and intermediate ideas." These deductions are either certain (and therefore constitute "knowledge") or merely probable (in which case they come under the heading of "opinion"). "In both these cases, the faculty which finds out the means, and rightly applies them to discover certainty in the one, and probability in the other, is that which we call reason." Where the mind does not perceive the connection between its ideas according to the method of reason, "there men's opinions are not the product of judgment, or the consequence of reason, but the effects of chance and hazard, of a mind floating at all adventures, without choice, and without direction."[14] It is evident that, although Locke frequently refers to the mind as a "white paper" on which sense experience writes, he views reason as performing an active role in arranging and ordering the ideas present to the con-

13. Ibid., chap. 17, sec. 1, p. 422.
14. Ibid., sec. 2, pp. 422–23.

sciousness as a result of both outward sensation and inner reflection ("inner sense").

Syllogisms. Although Locke praises Aristotle as "one of the greatest men amongst the ancients, whose large views, acuteness and penetration of thought, and strength of judgment few have equalled,"[15] much of his chapter on reason is taken up with an attack on excessive use of syllogisms. He admits that rational propositions can be reduced to syllogistic form, but he is skeptical of the utility of arguing in this fashion, and points out that syllogisms are frequently used by obscurantists (that is, the scholastic "philosophers") to defeat reason rather than to assist it. To Locke, reason is a native faculty, of which even the untutored and unsophisticated make use. Rational judgment is no abstruse or difficult affair, but a matter of steady, sober application by ordinary men of the intellectual faculties nature has given them.

Reason and Faith. Locke rejects the view that reason and faith are somehow opposed to each other. Faith, he declares, is "nothing but a firm assent of the mind: which if it be regulated, as is our duty, cannot be afforded to any thing but upon good reason; and so cannot be opposite to it."[16] This declaration forms the basis for a detailed assertion of the supremacy of reason over faith and revelation in the following two chapters. In the course of the discussion Locke roundly rejects the claims of "traditional revelation" to authority in its own right. His zeal for a new beginning in human affairs and his scant regard for tradition (except when it is useful for purposes of persuasion) are particularly apparent here. Liberalism's detractors have frequently criticized it as unhistorical, abstract, and narrowly rationalistic. A close reading of Locke, the father of liberalism, would appear to uncover some basis for the indictment.

That reason is the judge of the validity of revelation is a proposition Locke repeatedly endorses in the *Essay.* He distinguishes between original and traditional revelation. Original revelation is divine knowledge that a man (one of the prophets or apostles, for example) receives directly from God; traditional revelation is received indirectly, through the reports of others. Inasmuch as the age of original revelation is past, for all practical purposes, such revelation as is now afforded to man is traditional or indirect. In assessing the validity of traditional revelation, man is obliged to accept only what is not contrary to reason.

Locke says many times, in the *Essay* and in other works such as *The Reasonableness of Christianity,* that the true Christian teaching is fully

---

15. Ibid., sec. 4, p. 424.
16. Ibid., sec. 24, p. 435.

in accord with the dictates of natural reason. As we might expect, he has a low opinion of traditional revealed religions; presumably he exempts only the "rational" (i.e., his) interpretation of Christianity from the following indictment:

> For, to this crying up of faith, in opposition to reason, we may, I think, in good measure ascribe those absurdities that fill almost all the religions which possess and divide mankind. For men having been principled with an opinion, that they must not consult reason in matters of religion, however apparently contradictory to common sense, and the very principles of all their knowledge; have let loose their fancies and natural superstition; and have been by them led into so strange opinions and extravagant practices in religion that a considerate man cannot but stand amazed at their follies, and judge them so far from being acceptable to the great and wise God, that he cannot avoid thinking them ridiculous, and offensive to a sober good man. So that in effect religion, which should most distinguish us from beasts, and ought most peculiarly to elevate us, as rational creatures, above beasts, is that wherein men often appear most irrational and more senseless than beasts themselves.[17]

Reason, to Locke, is "natural revelation," and revelation is "natural reason enlarged by a new set of discoveries communicated by God immediately, which reason vouches the truth of, by the testimony and proofs it gives, that they come from God. So that he that takes away reason, to make way for revelation, puts out the light of both. . . ." The functions of revelation are thus absorbed by reason. To take away reason is to destroy revelation as well; it is as if one would persuade a man "to put out his eyes, the better to receive the remote light of an invisible star by telescope."[18]

Reason and Error. It has now become fully clear that, although Locke regards reason as humanity's defining characteristic, he considers that most men in most ages prior to his own made poor use of it. The true and proper age of reason is yet to begin. There are and have been "very few lovers of truth for truth-sake, even amongst those who persuade themselves that they are so."[19] This would seem to be a discouraging conclusion, and indeed it would be except for Locke's corollary belief that although most men are not diligent in using their reason to search out the truth, neither are they zealous in the pursuit of and assent to error. There are many erroneous and irrational opinions abroad in the

---

17. Ibid., chap. 18, sec. 11, pp. 440–41.
18. Ibid., chap. 19, sec. 4, p. 442.
19. Ibid., sec. 1, p. 441.

world, but only a small proportion of mankind—those who stand to profit from them—actively and seriously endorse them.

> Thus men become professors of, and combatants for, those opinions they were never convinced of, nor proselytes to; no nor ever had so much as floating in their heads: and though one cannot say, there are fewer improbable and erroneous opinions in the world than there are; yet this is certain, there are fewer that actually assent to them, and mistake them for the truth than is imagined.[20]

This conclusion bodes well for Locke's hope of reeducating men to support rational principles in politics. Because the old order's support is so tenuous, transforming it should not be such a difficult task as one might suppose. Once the partisans of obscurantism are routed, he seems to be saying, the majority of men, who have been attached to that order not out of conviction but out of opportunism and self-interest, may well convert to the new order, particularly when they are shown that it serves their self-interest much better than the old one ever did.

THE LOCKEAN LIBERAL CREED: THE POLITICAL MYTH OF A SEVENTEENTH-CENTURY RATIONALIST

We are now in a position to examine and, let us hope, to make sense of the argument of the *Second Treatise of Government*. We shall not expect it to be primarily a historical account of the origin of government. This is a subject that interested Locke only tangentially. From his point of view, most governments in most ages have been founded on error and unreason. He is concerned with the present and the future, not the past. His goal appears to be the political reeducation of man, beginning with his own country, England. He envisions the remaking of the political world as it has been known. In the process, however, not everything will be scrapped. The Christian religion, as rationally interpreted, and the practical maxims of private and civil probity handed down from classical antiquity will be preserved as the "common sense" of mankind. The transformation can be achieved with a minimum of violence. It will be a process of gradual, peaceful change, of the permeation of existing society with the clear, efficacious, and simple ideas of the rational man.

The State of Nature

Locke, like Hobbes, begins with man in a "state of nature." From this we are to understand that, *contra* Aristotle, society is not natural to man, but an artificial construct of man's reason. Man is the fabricator of society, and he need not endure a social structure that does not serve his

---

20. Ibid., chap. 20, sec. 18, p. 456.

interests and above all his desire for preservation of life and property in tranquillity. As he develops his argument, however, it becomes clear that Locke has some difficulty in recognizing the cultural, political, and economic arrangements of "uncivilized" peoples as phenomena of "society."

By nature, then, men are free (that is, independent of one another's control) and equal. If society is not natural to man, however, reason is. Reason, which is the "law of nature," "teaches all mankind, who will but consult it, that being all equal and independent, no one ought to harm another in his life, health, liberty, or possessions...."[21] The state of nature is a state of liberty, not of license. The law of nature, which reason discovers as self-evident, obliges every man to act so as to preserve himself and others. He has no right to another's person or possessions and can be secure in his own only so long as others recognize that they have no right to them.

The state of nature constitutes a predicament, however. Man is independent and equal but he is also insecure. This is so because there is no common authority to adjudicate violations of the law of nature and punish offenders. Each man in the state of nature is his own interpreter and enforcer of the law of nature. This fact results in a highly unstable situation. Inevitably, each man is partial to his own case; men become blind to any interpretation of reason's law but their own, and in fact act against that law. The state of nature (a peaceful state) is transformed into a state of war.

Government and the Law of Nature

Government per se is not the remedy for man's predicament in the state of nature; it must be a government in accordance with the self-evident principles of reason and the law of nature. That there is such a law is as

> intelligible and plain to a rational creature, and a studier of that law, as the positive laws of commonwealths; nay, possibly plainer; as much as reason is easier to be understood, than the fancies and intricate contrivances of men, following contrary and hidden interests put into words; for so truly are a great part of the municipal laws of countries, which are only so far right, as they are founded on the law of nature, by which they are to be regulated and interpreted.[22]

The chief purpose of Locke's *Second Treatise*, then, is to bring the governments of the world before the bar of reason. The natural law is the

21. Locke, *The Second Treatise of Government: An Essay Concerning the True Original, Extent, and End of Civil Government,* in *Works of John Locke,* vol. 2, chap. 2, sec. 6, p. 221 (Laslett, p. 311). Page references to the Laslett edition are also given because of its wide use and because it is the most recent critical edition.

22. Ibid., sec. 12, p. 223 (Laslett, pp. 315–16).

yardstick of legitimacy of states. Its content is definite and clear. It should govern men wherever they are, whether or not they have joined in political association with each other. Problems of interpretation and enforcement tend to make the state of nature anarchical rather than self-regulatory, however, and so civil government itself emerges as the remedy suggested by reason. However—and in this Locke departs decisively from Hobbes—tyrannical government is worse than no government at all, because the sovereign possesses far greater power for harm than a private person in the state of nature. Man leaves the state of nature and enters civil society to secure an impartial and regular interpretation and application of the law of nature; if instead he encounters a sovereign who systematically violates that law, he has gained no advantage over the state of nature. Indeed, he would be "much better" off in the state of nature, where the offender "is answerable to the rest of mankind."[23]

Locke contends that all men are in the state of nature and remain so "till by their own consents they make themselves members of some politick Society." All legitimate government thus rests on consent. Society is not natural, but conventional. Man's natural condition is pre-social. To enter into society is to perform an act of will. The basis of society is a contract whereby individuals consent to be bound by the laws of a common authority known as the civil government.

Stating the matter in this way, although justified by a number of passages in the text, implies a clearer concept of the state of nature than is actually expressed in the *Second Treatise*. Locke also cites Hooker in support of the view that men have a "natural inclination" to form societies, apparently quite independently of a rational calculation of advantage.

The State of War. In one respect it would appear that Locke, unlike Hobbes, sharply distinguishes between the state of nature and the state of war. It is because the peace of the state of nature is liable to deteriorate into a state of war (through lack of a common judge) that men are finally and decisively impelled into civil society. It is not clear, however, how the state of nature could conceivably avoid this unhappy result; for all practical purposes, therefore, Locke's concept of the state of nature is closer to that of Hobbes than might appear at first glance.[24]

Locke reverses Hobbes's assignment of guilt in the event of societal disorder. For Hobbes it is impatient, arrogant, and overweening subjects

---

23. Ibid.
24. This point has been made by Richard Cox in his *Locke on War and Peace* (Cambridge: At the University Press, 1964).

that ordinarily cause civil dissension. For Locke it is the rulers. If the rulers of society adopt a predatory position vis-à-vis the people, they have in effect abrogated their right to govern. It is they and not their dissenting subjects that have dissolved the commonwealth, for in seeking "absolute dominion" over subjects they establish themselves in a state of war.[25]

Government and the Social Contract

Just as the distinction between the state of nature and the state of war is blurred in Locke's presentation, so is his treatment of the nature of the contract by which men form societies and institute governments. Are there two contracts, one joining men together in a society and another forming a government, or are there merely two steps, one taken immediately after the other, or two clauses of a single contract? The issue is of some importance, because if there are two distinct contracts it is possible for men to overthrow a government without abolishing society and reverting to the state of nature with its inconvenience and insecurity. Although some commentators have said that Locke, in contrast to Hobbes, clearly distinguished between governmental and social contracts, I have been unable to find hard evidence for such a conclusion. It is possible that Locke left the matter deliberately ambiguous.

Liberty

Locke distinguishes between two types of liberty, natural and civil. Natural liberty, which man enjoys in the state of nature, is freedom from "any superior power on earth," and freedom to "have only the law of nature for his rule." Civil liberty, or "the liberty of man in society," consists in being "under no legislative power, but that established, by consent, in the commonwealth; nor under the dominion of any will, or restraint of any law, but what that legislative shall enact, according to the trust put in it." Freedom of men

> under government is, to have a standing rule to live by, common to every one of that society, and made by the legislative power erected in it; a liberty to follow my own will in all things, where the rule prescribes not; and not to be subject to the unconstant, uncertain, unknown, arbitrary will of another man. . . .[26]

---

25. Locke, *Second Treatise*, chap. 3, sec. 17, p. 225 (Laslett, p. 320): "And hence it is, that he who attempts to get another man into his absolute power does thereby put himself into a state of war with him." This applies both in the state of nature and in society. "He that, in the state of society, would take away the freedom belonging to those of that society or commonwealth, must be supposed to design to take away from them everything else, and so be looked on as in a state of war."

26. Ibid., chap. 4, sec. 22, p. 227 (Laslett, p. 324).

The similarity of this passage to Chapter 21 of Hobbes's *Leviathan* is striking. Filmer had characterized liberty as a lawless condition in which one
does as he pleases. Liberty for Locke is always bounded by law: by
the law of nature in the state of nature and by positive laws in accord
with the law of nature in society. As he says in a later chapter:

> Law, in its true notion, is not so much the limitation as the direction
> of a free and intelligent agent to his proper interest, and prescribes
> no farther than is for the general good of those under the law: could
> they be happier without it, the law, as an useless thing, would of
> itself vanish; and that ill deserves the name of confinement which
> hedges us in only from bogs and precipices.[27]

Slavery

After Locke's discussion of liberty, one expects him to denounce slavery;
but he leaves a loophole in his argument by observing that a man may
forfeit his natural liberty if, "having by his fault forfeited his own life,
by some act that deserves death," he is taken into slavery by someone
who, although having a right to take his life, chooses to "delay to take it."
This curious passage is attributed by Peter Laslett and others to the fact
that Locke served as administrator of slave-owning colonies in America.[28]
Whatever the reason for its inclusion, it is utterly inconsistent with
Locke's later statement that when a society's legislators reduce men "to
slavery under arbitrary power, they put themselves into a state of war
with the people, who . . . have a right to resume their original liberty.
. . ."[29] It may be argued that the "people" to whom Locke is referring
here are those who have chosen the legislators, not the men of other
societies; but he also clearly states that this "right" is "the common
refuge, which God hath provided for all men, against force and violence."
Locke has caught himself in a position impossible to defend on either
logical or humanitarian grounds.

Property

The argument on property in the long chapter that follows, while
supposedly a theoretical and critical inquiry into the subject, actually

---

27. Ibid., chap. 6, sec. 57, p. 239 (Laslett, pp. 347–48).

28. Ibid., chap. 4, secs. 23–24, p. 228 (Laslett, pp. 325–26; see also the note
on sec. 24, pp. 325–26). This conclusion seems quite alien to the tenor of Locke's
remarks on oppression of "primitive" peoples in "A Letter Concerning Toleration," in
Works of John Locke, vol. 2, pp. 367–68. However, he repeats it in the *Second
Treatise,* chap. 7, secs. 85–86, p. 250 (Laslett, p. 366).

29. Ibid., chap. 19, sec. 222, p. 302 (Laslett, pp. 460–61).

appears to be a rationalization of self-interest—that is, a defense of the rights of the English property-owning and commercial classes, if not of such classes generally. After reading such pages as these one begins to understand the socialist interpretation of Locke and Lockean liberalism advanced by Harold Laski, C. B. Macpherson, and others. This view holds that the primary concerns of early liberalism were the defense of middle-class economic interests and the securing of economic power for the bourgeoisie rather than political liberty for men in general. We have seen that Locke's perspective on political and social problems was broader than this; but at the same time, it must be noted that there is a certain narrowness to his humanism, and that when he speaks of "rational man" he often comes close to equating him with middle-class entrepreneurial man. No doubt there are more things in the life of man in society than are dreamed of in Locke's philosophy.

The chapter on property is a remarkable piece of writing. Locke begins by developing a theory that in some respects anticipates Marx's labor theory of value. It is by man's "mixing his labour" with the natural environment that economic worth is created; with it goes title to property over what a man has tilled, captured, or otherwise appropriated. In the beginning all the earth was common to all men; private property originated in the act of appropriating what nature commonly affords. For Locke, property is, therefore, a right antecedent to society: it is a right by nature rather than by convention. Originally this natural right was bounded by natural law: it is against the law of nature and reason to appropriate more of the bounty of nature than a man may use before it spoils. To do so would deprive another man of what he could use to maintain life (and therefore liberty). With the introduction of money as a medium of exchange, however, the spoilage limitation no longer applies. Money does not spoil or rot, and may be gathered in unlimited quantity. It is fully in accord with reason and the law of nature to sell one's surplus products for money once the system is introduced with man's tacit consent. The introduction of money ensures that there will be very considerable inequalities of possession in the state of nature, and these will be perpetuated in civil society. This too is fully in accord with reason, because God gave the world "to the use of the industrious and rational (and labour was to be his title to it), not to the fancy or covetousness of the quarrelsome and contentious."[30]

Unlimited Accumulation.   Locke's doctrine on property is unprecedented in the history of political thought. Many previous writers (Aristotle and Aquinas, for example) had defended the institution of

---

30. Ibid., chap. 5, sec. 34, p. 231 (Laslett, p. 333).

private property as not contrary to nature, but they always insisted with equal force on the social responsibility of the property owner. Wealth, furthermore, was a means to the good life, not an end in itself. No right to unlimited accumulation could conceivably exist; excessive wealth was a hindrance to the good life. Any society in which the disparities between rich and poor were too great was at once unjust and unstable.

Locke disagrees. The unlimited accumulation of nonperishable wealth is in accordance with reason and natural law. A man might "heap up as much of these durable things [gold, silver, and so on] as he pleased; the exceeding of the bounds of his just property not lying in the largeness of his possession, but the perishing of any thing uselessly in it."[31] It is plain, writes Locke,

> that men have agreed to a disproportionate and unequal possession of the earth, they having, by a tacit and voluntary consent, found out a way how a man may fairly possess more land than he himself can use the product of, by receiving in exchange for the overplus, gold and silver, which may be hoarded up without injury to any one.[32]

Government Regulation. Locke does seem to leave a loophole for the correction of excessive and unjust disparities in wealth when he notes that "in governments, the laws regulate the right of property, and the possession of land is determined by positive constitutions."[33] Actually, however, it is inconceivable that for Locke the government could properly undertake any redistribution of property, for as he later points out (in Section 124), the "chief end" for which men enter society is to preserve their property.[34] Government only secures natural rights; it cannot tamper with them and remain legitimate. This reference to the regulation of property rights by the laws was possibly introduced to justify government action in regard to certain property holdings (church lands, perhaps some vast feudal estates) regarded as inimical to the

---

31. Ibid., sec. 46, p. 236 (Laslett, p. 342).

32. Ibid., sec. 50, p. 237 (Laslett, p. 344).

33. Ibid.

34. Jacob Viner has pointed out that "Locke uses the term property in two different senses ... the narrow ... sense, meaning things salable for money ... and the broad sense, where it means an individual's right to anything (not merely any *thing*), as in the stock phrase of ancient origin: 'life, liberty, and estate ...'" ("'Possessive Individualism' as Original Sin," *Canadian Journal of Economics and Political Science*, 29 [November 1963]: 554–55). Viner thinks that C. B. Macpherson in particular has interpreted Locke's concept of property too narrowly. Viner has considerable respect for "bourgeois" liberalism and very little respect for socialism. Macpherson's views are just the opposite. See also Macpherson's reply to Viner, "Scholars and Spectres," ibid., pp. 559–62, and Viner's counterreply in ibid., pp. 562–66. This is an incisive and spirited exchange. I am indebted to Alpheus Mason for pointing it out to me.

development of the entrepreneurial spirit and the entrepreneurial class. As Locke says,

> This shows how much numbers of men are to be preferred to large-ness of dominions; and that the increase of lands, and the right employing of them, is the great art of government: and that prince, who shall be so wise and god-like, as by established laws of liberty to secure protection and encouragement to the honest industry of mankind, against the oppression of power and narrowness of party, will quickly be too hard for his neighbors. . . .[35]

Government and Religion

One of Locke's key objectives in the *Second Treatise* is apparently to define political power and to distinguish it from other forms of power and jurisdiction. In the process of doing so he significantly diminishes the political sphere as it had been known in classical political philosophy and, in a different sense, in Christian speculation as well. Locke seeks to define the boundaries between the political sphere and the areas of religion and the family ("paternal power"). The net result is a sharp line dividing the public and the private, a distinction that has been of crucial importance for later liberal thinking.

In his first "Letter Concerning Toleration," Locke had emphatically declared: "I esteem it above all things necessary to distinguish exactly the business of civil government from that of religion, and to settle the just bounds that lie between the one and the other." The "common-wealth" or political community, he wrote, is "a society of men constituted only for the procuring, preserving, and advancing their own civil interests." Civil interests are further defined as "life, liberty, health, and indolency of body; and the possession of outward things, such as money, lands, houses, furniture, and the like." The "care of souls" and the "care of commonwealth" are utterly diverse enterprises.[36]

Thus, for Locke, not only is religion ultimately a private affair of the individual conscience (in this Hobbes would have concurred), but churches, or the "outward regiment" of religion, are essentially private associations. A state church was thus a contradiction in terms. A church, like any other "spontaneous society," may "remove any of its members who transgress the rules of its institution; but it cannot . . . acquire any right of jurisdiction over those who are not of it." Locke, who is else-where so fond of quoting Richard Hooker in apparent support of his own views, makes no mention of him here as he goes completely opposite to the teaching of a man who still thought in terms of the "ecclesiastical

---

35. Locke, *Second Treatise,* chap. 5, sec. 42, p. 234 (Laslett, pp. 339–40).
36. Locke, "Letter Concerning Toleration," pp. 350–51.

polity." For Hooker, all Englishmen acquired membership in the established Church of England by birth (baptism could be assumed to follow as a matter of course). According to this earlier view, Jewish and other non-Christian minorities were regarded essentially as resident aliens, physically in but not politically of the society. This was, of course, a serious deficiency in the concept of the ecclesiastical polity, and one of the achievements of the modern secular state has been to affirm the principle of the equality of all men and citizens before the law regardless of religious or ethnic distinctions.

There were, as we shall see, anomalies in Locke's position. He did not begin to articulate the principle of civil equality as forcefully and unambiguously as would Hegel in a later day. But the principle is there in his writings, awaiting further development.

Religious Tolerance. To Hooker, Englishmen did not choose their church any more than they chose their society; they inherited it. For Locke, membership in both civil society and a particular religious association was voluntary, although there was only one political power to which one could be legitimately subject and it had coercive faculties absent in a modern religious body. Furthermore, although membership in society was optional in a sense (one could conceivably—before the age of twenty-one—contract out and emigrate to another political society or else to "America" and live in the state of nature), obedience to legitimate government was not optional if one chose or continued to live in society. Religious adherence was always optional, however. One could not live in society without adhering to its government, but one *could* live in society without adhering to the beliefs or practices of any religious organization.

Atheists and Catholics. After all this, Locke does an about-face and exempts atheists and Roman Catholics from toleration by the state— atheists on grounds that, lacking a belief in God, they allegedly would not keep their promises, and Catholics because they supposedly "deliver themselves up to the protection and service of another prince" (that is, the pope).[37] Locke's theory of toleration seems to be highly selective, but still it must be recognized that his views on freedom of conscience are relatively humane for his age.

Civil Theology. Perhaps a more interesting point is that Locke seems to have assumed that a "rational" and self-regulating civil theology would emerge in the private sphere. This civil theology would provide such social cement as the predominantly atomistic Lockean system permitted and would be maintained through social pressure rather than through legislation.

For Locke, although the *state* is in principle legally neutral on

---

37. Ibid., pp. 374–75.

questions of belief, members of *society*—including the "magistrates" of the state in their roles as individuals[38]—are committed to a common moral and political doctrine. We may characterize this doctrine as the liberal civil theology, creed, or ethos. Thus while Locke, unlike Hobbes before him and Rousseau after him, denies to the state or political magistracy the use of its powers of physical coercion to enforce a particular belief system in society (this is not the "business" of civil government), he does allow society itself the right to generate and maintain such a system by a variety of means, formal and informal, from political education to social pressure. This entire area is what we know today as political socialization.

Conformity. Locke assumes, therefore, at least a minimal consensus with respect to opinions necessary to "human society" and "moral rules necessary to the preservation of society" as determined by "rational and industrious men."[39] He is very little interested in employing the state's power to sustain this liberal creed, however, largely because he has found a far more efficacious power for this purpose: public opinion. Once the basic political and moral principles essential to human society have been demonstrated in such a manner that they are self-evident to the "rational and industrious men" who predominate in society, they will be self-enforcing, since most men tend to conform to the opinions of those who may advance their interests, especially their economic interests. Locke the liberal advocates toleration—on the assumption that it will lead to much more far-reaching agreement and conformity of thought than was known in preliberal society.

The conformist aspects of liberalism have not been sufficiently studied, especially in the United States, with the result that despite its procedurally free and open public debate, the American polity has generally been severely restricted in its consideration of alternative political styles and perspectives. The gain in critical freedom that is now taking place in this country through the growth of radical protest movements may entail some loss of political stability, but it may well result in a more open, and even a more just, political order.

THE LEGITIMATE GROUNDS OF "POLITICAL OR CIVIL SOCIETY"

Locke's master conception in the area of political legitimacy is consent: "Men being ... by nature all free, equal, and independent, no one can be

---

38. "In teaching, instructing, and redressing the erroneous by reason, he [the magistrate] may certainly do what becomes any good man to do. Magistracy does not oblige him to put off either humanity or Christianity" (ibid., p. 352).

39. Ibid., p. 373.

put out of this estate, and subjected to the political power of another, without his own consent." Men agree

> to join and unite into a community, for their comfortable, safe, and peaceable living one amongst another, in a secure enjoyment of their properties, and a greater security against any that are not of it. . . . When any number of men have so consented to make one community or government, they are thereby presently incorporated, and make one body politick, wherein the majority have a right to act and conclude the rest.[40]

Only consent can make a man a member of society and as such obliged to obey the laws set down, within the bounds of reason and the law of nature, by its civil government or legislative body. Only consent can morally oblige a man to join his own force to the common executive power of a society to assist it in defending the body politic from internal or external threat.

Majority Rule

This generalization is qualified in only two ways: (1) as C. B. Macpherson has pointed out,[41] slaves and servants are excluded, along with others who, in Toynbee's phrase defining the "proletariat," are presumably in society but not of it; and (2) it would be unreasonable to expect each member of the society to consent to every decision made by its representatives. Because of the variety of men's interests, such unanimity is rarely attained. Only the original decision to form a political community needs to be unanimous; for all subsequent decisions, the consent of the majority is sufficient. Therefore, in consenting to become a member of society, the individual automatically consents to be bound by the decision of the majority.

Locke's treatment of the concept of majority rule is one of the weaker aspects of the *Second Treatise*. In Section 98 he simply assumes that it is self-evident to "rational creatures" that "where the majority cannot conclude the rest, there they cannot act as one body, and consequently will be immediately dissolved again." Locke's only attempt at justification—and a feeble one at that—is found in Section 96, where he compares society to a physical body, which of necessity moves in the direction in which "the greater force carries it, which is [in the absence of unanimity—an impossibility in human affairs] the consent of the majority." On such a slender thread hangs the massive weight of Locke's argument for majority rule.

---

40. Locke, *Second Treatise*, chap. 8, sec. 95, pp. 254–55 (Laslett, p. 374).

41. C. B. Macpherson, *The Political Theory of Possessive Individualism: Hobbes to Locke* (Oxford: Clarendon Press, 1962), pp. 221–22.

Locke glosses over completely the danger to minority rights implicit in his virtually unqualified endorsement of majority rule. (Indeed, his endorsement is so little qualified that he might almost be called a proponent of majority absolutism.) The restraints that he places upon abuse of power, either by government acting in the name of the majority or by the majority itself when it resumes its "original" legislative power, are vague and inadequate. There is nothing in his political system comparable to the independent judiciary of the American system, with its power of judicial review. It is little to be wondered that sensitive interpreters of Locke, such as Alpheus T. Mason and the late Willmoore Kendall, have seen a danger of majoritarian tyranny inherent in the political principles he expounds in the *Second Treatise*. Particularly in the United States, where some elected political leaders have recently posed as champions of the "silent majority" in espousing insensitive and repressive policies, we are more vividly aware than ever of the conformist implications of majority rule. It is possible that today a minority of the people could prove to be the most authentic and effective exponents of substantive democracy; at the same time, that minority must be wary of any tendencies to confuse its own interests with the universal interest, and must resist the temptation to advance its cause through putschist tactics and adventurism.

Having deduced from the needs and interests of "rational and industrious men" the principles of consent and majority rule, and established them to his satisfaction as the foundation stones of all political legitimacy,[42] Locke makes clear that it was on these grounds that he earlier read absolute monarchy out of the ranks of governmental forms altogether: "Hence it is evident, that absolute monarchy, which by some men is counted the only government in the world, is indeed inconsistent with civil society, and so can be no form of civil government at all. . . ."[43]

---

42. "And thus that which begins and actually constitutes any political society, is nothing but the consent of any number of freemen capable of a majority, to unite and incorporate into such a society. And this is that, and that only, which did or could give beginning to any lawful government in the world" (*Second Treatise*, chap. 8., sec. 99, p. 256; Laslett, p. 377). From this and other passages it would seem that those writers who find in Locke (in contrast to Hobbes) clear evidence of two contracts—the social contract and a governmental contract—have little support in the text. The closest that Locke comes to distinguishing clearly between society and government is in chap. 19, sec. 211. Even here, however, there is no indication of a governmental contract. The social contract empowers the majority to erect a form of government and to set up a new one if that government abrogates its trust.

43. Ibid., chap. 7, sec. 90, p. 252 (Laslett, p. 369). This statement appears puzzling until one recalls the nature of the *Second Treatise* as an exercise in political reconstruction, the fabrication of a new "rational" political creed. When Locke says absolute monarchy is no form of government, of course he really means no *legitimate* form of government. But he is not speaking of government in a phenomenally descriptive sense—of government as it has been and is; he is speaking of government

Historical Evidence

Locke then proceeds to face the distasteful but inevitable question: If society originated in consent and contract, as he claims, why is there no evidence for any of this in history? His rejoinder is interesting. Although he clearly believes the historical issue is of scant relevance ("at best an argument from what has been, to what should be, has no great force"),[44] he nonetheless tries at some length to provide historical justification for his position.

Locke maintains that "government is everywhere antecedent to records," and so it cannot be surprising that mankind has been bequeathed few accounts of the origins of society. However, all those that have come down to us (excluding those of Israel, which is a special case "and which favors not at all paternal dominion") are "either plain instances of such a beginning as I have mentioned, or at least have manifest footsteps of it." To substantiate this assertion, Locke devotes one sentence to "the beginning of Rome and Venice" and one paragraph to Joseph Acosta's account of Peru.[45]

Government, then, is held both historically and normatively to rest on consent. The fact that most early governments are monarchical in form should not hide the fact that they also rest on consent and not on any "divine right" such as that fancied by Robert Filmer and others, Locke tells us.

LIBERAL GOVERNMENT

After blurring the issue of whether the state of nature is a logical construct following from his theory of man or a historical fact, Locke proceeds to the core of his argument: the exposition and defense of liberal government and the right of revolution to achieve it. Although, as we have observed, the term "liberalism" is a later invention, it is applicable to Locke's basic conceptions because those who later coined it were so clearly at one with him. Liberal government is government under law for limited objectives, above all for the preservation of the lives and property of the society's members. Liberal government is rational government: government of rational men, by rational men, for rational men. The obverse of liberal government is arbitrary or tyrannical government in

---

as it should and could be if only it conformed to clearly intelligible rational principles. The paradigm of classical political theory has become a program for practical political action.

44. Ibid., chap. 8, sec. 103, p. 257 (Laslett, p. 380).
45. Ibid., chap. 10, sec. 132, pp. 267–68 (Laslett, pp. 399–400).

any of its forms. Between liberal and tyrannical governments there is a gray area occupied by those intermediate governmental forms that, while legitimate in principle, are so structurally deficient as inevitably to be drawn in time toward tyranny. Only liberal government rests on correct principles, which ensure, if they are followed, freedom at once from the hazards and uncertainties of the state of nature and from the oppression of absolute dominion.

Locke's chief purpose in the *Second Treatise* is to establish the case for liberal government. In that sense the spirit of the work—despite the theoretical arguments on which it touches—is closer to that of a partisan tract than of a theoretical treatise. Locke has relatively little interest in discussing and evaluating the various forms of government or in propounding a paradigm of the best regime against which existing regimes can be measured. Liberal government can be established within time, and once established can govern wholly in accord with the law of nature, which means the law a "rational" man sees as conducive to self-preservation.

Forms of Legislative Power

What Locke says about the various forms of government is of some interest because of his perfunctory treatment of any alternative to liberal constitutionalism. The social contract, we shall recall, entailed (1) a unanimous agreement among those concerned to leave the state of nature and unite in society, and (2) the corollary principle that every member agrees to be bound by the decision of the majority as to the precise form of government adopted. According to Locke, the second principle is implicit in the first, because the community that has been established cannot move and decide matters of public concern on any basis other than majority vote. Because of the variability of men's interests and dispositions, unanimity is impossible. A minority decision would be unacceptable because it violates the fundamental principle, derived from the state of nature, of the equality of the society's members. Inasmuch as all government rests on consent, only the consent of the majority can make a government legitimate. If there is a "sovereign" in Locke's system, it is the sovereign majority.

In principle, this majority may designate a legislative power—seemingly the core of government to Locke—in any number of forms. It may opt for a "perfect" or direct democracy, in which all the people assembled constitute the legislature. Or it "may put the power of making laws into the hands of a few select men, and their heirs or successors," in which case it is an oligarchy. Another solution is to place that power "into the hands of one man and then it is a monarchy: if to him and his heirs, it is an hereditary monarchy: if to him only for life . . . an elective monarchy." Finally, the community by majority decision may opt for a mixed form of government. Locke does not make clear how the mixed form is consistent with the "supremacy" of the legislative power. It might be said that Locke is simply abridging the English constitution, but he is not. He is here writing of the mixed form in general as a species, of which the English constitution would presumably be a genus. The only problem is that this constitution was and is not a mixture of pure democracy, oligarchy, and monarchy, or of any two of these, as Locke describes them. Furthermore, the notion of the mixed regime clashes with the constitutional principle of parliamentary sovereignty and the subordination of the monarch to parliament, which was to be the principal outcome of the revolution of 1688, even while preserving the formula of the king-in-parliament. Therefore, although Locke was of course profoundly influenced by specifically English political developments, and although the results of 1688 were in harmony with his political objectives, it seems doubtful that he was writing with only England in mind. On one level at least, the *Second Treatise* is a call for universal political reform in accordance with what were later to be called the principles of liberalism.

Legislative and Executive Powers

The social contract, then, creates a community, or "commonwealth," which proceeds to devise its form of government. Forms of government have historically been of diverse types. *All* forms of government, however, are bound by the "trust . . . put in them by society, and the law of God and nature," (1) "to govern by promulgated established laws," (2) "to enact only laws which are necessary and for the good of the people," (3) "not to raise taxes on the property of the people, without the consent of the people, given by themselves, or their deputies," and (4) not to "transfer the power of making laws to any body else, or place it anywhere, but where the people have."[46] The very terms by which the laws of reason are to bind all governments point in the direction of a government organized in two branches, a representative assembly (the "legislative" proper) and an executive with broad powers of administration and enforcement.

Locke insists on the need to invest the legislative and executive powers in distinct entities. (He is sometimes said to have argued for the "separation of powers," but as we shall see when we come to consider Montesquieu, this is something of an exaggeration.)

Given the tendency of uncontrolled power to aggrandize itself,

---

46. Ibid., chap. 11, sec. 142, p. 273 (Laslett, p. 409).

Locke sees the distinction of powers between the legislature and the executive as a lesson learned by reason from experience. He does not intend the distinction of powers to compromise the supremacy of the legislative power, for the executive is to be subject to the laws enacted by the legislature. On the other hand, the requirements of effective administration and the survival of the commonwealth require that the executive possess substantial power and discretion.

Supporters of a weak executive will find little encouragement in Locke. He shores up the power of the executive in three ways: (1) by annexing the "federative" power (or the power over foreign relations); (2) by investing the executive with the authority to maintain the representativeness of the legislative body by altering its composition (that is, by redrawing the boundaries of electoral constituencies to eliminate "rotten boroughs") if necessary; and (3) by ascribing to the executive an inherent "prerogative" power to "provide for the publick good, in such cases, which, depending upon unforeseen and uncertain occurrences, certain and unalterable laws could not safely direct...."[47]

Liberal Optimism

Locke's political "rationalism" is revealed with particular clarity in his remark on the executive's prerogative to carry out legislative reapportionment: "If therefore the executive... observing rather the true proportion, than fashion of representation, regulates, not by old custom, but true reason, the number of members... [he] cannot miss the consent and approbation of the community."[48] In his touching faith in the ability of "true reason" to cut through the complexities of a matter like representation and his assumption that such a solution would automatically receive the "approbation of the community" we have the measure of Lockean liberal optimism, an optimism of an exceedingly sanguine variety despite its bows in the direction of "human frailty." Along with Locke's faith in

---

47. Ibid., chap. 13, sec. 158, p. 277 (Laslett, p. 420). Locke introduces his discussion of prerogative by suggesting as an example the power of the executive to alter the composition of the legislature by reorganizing the electoral districts if it becomes unrepresentative. Inasmuch as this provision specifically affects the relationship of the executive to the legislative assembly, however, I am listing it separately. It is not too difficult to foresee, even from Locke's plan for a liberal political order, the eventual "decline" of parliament vis-à-vis the executive power. From this passage, however, Locke may not be interpreted as a forerunner of the "one man, one vote" principle endorsed in *Baker* v. *Carr*. Although he does not explicitly say so, it may be assumed from his emphasis on property that he regarded only property holders as full participating members of society. Therefore such legislative reapportionment as is carried out would take into account the distribution of property owners and not simply the distribution of population. Again, it would seem that Locke wishes to increase the power of the commercial class as opposed to the landed aristocracy.

48. Ibid., chap. 14, sec. 160, p. 280 (Laslett, p. 422).

the reasonableness of the majority, this optimism testifies to an impressive confidence in men's capacities for rational decision. While Sheldon Wolin and others rightly object that to portray liberalism as naively optimistic is to distort the position of early liberal writers, it remains true that those writers display a confidence in the victory of pragmatic rationalism not substantiated by the more profound psychologies of Machiavelli and Freud. One of the principal requirements for a revision of liberalism today is a deepening of its psychological insights.

A Powerful Executive vs. Tyranny

Commentators on Locke frequently, and properly, stress his advocacy of limited government. It is less frequently noted that Locke's limited government can under no circumstances be equated with weak government. This is evident in his extremely broad definition of political power ("a right of making laws with penalties of death, and consequently all less penalties, for the regulating and preserving of property, and of employing the force of the community, in the execution of such laws, and in the defence of the commonwealth from foreign injury"[49]), and particularly in his insistence on a broad "prerogative" power for the executive.

The Executive's Prerogative. "Prerogative" is defined in Chapter 14 as the "power to act according to discretion, for the publick good, without the prescription of the law, and sometimes even against it. . . ." This power properly belongs to the executive because in "well-framed governments," in which the legislative and executive authorities are in "distinct hands," only the executive functions at all times and thus is able to act swiftly as the occasion demands. Locke has in mind here what have since come to be known as "emergency powers." Inasmuch as it is impossible for legislators "to foresee, and provide by laws, for all that may be useful to the community, the executor of the laws . . . has by the common law of nature" a right to use his discretion to see that the commonwealth is preserved. In temporarily setting aside specific positive laws for such a purpose, the executive is not acting against law as such, but rather following the dictate of the "fundamental law of nature," which counsels self-preservation.[50]

Having allowed as much, however, Locke proceeds without much consistency to point out that prerogative may legitimately be defined in part by positive law. Concern by a people to define the precise powers and duties of government by positive law is for Locke a relatively late

---

49. Ibid., chap. 1, sec. 3, p. 220 (Laslett, p. 308).
50. Ibid., chap. 14, sec. 159, pp. 279–80 (Laslett, p. 421).

development in political history. In a society's infancy, when its needs are simple and its population is small, there is close contact between the rulers and the ruled. The people are therefore content to trust the "magistrate" to govern as he thinks best, without laying down detailed and specific rules and procedures for the conduct of his office. Modern society, however, with its vastly increased size and complexity, recognizes a need for greater specificity of functions. In any event, for Locke the decisive test of the proper use of the executive's prerogative is the judgment of the people—the "society of rational creatures." If they judge that he is not using it well and the abuse continues, they may "appeal to heaven"—that is, resist by force if necessary—against what is no longer legitimate prerogative, but arbitrary power.[51]

Forms of Power. Locke distinguishes among "paternal, political, and despotical power." *Paternal* power is the power exercised by parents over children. As he argued at great length against Sir Robert Filmer in the *First Treatise,* it is not a proper model for political relationships. *Political* power, properly speaking, is "that power, which every man having in the state of nature, has given up into the hands of the society ... with this express or tacit trust, that it shall be employed for their good, and the preservation of their property...." It "cannot be an absolute and arbitrary power," and, unlike paternal authority, which rests on nature, is derived *only* from "compact and agreement, and the mutual consent of those who make up the community." *Despotical* power is "an absolute, arbitrary power one man has over another, to take away his life, whenever he pleases. This is a power which neither nature gives ... nor compact can convey...." Finally, Locke observes, anyone who "shall consider the distinct rise and extent, and the different ends of these several powers, will plainly see, that paternal power comes as far short of that of the magistrate, as despotical exceeds it...."[52]

Conquest. Conquest alone cannot establish a government, for there can be no other basis of political power than the "consent of the people." Conquest "often makes way for a new frame of a commonwealth, by destroying the former; but, without the consent of the people, can never erect a new one." Locke is plainly troubled by the problems this topic poses for his doctrine of consent. In general he argues that force makes no right, although those who are vanquished in a just war are rightfully at the mercy of their righteous victors. Even the power over captives taken in a just war is not purely despotic, however; it seems to exist in a limbo between political and despotic power. The conqueror in a just war

---

51. Ibid., sec. 168, p. 282 (Laslett, p. 426).
52. Ibid., chap. 15, secs. 168–74, pp. 282–85 (Laslett, pp. 427–31).

may rightfully dispose of the lives of the conquered or punish them in various ways, even keeping them in perpetual servitude.[53] He may not, however, confiscate their property or harm their wives and children (who, as noncombatants, are not responsible for the waging of the war). If the conquered populace as a whole does not freely consent to the new government, then government will exist there only in name; in fact, a state of war will exist between a populace held in subjection and an occupying power. Locke's position on the matter is summarized in the statement that "the government of a conqueror, imposed by force on the subdued, against whom he had no right of war, or who joined not in the war against him, where he had right, has no obligation upon them."[54]

Usurpation. Locke describes usurpation as a "kind of domestic conquest." A usurper is one who gains power "by other ways than what the laws of the community have prescribed." He has "no right to be obeyed." Like conquest, however, usurpation can subsequently be invested with legitimacy if the people freely consent to it.[55] It would appear that the principle of consent is used to cover a multitude of things more properly classified as coercion. Perhaps this is what Eric Voegelin had in mind when he spoke of Locke's "swindle of consent."[56]

Tyranny. "As usurpation is the exercise of power, which another has a right to; so tyranny is the exercise of power beyond right, which no body can have a right to." Tyranny occurs when the governor, "however entitled, makes not the law, but his will the rule."[57] Tyrannical rule is not an occasional arbitrary action by a society's governor, but a "long train of actions" indicating a deliberate and consistent design to flout the laws of both men and nature and to deprive the subjects of life and property. Just as legitimate government is always to be obeyed, so tyranny may always be rightfully resisted by force. The problem, of course, is to determine who shall judge when a government has become tyrannical and when the right of resistance may thus be invoked. This problem is discussed at length in the important concluding chapter of the *Second Treatise.*

---

53. In ibid., chap. 16, sec. 189, p. 291, Locke circumscribes his earlier justification of slavery as a result of rightful conquest. Here he observes that the conquerer has a right to enslave the captives but not "their children." Locke thus supports the institution of slavery as it existed in ancient Greece and Rome but not as it was developing in the English colonies of North America.

54. Ibid., sec. 187, p. 290 (Laslett, p. 440).

55. Ibid., chap. 17, secs. 197–98, p. 293 (Laslett, pp. 445–46).

56. Eric Voegelin, *New Science of Politics* (Chicago: University of Chicago Press, 1952).

57. Locke, *Second Treatise,* chap. 18, sec. 199, p. 294 (Laslett, p. 446).

THE PROBLEM OF REVOLUTION

Chapter 19, entitled "Of the Dissolution of Government,"

> contains those statements of Locke's which associate his book most closely with the events of 1688–89. It is lacking in structure and obviously the result of successive corrections and additions. . . . The first part of the chapter, up to ¶ 218, seems clearly to have been written well before 1688. . . . Then come two paragraphs which were added in 1689 (¶¶ 219, 220), followed by a passage mainly belonging to the original text. . . . The final paragraphs seem to belong to the original, but were obviously modified and extended after the Revolution.[58]

That the chapter is a mixture of general propositions relating to the right of resistance and observations appropriate to the Glorious Revolution is quite evident.

The Supreme Power of the People

Interestingly enough, Locke does not refer to a "right of revolution" by the people. Earlier he established the doctrine that although in well-constituted regimes the people have conferred the legislative power on a particular organ of government, they retain ultimate control over it, since the legislative power is granted in trust (it is a "fiduciary power") and may be recalled by the people if the governors break that trust. Thus "the community perpetually retains a supreme power of saving themselves from the attempts and designs of any body, even of their legislators, whenever they shall be so foolish, or so wicked, as to lay and carry on designs against the liberties and properties of the subjects. . . ."[59] As a result of their always latent "supreme power," when the people resist tyrannical rule by force, they do not rebel, but rather assert their legitimate rights. Locke thus turns the tables on those who demand justification for revolution by denying that the people are engaged in revolution in the first place. It is not the people that have rebelled, but the government.[60] When government consistently acts in a tyrannical fashion, it ceases to be legitimate. It is a body of men exercising force without right; it has placed *itself* in a state of war with the populace. The "rebel," the "violator of law and order," to Locke is the tyrannical govern-

---

58. Laslett, p. 454n.

59. Locke, *Second Treatise*, chap. 13, sec. 149, p. 275 (Laslett, p. 413).

60. Ibid., chap. 19, sec. 226, p. 304 (Laslett, p. 464).

ment and never the people when they act according to the reasoned judgment of the majority to curb arbitrary rule.

Locke gives examples of violations of legislative and executive power that lead to the "dissolution of government" in fact, if not in name. When serious infringements occur, the majority may "appeal to heaven" and resist illegitimate force with just and rightful force. If chaos and civil war result, the fault is in society's tyrannical governors, not in the resisting people. The people to Locke are the repository of political virtue. They will endure grievous errors and imperfections of government and will act only after their patience is exhausted.[61] To demand, like some proponents of divine right, that the people endure tyrannical acts with infinite patience (although Locke shows that even Robert Barclay had conceived of some extreme situations in which resistance was legitimate[62]), is to demand that free and rational men act like slaves. Locke thus propounds a "doctrine of a power in the people of providing for their safety anew, by a new legislature, when their legislators have acted contrary to their trust, by invading their property. . . ."[63]

Who Shall Be Judge?

Having resoundingly vindicated what later came to be known as "popular sovereignty" (a phrase Locke does not use), he assures his readers that this power will always lie dormant under a well-constituted, just, and prudent government—that is, a government according to law, which places the preservation of its citizens' lives and possessions (Locke's use of "property" includes both these terms) before all else. When a government fails to act justly and prudently, the people may use force against it for a specific and limited objective: to reestablish a liberal society in which the person and goods of each member are safeguarded and each individual can proceed with his work in the world in freedom under law.

But who is to decide whether a government is acting justly? Who is the judge? The majority of the people. (Locke nowhere clearly specifies who is included in the ranks of "the people," but we may assume he meant only full-fledged members of society, or property owners.) Paradoxically, to ensure the prospects for survival of an individualist society, a supreme moment of collectivism is necessary. Individuals are not themselves authorized to use force against a government they deem tyranni-

---

61. Ibid., sec. 225, p. 303 (Laslett, p. 463).

62. Ibid., secs. 232–33, pp. 306–7 (Laslett, pp. 468–70). Interestingly enough, Locke does not cite Hobbes at all; those who see this omission as significant are surely correct.

63. Ibid., sec. 226, pp. 303–4 (Laslett, p. 464).

cal; only the collective judgment of the greater part of the people can sanction the use of force against those who claim to be in authority. If an individual or group attempts to move by force against the established government without the approval of the majority, that individual or group is guilty of subversion and treason.

Over and over Locke asks, "Who shall be judge?" and the answer is always the same: the majority of the people. When those constituting the majority have been victorious in their appeal to heaven, they shall have the power to make a new beginning, "and continue the legislature in themselves, or erect a new form, or under the old form place it in new hands, as they think good."[64]

CONCLUSION: LOCKE'S AMBIGUOUS LEGACY

Dunning's harsh judgment on Locke's lack of consistency, already noted,[65] has been echoed by numerous commentators. Consistency, however, is not the greatest virtue in a serious political writer. If it were, then ideologists, who reduce all their analyses to one abstract idea and remorselessly impose their dream constructions on a recalcitrant reality, would be the greatest political thinkers. All writers who grapple with political complexities encounter difficulties in their analyses and may be downgraded by a hasty reader for their "inconsistency." Emerson said something profoundly true when he acidly observed that "a foolish consistency is the hobgoblin of little minds, adored by little statesmen and philosophers and divines."

So let us not be overly concerned about Locke's lack of consistency. It is rather in the narrowness of his psychology and the oversimplicity of his political psychology that he led himself and others astray. For all his impressive common sense, acute perception, moderation, and commitment to a more humane society, Locke glosses over many difficulties that one would expect a full-fledged political theorist to tackle. We do not have to refer to the later insights of Freud to discover that men are not so rational or political solutions so "self-evident" and straightforward as Locke claimed them to be. Augustine, Machiavelli, and, indeed, Hobbes himself provide the balance lacking in Locke's rationalism. Despite his sober temperament and the insights that not infrequently appear in his work, Locke is fundamentally an exuberant optimist to whom the most exuberant optimists of the Enlightenment turned for inspiration.

---

64. Ibid., sec. 243, p. 312 (Laslett, p. 477). This is the concluding sentence of the work. In sec. 168, however, Locke unaccountably says that not only the people, "but any single man" has a "liberty to appeal to heaven."

65. See p. 118 above.

Locke sweeps many problems under the rug. He tells us that government rests on consent, but fails to show that consent is often manipulated so that many things that are said to originate in the consent of the governed actually stem from the interests of the economically privileged. With his concept of "tacit consent" he makes the idea of consent itself so loose that it can cover a multitude of sins. He tells us that the people are the judges of justice and injustice in government without indicating the difficulty in identifying "the people" and of ascertaining whether the majority has in fact rendered a judgment. He assumes that the majority's judgment will be uncorrupted and in accordance with reason without apparently recognizing the danger of majority suppression of minorities or the possibility of an irrational and hysterical majority. He informs us that the problems of basic political arrangements and decisions can be solved simply and rationally, without considering the complexities and imponderables—and the frequent need to choose the lesser evil—that often emerge when these problems are submitted to hardheaded analysis. He acknowledges only one set of political arrangements and rationalizing principles—that is, his own doctrine of what has come to be known as liberalism, based on individualism, consent, the contractual basis of society, the rule of law (as he understood it), the distinction of powers, the primordial importance of individual property rights. He sees all these as valid for all men and societies, without perceiving the worth of alternative political myths grounded on a more solidaristic concept of man's relation to the community and on aesthetic and contemplative values in some ways at variance with the productive ethos he had subsumed under the name of property.

Today, as the United States finds itself bogged down in a tragic and—many would cogently argue—immoral war in southeast Asia, the deficiencies of the Lockean legacy stand out in stark clarity. Locke's political teaching has remarkable strength and resilience, which comes from its rational simplicity, its inherent efficiency, and its implicit universalism and humanism. It also possesses weaknesses, which are especially evident when Western societies attempt to transpose their objectives to civilizations and cultures with different political styles and greater receptivity to mythopoeic symbols. These weaknesses are also becoming increasingly evident in the West itself, where a revolt is taking place against the productive ethos and property fixation of the liberal creed. Lockean liberalism shares with Marxism a fundamental arrogance: both doctrines claim to have discovered the political system to be adopted by all rational men. Both Locke and Marx, however, were more flexible in their political thinking than many of their followers.

For all its achievements, Locke's vision is a restricted one and needs to be supplemented by insights that he either neglected[66] or had no opportunity to discover. Today we have available, both from the tradition that begins with Plato and from sensitive contemporary investigations, a deepened knowledge of the potentialities and aspirations of the human psyche and its relation to society. We therefore possess the insights to revise, fundamentally if necessary, the teaching of Locke so that it may become more adequately attuned to the complex and multiple reality that is human political existence.

---

66. As we have seen, Locke read extensively in Hooker, and this alone would have been sufficient to make the insights of theocentric humanism available to him.

6

The Enlightenment in
Modern Political Thought

What is "the Enlightenment"? Is it a coherent period in the history of
political thought, or has it become a slogan to be defended by political
writers who see merit in the principles it embodies and to be attacked
by those who do not?

In considering our answers we may usefully begin with the analysis
of Peter Gay, one of the Enlightenment's best-known historians, who
recently brought out a comprehensive two-volume study of the period.[1]
As early as 1954, however, he published an important article dealing with
the specifically political implications of the Enlightenment. Gay's conception of this period is succinctly stated at the beginning of the article:

> The Enlightenment—the age that extends from Locke to Condorcet
> —was one of the most creative ages in the history of political theory.
> Its leading writers brought the conception of natural law to its cul-
> mination, created the foundations of modern sociology, developed
> utilitarianism, anticipated socialism, and gave democratic theory
> the most profound formulation it has ever received.[2]

He then goes on to attack what he holds to be caricatures of the
Enlightenment—the views that it was an age of naive "faith in reason,"
that its philosophers "believed in the inevitability of progress," that its
thinkers possessed no "sense of history," and that they were advocates of
"enlightened despotism."

Gay is largely successful in refuting the oversimplified versions of
the Enlightenment that have been offered by some scholars, though he is

---

1. Peter Gay, *The Enlightenment: An Interpretation,* 2 vols.: 1, *The Rise of
Modern Paganism;* 2, *The Science of Freedom* (New York: Knopf, 1966, 1969).

2. Gay, "The Enlightenment in the History of Political Theory," *Political
Science Quarterly,* 69 (September 1954): 374.

at times too militantly secularist to allow us a clear vision of the period as a whole. Gay argues that the Enlightenment marks the true beginning of the modern period, and he shows a distinctly limited appreciation for the contributions of premodern writers who worked within the Greek and Judeo-Christian traditions. As a result, his view of the Enlightenment is out of focus. Nonetheless, Gay's two-volume work is valuable, for it ranges widely over the entire literature of the period and contains many sensitive and careful judgments of individual works. After reading Gay one has a good feel for the climate of the period and is convinced of the usefulness, if not the indispensability, of regarding the Enlightenment as a distinctive phase in the intellectual development of modern man.

Near the conclusion of his 1954 article Gay provided a useful summary of Enlightenment political ideals:

> Enlightenment philosophers had a set of ideals . . . : they championed free inquiry, they upheld the right to free thought and expression, they believed in diversity, they were secular, they despised superstition and fanaticism, they believed in the possibilities of reform, and they were passionately humane. Indeed, if Enlightenment thinkers could be summed up in one phrase, I would call them "the party of humanity."[3]

Gay properly points out, in effect, that what binds most Enlightenment political thinkers together is precisely their secular liberalism. I prefer this characterization to his later description of the Enlightenment as an expression of "modern paganism."[4] The Enlightenment period gave strong emphasis to the drive for what we know today as a secular society based on the separation of church and state. Thinkers of the period differed on many matters, and in the heat of the moment (for most Enlightenment intellectuals were fiercely partisan) they often made exaggerated statements with an unconvincing ring to them. Viewed from the perspective of today, they appear less radical than they did at the time. We live today in the midst of secular institutions and tend to forget the context in which Enlightenment writers forged their ideas. The social order in which they lived was far from liberal; although the "old regime" was rather less oppressive than they often painted it (otherwise these intellectuals could not have survived as well as most of them did), there can be no doubt that the alliance of the official church with an aristocracy that could no longer justify its privileges produced an intellectual and institutional climate stifling to the development of the best in man.

---

3. Ibid., p. 389.
4. Gay, *The Enlightenment,* vol. 1.

ENLIGHTENMENT LIBERALISM IN FRANCE:
THE *PHILOSOPHES* AND PHYSIOCRATS

A period as diverse as the Enlightenment defies easy summarization, and there are exceptions to most generalizations. We will not expect, then, to find total agreement on the details of a political program among the period's leading representatives; but there is a unity of style and mood among them, which has important implications for the intellectual and spiritual climate of our civilization.

Many of the Enlightenment spokesmen were liberals, and the center of Enlightenment liberalism in the eighteenth century was France. Locke's ideas, both epistemological and political, crossed the channel and in various and sometimes unpredictable ways helped to inspire a multitude of continental writers to enter the lists in behalf of a more egalitarian, secular, and individualistic social order. It was Voltaire who said that "anybody who has read Locke must find the Platos mere fine talkers and nothing more."

French liberal thought battled a regime that accorded considerable freedom of expression to its opponents but proved incapable of reforming itself without violent upheaval. Accordingly, Locke's political ideas were revolutionary in the context of eighteenth-century France. The *Second Treatise,* published to justify nonviolent political reform in England, helped to prepare the way for total revolution in France a century later.

The *Philosophes*

The French *philosophes* (who were scarcely philosophers in the traditional sense) were fierce polemicists and partisans of change who were determined to use the power of the pen to bring about a new social order. Men like Voltaire, Diderot, and Alembert were highly conscious of writing for a mass audience. "Our philosopher does not count himself an exile in the world," wrote Diderot. Rather, he is "full of humanity. Civil society is . . . a divinity for him on earth." He is one who brings "light" to the people, for "the more reason . . . people have, the better fitted they are . . . for the common intercourse of life."[5] Far from being content with the philosopher's role of thinker, confined primarily to the study and the academy, Diderot saw the philosopher's mission as communication with the broad masses of the people:

> Let us hasten to make philosophy popular. If we want the philosophers to march on before, let us approach the people where the

---

5. Cited in Ernst Cassirer, *Philosophy of the Enlightenment,* trans. Fritz C. A. Koelln and James P. Pettegrove (Princeton: Princeton University Press, 1951), p. 268.

philosophers are. Will they say there are works which will never come within the reach of everyone? If they say so, they only show they are ignorant. . . .⁶

By disseminating the critical spirit of the new secular philosophy, the *philosophes* hoped to achieve a society in which ignorance, superstition, and privilege would be eliminated or at least vastly reduced. Although they were aware of the power of human passions, they believed that the basic outline of a free and decent society was readily discernible to all men of reason. The *philosophes* maintained that no lengthy inquiry into first principles was necessary to prove that the old order was irrational, cruel, and repressive, and that men must be given political and economic freedom to make the best of themselves. Accordingly, they favored removal of all censorship limitations, archaic trade restrictions, and hereditary privileges.

In place of the "empire of custom," the *philosophes* proposed the "empire of nature." They agreed with the basic Lockean liberal postulates that a political order in conformity with the "law of nature" was individualist, secular, protective of property rights, and grounded on the consent of the people.

The *philosophes* regarded themselves primarily as practical political reformers, not as theorists. (Their own views of their political roles thus contrasted markedly with the views of their later conservative opponents, who saw them as purely abstract and deductive intellectuals.) Voltaire, in comparing himself to Rousseau, who incurred the animus of the *philosophes* for his pessimism regarding the effect of modern society on human freedom and dignity, observed that *"Jean Jacques n'écrit que pour écrire, et moi j'écris pour agir"*⁷ ("Jean Jacques writes only for the sake of writing; I write in order to act"). "To overturn the colossus," he wrote to Alembert in 1757, "we need only five or six philosophers who understand each other."⁸

Voltaire's *Lettres philosophiques* of 1734, written during his stay in England, has been called "the first bomb thrown at the Old Regime." In this work and in other pamphlets such as his *Idées républicaines* and *L'A,B,C* he propounded a program for a secular liberal political order which had revolutionary implications for the old regime.

Religious Views. High on the list of reforms advocated by the *philosophes* was the destruction of the privileged legal position of the

6. Cited in Kingsley Martin, *French Liberal Thought in the Eighteenth Century: A Study of Political Ideas from Bayle to Condorcet* (Boston: Little, Brown, 1929).

7. Cited in Peter Gay, *Voltaire's Politics: The Poet as Realist* (Princeton: Princeton University Press, 1959), p. 3.

8. Cited in ibid., p. 188.

Catholic church. They were not so much for separation of church and state as for control of the church by an "enlightened" state. Although they were convinced that in taking this position they were unequivocally striking a blow for human freedom, they were less than sensitive to the threat to religious freedom and to the independence of churches implied by their position. The intransigence of conservative spokesmen of the church, determined to preserve the ecclesiastical polity of the old regime, only served to convince the *philosophes* that no compromise with "*l'infâme*" was possible. There is little doubt that this was the burden of Voltaire's famous slogan "*Écrassez l'infâme*" ("Crush the infamous thing"). The conflict between the two irreconcilable positions, clerical and anti-clerical, is the basis for much of the great instability that has so often characterized French politics.

Because of the *philosophes'* anticlerical and indeed anti-Christian pronouncements, it has often been assumed that they were atheists; but a consistently atheistic position was typical only of the extreme left wing (Helvétius, Holbach). Men of the center of French Enlightenment thought were deists and advocated a "natural theology." "I shall always be convinced that a watch proves a watchmaker and the universe proves a God" is one of Voltaire's more famous epigrams. The argument from design was frequently invoked by the *philosophes*. The concept of the universe as a machine set in motion by a divine first cause was congenial to what they conceived to be respectable scientific thought at the time.

There is also a sense in which the *philosophes* regarded religion as an *instrumentum regni*, necessary for the masses even if dubious or debatable on philosophic and scientific grounds. Thus we have Voltaire's pungent and rather cynical observations "If God did not exist, one would have to invent him," and "I want my attorney, my tailor, my servants, even my wife to believe in God, and I think I shall then be robbed and cuckolded less often."

Social Views. Men like Voltaire, Diderot, and Alembert, then, cannot be considered advocates of a radically egalitarian revolutionary movement. They were skeptical about the possibility of universal enlightenment and they feared the power and prejudice of the masses. They never advocated a popular revolution as the means of achieving the political changes they sought.

While it is incorrect to conclude that the *philosophes* were unequivocal champions of monarchical rule and enlightened despotism, it is clear that they envisioned their reforms as spreading from the top down. Voltaire was on friendly terms with Frederick the Great of Prussia, for example, a man who was in many respects a model of the enlightened monarch. It is not strange, therefore, that he and other *philosophes* should have advocated the strengthening of existing monarchies when they had hopes of converting the monarch to their program. To conclude from this that they were monarchists in principle, however, would be to go too far. In the writings of men like Voltaire one encounters both monarchical and republican preferences, according to the context. The fact is that the question of the form of government was secondary for the *philosophes* and their allies; what they were primarily interested in was the creation of a new society on a liberal basis. Being good liberals, furthermore, they did not champion a strong state as an end in itself. Enlightened despotism was regarded as necessary for the transition period from the old order to the new. The power of the old regime could be broken only by greater power. In the enlightened society men would be left as free as possible to pursue their own felicity; like the deist God presiding over the natural universe, the state would supervise the proper working of the political machine.

The Physiocrats: Laissez-Faire Economics

Enlightenment liberalism in France espoused neither radical political democracy (one man, one vote) nor economic equality. On the economic front the *philosophes* and their allies were champions of some form of economic laissez-faire and opponents of both feudalism and mercantilism. They wanted to remove existing barriers to trade and were opposed to the feudal economic structure, but they did not favor state planning and management of the economy either. The eighteenth-century French liberals who concentrated on the economic sphere were known as the physiocrats. Among them were François Quesnay, economist and physician to Louis XV; Pierre Samuel Du Pont de Nemours, economist and politician; Paul Pierre Mercier de la Rivière, associate of Quesnay; and Jacques Turgot, who became minister of finance in 1774 and wrote a number of works on history and economics.

The physiocrats were relatively uninterested in the development of industry; they saw agriculture as the key to economic prosperity. They favored free trade, both within and between nations, and they did succeed in lifting some of the barriers to trade within France. Their influence was at its height when Turgot became finance minister; his tenure of office was brief, however, as he was replaced in 1776 by the mercantilist Jacques Necker, who stressed the importance of manufacturing and the acquisition of colonies.

It is to the physiocrats that we owe the untranslatable phrase *"Laissez faire, laissez passer,"* meaning in substance "Leave things alone, let men act unhindered." They were at one with Adam Smith (whose *Wealth of Nations* appeared in 1776) in subscribing to the notion that economic relations are governed by "natural laws of supply and demand," and that if the process were let alone, the economy, as if guided by an "invisible hand," would produce maximum prosperity for all those who labored productively. (What happens to those who lose out in the economic race was of no apparent concern to the physiocrats.) As we shall see later when we consider the welfare-state liberalism of the nineteenth century and its criticism of the laissez-faire position, the physiocrats, however much they intended to advance freedom, were in effect advocating a new ruling class based on commerce to replace the old one based on landed wealth.

THE MATERIALIST AND SENSATIONALIST WING OF THE ENLIGHTENMENT

The moderates of the Enlightenment both in France and elsewhere made much use of the concept of natural rights, which has a lengthy history in Western thought. It can be traced at least as far back as Aristotle, who wrote of things that are "right by nature" as opposed to things that are right by convention or by agreement. As we have seen, however, the idea of natural right or natural law was given a decidedly new twist in the modern period by Hobbes and Locke.

The spokesmen for Enlightenment liberalism, including Thomas Paine and Thomas Jefferson in America and Christian Wolff in Germany, contributed to the trend toward a secular and individualist interpretation of natural law. In the evolution of the concept of natural law, emphasis is shifted from duties to rights, from the natural basis of the community to the inviolable claims of the individual, from a theologically related natural law (Aquinas' dictum that "grace does not annul nature but perfects it") to norms that emanate from world-immanent autonomous reason. Man's "natural" condition, the state of nature prior to the formation of society, is seen as a condition of freedom and equality. As Locke admits, this condition has "inconveniences," but they can be overcome by creating a society that ensures a predictable environment through the rule of law rather than force while still conforming as closely as possible to the natural condition. The American Declaration of Independence is a classic expression of the Enlightenment view of natural rights: "We hold these truths to be self-evident, that all men are created equal, that they are endowed by their Creator with certain unalienable Rights, that among these are Life, Liberty, and the pursuit of Happiness." The French Declaration of the Rights of Man of 1789 is also representative of Enlightenment thinking on natural rights, with some touches of Rousseau (the "sovereignty of the people").

Voltaire himself frequently resorted to the language of natural rights and natural law, even if he used the terms loosely,[9] and it is clear from the treatment of the law of nature in Locke's *Essay Concerning Human Understanding* (see Chapter 5) that Locke's followers had no reason to feel uneasy on this score. The "empiricism" in his epistemology did not lead him to reject the natural law, which could be discovered through the active employment of man's reason.

Not all of Locke's followers went along with him in this regard, however. The sensationalist and materialist school of writers condemned the concept of natural rights as "metaphysical" and transformed Locke's doctrine that ideas originate in sensation *and* experience (including inner experience) into an epistemology proclaiming that all ideas are derived from sensation alone. They took quite literally Locke's statement that the mind is a "white paper" upon which experience writes, denied a constant human nature, and embraced an extreme environmentalism. They also embraced an explicitly materialist conception of reality. Baron Paul Henri Dietrich d'Holbach and Claude Adrien Helvétius were among the leading French proponents of materialism and sensationalist epistemology.

Helvétius

Of the two, Helvétius was perhaps the more interesting and important. For one thing, he was a key figure in the development of utilitarianism, which was to replace the concept of natural rights among English liberal intellectuals in the nineteenth century and provide the basis for the liberalism of Jeremy Bentham and James Mill. In fact, it was Helvétius who originated the idea that the good is identified by the "greatest happiness of the greatest number," which Bentham developed with such success for social reform.

Pleasure and Pain. Helvétius was convinced that human behavior is motivated by the desire for pleasure and the avoidance of pain. "Good" and "evil" are simply synonyms for "pleasure" and "pain." All men are equal in this respect; such differences as exist among them are attributable to environmental influences. If all men had the same educational opportunities and if their physical needs were adequately taken care of, there would be no decisive differences in their intelligence and performance.

Helvétius' most significant work is *De l'esprit* (*Of the Mind*), in which he wrote that man is by nature selfish and indifferent to the fate of his fellows. Men care only for the increase of their own pleasure, which is

---

9. See ibid., p. 346.

achieved by the domination of others. Helvétius' psychology, far from exemplifying the naive optimism associated with the Enlightenment, is thus quite grimly "realistic," even pessimistic.

Utilitarianism and Social Reform. Helvétius' comprehensive psychological teaching does have an optimistic element, however, because he in no sense considered this bleak picture of man's natural condition unalterable. Education could remake man from a hostile and destructive animal into a cooperative and productive one. Proper psychological management and wise legislation could bring about an "artificial identity of interests" that would lead men to see that their desires can best be satisfied in society. For Helvétius, then, obedience to the laws rests ultimately on utility rather than on some fancied obligation to an objective moral law of nature. Basic to his political thought was the conviction that society had to be reformed so as to maximize individual pleasure and minimize pain. It was only a short step from this position to a demand for the complete revamping of penal codes. Cesare Beccaria in Italy and Jeremy Bentham in England were two who took this step, arguing that if men knew in advance that punishment or pain was always greater than the benefit or pleasure to be expected from a criminal act, they would be deterred from committing such acts. The determinate sentence and the concept of punishment as a deterrent, major social reforms in the nineteenth century, are still very much with us today.

Helvétius never faced squarely the elitist implications of his thought and the dangers inherent in the manipulation of human beings by those who took upon themselves the task of remolding man's psychic constitution in the "right" form. He took it for granted that the manipulators would be benevolent and self-controlled, and that they could easily discover the "true" needs and interests of humanity—assumptions that both common sense and a more complex psychology would incline us to doubt.[10]

Holbach

Baron d'Holbach was a co-worker of Helvétius in the vineyards of materialist and sensationalist political thought, and was another forerunner of utilitarianism. His writings are neither systematic nor profound, and in intellectual quality they are inferior to Helvétius', though they exhibit the same tensions and contradictions between democracy and elitism. The end of political association is "the happiness of the people." If "the people" are ruled arbitrarily and unjustly over a pro-

---

10. For more on Helvétius, see Eric Voegelin and Peter Leuschner, "Helvetius," in *Aufklärung und Materialismus im Frankreich des 18. Jahrhunderts,* ed. Arno Baruzzi (Munich: List, 1968), pp. 33–97.

tracted period, they can legitimately turn out the despotic governors; in fact, he held, tyrannical government automatically produces its own dissolution. Holbach is unclear, however, about the mechanism for deciding upon and conducting a legitimate revolution. He condemns tyrannicide by isolated individuals; only society as a whole has a "right" to revolt. Holbach was far from being an anarchist; on the contrary, there was a strong streak of the social engineer in him. He seemed ultimately to imply that unjust governments were those of the old order and just governments were those of the new individualist and utilitarian dispensation. Against the new sort of government, it was clear, there could be no legitimate rebellion. Rather, the power of the government was to be vigorously asserted and the people were to be obedient:

> Governing means obliging the members of a society faithfully to fulfill the terms of the social covenant. It means inviting or forcing them to work together for the public good or for the practice of virtue. If men had been reasonable there would have been no need for them to submit to authority. . . . But men are born with passions, some of which, when restrained or driven by reason, i.e., by enlightened self-interest, become useful, while others, guided by blind interest, imagination, ignorance, and imposture . . . make their possessors lose sight of the end of the association in which they live. . . ."

Holbach, as has been mentioned, was an avowed atheist; this position, coupled with an egalitarian bent in economic matters[12] and a sensationalist epistemology, combined to put him in the radical left wing of the Enlightenment. The iconoclastic baron held that anyone who would "deign to consult common sense" would "easily perceive" that religious beliefs "have no foundation; that all religion is an edifice in the air; that theology is only the ignorance of natural causes reduced to system; that it is a long tissue of chimeras and contradictions."[13]

Although Holbach, like Helvétius, was darkly pessimistic about men's selfishness and antisocial behavior in an "unenlightened" epoch, he was exuberantly and even naively optimistic about the prospects for reversing this state of affairs:

> Let men's minds be filled with true ideas; let their reason be cultivated; let justice govern them; and there will be no need of opposing to the passions, such a feeble barrier, as a fear of gods.

---

11. Quoted in W. H. Wickwar, *Baron d'Holbach: A Prelude to the French Revolution* (New York: A. Kelley, 1968), p. 190.

12. See ibid., pp. 178–80.

13. Paul Henri Dietrich d'Holbach, "Common Sense, or Natural Ideas Opposed to the Supernatural" (1772), in *The Enlightenment*, ed. Frank E. Manuel (Englewood Cliffs, N.J.: Prentice-Hall, 1965), p. 58.

> Men will be good, when they are well instructed, well governed, and
> when they are punished or despised for the evil and justly rewarded
> for the good, they do to their fellow creatures.
>
> In vain should we attempt to cure men of their vices, unless we
> begin by curing them of their prejudices. . . .[14]

Although there is justice in Peter Gay's strictures against viewing
Enlightenment thought as wholly abstract, ahistorical, and simplistic,
such passages as the following from Holbach at least establish some
basis in fact for these one-sided interpretations:

> Truth is simple; error is complex. . . . The voice of nature is intelli-
> gible; that of falsehood is ambiguous, enigmatical, mysterious; the
> way of truth is straight; that of imposture is crooked and dark. . . .
> Men are unhappy only because they are ignorant; they are ignorant
> only because everything conspires to prevent their being enlightened;
> they are so wicked only because their reason is not yet sufficiently
> unfolded.[15]

STUDIES IN ENLIGHTENMENT POLITICAL THOUGHT: CONDORCET, TURGOT, MONTESQUIEU, HUME

Among the many political writers of the Enlightenment period, four men
stand out for the interest and quality of their thought: the Marquis de
Condorcet, Jacques Turgot, the Baron de Montesquieu, and David
Hume. One cannot entertain the idea that the Enlightenment was a
monolithic unity after reading about these four men.

Condorcet

Condorcet's remarkable work, *Esquisse d'un tableau historique des
progrès de l'esprit humain* (*Sketch of a Historical Portrait of the Progress
of the Human Mind*) has on the whole received insufficient attention in
histories of political thought. As one of the most eloquent and succinct
expressions of the eighteenth-century French Enlightenment world view,
it is a document of the first importance in the unfolding of the modern
political consciousness. While admittedly it takes an exuberant view of
political possibilities, and is more optimistic about the prospects of mankind than the writings of most of the *philosophes*, the *Esquisse* is still not
so immoderate as it is often said to be. It is not really surprising that
Condorcet ended by sympathizing with the Girondists rather than the
Jacobins in the French Revolution. He was a true liberal, and he ab-
horred violence. He refused to vote for the execution of Louis XVI

---

14. Ibid., pp. 60–61.
15. Ibid., p. 62.

and publicly criticized the Jacobin constitution of 1793. For these courageous actions he was driven into hiding and ultimately arrested by the Jacobins. He died in prison, presumably by taking poison.

The *Esquisse* was written while Condorcet was in hiding during 1793 and 1794 and was published posthumously in Paris in 1795. It is a work of considerable learning and ranges over all fields of Western intellectual history; at times it includes interesting asides on Asian and Islamic speculation, although on the whole it touches only lightly on the achievements of nonwestern thought. It reveals Condorcet as a compassionate and generous man who was committed to the fundamental equality of all men. He explicitly rejected arguments based on the assumption of the innate inferiority of nonwhite peoples.

Condorcet's political psychology is expressed very briefly in the Introduction to the book; it is clear that what he had to say on this subject was in no way original, but was derived from the writings of the French sensationalist school, above all from Condillac and Helvétius. For Condorcet (as for Condillac and Helvétius), sensationalist epistemology, which assumed that all ideas originated in sense experience, pointed straight to political reform. If the mind was essentially a blank sheet (*tabula rasa*) written upon by sensations, then the specific milieu in which men found themselves decisively determined consciousness. If socioeconomic conditions and educational opportunities could be made more equitable, presumably many existing inequalities in intelligence level, energy, the capacity to work productively, and so on could be substantially reduced. Although Condorcet clearly thought environment far more important than heredity in determining performance, he did not discount heredity altogether. (He did, however, anticipate Lamarck's highly dubious scientific theorizing in asserting a belief in the heritability of acquired characteristics.) Nor did he believe that a time would come in which *all* distinctions in ability would be eliminated among human beings. This is evident in the following rhetorical question from the last chapter of the *Esquisse*, which attempts to foresee the future "tenth stage" of human history:

> Will they [existing differences among men] necessarily decrease and ultimately make way for a real equality, the final end of the social art in which even the effects of the natural differences between men will be mitigated and the only kind of inequality to persist will be that which is in the interests of all and which favors the progress of civilization, of education and of industry, without entailing either poverty, humiliation, or dependence?[16]

16. Marie Jean Antoine Nicolas de Caritat, Marquis de Condorcet, *Sketch for a Historical Picture of the Progress of the Human Mind*, trans. June Barraclough (London: Weidenfeld & Nicolson, 1955), p. 174.

Condorcet's position, then, was that irremediable natural inequalities had been vastly magnified by a corrupt society.

Historical Progress. Condorcet saw a beneficent and progressive tendency at work in history, a tendency that was now past halting or reversing, as he intended to make clear in his book:

> Such is the aim of the work that I have undertaken, and its result will be to show by appeal to reason and fact that nature has set no term to the perfection of human faculties; that the perfectibility of man is truly indefinite; and that progress of this perfectibility, from now onwards independent of any power that might wish to halt it, has no other limit than the duration of the globe upon which nature has cast us. This progress will doubtless vary in speed, but it will never be reversed as long as the earth occupies its present place in the system of the universe, and as long as the general laws of this system produce neither a general cataclysm nor such changes as will deprive the human race of its present faculties and its present resources.[17]

Condorcet, then, found a universal reason at work in nature and human history, although it was a reason that, unlike Hegel's, arrived very late on the scene. Although Condorcet was in no sense ignorant of history—in fact, the *Esquisse* is essentially an attempt at a theory of history—the book is also a condemnation of most of what had hitherto occurred in history. Condorcet concluded that "enlightenment" had come slowly and painfully to only a small group of men; although other civilizations had made some contribution to the growth of man's capacity for rational thought and hence control over his environment, on the whole it was only the West, specifically ancient Greece and modern Europe, that had achieved a true breakthrough toward the indefinite future progress and perfectibility of the human race.

Like Voltaire and the *philosophes* generally, Condorcet considered the Middle Ages a total loss—in fact, a retrogression—in the history of the human mind. *Écrassez l'infâme* was his motto, too. In his eyes the church and the feudal system had united for centuries to crush the power of the human mind and prevent any real increase in knowledge. Only with the development of modern natural science—above all with Copernicus, Galileo, and Newton—and the emergence of political liberalism in the Netherlands, England, and Sweden was the groundwork laid for a transition into a rational, progressive world order.

The Rights of Man. Condorcet's liberal political creed was anchored in what he called "the true rights of man," which are all "deduced from

---

17. Ibid., pp. 4–5.

the single truth, that *man is a sentient being, capable of reasoning and of acquiring moral ideas.*"[18] (It is interesting that he managed to combine both the psychological or "empirical" ["man is a sentient being"] and the rational ["capable of reasoning"] in a metaphysical formulation of "the true rights of man." Although Enlightenment thinkers can be classified as either rational or empiricist, the two strands of thought were never completely separated, and this is perhaps not surprising in view of the fact that both rationalists and empiricists claimed to trace their ideas back to Locke, who used both approaches.)

Condorcet's liberalism is a blend of diverse elements, and reflects in an unusual degree the tensions that have plagued the liberal ethos since its inception in the seventeenth century. Condorcet speaks of the "rights of men"; the preservation of these rights constitutes the "sole object of men's coming together in political societies." Yet simultaneously he maintains that it is the majority that determines the "common rules" that the members of the society obey. The "majority alone" can "impose an obligation upon all." And yet, he says, the majority itself may err and transgress the rights of man; if it fails to respect these rights, its commands are not legitimate and the individual is not bound to obey them. Condorcet is trapped in a hopeless dilemma, and it is only his optimistic faith in enlightened men that leads him to assume that the entrusting of power to the majority will ultimately ensure and preserve human rights.[19]

The New World Order. The political rationalism that we detected in Locke, but which Locke applied specifically only to England, emerges in uncompromising form in the work of Condorcet. If "all men possess equal rights by nature," it follows that there is only one just political order, which applies universally to all nations. Condorcet explicitly rejected the arguments advanced by Edmund Burke and the conservatives that political arrangements must vary in accordance with social customs and traditions, and that within any society there are various orders with distinct interests and privileges. Yet he also rejected any notion that the natural order should be *forcibly* imposed on the recalcitrant historical order, which would continue to exist for a time as an irregular and partially irrational patchwork. He anticipated that with the spread of Enlightenment ideas and the technical advances made possible by modern natural science, political regimes all over the world would come increasingly to respect the fundamental rights of man, natural boundaries would gradually lose their significance, and a new world order committed to human equality would emerge.

18. Ibid., p. 128 (italics in original).
19. Ibid., pp. 128–29.

Despite the obvious humanity of the man and the touching sincerity with which he argued his convictions, there is a certain troubling simplicity to his thought. Condorcet wrote of the "simple truths and infallible methods" that the West had discovered, and which peoples in other parts of the world had only to adopt in order to achieve a progress "more rapid and certain than our own." Although he condemned the intolerance and fanaticism that too often accompanied the spread of Christianity in Latin America and elsewhere, he was blind to the equal fanaticism with which he benevolently preached "progress." The shape of the new rational order was self-evident to him, and it did not occur to him that other peoples might not wish to give up their cultural and religious traditions for the new society he envisioned. Despite his admirable sympathies for peoples of different skin pigmentation, physiognomy, and cultural traditions, and for the plight of racially oppressed minorities within the West, Condorcet was really quite narrowly ethnocentric. If we are to judge from his characterization of Asia, its only products have been "oriental despotism"[20] and religions that fetter the mind.

In his zeal to affirm the unity of mankind, Condorcet showed little appreciation of mankind's rich variety. Any theory of human development that does not respect the cultural diversity of the human family will lead at best to a well-meaning but enervating paternalism and at worst to a destructive and deadening imperialism.

The Ideal of Progress. In his description of the Tenth Epoch, or final stage of world history, upon which he believed mankind about to embark, Condorcet combined a mixture of fantasy and plausible conjecture that at once commands the serious attention of modern readers and strikes a historian of political thought as flawed by certain major weaknesses. He sagaciously anticipated scientific and technological advances that would enable men vastly to improve their management of scarce resources and their health, thereby greatly lengthening their lives. Yet while he accurately foresaw a substantial increase in food production, he failed to foresee the terrifying expansion of population that would inevitably accompany improved health measures and living conditions. Much of what he had to say, which appeared fantastic then, today seems well within the range of possibility over the next century, if man manages not to destroy himself with the effects of overpopulation or with nuclear weapons, a development that Condorcet could of course not have predicted.

The most serious defect of Condorcet's book, however, does not lie in his assessment of future possibilities or even in his failure to foresee

---

20. Ibid., p. 172.

the development of countervailing factors; his real failure was his inability to see that his grand political dream might turn out to be a nightmare. Condorcet held that the tenth stage of history would be one of indefinite progress, in which the frontiers of knowledge would be constantly pushed back, only to reveal new vistas of territory waiting for conquest by the human mind:

> No one has ever believed that the mind can gain knowledge of all the facts of nature or attain the ultimate means of precision in the measurement, or in the analysis of the facts of nature, the relations between objects and all the possible combinations of ideas. Even the relations between magnitudes, the mere notions of quantity or extension, taking in its fullest comprehension, give rise to a system so vast that it will never be mastered by the human mind in its entirety, that there will always be a part of it, always indeed the larger part of it, that will remain for ever unknown.[21]

In his last days, when he was under a threat of death, Condorcet comforted himself with the thought of mankind on an escalator of indefinite progress and perfectibility. He failed to foresee that the escalator might ultimately turn out to be a treadmill for those who traveled on it (as distinct from himself, who only contemplated it).

The prospect of indefinite advances in the material conditions of life, while in one sense profoundly exhilarating and comforting, can be profoundly disquieting to the psyche. Condorcet's vision is wide and humane, but it is directed toward the future—and an infinitely receding future, at that—and not to the present. Yet it is in the present that man exists, and to be oriented at the very core of his being toward an infinite series of future expansions of human knowledge and control ultimately deprives him of his ability to find meaning in his life here and now. When a man exhorts others to make the world better tomorrow, he tends to lose sight of the delights of the multidimensional human experience today. Condorcet dramatically illustrates the limitations of the liberal ideal of progress and points up the problem of those liberals who today continue to speak of unlimited "progress" for mankind.[22]

Turgot

In 1750 Jacques Turgot delivered two lectures in Latin on world history at the Sorbonne. The lectures, Frank Manuel has observed, "framed a new conception of world history from remotest antiquity to the present and constituted the first important version in modern times of the

21. Ibid., p. 184.

22. See, for example, some of Lyndon Johnson's earlier pronouncements on the "Great Society," with their references to the "unlimited development" of America and ultimately all mankind.

ideology of progress." They were "more potent than the wit of Voltaire and the mechanistic materialism of La Mettrie in deflecting Western consciousness from a religious to a utilitarian earthly morality."[23]

In the second of his Sorbonne lectures (or *Sorbonniques*), *Tableau philosophique des progrès successifs de l'esprit humain,* Turgot contrasted human history with the realm of nature: whereas nature follows a cyclical pattern, history is essentially cumulative and progressive, each generation building upon the knowledge acquired and transmitted by the previous generation.

Unlike most Greek political thinkers, who valued stability, Turgot gloried in change, novelty, and movement. He was oriented toward activism and reform, and he called for an expansive civilization in which the increase of births would be accompanied by an increase of geniuses.

The Straight Line of Progress. As Turgot saw it, the history of the world progressed in a straight line. Within this overall scheme, however, individual nations and even whole civilizations went through cycles of development, the torch of progress being passed from one to another as each torchbearer in turn became exhausted. Thus not all peoples of the world have advanced at the same rate, but mankind as a whole, represented by the society that is in the vanguard at any particular moment, always advances.

Turgot held that progress could be measured in four areas: the scientific, technological, moral, and artistic. The uneven rates of progress on the four fronts accounted for the "extraordinary diversity of human experience, despite the identity of mankind's underlying historic destiny."[24]

The Three Stages of Intellectual Development. Turgot has rightly been credited with anticipating Auguste Comte's three stages of human intellectual development. There are important differences, however, between their ways of elaborating this concept. It did not have the same cosmic significance for Turgot as it did for Comte, and Turgot did not envisage a smoothly functioning and coordinated "positivist" society in the third stage. Finally, although he was critical of certain practices of the church, he was not anti-Christian and did not proclaim, as Comte did, the necessity of a new religion. With these qualifications, it is possible to agree with J. B. Bury's view of the similarity between Turgot's concept of a three-stage development of intellectual history and that of Comte:

---

23. Frank E. Manuel, *The Prophets of Paris* (Cambridge: At the University Press, 1962), p. 13. I am greatly indebted to Manuel's discussion of Turgot in this section.

24. Ibid., pp. 36–37.

Turgot ... anticipated Comte's famous "law" of the three stages of intellectual evolution, though without giving it the extensive and fundamental significance which Comte claimed for it. "Before man understood the causal connection of physical phenomena, nothing was so natural as to suppose they were produced by intelligent beings, invisible and resembling ourselves; for what else would they have resembled?" That is Comte's theological stage. "When philosophers recognised the absurdity of the fables about the gods, but had not yet gained an insight into natural history, they thought to explain the causes of phenomena by abstract expressions such as essences and faculties." That is the metaphysical stage. "It was only at a later period that, by observing the reciprocal mechanical action of bodies, hypotheses were formed which could be developed by mathematics and verified by experience." There is the positive stage. The observation assuredly does not possess the far-reaching importance which Comte attached to it; but whatever value it has, Turgot deserves the credit of having been the first to state it.[25]

The Limits of Progress.   Turgot believed that he had demonstrated the inevitability and irreversibility of progress. Knowledge was cumulative in all areas save literature and the fine arts, and with the increasing mathematization of the sciences the rate of intellectual progress was becoming rapidly accelerated. Mankind was on the threshold of a great leap forward comparable to the abrupt transition from the mythopoeic stage to the abstract, rational stage. Turgot's optimism was not unbounded, however. Although he held retrogression to be impossible and believed that further moral progress would bring an end to war, cruelty, and crime on a large scale, he did not think that all evil, error, and suffering would disappear. The human condition could and, barring some wholly unanticipated development, would be improved, but it would not be qualitatively transformed. Compared with the programs and predictions of nineteenth-century radical humanists such as Fourier and Marx, Turgot's progressivism was relatively moderate and realistic. All the same, the dividing line between his outlook and theirs was not altogether sharp and neat. The progressivism of Turgot and Condorcet merges into the radicalism of the succeeding two centuries.

Montesquieu

Among Montesquieu's works three deal directly with his political theory: *The Persian Letters* (1721), *Considerations on the Causes of the Greatness and Decline of the Romans* (1734), and *The Spirit of the Laws* (1748). As Melvin Richter has commented,

25. J. B. Bury, *The Idea of Progress* (New York: Dover Publications, 1955), p. 157.

Certain points made in the *Persian Letters* anticipated what Montesquieu later argued more extensively—that men are always born into a society and that it is therefore meaningless to discuss the origin of society and government; that self-interest is not a sufficient basis for human institutions as Hobbes had asserted; and that, instead, the possibility of good government depends on education and example, in short, on civic virtue.[26]

Richter might have added that *The Persian Letters* also contain the first formulation of Montesquieu's deist views and his essentialist and objectivist view of justice.

The *Considerations* is also of interest to students of political thought. Montesquieu's fascination with Roman politics is reminiscent of Machiavelli's. Indeed, the theme of classical republicanism runs through the political writings of the *président à mortier* of the parlement of Guyenne as it does through those of the Florentine secretary. Like Machiavelli, Montesquieu saw differences of opinion as the strength of republics: Rome's divisions were "necessary" to its strength and vitality. "As a general rule, it may be assumed that whenever everyone is tranquil in a republic, that state is no longer free." Montesquieu drew a sharp distinction between union and unanimity: "union may exist in a state, where apparently only trouble is to be found," and beneath the surface unanimity of a state ruled by a despot or an immoderate government there is "division of another kind. The peasant, the soldier, the merchant, the noble are related only in the sense that some of them oppress others without meeting any resistance."[27]

It is *The Spirit of the Laws*, however, that is Montesquieu's political masterpiece. For twenty years, the author informs us in his remarkable preface, he labored over this vast treatise. He professes to discover regularity in human affairs; all variety and diversity of manners and institutions are traceable to a particular law, and all laws taken together make up an intelligible whole.

Enlightenment. Montesquieu has frequently been described as out of harmony with the Enlightenment. But while he and Voltaire never got along well personally, many of his leading ideas are wholly compatible with the spirit of the Enlightenment; and though not himself a *philosophe* in the strict sense, he was, intellectually, as his biogra-

26. Melvin Richter, "Montesquieu," in *International Encyclopedia of the Social Sciences* (New York: Free Press, Macmillan, 1968), vol. 10, p. 469. I am indebted to Richter's lucid treatment of Montesquieu's political theory.

27. Ibid., p. 470.

pher Shackleton has pointed out, "very close to the deist wing of the *philosophes.*"[28] But let us permit Montesquieu to speak for himself:

> It is not a matter of indifference that the people be enlightened. The prejudices of the magistrates originate in the prejudices of the nation. In an age of ignorance they have perpetrated even the greatest evils without the least hesitation; in an age of enlightenment they tremble even while accomplishing the greatest benefits.[29]

Enlightenment, then, was Montesquieu's goal. By enlightenment he meant the liberation from prejudice of both rulers and ruled. By prejudices he meant "not what makes men ignorant of certain things but what makes them ignorant of themselves."[30] Montesquieu shared the Enlightenment's confidence in the power of education to liberate man. To instruct men in the nature of their condition was to practice "that general virtue which includes the love of all." But this sort of instruction was not easy to accomplish, because if man—"that flexible being"—is "capable of knowing his own nature when it is demonstrated to him," he is equally capable of losing or being deprived of his understanding.[31]

Montesquieu was both an Enlightenment man and a modern man in his claims to have made a new beginning in political speculation. As Richter points out, he introduced one of the editions of *The Spirit of the Laws* with the epigram *Prolem sine matrem* ("A child born of no mother").

Rationalism and Empiricism. Montesquieu begins his work with a discussion of "Laws in General." The rationalism of Book 1 (and not only Book 1, for he returns to his general theory of law in Book 26) has often been called inconsistent with the empiricism and even relativism of the remainder of the work. I see no such profound contradiction. Despite his claim to novelty—and certainly in his analysis of forms of government and the separation of powers he did make a very original contribution—Montesquieu was in the great tradition of political theory both in his elaboration of a paradigm of right action for man and in his description of the variety of political structures that have existed in the world. Without a paradigm there could be no effective evaluation of the conditions he described. Without evaluation there could be no

---

28. Robert Shackleton, *Montesquieu: A Critical Biography* (London: Oxford University Press, 1961), p. 386.

29. Montesquieu, *De l'esprit des lois,* in *Oeuvres de Monsieur de Montesquieu,* 3 vols. (London: Chez Nourse, 1777), Preface, p. lxi.

30. Ibid.

31. Ibid., p. lxii.

hope for reform. To Montesquieu, therefore, descriptive "political sociology" was an important part, but only a part, of political science as a
whole. In espousing this view he was in substantial agreement with
Aristotle.

   Stoicism.   Shackleton has called Montesquieu a "deist." We might
with equal accuracy and greater specificity describe him as a modern
Stoic. Like the ancient Stoics he saw the universe as ordered by reason,
and the source of order for him was an "original reason" (*une raison
primitive*) that informs all relations, physical and spiritual. In this respect
his thought echoes the Stoic conception of the *spermatikos logos* (seminal
reason) which is the ground of all things:

> Laws, in their most comprehensive signification, are the necessary
> relations which derive from the nature of things; and, in this sense,
> all beings have their laws: the divinity has its laws, the material
> world its laws, intelligences superior to man their laws, beasts their
> laws, man his laws.
>   Those who have said that a blind fatality has produced all the
> effects which we see in the world have uttered a great absurdity: for
> how can there be greater absurdity than the notion that a blind
> fatality could have produced intelligent beings?
>   There is, then, an original reason, and laws are the relations
> which obtain between it and the different beings, and the relations
> of these divers beings between themselves.[32]

Montesquieu, then, represents what might be called the Stoic wing
of Enlightenment thought, as Hume represents the Epicurean. It is not
surprising, therefore, that Hume, while praising Montesquieu as a writer
of "great genius" in his *Enquiry Concerning the Principles of Morals*
(1751), attacked Montesquieu's "abstract theory of morals," which "pretends to found everything on reason."[33] Montesquieu continues the
venerable natural-law tradition in his insistence that justice is an objective standard of right action and is "antecedent to positive law." Justice
to him is the "proper relation" between "intelligent beings."

   Reason and Law.   While man, like every other part of creation, is
bound by physical laws, as an "intelligent being" he is free to disregard moral laws. His intelligence is finite and he is subject both to
ignorance and to the sway of "a thousand passions." Such a being

> can at any instance forget his creator; God has reminded him
> through laws of religion. Such a being can at any instance forget
> himself; philosophers have warned him through laws of morality.

---

32. Ibid., bk. 1, chap. 1, pp. 1–2.
33. Cited in Shackleton, *Montesquieu,* p. 245.

Fashioned to live in society, he is able to forget others; legislators have recalled him to his duties through political and civil laws.[34]

Montesquieu held that although reason and justice are universal and morally binding on all men alike, a uniform world of identical customs and institutions is neither likely nor desirable. Reason requires adaptation to particular cases, and a wise and enlightened legislator would take into account the special circumstances confronting him. Human laws, then, must be adapted to the "nature" and "principle" of the society for which they are designed. The "nature" of a government is its structure, the institutions in which "sovereign power" is lodged. The "principle" of a government concerns "the human passions which cause it to move." Laws "should relate as much to the principles of each government as to its nature."[35] As Richter says, "By the 'nature' of a government he meant the person or group of persons holding sovereign power; by 'principle' that passion which must animate those involved in a form of government if it is to function at its strongest and best."[36]

Republics, Monarchies, and Despotisms. Montesquieu held that there are three types of government: republics (subdivided into "democratic" and "aristocratic"), monarchies, and despotisms. The *nature* of republics requires that either the whole or a part of the people hold "sovereign power"; of monarchies, that a prince rule by established laws and channels; and of despotisms, that a single individual rule arbitrarily, unrestrained by any laws or any intermediary power between the despot and the people. Only religion can have a moderating effect on a despotism. The *principle* of republics is civic virtue, of monarchies honor, and of despotisms fear. Montesquieu did not mean to imply that virtue is wholly absent in monarchies or honor in republics, but that these passions are the "mainsprings" of their respective regimes.[37]

Although Montesquieu admired republics, he doubted that they were appropriate except to small states. He was not an ultrademocrat, and seemed to believe that even in a democracy the unthinking masses should be accorded only civil liberty; political participation was best reserved for the more intelligent and active citizens. What is most clear from his analysis is his hatred of tyranny. He called despotisms "monstrous governments."

The Separation of Powers. Although Montesquieu spoke of moderate governments of any kind—including monarchies—as legitimate, his para-

---

34. Montesquieu, *De l'esprit des lois,* bk. 1, chap. 1, p. 4.
35. Ibid., bk. 3, chap. 1, p. 25.
36. Richter, "Montesquieu," p. 471.
37. Montesquieu, *De l'esprit des lois,* bk. 2, chaps. 2–5; bk. 3, chap. 9.

digmatic constitution was based on his famous doctrine of the separation of powers. After an extended stay in England he had concluded that the key to the liberty of Englishmen was the division of political power among three distinct power-holding bodies. Montesquieu thus disagreed with Hobbes on the indivisibility of sovereignty. In fact, he argued strongly that only in a regime in which power is divided can the citizens enjoy true liberty. Every government, he wrote, has three sorts of power: legislative, executive, and judicial. There can be no liberty if all three are united in one person. To Montesquieu, liberty was "a tranquillity of mind arising from the opinion each person has of his own safety."[38]

There are certain affinities between Montesquieu and the earlier classical republicanism of Machiavelli; but his doctrine of the separation of powers and his conception of liberty as "tranquillity of mind" introduce a new strain. In his reverence for the rule of law, Montesquieu was much more fearful than Machiavelli of the populism to which ancient republics had been prone. Although Machiavelli was also a strong champion of the rule of law and an opponent of tyranny, his conception of political participation was more consistently activist than Montesquieu's. He too believed in a "mixed state" (*Discourses*, Book 1, Chapter 2), but it is not at all certain that he would have accepted the separation of powers, because of the inherent dangers of immobility. Montesquieu also was aware of these dangers, but he considered them unavoidable if liberty was to be maintained. Robert Shackleton has well summarized the difference between Machiavelli's mixed state and Montesquieu's separation of powers:

> The supporters of the mixed state urge that a desirable and lasting constitution can be obtained by assigning legislative power, which for them is sovereign, to kings, nobles, and people *jointly*, and by securing a harmonious balance between these three, while supporters of the separation of powers claim that liberty can be secured only by dividing political authority (which being divisible cannot be sovereign) into its three constituent functions, and by assigning these functions to different bodies or individuals, who will exercise their powers separately and without collusion.[39]

Liberty. Montesquieu's discussion of liberty is quite confused. On the one hand he seems to approximate a negative concept of liberty quite characteristic of early liberal thought: that is, liberty as absence of restraint by governmental authorities. As a result, therefore, he advocates minimal restraints for all citizens, imposed by the laws precisely

---

38. Ibid., bk. 11, chap. 6, pp. 207f.
39. Shackleton, *Montesquieu*, pp. 288–89.

to protect the individual in his "tranquillity." Such a concept of liberty stresses the private or nonpolitical life of the individual; it does not focus on public participation and sacrifice for the common good (republican *virtù*). And yet Montesquieu did not abandon the older identification of liberty with civic virtue, and in one place observed that liberty can in no sense be equated with the ability to do what one wills, but "can only consist in the ability to do what one ought to will, and in not being constrained to do what one ought not to will."[40]

Montesquieu seems never to have fully resolved the tension between the concepts of liberty as independence and as active pursuit of civic virtue. He is a transitional figure, a brilliant theorist who serves as a connecting link between classical republicanism and modern liberalism.

Hume

David Hume, a Scotsman, was born in 1711 and died in 1776, the year of the appearance of Adam Smith's *Wealth of Nations*, Jeremy Bentham's *Fragment of Government*, and, of course, the American Declaration of Independence. He shared many of the social and political views of the *philosophes*, but for him these views had a different philosophical basis. He was a man of moderation and common sense and a champion of independent critical inquiry. Although famous as an iconoclast among philosophers (he argued half-seriously in his *Enquiry Concerning Human Understanding* that previous works on metaphysics should be consigned to the flames as worthless), Hume was by no means a total skeptic; rather he saw a rigorous and refined metaphysics and moral philosophy as contributing substantially to the improvement of man's estate.

Hume's writings range widely over the areas of epistemology, ethics, economics, religion, and political history. For him the pleasures of critical inquiry surpassed those of any other human activity, and he would have agreed with Hobbes's observation that "voluptuous men" would engage in philosophy if they only knew the delights to be had from it.

Hume would have none of the talk about "natural rights" or the "social contract," and in his criticism of these familiar concepts of eighteenth-century liberalism he anticipated the utilitarianism of Jeremy Bentham. He held that there were strict limits to the lengths to which human reason could go, and that to postulate a state of nature antecedent to society in which isolated individuals came together to forge a social contract was a fiction that was of no use in explaining how or why men behave as they do in society. Yet it would be a mistake to conclude that Hume broke fundamentally with Locke in either philosophy or politics;

---

40. Montesquieu, *De l'esprit des lois*, bk. 11, chap. 3, p. 205.

rather he sought to reformulate the basis of moderate political reform in more cautious terms. In doing so he produced a mildly conservative variation on an Enlightenment rationalist theme.

According to Hume, the "science of man," which Locke had attempted to put on a "new footing," is comprised of four types of inquiry: logic, morality, criticism, and politics. Such a science, which rests on experience and not on abstract, *a priori* principles, can flourish only in "a land of toleration and of liberty."[41]

The Limits of Knowledge. Hume's epistemology contains the germ of the later logical positivist division of knowledge into logical statements, on the one hand, and factual statements, subject to verification by sense experience, on the other. A good many apostles of positivism also credit Hume with having originated the attack on the so-called naturalistic fallacy—the attempt to derive a normative judgment from a factual observation, or an "ought" from an "is."

To be sure, in the famed *Treatise of Human Nature* (written in France in the 1730s), Hume observes:

> In every system of morality which I have hitherto met with . . .
> the author proceeds for some time in the ordinary way of reasoning
> . . . when of a sudden I . . . find that instead of the usual copulations
> of propositions, *is* and *is not,* I meet with no proposition not connected with an *ought* or an *ought not.*[42]

He finds it "altogether inconceivable" that an "is" can suddenly become an "ought."

These statements of Hume's have often been invoked to sustain an emotive theory of ethics, which maintains that ethical judgments rest on nothing but individual taste and inclination. But it is doubtful that Hume would have approved of such a radically subjectivist interpretation of his views. As Alasdair MacIntyre has pointed out, Hume did not mean to deny that moral conclusions can be derived from factual observations, but was simply arguing that facts per se do not point to any moral conclusions; these have to be wrested from the facts by the active human mind.[43]

Hume contended that it was beyond the powers of human reason to demonstrate the truth of either the idea of causation (as used in science) or moral ideas of good and evil. All that understanding can

---

41. David Hume, *A Treatise of Human Nature,* ed. L. A. Selby-Bigge (Oxford: Clarendon Press, 1888), Introduction, pp. xix–xxi.

42. Ibid., bk. 3, pt. 1, sec. 1, p. 469.

43. Alasdair MacIntyre, *Hume's Ethical Writings* (New York: Collier, Macmillan, 1968), p. 457.

tell us is that one event follows another. No matter how many times a given event is followed by another given event, we have no proof that the second is caused by the first. As far as moral judgments are concerned, from a strictly logical point of view there is no reason to prefer the "destruction of the world to the scratching of your finger."[44]

Nature. Hume thus maintained that there is no such thing as an immutable moral "law of nature" discoverable by "right reason." Moral norms, like scientific concepts, are artificial, the deliberate inventions of men. This did not make such propositions arbitrary, however, for in another sense principles of justice *are* natural "if by natural we understand what is common to any species, or ... what is inseparable from the species."[45] Thus what Hume casts out by the front door of dissolving philosophical criticism he readmits through the back door of philosophical reconstruction.

It is by means of his conception of nature (and in this he remains very true to the Enlightenment) that Hume avoids a sterile and crippling relativism. What human reason cannot fathom, an obliging nature supplies. "Most fortunately it happens," he informs us, "that since reason is incapable of dispelling these clouds [of skepticism], Nature herself suffices to that purpose. ... I find myself absolutely and necessarily determined to live, and talk and act like other people in the common affairs of life."[46]

Although for Hume (in contrast to the psychologies of Plato, Aquinas, and Hooker), "reason is and ought only to be the slave of the passions, and can never pretend to any other office than to serve and obey them,"[47] these very passions are then differentiated as "calm" and "violent." Nature teaches men by the active use of their reason to prefer the calm to the violent passions, since the calm passions are conducive to their self-interest and consonant with their feelings of benevolence toward other men (which are implanted in them by nature).

Thus despite his apparent rejection of the law of nature, it would be more accurate to say that he reformulates it; and his writings on morals and politics repeatedly invoke the idea of a constant "human nature," which may be consulted to give meaning and direction to man's life. In other words, there are certain observable propensities of human behavior that are "inseparable" and "necessary" to man as a species.

---

44. Hume, *Treatise of Human Nature*, bk. 2, pt. 3, sec. 3, p. 416.
45. Ibid., bk. 3, pt. 2, sec. 1, p. 484.
46. Ibid., bk. 1, pt. 4, sec. 7, p. 268.
47. Ibid., bk. 2, pt. 3, sec. 3, p. 415. (Note the "ought.")

Hume declares that mankind "is an inventive species, and where an invention is obvious and absolutely necessary, it may properly be said to be [as] natural as anything that proceeds immediately from original principles, without the intervention of thought and reflection. Tho' the rules of justice be *artificial*, they are not arbitrary."[48] Burleigh Wilkins, commenting on this passage, has noted the similarity between Hume's idea that rules of justice are "absolutely necessary" to the species and traditional thinking on natural law.[49] We might say that here we have a dramatic instance of what Heinrich Rommen has called the "eternal recurrence of natural law."

The Conservative Reformer. Hume, of course, does not speak the language of Aquinas or Locke or any of the older natural-law theorists. He sounds rather more like a utilitarian in his insistence that principles of justice are grounded in the "interests" of men. But he links these interests to the nature of man, and discovers in that nature the twin impulses of self-preservation and benevolence, which had been the mainstay of the political psychologies of the great moralists since Aristotle. Hume, in sum, is a moderate in revolutionary's clothing.

Hume obviously does not lend himself easily to the conventional categorizations. A highly independent thinker, he could appear liberal or even radical in some respects and conservative in others. His views on economics put him very much in the mainstream of liberal free-trade, antimercantilist views.[50] In politics he is often classed as a Tory, largely because of his attempt in his famous *History of England* to correct what he regarded as excessively Whiggish, antimonarchical views of the revolution of 1688 and other events. Actually, Hume was neither Whig nor Tory, but held to a belief in strong but limited constitutional government in which the crown preserved sufficient power to contribute to the growth of a free and vital nation.[51] Insofar as England was concerned, he favored the reconciliation of royal power to the newly asserted powers of parliament.

David Hume was at once *sui generis* and an offspring of the best in Enlightenment thought and criticism. He was *sui generis* because no thinker of his age had a greater capacity for being his own man and

---

48. Ibid., bk. 3, pt. 2, sec. 1, p. 484.

49. Burleigh T. Wilkins, *The Problem of Burke's Political Philosophy* (Oxford: Clarendon Press, 1967), p. 52.

50. See Gay, *The Enlightenment*, vol. 2, pp. 355f.

51. See R. W. Harris, *Reason and Nature in the Eighteenth Century* (London: Blandford Press, 1968), pp. 361–68, for a succinct account of the argument in Hume's *History*. The Harris volume is a useful supplement of and corrective to Peter Gay on the general tenor and development of Enlightenment thought.

reaching his conclusions through his own careful, independent reflection. (Rousseau and Kant were his peers in this respect, however.) He was representative of the Enlightenment in his tendency to question everything in the name of reason and nature (as he defined them) and in his intense aversion to received or established religion (or to what Thomas Jefferson somewhat uncharitably called "priestcraft"). Even in his reformism he demonstrated considerable reticence and sobriety, however. He could write a book called *The Idea of a Perfect Commonwealth* and in it advise the rising generations to "conform themselves to the established constitution," and in a book called *The Natural History of Religion* he could write that the "whole frame of nature bespeaks an intelligent author."[52] Hume was above all eager "happily [to] ... escape into the calm, though obscure regions of philosophy" from the furious contentions of opposing theological opinions. His reaction to the religious disputes of his time was evidently one of urbanity, not of atheism.[53]

As we noted earlier, Hume aspired to contribute, among other things, to the elaboration of a "science of politics." His conception of such a science, however, has little in common with that of some of his avowed present-day disciples, who are addicted to a methodology grounded on the assumptions of a dogmatic and arid logical positivism. For the good Scotsman knew too much history and had too much common sense to think that the propositions of political science could be as precisely formulated and could reach conclusions as definite as those of the physical and natural sciences.[54] A humanist to the end, Hume concluded that in their relations with one another, men dwelt only in the twilight of probability.

CONCLUSION

Peter Gay has described the Enlightenment as the age of "criticism and power." Hume's intellectual orientation is consistent with Gay's summation. Despite Hume's very genuine commitment to constitutionalism and limited government, he was loath to see the powers of the crown weakened. Yet his preference for monarchy, although couched in tra-

---

52. Cited in Gay, *The Enlightenment*, vol. 1, pp. 412–13.

53. It is therefore reading far too much into the gentle Scotsman to claim, as Gay does, that in Hume "the last threads are torn; his philosophy embodies the dialectic of the Enlightenment at its most ruthless—it appeals to antiquity at its most disenchanted, its tension with Christianity is wholly unappeasable at all points, and it pursues modernity most courageously" (ibid., p. 418).

54. For a discussion of contemporary logical positivism in the social sciences, see Dante Germino, *Beyond Ideology* (New York: Harper & Row, 1967), pp. 67–84 and 198–202.

ditionalist terms, has echoes of the "enlightened despotism" of other, more radical writers of the period. Gay is right in saying that at the heart of the Enlightenment we find a commitment to increasing man's control over his environment. Criticism—the exercise of autonomous, creative intellectual faculties independently of all concern for authority—was to prepare the way for a more efficient exercise of human power.

The Enlightenment, however, was known not only for its achievements; it also had its failures. It is surely an exaggeration to call Enlightenment thinkers, as Gay does, "*the* party of humanity." The Enlightenment is an important voice in the conversation of mankind, but still only a single voice. Even its most sophisticated thinkers suffered from a certain insularity of perspective; they thought they understood man and his limitations better than they did. Perhaps the arrival of Kierkegaard and Freud was necessary to reveal the overly optimistic and even simplistic side of Enlightenment psychology. The depths of the psyche and its requirements of solidarity and dependence were largely ignored by even the most balanced thinkers involved in the Enlightenment quest for mastery over the self and the world. "Criticism and power," yes; but also criticism *of* power—and not only of power's specific abuses, but of the power ethos itself. For the criticism of power, however, we must look beyond the confines of the Enlightenment. We must look to both the pre- and postmodern worlds.

7

Rousseau

Jean Jacques Rousseau was born in Geneva in 1712 and died in France in 1778. He led the life, as the title of his last attempt at autobiography expressed it, of a "solitary wanderer." He was an unhappy and neurotic man, at times suffering from extreme paranoid delusions. He could hardly be described as an integrated personality, and many incidents and escapades in his life were not attractive and indicated an inability to establish stable and responsible personal relationships. Our purpose here, however, is not to judge him as a person, but to explore his contribution to political thought. He was a political thinker of the first rank; indeed, he is one of the four or five great political writers of modern times.

Scholars differ tremendously in their interpretations of Rousseau. In recent years some have identified him as a proponent of totalitarianism. Others find profoundly liberal elements in his teaching. Many hold him intellectually responsible for the excesses of the French Revolution. Still others see conservative tendencies in his thought and even link him to the romantic reaction. To some he is an extreme individualist, to others an archcollectivist. Some hail him as a champion of progressive forms of democracy, while others condemn him as an advocate of a cynical and brutal dictatorship.

Insofar as possible, I shall attempt to leave aside this mountain of conflicting interpretations and simply consider the leading ideas of Rousseau as a political theorist, concentrating on the argument of his political masterpiece, *The Social Contract*. Rousseau wrote many works. Besides *The Social Contract* (1762), the political writings in the strict sense include *A Discourse on the Moral Effects of the Arts and Sciences* (1750), *A Discourse on the Origin of Inequality Among Men* (1755), *A Discourse on Political Economy* (1758), and *Considerations on the Government of Poland* (published posthumously). Other writings include *Émile* (1762) and the *Confessions* (also published posthumously). While references will be made to some of these works as they bear on the discussion of *The Social Contract,* no extensive treatment of them will be attempted here. It is in his master treatise that we find Rousseau's political teaching most fully developed. Its scope is so vast and its argument so compactly expressed that we dare not fail to give this work the most careful attention in a history of political theory.

The decision to concentrate on *The Social Contract* is in no way meant to imply that the other works are unimportant to an understanding of Rousseau's political thought. It would be particularly helpful to read the *Discourse on Inequality* along with *The Social Contract,* because the former work deals at length with Rousseau's concept of the state of nature, a subject that receives only brief attention in *The Social Contract.*

MAN AND SOCIETY

Some writers find a basic contradiction between the views expressed in the *Discourse* and those expressed in *The Social Contract.* The *Discourse* is supposedly an idyllic account of the state of nature and a rejection of societal existence on principle. It purportedly idolizes primitive man, or the "noble savage." It is held to be a cry for untrammeled independence and the liberation of man from all social conventions. It represents Rousseau's flight from society, an anguished expression of anarchic individualism. *The Social Contract,* on the other hand, is judged to have reversed the teaching of the *Discourse* and to have made of the state a god on earth and natural man a contemptible creature whose happiness consists in the negation of his natural condition.

There is undoubtedly some variation between the teachings of the two works, and this is scarcely surprising. We need not resort to dubious psychologizing (e.g., Rousseau was unable to decide whether he loved or hated the company of his fellows and so wrote one book attacking society and another extolling it) to understand why these differences should exist. Rousseau engaged in a lifelong inquiry into the principles of a just political order; the *Discourse on Inequality* and its predecessor the *Discourse on the Arts and Sciences* were early attempts to set down his reflections on the subject. The guiding thought of all his works was that most societies as they were then constituted were unjust and corrupt. It was necessary for his teaching that he attempt to show both how society had corrupted the natural man and how a good society, which would ennoble man rather than debase him, might be erected. The two works (the second *Discourse* and *The Social Contract*) are related, but they focus on different questions, and the emphasis of the argument shifts in the later work to the question of the good society.

Natural Man

In the *Discourse on Inequality* Rousseau takes issue with Hobbes regarding man in the state of nature—the hypothetical precivil state, which "no longer exists, perhaps never did exist, and probably never will exist."[1] In addition to the desire for self-preservation, which Hobbes had found basic to man, Rousseau added compassion, the instinctive abhorrence felt at the sight of another living being, and especially another man, suffering pain and death.[2] Man is, then, not the enemy of his kind.

Yet Rousseau did emphatically agree with Hobbes that man was not sociable by nature. Society rests on convention rather than on nature; it is the product of deliberate contrivance. It gives to man a second nature. Because society rests on convention, it is essential to consider the question of what constitutes a right or legitimate convention.

Although Rousseau displays sympathy for natural man in the *Discourse on Inequality*, he by no means showers him with uncritical adulation. Natural man is "wild rather than wicked"; he is lacking in vanity, in the desire to harm others, in ambition, and in covetousness (he has nothing and in fact does not even know the meaning of possession, of "mine" and "thine"). But although he may be said to lack vice, it can hardly be maintained that he possesses virtue. Reason, speech, and the concept of justice are foreign to him. So is love except in the most carnal sense; in fact, it is indistinguishable from a merely physical impulse and need.[3]

His portrait of man in the state of nature—man as he had been—was scarcely meant to stand alone in the gallery of Rousseau's ideas. Another work was needed to hang beside it, and it would reveal what man could become. The composition of this second portrait is the task Rousseau assigned himself in *The Social Contract*. Thus his two major political works may be said to complement rather than to contradict each other.

THE SOCIAL CONTRACT

Du Contrat social (*Of the Social Contract*), Rousseau's masterpiece of political theory, is astonishingly brief and compact. In his preface the author modestly refers to the work as "this little treatise" and remarks that

---

1. Jean Jacques Rousseau, *A Discourse on the Origin of Inequality,* Preface, in *The Social Contract and Discourses,* ed. G. D. H. Cole (New York: Dutton, 1950), pp.190–91.

2. Ibid., p. 193.

3. Ibid., pt. 1, pp. 227–29.

it is "the least unworthy" section of a longer manuscript that proved too ambitious to be completed. This statement is in striking contrast to Machiavelli's assertion regarding his two masterpieces, *The Prince* and the *Discourses*—that they contain "all that I know and all that I have learned" about politics.

The subtitle, *Principes du droit politique,* is more indicative of the scope and contents of the work than either the main title or the explanation given in the modest preface. Within its brief compass the treatise addresses itself to the central question of political theory—the nature of the good society. It is in *Du Contrat social* that we find Rousseau's conception of the paradigm. The essay has a place and importance in its author's political teaching roughly equivalent to that occupied by *The Republic* in Plato's philosophy of politics.

To read *The Social Contract* is an exciting intellectual adventure. The depth of penetration into the topics considered, the masterful economy of style, the closeness of the reasoning, the originality of the concepts employed, all combine to make it one of the great works in the history of Western political speculation. Even if Rousseau had written nothing else, his claim to literary fame would have been secure on the basis of this treatise. Because its central ideas (the general will, popular sovereignty, the critique of representation) have so frequently been lifted out of context and transformed into symbols of the political struggle, it is important to pay particularly close attention to their place in the essay's overall argument.

Introduction to General Principles

The first of the four books of *The Social Contract* begins with the famous epigram "Man is born free, and everywhere he is in chains." Even those in ruling positions, who "believe themselves to be masters of others," are slaves—in fact, to a greater degree than others. "How did this transformation come about? I do not know. What can render it legitimate? I believe I can resolve that question."[4]

Rousseau sharply distinguishes between force and right. If a society is based only on force, it has no moral claim on the obedience of its subjects, who may overthrow it when the opportunity presents itself. "But the social order is a sacred right," which is the foundation of "all other" rights. This right "does not come from nature" but is grounded on "conventions." It is a question of knowing what these conventions are.[5]

---

4. Rousseau, *Du Contrat social,* ed. and introduced by Bertrand de Jouvenel (Geneva: Éditions du Cheval Ailé, 1947), bk. 1, chap. 1, p. 173.

5. Ibid., p. 174.

Rousseau thus agrees with Hobbes and Locke that society exists by convention rather than by nature. The only natural association is the family, and this only so long as the children are too young to care for themselves, to preserve their own lives. Innately, men are free and independent; they share a "common liberty," which is the "consequence of the nature of man." Man's first law is to "look to his own preservation"; his first obligations are those he owes to himself. Every man is "his own master," and once he reaches the age of reason he is "the sole judge" of the proper means of preserving himself.[6]

Rousseau criticizes Grotius and Hobbes severely (and unfairly) for deducing "right from fact" and for assigning men to be slaves of rulers, claiming that to them "the human race belongs to a hundred men" rather than these hundred men to the human race.

Human Association. With these introductory considerations in hand, Rousseau then moves on to consider "the original convention," or that act which alone can give legitimacy to the civil order, which can make men members of a true association rather than a mere aggregation. Before considering the institution of government—"the act by which a people elects a king"—it is essential to inquire into "the act by which a people is a people." The constitution of society is "necessarily anterior" to the constitution of government.[7]

Rousseau begins—inevitably, since he has insisted society rests on convention alone—with man in a state of nature. He is not so clear as Hobbes in proclaiming that such a state is a hypothetical device rather than a historical or anthropological truth. Nonetheless, it seems clear that whether or not men ever actually existed as isolated individuals in a state of nature, the concept itself implies a profound truth about man. As we noted in the discussion on Hobbes, the view of man in the state of nature is offered as a portrait of the irreducible components of man's own nature—man divested of his civilizational garments, of all the attitudes and inclinations resulting from his societal existence, from his culture.

In the *Discourse on Inequality* Rousseau presented a detailed portrait of presocietal man as isolated, self-sufficient, alone, without speech, needing nothing and desiring nothing beyond the things he considers necessary for his self-preservation. Unlike Hobbes, he did not hold man to be by nature an enemy of his fellows. *The Social Contract*, however, makes little of the state of nature aside from mentioning its existence and the fact that at a certain point "obstacles"—presumably such natural calamities as floods and earthquakes—make it necessary for isolated

---

6. Ibid., chap. 2, p. 175.
7. Ibid., chap. 5, pp. 187–88.

individuals to unite and combine forces in order to survive.[8] Such union brings about a major theoretical problem: how to form an association without endangering man's own existence, protected in the natural state by his strength and independence ("liberty"). Rousseau states the problem in the following famous passage:

> "To find a form of association which defends and protects with the entire common force the person and goods of each associate, and in which each uniting himself to all obeys only himself and remains as free as before"—such is the fundamental problem of which the social contract gives the solution.[9]

The Clauses of the Social Contract. The "clauses of the social contract" flow from the act of association and serve the purpose of at once forming a community where before there were only isolated individuals, and of protecting those individuals. If there is the "slightest modification" the contract is rendered null and void, and if it is violated each returns to the state of nature and "resumes his natural liberty."[10] Rousseau nowhere mentions a right of revolution, but in this idea of "violation" of the contract the question of the dissolution of the societal order is implicitly confronted.

Although the clauses of the social contract may not be "formally enunciated" and may only be "tacitly recognized," yet they are everywhere the same. They reduce themselves to a single one: "the total alienation of each associate with all his rights to the whole community." This astonishing conclusion—that giving oneself without reservation to the community enables one to retain his freedom and security—is reached by arguing that since everyone has made the same renunciation and the conditions laid down by society will be the same for all, no one will have an interest in making them burdensome.

Total renunciation of rights is necessary because otherwise a true community cannot exist. It is beneficial because, since everyone makes a similar renunciation, no one gains power or advantage; the rights are given up not to a person or persons but to the entire community, of which the individual is a part. Everyone "gains the equivalent of what he loses and increased force to conserve what he has." In "giving himself to all he gives himself to no one."

At this point Rousseau reformulates the kernel, or essential core, of the contract: "Each of us puts in common his person and all his power [there is no mention of "rights"] under the supreme direction of the

---

8. *Ibid.*, chap. 6, p. 190.

9. *Ibid.*, p. 191.

10. *Ibid.*

general will; and we receive at the same time each member as an indivisible part of the whole."[11]

The Social Entity. The social contract or "act of association" creates a "moral and collective body" that "receives from this same act its unity, its common ego *[son moi commun]*, its life and its will."[12] All participants are members of one body; a "public person" is established where before there were only individual persons. This public person is called alternatively either "state" or "sovereign," depending on whether it is "passive" or "active." It is referred to as "power" in relation to other similar entities. The individual members are citizens when participating in the sovereign authority and subjects when "submitting to the laws of the state."[13] The true meaning of "citizen" has been "almost wholly lost" by "modern peoples" *[chez les modernes]*. An inhabitant is not synonymous with a citizen, nor is a town—a collection of buildings—identical with a city. It is significant that those who live under a monarch are called subjects and not citizens; this is true even of the English, although they are "closer to a condition of liberty" than "all the others" (presumably than all the other monarchies). Citizenship involves the active exercise of a "right"; it is enjoyed by certain orders of people in a republic (as for example in Rousseau's own Geneva, where there were four orders of inhabitants, only two of which could be styled citizens).[14]

The act of association implies a "mutual obligation" between "the public" that is created by the act and "the individuals" who perform it. Each individual "contracts with himself, so to speak," and incurs obligations to the whole of which he is a part. A dual relationship morally binds him to other individuals as a member of the sovereign and to the sovereign as a member of the state.

Sovereignty and the General Will. The individuals, then, are bound to accept the decision of the sovereign after public deliberation; it is in any event their decision, in which they have shared as members. The sovereign, however, considered as the expression of the will of the whole community, is not obliged to be bound by itself. It is contrary to the very concept of sovereignty and to the "nature of the body politic" that the sovereign impose a law on itself which it cannot break. There can be "no kind of fundamental law obligatory for the whole body of the people *[le corps du peuple]*, nor even the social contract itself."[15]

It is not sovereignty but the general will, however, which constitutes

11. Ibid., p. 192.
12. Ibid., p. 193.
13. Ibid.
14. Ibid., n.
15. Ibid., chap. 7, pp. 194–95.

the keystone of Rousseau's political thought. The general will is the interest of the community, and nothing may legitimately be done against that interest; otherwise a society ceases to be a community and becomes a mere "aggregation." The general will reconciles liberty and authority, interest and duty, individuality and universality. It is because the sovereign "is made up only by individuals who compose it" that it "neither has nor can have any interest contrary to theirs." Therefore, the "sovereign power" needs no "guarantees" or restraints built around it. The guarantee against its abuse is contained within itself; the sovereignty is bound by the collective goodwill of citizens dedicated to the community's preservation and to the equal sharing of burdens, public undertakings, and the common life in all its dimensions. Sovereignty is always the exercise of authoritative power, not force without right. It cannot harm the individual, for it "is always what it ought to be."

The sovereign power cannot harm the citizens because it emanates from their common goodwill, their will to maintain the community, to act for the universal advantage. The sovereign power is a reflection of their best selves, of the noblest and most disinterested aspect of their character. But individual members can harm the sovereign when they fail voluntarily to take upon themselves their obligation as citizens of participating disinterestedly and objectively in making the laws, and their duty as subjects to obey them once they are made. The sovereign does need a guarantee, or "security," that the individual members will faithfully fulfill their obligations.

The Particular Will. The difficulty lies in the particular will. In the disordered person the "particular will" (*volonté particulière*) which he "possesses as a man" expresses itself in opposition to the "general will" (*volonté générale*) which he "possesses as a citizen." If the particular will is accorded precedence over the general will instead of being understood to exist in harmony with it, then it becomes the great disease of commonwealths. Those who accord primacy to the individual will and fail to understand that the true individual will of every man is realized within the context of the general will (for the realization of the latter simultaneously secures the former as well) seek to enjoy the rights and privileges of the citizen without fulfilling the duties of the subject. Such actions destroy the equality that is the indispensable condition of the act of association and constitute "injustice," an injustice which if sufficiently widespread will bring about the "ruin of the body politic." Thus Rousseau thoroughly grasps the truth that for the assertion of rights to be effective, the obligation to fulfill corresponding duties must be recognized. Rights and duties are two sides of the same coin. (Hegel will later reiterate this point.)

"Forced to Be Free." It is in this connection that Rousseau introduces his famous and controversial concept of being "forced to be free."
The passage is worthy of quotation in full:

> So that the social pact will not be an empty formulary, it includes
> tacitly the following obligation which alone can give force to all
> the others: whoever refuses to obey the general will will be con-
> strained to do so by the whole body. This signifies nothing else than
> that he will be forced to be free. Such is the condition that gives
> to each citizen the guarantee against all personal dependence, which
> insures the construction and flexibility of the political machine and
> which alone renders civil obligations legitimate and without which
> they would be absurd, tyrannical, and subject to the most enormous
> abuses.[16]

Rousseau is no utopian, although he is frequently mistaken for one.
Even in *The Social Contract*, where he presents his paradigmatic society,
the reader encounters generous doses of realism. Man, even in the good
society, is still man and not angel. Even with the best political education,
institutions, and laws he is constantly prey to the temptation to place his
own individual interest ahead of the public interest. In the rightly
ordered polity the true citizen will not need the constraint of force. He
will think of himself first as a member of a political body. He will be like
the citizen of Rome who thought of himself first of all "not as Caius or
Lucius but as a Roman."[17] He will be, Rousseau might have said, like
Machiavelli, who declared that he loved his country more than his soul.
But as a guarantee that devoted citizens will not be tyrannized over by
those who seek only their own advantage—which means taking advantage
of their fellow citizens—force must be available for employment against
destructive individuals who refuse to abide by the conditions of social
solidarity. In constraining such individuals to act in accord with the
general will, they are being forced to be free, because there is no true
freedom to be found in society except by general obedience to the dictates of the general will.

The Social Nature. In the course of passing from the "state of
nature" to the "civil state," a "very remarkable transformation" takes place
in man. He acquires a second or social nature; a sense of justice replaces
instinct in his conduct and "gives to his actions the morality which they
lacked before."

This "very remarkable transformation in man" means that instead of
acting out of desire and instinct, he "consults his reason." (The "irra-

---

16. Ibid., p. 197.
17. From Rousseau, *Émile,* chap. 9, cited by Jouvenel in *ibid.,* p. 196n.

tional" or "romantic" Rousseau of many interpreters does not seem to square with the text.) In the place of total absorption in the self and its needs, he becomes sensitive to and aware of the needs and rights of others. His "whole soul becomes so elevated" and ennobled that were it not for the fact that the "abuses of this new condition did not often result in degrading him" below the level of the state of nature, he would be bound to "bless without ceasing" the happy moment when he left that state forever and "instead of a stupid and limited animal" became "an intelligent being and a man."[18]

This striking passage has often been contrasted with the portrait of man as a "noble savage" in the *Discourse on Inequality*. When the qualifying phrase about the degrading effect of "the abuses" of the civil state is taken into account, the contrast is perhaps not so marked. It is not *any* society that consistently ennobles man, but only the good society. Compared with the man of the corrupt society, "primitive" man is to Rousseau indeed "noble" in many respects.

Property. The final chapter of Book 1 concerns property. In the state of nature there is only possession, derived from the "effect of the force or right of the first occupant." Civil society legitimizes mere possession and turns it into property. In stating that there is possession but no property in the state of nature, Rousseau differs markedly from Locke. For Rousseau, the ownership of property is a privilege accorded by society, not a natural right. There is no absolute right to one's property: "the right which each individual has to his own estate is always subordinate to the right which the community has over all: without this the social tie would not hold and there would be no real strength in the exercise of sovereignty."[19]

The individual upon entering society gives up all his possessions only to receive them back again as property. The chapter is brief and schematic on the subject of inequality of possession. In general, Rousseau is not dogmatic on the subject; in *The Social Contract* he certainly does not prescribe communism as mandatory for the good society, and seems to regard a regime based on private property as the rule rather than the exception. In concluding the social contract each individual gives over his possessions to the body politic and receives them back, no longer as possessions but as legitimate property to which he has title in positive law and for which he enjoys protection by the public force. However, it may turn out that the contracting parties have no possessions, in which event they may enjoy property "in common or distribute it among them-

---

18. Rousseau, *Du Contrat social*, bk. 1, chap. 8, p. 199.
19. Ibid., chap. 9, p. 204.

selves either equally or in accordance with proportions established by the sovereign."[20] The point is that there can be great flexibility of property arrangements, ranging all the way from common ownership to a system based on unequal private ownership. Any given arrangement is subject to abrogation or revision as determined by the community as a whole acting in its sovereign capacity under the direction of the general will.

Although in *The Social Contract* Rousseau does not see private property as the source of all evil and as incompatible with the good society (a view he seemed to approximate in the *Discourse on Inequality*), he sees the moral and legal equality that is the basis of any legitimate political association compromised and endangered by excessive disparities of wealth. The purpose of the social system is not to destroy "natural equality," but to replace it with a "moral and legitimate equality" that makes all men "equal by convention and right," even if they are "unequal in physical strength or intelligence."[21] Civil society is "advantageous to men only so long as all have something and none has too much."[22] Thus under the direction of the general will a real, substantive, and meaningful equality is established that is superior to the equality of independence prevailing in the state of nature. The general will is not oppressive but is the guarantee of true equality, equality of participation and respect, just as it is the realization of true liberty.

The General Will

Book 1 prepares the way for an extended discussion of sovereignty and the general will in Book 2. Book 2 may be regarded as the kernel of the entire work, for the general will is without doubt the leading idea of the treatise.

"The primary and most important consequence of the principles so far established," Rousseau declares in the opening sentence of Book 2, "is that the general will alone is capable of directing the forces of the state according to the end of its institution—which is the common good." The "opposition" of individual interests makes society necessary; their "agreement" makes society possible. "It is that which is common in the different interests which forms the social tie, and if there were no point on which all the interests agreed it would be impossible for any society to exist."

Sovereignty is "nothing else than the exercise of the general will."

---

20. Ibid.
21. Ibid.
22. Ibid., n.

Sovereignty can "never alienate itself," for it is a "collective being" and "can be represented only by itself." It has been shown that it is impossible for there to be no basis of agreement between individual wills. The mere existence of society demonstrates that the general will and the particular will are not opposed on all points. This accord will not automatically support and maintain itself, however. There is a natural tendency for the particular will to pull in the direction of partiality and the general will toward equality.[23]

The identity of the general will and the particular will can be guaranteed only under the condition that sovereignty remain with the community as a whole and not be relinquished to any group or individual. Were such a surrender to occur, the will of the individual or group accorded this submission would dominate over the collectivity; the body politic would have "a master" and would be destroyed because the general will would no longer be in command. Only if the entire body politic retains the right and capacity to abrogate and oppose any decision by a given segment of the community (with its particular will) can there be a guarantee that such a decision will be in conformity with the general will. "Universal silence" implies the consent of the people.[24] Thus, although the individual wills, if unimpeded, can and will destroy the general will, the general will, if unchecked, always preserves the legitimate expression of the individual wills; it cannot be tyrannical and its operation is beneficial. There is no need to seek a balance between the common will and private or individual wills, because the former always protects and sustains the permissible claims of the latter.

An indispensable condition for the maintenance of true community is the effective operation of the general will; this operation can be secured only if sovereignty remains with the whole community and is not transferred to any part. Nor can sovereignty be divided. Sovereignty must remain with the whole people, entire and intact. Laws are acts of sovereignty—that is, declarations of the general will. They cannot be the acts of magistrates or government officials only; such acts are not laws, but at best decrees or applications of laws to specific circumstances. For a will to be general it is "not always necessary that it be unanimous, but it is necessary that all the votes be counted"; any arbitrary exclusion of voters "destroys the generality" of the decision.[25] That a decision is based on a unanimous vote, or on a majority vote that has not excluded any members arbitrarily from participation, fulfills the minimum condition for expressing the general will; even this does not guarantee that expres-

---

23. Ibid., bk. 2, chap. 1, pp. 205–6.

24. Ibid., p. 207.

25. Ibid., chap. 2, p. 208n.

sion, however. The general will is always right, and needs to be declared by the whole people or a majority thereof to find expression in law, but the majority does not always will the general will. Even a whole people may will not the general will, but some particular will that has found acceptance, or the "will of all"; for the general will is discovered only after each man asks himself what is the general will with regard to the matter at hand; if instead he asks what is his private preference or the preference of his group, then the result would be a falsification of the general will. The general will is the enlightened interest of the whole and not the mere imposition of the will of a numerical majority.

The General Will and Natural Law. It would appear that the concept of the general will has a place in Rousseau's political thought similar to that occupied by the concept of natural law in the teaching of such earlier thinkers as Aquinas and Hooker. It is a moral standard beyond the reach of unstable majorities which serves as a measure of right and just action in a society. Not all enactments called laws are truly laws. To be a true and just law, an enactment must be in accord with the general will, which means that substantively it must affect all equally as realizing the common good and that formally it must be approved by all equally because it is recognized as rightfully binding upon them. The general will is the communal ethos of a society; it is a latent moral force that, when given concrete expression and actualization, becomes embodied in laws, or in general principles that reveal the purposes, objectives, and institutional framework of a body politic. Only basic, general, comprehensive laws are properly laws; detailed enactments within the framework laid down by the sovereign are properly acts of government. These decrees and decisions, whether of administrative officials or of courts, are directed toward particular, specific cases rather than at general categories and common problems.[26]

A law that may reflect the general will at one stage in the life of a society may not so reflect it, or may inadequately reflect it, at another stage. The general will is not a vain and empty phrase, but it is not a detailed institutional and policy blueprint either (another point that the concept of the general will has in common with the traditional idea of natural law). It is the spirit of common purpose in a society, the "best sense of the community," as T. H. Green was later to interpret it.

Although there are similarities between the natural law and the general will, there are also differences. The general will is the binding moral force of a particular society, and presumably there are as many general wills as there are political communities in the world. There is

---

26. Ibid., chap. 6, p. 224.

only one natural law, however, knowable by right reason and binding on all men at all times. One could deduce that there is a latent universal general will making for a world community, but this would be counter to Rousseau's insistence that the good society must be small; the world would therefore optimally be composed of innumerable self-supporting and sovereign communities, each with its own general will, which would constitute an individual will in regard to the general wills of the others. Finally, the natural law—as its very name implies—is an entity independent of society. It is born of and imposed by nature, and man is bound by it even outside the community. Rousseau's general will is not imposed by nature but becomes a reality only through convention—the basic convention of the social contract. It does not exist in the state of nature but comes into being in the very process of making, of willing, a community where before there was none.

Rousseau nowhere indicates that he advocates rejecting the reality of a universal moral order, and even contradicts his earlier assertion that justice is grounded on convention when he states that "what is good and conforms to order is so by the nature of things and independently of human conventions." "All justice comes from God," he continues, "who alone is its source." Without doubt there is a universal justice emanating from reason alone.[27] In these and other references Rousseau seems to be reviving the premodern tradition of higher law. No sooner has he made these statements, however, than he continues in a vein very reminiscent of Machiavelli. Absolute justice, a transhistorical standard of right and wrong, exists, but it is irrelevant to the conduct of men unless it is interpreted and enforced by political authority. Men who follow the just by nature in a situation where there is no power to compel obedience court their own ruin.

Rousseau goes on to dismiss natural law as lacking basic significance for political theory: knowledge of what is a "law of nature" will not enable us to understand better our true task, which is to grasp what is a "law of the state."[28] This brings us back to the general will, for the law of the state is nothing else than the authentic declaration by the sovereign people of the general will.

The General Will and the Will of All.   An important distinction for Rousseau is that between the general will and the "will of all" (*volonté de tous*). While the former is concerned only with the common interest, the latter is the "sum of particular wills" and results from the interplay of competing private interests in a society. The optimal condition for the

---

27. Ibid., chap. 6, pp. 222–23.
28. Ibid.

general will would be one in which each individual, consulting only himself, declared what he conscientiously held to be the general will on a given issue. The differences of view between individuals would cancel each other out and the result would be the general will. If partial associations are formed, however, each of them expresses not the general will, but the particular will of the group itself. The larger and more powerful the subsidiary groups in the state, the smaller the opportunity for the general will to assert itself. The paradigmatic society would have no partial groups complicating the process of eliciting the general will; but if their existence is unavoidable, they should be as numerous and as equal in power as possible, so that none is able to dominate the others. The least desirable situation is one in which a partial association (or special interest) becomes so powerful that it is able to engineer the declaration of its own will as the general will. In that event the general will is completely lost sight of, and the "prevailing opinion" has no more validity than if it were that of a single individual.[29]

It is clear from this discussion that Rousseau would have little sympathy with what has since come to be called interest-group politics. He most certainly would not agree with the "group theory of politics" school that emerged in the United States under the inspiration of Arthur Fisher Bentley's writings, or at least not with the implication that the interest-group struggle is in principle beneficent and an indispensable ingredient to a healthy or developed polity. To Rousseau, it was highly unlikely that the public interest would emerge from the process of bargaining between interest groups. The public interest, or the general will, was a moral reality over and *against* the expression of particular wills or of any combination of them. Only if primacy were accorded the general will could a just and ordered society prevail. Otherwise, one is left with an aggregation of divided and hostile groups, a society whose decisions would be certainly detrimental to those groups that lost out in the power struggle and which would ultimately prove harmful even to the victors, whose true interests as men would not be served in the enjoyment of unjust domination.

The Legislator. The general will does not automatically emerge from the deliberations of a people, for individuals may be seduced by the temptation to accord primacy to their own interests. And even if this temptation is overcome and the people called into assembly conscientiously seek the general will, their judgment about it may be mistaken. Consequently, the judgment of the people is in need of "enlightenment." From such "public enlightenment," from the "union of understanding and

---

29. Ibid., chap. 3, pp. 212–13.

will," come decisions in conformity with the general will. But such illumination of the collective judgment of a people will take place only under the proper guidance. This is why a legislator is necessary.[30]

Rousseau's legislator recalls both the founder-prince of Machiavelli and the Platonic lawgiver. He is a wholly extraordinary man who is capable of transcending his environment and shaping it for higher purposes. He is a god among men, a "superior intelligence, who is aware of all the passions of men but who himself does not experience any of them," a creature who "has no relation to our nature but knows it thoroughly." He has remarkable foresight and works for a distant glory rather than momentary fame.[31]

The legislator is not a ruler, but the man who constructs the framework within which all future governors will act. He "invents the machine," whereas the ruler or prince is only the workman who makes it run. The legislator is the man who brings a society into being. He should "so to speak feel himself capable of changing human nature, of transforming each individual . . . into a part of a larger whole . . . [and] altering man's constitution so as to strengthen it." Man must lose his natural self and acquire a social self; he "is nothing, can do nothing, except through all the others." Only if man and community are thus completely integrated can it be said that "legislation has achieved the highest possible degree of perfection."[32]

The legislator is not a permanent institution of the state. He is not the head of the government, as Rousseau understands the term. He is not the sovereign—that can be only the whole people. The legislator is the rare and superior individual who creates the conditions under which a community of men may flourish as it should. His office has "no place in the constitution" of the state; his role is altogether extraordinary and exceptional.

The legislator, then, does not make the laws, but rather proposes the initial, fundamental laws to the people. In a sense the term is a misnomer; the people as a whole remain the true "legislator."

Every society has its national heroes who played decisive roles in the events leading to the creation or restructuring of the body politic. The legislator is Rousseau's term for the individual (or individuals) fulfilling this role. It is therefore somewhat excessive for J. L. Talmon to argue, as he has done, that the legislator prefigures the contemporary totalitarian

---

30. Ibid., p. 226.
31. Ibid., chap. 7, p. 227.
32. Ibid., p. 228.

dictator,[33] even though it must be admitted that Rousseau used extravagant language, which could be easily subject to misinterpretation, in describing this important figure.

The legislator, or founding prince, draws up the laws to be considered in the formative period of a community's existence, but he "has no right of legislation"; even if they wished, the people could not "divest themselves of this right." This is because "only the general will obliges individuals" to obey a law, and one can be assured of the conformity of an individual will (even that of the legislator) to the general will "only after having submitted it to the free vote of a people."[34] Rousseau explicitly repeats this point in the section on the legislator, and there can be no doubt of his intention that this figure should function not as a dictator or manipulator of plebiscites, but as a supremely democratic leader whose authority rests on the freely given consent of a people that reposes its confidence in him and can withdraw it at any moment.

For a society in the making (*un peuple naissant*), which lacks experience in participation in political affairs and is in need of guidance, an appeal to the quasi-religious basis of the legislator's authority is essential. This is an authority that, while not counter to reason, invokes metarational or mythical imagery. This appeal to metarational symbolism enables the legislator to "constrain without violence and to persuade without convincing [through] the force of reason alone." Rousseau expresses his idea of the usefulness of religious symbolism in founding a political order in words reminiscent of Machiavelli:

> There we have what forces the fathers of nations in all ages to have recourse to the intervention of heaven and to honor the gods by attributing to them their own wisdom, to the end that the peoples, submitting to the laws of the State as to those of nature, and recognizing the same power in the formation of both man and the city, might obey with liberty and bear obediently the yoke of the public happiness.
>
> This sublime reason, which soars above the reach of ordinary men [*les hommes vulgaires*], enables the legislator to put decisions into the mouth of the immortals, in order to constrain by divine authority those who cannot be moved by human prudence. It is not every man who has the gift of making the gods speak, nor is it every man who can make himself believed when he declares himself

---

33. J. L. Talmon, *The Origins of Totalitarian Democracy* (New York: Praeger, 1960), pp. 42, 49. Rousseau explicitly distinguishes between a legislator and a "tyrant" in *Du Contrat social,* bk. 2, chap. 10, p. 243.

34. Rousseau, *Du Contrat social,* bk. 2, chap. 7, p. 230.

their interpreter. The great soul of the legislator is the true miracle, and that which should serve as proof of his mission.[35]

Rousseau cites with profound respect three great religious figures who were also founders of commonwealths: Moses, Mohammed, and Calvin. It is as a political genius who codified the laws of Geneva rather than as a theologian that Rousseau values Calvin. Like Machiavelli, Rousseau is concerned principally with the political utility of religion rather than with its truth. In fact, he comes closer than Machiavelli to explicitly denying the claim of truth of any revealed religion.

These remarks about the legislator omit discussion of one important qualifying factor: the role of the general will as a restraint on the legislator himself. The general will does not exist in nature—otherwise Rousseau would surely not have abandoned the natural law concept. But neither is it the imposed will of a single man (that is, the legislator). The general will is a willing of a collectivity that has become a people. The legislator evokes the general will and his evocative role is essential for its proper manifestation. He himself is not above it. In some way that is not rationally explicable—Rousseau deliberately employs the word "miracle" to describe the event—throughout history extraordinary and heroic men emerge who are themselves the prototype of what the new man of the community can become. The legislator is more than human but not more than what humanity can become if it is organized into the right kind of community. The new man, of whom Rousseau's legislator is the prototype, is not a superman, not an *Übermensch* in Nietzsche's sense. The new man is more than human only with reference to the natural man; he is the model, the paradigm of what man can become under the proper conditions. He anticipates the development of such a man, who through his foresight, sagacity, and example will help to elicit the general will in the well-ordered community. The new man will be disciplined, tempered, and liberated by the general will—just as the legislator has freed himself from personal ambition and the slavery of appetite and is willing to give himself for his people.

Necessary Conditions. The Social Contract is primarily concerned with Rousseau's theory of the paradigmatic society. He is under no illusion that the paradigm is directly applicable to all circumstances, however. As Plato and Aristotle had been, he is careful to point out that the paradigm is essentially a standard by which existing regimes may be evaluated. The paradigm may be realized or approximated only under

---

35. Ibid., p. 231. Rousseau quotes Machiavelli (*Discourses*, bk. 1, chap. 11) in support of the importance of claiming religious authority in founding a commonwealth.

exceptional conditions. If an attempt is made to erect the good society on a faulty base it will surely fail. Rousseau was no utopian, if by a utopian we mean one who believes that the world may be restructured according to an abstract blueprint regardless of the diverse traditions and aspirations of men and of the concrete obstacles that stand in the way of sweeping renovation in society. He had in common with Plato a vivid awareness of the difficulties to be overcome before a decisive advance in the quality of man's social existence could be attained. He was not an advocate of change and revolution for its own sake. An attempt to introduce sweeping changes when conditions are inappropriate will only produce harm, perhaps even a condition of terror and violence that would make the order that was overthrown look like a paradise. Rousseau's caution on this subject has not always been heeded by those influenced by his teaching, but it is an important and basic element of his belief. Most constitutions are bad,[36] and it is important that we know they are and why they are. (The major task of political theory is to provide us with the intellectual tools with which to subject them to critical scrutiny.) And the fact that they are bad does not necessarily mean that they can become good. There may be little we can do about society as a whole at a particular stage except wait out the storm and seek to act in our personal situations so as to spread awareness of the need for a new critical perspective for our times.

Still, Rousseau did not abandon hope that paradigmatic conditions might be attained in his time in certain areas with which he was familiar. He frequently spoke with praise of his native Geneva, and sometimes of Switzerland in general and the Netherlands. Corsica he declared to be a "country capable of legislation" and a "small island that will some day astonish Europe."[37] He was generally negative in his judgments of England, France, and Russia.

Rousseau did not believe it possible for the paradigm to be realized in a large state, because realization required every member to have a face-to-face relationship with every other member—an impossibility in a vast multitude. All the people should be capable of being assembled in one place, where they could authentically exercise their sovereignty under the general will. Such assemblies are impossible in the large nation-state, where many people live great distances from the center of government and where it would not be possible to find a meeting place vast enough to hold them all. Even if they could be brought together

---

36. "Aussi voit-on peu d'états bien constitués" (*Du Contrat social*, bk. 2, chap. 10, p. 244).

37. Ibid.

they would not know each other; their physical separation overcome, they would remain psychically apart. A large multitude spread out over a vast territory divides itself into various social units with diverse customs and practices. People from one province are often incapable of fully understanding and sympathizing with the traditions and customs of those from a different one.

In addition to smallness—and here he clearly takes as his model the Greek *polis*—Rousseau observed that certain other preconditions were essential to the full attainment of the good society:

> What people, then, is suitable for legislation? One which, finding itself already bound by some union of origin, interest, or convention, has not yet felt the true weight of laws; which has no deeply-rooted customs or superstitions; which does not fear being overcome by a sudden invasion and which without being involved in its neighbors' quarrels, is capable of resisting each of them taken singly, or of aiding one in repulsing the attack of another; in which each member can be known by all others and where no man is made to carry a greater burden than he is able to bear; which can get along without other peoples and which every other people can also do without; which is neither rich nor poor, and can suffice for itself; and, finally, which unites the firmness of an ancient people with the docility of a new one. What makes the work of legislation so arduous is not so much that which must be established as that which must be destroyed, and it is the impossibility of finding the simplicity of nature joined to the needs of society that makes success in the enterprise so rare. All of these conditions, it is true, are difficult to find present at the same time. Thus, there are few states that may be considered to be well constituted.[38]

Government and Its Forms

Book 3 of *The Social Contract* treats of government and its relation to the sovereign. Rousseau's sharp dissociation between sovereignty and government is not always properly understood. As we shall see, Rousseau advocated a democratic *society* or *state*—under the proper conditions—but not a democratic *government*. He thought it inevitable that government should be by the few, although it should be under the control of the general will as expressed in the rightly conducted deliberations of the whole people. Government should not legislate but should act within the framework of legislation enacted by the whole people.

Of government in general, Rousseau observes that it is "an intermediary body established between the subjects and the sovereign to pro-

---

38. Ibid., pp. 243–44.

mote their mutual agreement, which is charged with the execution of the laws and the maintenance of civil and political liberty."[39] Individual members of this body are called magistrates, kings, or governors; taken as a whole the body is known as the prince. The act by which a people agrees to submit to a given form of government is not a contract but a "commission." The power of government can be recovered or limited at any time by the sovereign people; governors are simply "officials of the sovereign." "I call then *Government*, or supreme administration, the legitimate exercise of the executive power, and Prince or Magistrate the man or body of men charged with that administration."[40]

Political Components. There are three components of the political equation: sovereign, government, and subjects. "If the Sovereign wishes to govern or if the Magistracy wishes to give laws, or if the subjects refuse to obey, disorder replaces regularity, force and will no longer act in concert, and the State, in dissolution, falls into either despotism or anarchy."[41] Will, or legislative power, belongs to the people; force, or executive power, is exercised by the government. The latter is a physical force, the former a moral one. Government only executes, or puts into effect, the decisions of the legislative power, which "belongs to the people." That power itself, to be legitimate, however, must be exercised "according to the direction of the general will."

Governmental Forms. Every society must have a governmental power, but there is no single form of government that is everywhere the best.[42] The form of government will depend upon the size (both in population and territory) of the state, the degree of social and economic equality among the citizens, its particular customs, geographic position, military requirements, and so on. In general, the more numerous the governing body (the prince or magistracy), the less force possessed by the government. The larger the society, the greater is the need for a strong government. This means that a democratic government (composed of all or a majority of the citizens) is conceivable only in a very small society and that monarchy (the government of a single man) is the unavoidable form for large states. Aristocracy, or the government of a minority of the population, is suitable for states in the middle range. Within these three basic types there are many subforms and possible gradations. Rousseau could easily have expanded this section to range over as much detail as did Aristotle in the *Politics*. His major point, how-

---

39. Ibid., bk. 3, chap. 1, p. 252.
40. Ibid., p. 253.
41. Ibid., pp. 253–54.
42. Ibid., p. 255.

ever, is to warn of the impossibility of asserting *a priori* that only one governmental form is suitable for all conditions and men. This warning always needs to be considered but was particularly pertinent in Rousseau's own day, when the *savants* of the Enlightenment were prone to offer up universal blueprints for governing mankind with singular disregard for diversities among nations.

The social order demands that the general will of the whole people predominate, that the will of the government be strictly subordinated to it, and that the personal will of the individual have no effect (*doit être nulle*). In "the natural order," however, the reverse priority holds, and man thinks of his own interests first, then of himself as a government official, and of his duty as a citizen last.[43] These considerations recall, even in the midst of discussions about governmental forms, the importance of public morality, or the laws engraved on the hearts of the citizens. Only through sound political education in all its aspects can men be induced to go against the inclinations of their primary natures, adopt second natures, so to speak, and act in accordance with the general will.

Democracy. Of the three basic governmental forms, democracy, conceived of in the literal sense of government of all or a majority of the people, must be set aside as impracticable.

> If we take the term in a strict sense, there has never existed a true democracy, and one never will exist. It is against the natural order that the greater number governs and the minority is governed. It is unthinkable that the people would remain perpetually assembled in order to devote its attention to public affairs. . . .[44]

Only if there were a "people of Gods" would democratic government be possible. "So perfect a Government is not suited to men."[45]

In such remarks as these, the supposedly democratic Rousseau sounds very much like Gaetano Mosca, Roberto Michels, or Vilfredo Pareto. Every society, he declares, must have a governing class, and that class comprises a minority of the population. Where is the Rousseau who supposedly fathered the concept of populistic democracy, of a society directed by the people without recourse to any leaders? Even a moderately careful reading of *The Social Contract*, beginning with the chapters on the legislator in Book 2 and proceeding to Book 3 with its consideration of government, would show that, far from ignoring the

---

43. Ibid., bk. 3, chap. 2, p. 260.
44. Ibid., chap. 4, p. 266.
45. Ibid., p. 267.

problem of leadership, Rousseau particularly emphasized its importance.

Government and the General Will. However, a nagging problem remains. If it is "against the natural order" for the greater number to rule and the lesser number to be ruled, how is it that government in general —viewed realistically as either an aristocracy or monarchy—can be brought under the direction of the sovereign assembly of the whole people? Why is it not inevitable that minority governments not only will perform their *executive* functions but will seek to usurp the *legislative* power as well? If it is true that the larger the assembly or committee, the weaker its effective authority,[46] why will not the whole assembly of the people always be dominated and manipulated by a small governmental elite that is well organized, disciplined, and prepared for effective action?

Rousseau cannot have been unaware of these harsh sociological realities. The facts of "the natural order" did not deter him from proclaiming his conviction that under exceptional circumstances a social order could be erected which would reverse these priorities and proclivities. Government could not and should not be eliminated, but it should be made responsible to the general will. A wise legislator could preside over the construction of a well-ordered society, one in which the centrifugal tendencies of primary nature are overcome. In this society, the strength of customs and conventions, a society's shared public morality and ethos, the "laws engraved on the hearts of the citizens" would act as inner restraints on magistrates and subjects alike. A minority is needed to govern, to make the specialized, particular judgments and applications essential to the day-to-day running of society and to frame basic questions for discussion and voting in the assembly. But this need not be a dominating and exploiting minority; it can be a minority that serves the public interest and leaves the general will—the best sense of the community—as the ultimate judge of its plans and actions.

Aristocracy. By aristocracy, Rousseau means an elected government that is composed of a minority of the population—usually a small minority. He rejects hereditary aristocracy as "the worst of all governments," and he regards natural aristocracy as a form suitable only for "simple peoples." Elective aristocracy is the best of all governments, provided that the proper conditions prevail for its adoption. Aristocracy is for states of moderate size and of moderate disparities of wealth. It is the "best and most natural" order of things that "the wisest men govern

---

46. Ibid., p. 266.

the multitude." There is, however, the constant danger that the governing minority will form a corporate will of its own that pulls its deliberations away from the general will.

Monarchy. Rousseau is very negative in his judgment on monarchy. He cites Machiavelli's preference for a republican regime in the *Discourses* and the *History of Florence,* attributing the apparent "opposition" between the teachings of these works and the maxims of *The Prince* to the author's need to "disguise his love for liberty" while he was living under the oppressive reign of the Medici.[47] *The Prince* is declared to be truly "the book of republicans." Machiavelli is said to have chosen such "abominable heroes" as Cesare Borgia for *The Prince* in order to mask his "secret intention" of advocating through his writings the liberation of his people from tyrannical oppression.

"Kings desire to be absolute," Rousseau declares. It is in vain that they are advised to govern so as to enable their people to become strong and prosperous. Monarchs wish their people to remain weak in order that they may be more secure in their mastery over them.

Monarchy as a governmental form is suitable only for large states. The strength of a government must increase in proportion to the population, and if governmental power is concentrated in a single hand, it has the greatest possible strength and unity of direction. The size of a nation-state also necessitates that "intermediary orders" be established to serve as liaison between the monarch and the people. Such "differences of rank" would spell the death of a small state, which thrives on equality. It is clear that, although Rousseau discusses monarchy as one of the possible legitimate forms of government—assuming that it operates under the direction of the general will—neither the large state nor the monarchical form is truly compatible with the principles of a good society. The large state is too vast to allow periodical assembling of the people to declare the general will, and government by a single man irrestibly pulls toward tyranny or personal domination. Rousseau in effect declares that all the major states of his time, which were monarchies, lacked legitimate foundations. In that sense, even though he warns against the dangers of indiscriminate revolution, or revolution for its own sake, his teaching may be held to have encouraged revolutionary sentiment. Political activists have a tendency to take the most striking expressions and phrases in a political book without paying heed to the qualifications.

In view of the way that monarchies, and particularly hereditary monarchies, work in practice, Rousseau ranked them beneath republics

---

47. Ibid., chap. 6, p. 273n.

even in stability of direction and policy. Hereditary monarchs are often not suited to the job and they depend on ministers who are petty intriguers and swindlers. Republics, "which must always rank above monarchies," tend to elevate their most able and enlightened members to ruling positions, for the people is "not mistaken in its choice of leaders nearly so frequently as the prince."[48] There is "more wisdom" in a senate than in the court of a king, and the policies of republics are "more constant and better executed." In a monarchy, on the other hand, each change of ministers produces a major shift in public policy.

To evaluate monarchy correctly, one must consider princes to be evil or incompetent; for they "either are so when they ascend to the Throne or the Throne makes them so." It is not sufficient to advise the people simply to endure a bad government on the supposition that God has willed it because of the faults of men. "The question is to find a good one."[49]

Mixed Governments. In addition to the three simple forms of government (monarchy, aristocracy, and democracy), Rousseau has a brief chapter on mixed governments. Because he recognized that while theoretical distinctions are crucial in aiding us to understand reality, they cannot pretend to prescribe specific historical situations in all their variety, Rousseau was led to observe that strictly speaking "there are no simple forms of government," and that every monarch must have subordinates to assist him in governing and every popular government must have a head.[50] There is then in every government a gradation of authority, with authority being weighted in favor of one man in a monarchy and of a greater number of officials in the other two forms. Occasionally the distribution of power among the elements (one, few, and many) is balanced; if the parts are in mutual dependence (as in England), the result is beneficial, while if the "authority of each part is independent but imperfect, as in Poland," the effect is harmful because it leaves the government incapable of action. (Presumably he saw the English regime through the mirror of Montesquieu—that is, based on the separation of powers.)

The Paradigmatic Government. To Rousseau, the best form of government for his paradigmatic society is clearly an elective "aristocracy," a government of the best men as chosen for fixed terms by the free vote of the citizenry. Such a government is otherwise known as a republican form.

---

48. Ibid., p. 275.
49. Ibid., p. 279.
50. Ibid., chap. 7, p. 280.

However, Rousseau is most insistent that a single form of government is not suitable for all conditions, and he cites Montesquieu with approval in support of this contention. "Liberty," he writes, "not being a fruit of all climates, is not within the grasp of all peoples."[51] A good society, small enough to ensure effective popular participation in making the laws and yet large enough to be economically and politically viable, will produce a good government and has a fairly wide choice of governmental arrangements. There are various types of republican (or aristocratic) government. Unfree societies will not have good governments, because their governments in varying degrees encroach upon and usurp the sovereignty of the people. The precise governmental structure of each concrete society in history will vary in relation to its population, geography, size, climate, and traditions.[52]

Much of the material in Book 3 is suggestive of Aristotle and Machiavelli. Here we encounter very definitely Rousseau's "empirical" side. Affinities with Montesquieu are also evident. It is important to note this aspect of Rousseau, because he is frequently interpreted as an abstract, utopian writer. Even in *The Social Contract*, his most "idealistic" work, large doses of "realism," or empirical description as conventionally defined, may be found. In other words, he not only asks the question: What is the good society? He also considers the question: What are the conditions and governments in human history? His political teaching includes a theory of the paradigm and a political sociology.

The Return to the Paradigm

After this *excursus* on the condition of actual states and governments, Rousseau returns to the paradigm and the problem of its realization. The consideration given to this topic in the remainder of the work is thoroughly realistic, and is prefaced by the warning that even if the good society should be established, it could not indefinitely endure. It is the "natural and inevitable tendency" of even the "best constituted governments" to decay and ultimately fall into ruin. Rousseau echoes Machiavelli's conclusion that a "perpetual republic" is an impossibility. The state is a "work of art" fashioned by man, who is a mortal creature. If a state were to endure forever, the work of man would have to be endowed with "a solidity of which human things do not admit."[53]

Popular Assemblies. As we have seen, for Rousseau the indispensable condition for the maintenance of the sovereign power was to have

---

51. Ibid., chap. 8, p. 282.
52. Ibid., p. 285.
53. Ibid., chap. 11, p. 296.

the people assemble periodically, for the "sovereign can act only when the people is assembled." He refuses to admit that periodic assemblies of the whole people are impractical, citing the Roman republic as an example of a vast society that was able to conduct them efficiently. Popular assemblies have been features of the early histories of many peoples. It is therefore feasible to hope to hold them in modern times. These meetings of the whole people must take place at "fixed and periodic" intervals; it is "not sufficient to have decided on the form of Government or to have settled once and for all the election of magistrates."[54]

Rousseau explores the problem of how to bring together citizens of a large contemporary nation-state. The paradox is that the larger the state, the stronger its government should be to maintain its unity and cohesion. The stronger the government, however, the more important it is "for the Sovereign to show itself frequently." If the state includes a number of cities, there are three possibilities: (1) to have one city, the capital, dominate the rest; (2) to divide the sovereignty of the nation among various regions or cities; and (3) to have no capital city, but have the government move from town to town in order to assemble the citizens of each one in turn. Of these solutions, 3 is clearly preferable to 1 and 2, which are unacceptable. In fact, 2 is impossible, because sovereignty cannot be divided.

However, Rousseau's general argument raises doubt that he would have been satisfied with 3 as a solution either. He simply rejected large states on principle. To have a society of many towns, some far distant from others and situated in regions with a variety of customs and traditions, would be to have not one state, but a society of several, or many states. This could not result in a true political community.

Representative Assemblies. Rousseau's rejection of representative assemblies, composed of a limited number of men who have been elected to make laws in behalf of the people—to "stand in their place"—is well known. He summarizes his objections to the idea that the people can be represented in their legislative capacity in the following passage:

> Sovereignty cannot be represented for the same reason that it cannot be alienated; it consists essentially in the general will, and will is not represented (it is either this or that, there is no middle position). The deputies of the people, then, are not and cannot be representatives; they are only its stewards or commissioners and can conclude nothing definitively. Every law which the people in person has not ratified is null and void; it is not a law. The English people think

54. Ibid., chap. 13, p. 300.

they are free, but they are strongly mistaken; they are so only during the election of members of Parliament. Once the election is over they are again slaves—they are nothing. Considering the use they make of their freedom during the brief moments when they exercise it, they well deserve to lose it.[55]

The principle of representation was unknown to the ancients; the citizens of the Greek *polis* cared too much for their liberty to entrust it to others. It is true that they possessed the institution of slavery, which enabled them to remain more or less constantly assembled to consider public affairs. The difference between ancient and modern times on this point is not that slavery has been abolished but that it has been extended. Modern peoples do not have slaves, but they are slaves.[56] Representative institutions are a modern invention; they go with the feudal system, "under which the human species is degraded and the name of man dishonored."[57]

At the moment when a people gives itself representatives, "it is no longer free, it no longer exists." This is why a small society is essential, for

henceforth I do not see how it will be possible for the sovereign to preserve among us the exercise of its rights if the City is not very small. But if it is very small, then will it be subjugated? NO. I will show hereafter how one can unite the external power of a great people with the wise policy and good order of a small state.[58]

Rousseau concludes the chapter from which this quotation is taken by posing the question of whether the paradigmatic society—the small state in which the people can easily come together under conditions conducive to legislation in accordance with the general will—is a pragmatic possibility. His answer is affirmative. He proposes to treat external relations and the whole question of confederations in another work. Apparently he envisaged the modern city-state, like its ancient Greek counterpart, as defending itself in the international arena through the formation of a confederation with other small societies to ensure the survival of all the member states.

Popular Sovereignty and the General Will

Rousseau discusses the implications of his idea of the sovereignty of the people in the concluding chapters of Book 3 and in much of Book 4.

55. Ibid., chap. 15, p. 307.
56. Ibid., p. 309.
57. Ibid., p. 307.
58. Ibid., p. 310.

Sovereignty must always reside in the people and never in the government. The institution of government is a law and not a contract; all government is provisional in nature and its form and/or personnel may be altered at any time. It is true that a change of government is "always dangerous," and a society would be well advised not to tamper with its government unless it turns out to be clearly "incompatible with the public good." This, however, is a "maxim of policy" rather than a "rule of right." From the perspective of right and law, the sovereign people have unlimited authority to change the government at any time.[59]

As we have seen, however, the people are rightfully sovereign only when they act in conformity with the general will. The majority may err in its decisions; indeed, not even a unanimous vote guarantees that it will be in conformity with the general will. For Rousseau there must be, as J. L. Talmon has suggested, a "marriage" of popular sovereignty and the general will.

Rousseau refers with great frequency to the general will in Book 4. He observes that no great subtlety is required to fathom it. The best governed states need only a few laws to govern them, and the necessity for new laws is "universally understood." Then the "first person who proposes them says only what all have already felt."[60]

Unanimity. When devotion to the general will achieves its maximal saturation in a society, spontaneous unanimity prevails. When the social tie begins to loosen and particular interests increasingly make themselves felt, unanimity gives way to disputes and lengthy debates. Finally, the general will becomes "mute" after the social tie is "broken in every heart" and "pernicious interests" take the place of the public good. "Iniquitous decrees" are passed "under the name of laws." When that happens, it is not the general will that has changed, however; it remains there, "unalterable and pure," waiting to be interrogated.

"At the other end of the circle," Rousseau observes, unanimity returns. When the citizenry has fallen into a condition of servitude, it votes by acclamation for the powers that be out of either fear or the wish to flatter. This is an utterly false kind of unanimity and is completely opposite to the general will.

Minority Views. Under the proper circumstances the vote of the majority may be assumed faithfully to express the general will. Unanimity is essential only for the social contract itself. Each individual, either in an overt act or by voluntarily consenting to reside continuously in a given society, freely binds himself to become part of the community.

---

59. Ibid., chaps. 16–18, pp. 312–13, 315–16.
60. Ibid., bk. 4, chap. 1, p. 320.

This means that he gives himself up to the direction of the general will. In the deliberations of the assembly he and all others express their views as to the demands of the general will for dealing with the problems at hand. If his view is not accepted—if he is in a minority—after mature and conscientious deliberation by a dedicated citizenry, itself formed by proper education and by good laws enacted under the guidance of a sagacious founder, then it can only mean that he was (sincerely) mistaken about the general will. In following the majority the individual does not yield to an alien force but discovers his own true interest, his own true will—the general will as declared by the majority. Thus, "excluding the social contract, the views of the majority always oblige all the others." This is implicit in the contract itself.[61]

Rousseau makes abundantly clear, however, that not every decision of the majority (or even of the entire people) is right and legitimate. While it is clear that majority approval is essential for a law to be binding, that approval is only the minimal condition for its being truly a law; "the characteristics of the general will must be present in the plurality."[62]

From this passage it would seem to follow that a minority, even if it should express the true general will against an erring majority, can never legitimately impose its view. If the general will does not reside in the majority opinion, then "whatever side one takes liberty no longer exists."[63] Minority domination is unjust *even on behalf of the general will*. This conclusion is of considerable importance, for some of Rousseau's interpreters have declared or implied that the author's true intention was to establish a dictatorship of an ideologically committed elite or vanguard. Actually, throughout *The Social Contract* he insists that the freely accorded consent of the majority is indispensable. If the majority has forsaken the general will, then a free society becomes impossible.

The Roman Republic. The middle chapters of Book 4 consider in detail the institutions of the Roman Republic, with particular emphasis upon the assemblies of the people and the tribunate.[64] There is also a defense of the constitutional dictatorship devised by the Romans to cope with emergency situations. Rousseau follows Machiavelli in praising the Romans' short-term constitutional dictatorship, and holds that this institution, far from violating popular sovereignty, actually up-

61. Ibid., pp. 321–22, and chap. 2, pp. 324–25.
62. Ibid., p. 326.
63. Ibid.
64. Ibid., chaps. 4–7.

holds it, for it is the true will of the people (and therefore the general will) that the society be preserved. The discussion in Chapter 6 of Book 4 is relevant to the problems of twentieth-century constitutional democracies and their provisions for meeting crisis situations that threaten the constitutional order itself (Weimar Germany, for example, with its Article 48, and the French Fifth Republic with its Article 16). In general, Rousseau is lavish in his praise of the Roman Republic and concludes that in its popular assemblies "the Roman people was truly sovereign both by right and by fact."[65] He disagrees with Cicero on the question of whether a change in the voting procedure (from a public to a secret ballot) brought on the ruin of the republic. He maintains that it was the corruption of the people and not changes in their political arrangements that resulted in the destruction of the republic. Good laws are appropriate only for a good people; if the people become corrupt, there is no alternative to an altering of the laws. Good laws alone cannot save a corrupt social order.[66]

Public Morality

The final two chapters of *The Social Contract* have to do with the public morality, or the "laws written on the hearts of the citizens." We shall recall that these "laws" were viewed by Rousseau as absolutely fundamental to keeping a true community in being and responsive to the general will. Man to Rousseau is not a social being, but a being fashioned by society. He can be either ennobled or corrupted by society. It is not nature but "opinion" that guides societal man in his choice of pleasures. It is the ethos of a society that impels men in their moral commitments to this or that end. Although law does not regulate public morality (which, in fact, serves as the basis of good laws), wise legislation in the formative period of a society "gives birth" to such morality.[67]

Censorship. The institution of censorship may, then, be useful in "conserving morality but never in restoring it." While the laws are observed in full and a people is young and virtuous, the censorship should be instituted to check and retard the inevitable retrogression that will set in. A public censorial tribunal, "far from being the arbiter of the opinion of a people, is only its expositor." If such a body attempts to impose customs and opinions not rooted in public morality, "its decisions are vain and without effect."[68]

---

65. Ibid., chap. 4, p. 339.
66. Ibid., pp. 343–44.
67. Ibid., chap. 7, p. 354.
68. Ibid.

Civil Religion. In the concluding chapter of the work Rousseau discusses at some length the need for the good society to possess a civil religion. Both civil religion and censorship are features of the polities of classical antiquity which Rousseau has incorporated into his political theory. The chapter on civil religion has aroused much controversy and apparently was not included in the first version of *The Social Contract.*[69]

Rousseau makes it clear that he considers Christianity destructive of good polity and the civic spirit. The ancient pagan cults were grounded on the union of religion and politics. Each "nation" had its gods, and the gods served men rather than being served by them. Religious belief was conducive to civic dedication. There was only one loyalty, to the state. With the coming of Christianity, "everything changed its aspect." Christianity introduced the "new idea" of an otherworldly kingdom to which men owed loyalty in addition to the visible earthly community. Once the victory of Christianity over paganism was secured in the Roman Empire, this "otherworldly" community took the form of a powerful organized church with its own clergy which constituted a separate corporation within the state. This "double power" of the church and the civil order has produced a "perpetual conflict" which has made all good polity impossible in Christian states."[70]

Civil religion is discussed within the context of the principles of right which Rousseau has elaborated throughout the work. The social contract gives to the sovereign the power to regulate the behavior of the citizen "within the limits of public utility." Individual subjects are accountable to the community only for those beliefs that have a bearing on social solidarity. It is the concern of the state that each individual have a religion, because religion "makes him love his duties." However, the dogmas of that religion concern the state only insofar as they have implications for the individual's behavior as a citizen and the recognition of his duty to the community and his fellow citizens. Beyond the minimal dogmas necessary for social solidarity, each individual may have whatever additional religious beliefs he chooses to hold. The community is concerned only with the role of the citizens in this life and has no competence to legislate in theological terms about the destiny of man in the next world.

Rousseau calls for a "purely civil profession of faith" for which the sovereign determines the articles of belief not as religious dogmas so much as "sentiments of sociability without which it is impossible to be either a good citizen or a faithful subject." No one may be obliged to

---

69. See Bertrand de Jouvenel's appendix on this chapter in ibid., pp. 373f.
70. Ibid., chap. 3, p. 361.

believe in the articles of the civil religion if he cannot do so conscientiously. But in that event he must withdraw from the community; if he does not, the community has the right to banish him. His banishment would not be for the crime of impiety (as with the civil religions of antiquity) but for offending against the duties of citizenship and for being incapable of loving justice and the laws. Anyone who remains in the society and, having sworn allegiance to the articles of the civil religion, "acts as if he does not believe them will be punished with death; he has committed the greatest of crimes, he lied before the law."[71]

Rousseau then lists the "dogmas of the civil religion," which "ought to be simple, few in number, and precisely stated without explanations or commentaries." These provisions are: (1) belief in the existence of a "powerful, intelligent, beneficent Divinity endowed with foresight and providence"; (2) belief in an afterlife wherein the just are rewarded and evildoers punished; and (3) belief in the "sanctity of the social contract and the laws." To these positive dogmas there must be added a negative one. Citizens are forbidden to hold religious beliefs grounded on theological intolerance.[72] (Religions that hold that "outside the Church there is no salvation" are not to be tolerated. The civil religion endorses an intolerance of its own.) If proponents of a particular religion thought that nonbelievers in the society were damned on principle, then this belief would be a grave barrier to social solidarity and would draw a sharp line between believers and nonbelievers in the same society. In modern times, Rousseau explains, it is no longer possible to have an "exclusive, national religion" along the lines of the ancient pagan societies. (We have already seen that the "religions of the citizen" were defective because they were too parochial and bloodthirsty.) This means that society should tolerate all religions that themselves are tolerant of other religions and whose teachings are not contrary to the civil religion and the duties of the citizen.[73]

The Problem of the Closed Society

The Social Contract ends on a repressive note, with the harsh reference to the death penalty for offenders against the civil religion. This remark is regrettable, for it leaves the way open for a possible reign of terror, however contrary this was to Rousseau's intentions. Even Plato in an earlier time and age, which lacked the insights of modern liberalism regarding the fallacy of attempting to enforce religious faith by legisla-

---

71. Ibid., p. 370.
72. Ibid.
73. Ibid., p. 371.

tion and the importance of procedural safeguards for the individual citizen, had in the *Laws* introduced the death penalty for offenders against the civil religion only as a last resort, after all attempts at persuasion had failed. Rousseau does not even spell out the procedures and conditions for determining when a violation of the civil religion has in fact occurred.

Philosophically speaking, Rousseau ends the work at midpoint between the closed and the open society (to employ the terminology of Henri Bergson). His concern to narrow societal man's moral horizon to the general will and to reduce to a secondary position all loyalties conflicting with the duties of citizenship constitutes a move in the direction of the closed society. At the same time, he does not absolutely deny the reality of a universal morality and a common, universal human nature. In many respects he captures the dilemma of the contemporary ultranationalist intellectual who seeks to build a new, more intensely ethnic community at the national level but at the same time envisages the restructuring of the international order, making possible cooperative ventures for the maintenance of peace and the promotion of the well-being of peoples.

Rousseau sought desperately to overcome through a rightly ordered polity the alienation that he detected in the situation of modern man. He devised a new language through which he could express his conviction regarding the social origin of morality. The idea of the general will does not necessarily deify society, however, as some writers have claimed.

Rousseau yearned for a kind of human intensity and depth of participation in a concrete body politic which is impossible to attain under even the most favorable conditions. In this sense there is a certain affinity between his teaching and the various forms of political messianism that were to develop later. Nonetheless, there is a sense of limit evident in his works, and a recognition that social unity cannot be achieved without discipline and sacrifice. The new collective freedom of man in the good society would not be without cost. Rousseau thought the price well worth paying, but he never maintained that egalitarian social solidarity and spontaneity could be effortlessly combined—or would be the end result of some inevitable historical process.

Rousseau made extensive demands on the temporal political order, but he was not a wild utopian. His paradigmatic society was first of all just that—a paradigm against which the relative defectiveness of existing regimes could be measured. He should have been clearer about the alternatives available to men if, as was likely, the miracle of the paradigm's realization in history failed to occur. Would he have preferred a large mass democracy (if necessary, established by violent revolution) to a representative regime based on imperfect institutions, relative inequality of wealth and status, constitutionalism, and intermediary powers between the individual and the government? Or would he have been content to hold up his paradigm as a model for either of the two main types of contemporary democracy (constitutional and populistic) to approximate insofar as possible? In a sense, *The Social Contract* can be viewed as a piece of hypothetical advice to all societies to strive to conform to the public interest or the general will in their deliberations and decisions. Rousseau did not uncritically extol popular participation as an end in itself; it was the *quality* of the participation that mattered most to him. And yet he clearly would have favored the extension of that participation as widely as possible. For him, to be a citizen is a heroic affair. Perhaps this is the final, enduring legacy of his political thought. Only a relatively small number of people can meet the strenuous demands of authentically democratic citizenship. The paradigmatic society, unrealizable in full in the actual world of men and regimes as it is, can be achieved by a saving remnant *within* a larger community, such as the contemporary nation-state. No more than Bergson did Rousseau conceive of democracy as a society of mediocrities. What he did not see so well as Bergson is that the saving remnant must also exist *between* societies. For mankind is one, and the advancement of the world community is a goal worthy of the highest dedication. The growth of an organic world consensus can also be the work of those with the heart and mind of the legislator.

8

Burke and the Reaction
Against the French Revolution

The French Revolution is one of the great watersheds of Western history. Both protagonists and opponents were aware that the Revolution involved much more than a mere change of regime; nor did it bear implications for France alone. As it progressed from its moderate to its extreme phase, it came to mean the victory—brief but unforgettable—of a radical style of political thought and action. The most secularist and egalitarian tendencies of Enlightenment political thought gained the day; the cry of *liberté, égalité, fraternité* resounded throughout Europe, which reacted with both apprehension and expectation.

Inevitably, there emerged a body of serious political thought arrayed in opposition to the new order. In every country of Europe eloquent and gifted spokesmen denounced the revolution and most, if not all, of its works. Edmund Burke in Great Britain, Comte Joseph de Maistre and Vicomte Louis de Bonald in France, Juan Francisco Donoso-Cortés in Spain, Friedrich von Gentz and Friedrich Karl von Savigny in Germany, Vincenzo Cuoco in Italy—these names comprise only a fraction of the list of those who undertook the task of refuting the principles on which the revolution was based and of arguing for a political order in Europe which maintained its contact with the institutions and practices prevailing before the fateful year of 1789.

Collectively, these opponents of the revolution have been dubbed "the Reaction," or even "the Romantic Reaction." This label is both suggestive and misleading: suggestive in that the movement, particularly on the continent, was first and foremost a reaction against radical Enlightenment ideas, and misleading in that by no means all the thinkers involved despised reason and its works (as the adjective "romantic" is held by some to imply), nor were they all political reactionaries. As with the Enlightenment itself, this "counterenlightenment" was a synthesis of diverse elements, ranging from the ultratraditionalism of Maistre to the moderation of Cuoco.

Of all the men of the counterenlightenment, Edmund Burke was the most gifted and the most influential. Self-conscious conservatism, in the English-speaking world at least, traces its lineage to him. Although at times prone to massive rhetorical overkill, Burke demonstrated in his writings a generosity of temperament, imaginativeness, and flexibility all too rarely found among those who today call themselves conservatives. Indeed, his flexibility was the source of frequent misinterpretation of his teaching by nineteenth-century historians and moralists, many of whom regarded him simply as a champion of expediency or "utility" in the vulgar sense. Only in recent years has the rationalist or "natural law" side of his thought been given due recognition.[1]

REASON

One detects in Burke an important anticipation of the distinction Hegel was to make between *Verstand* (understanding) and *Vernunft* (reason). Reason to Burke is not a mechanical, logic-chopping, *a priori* exercise; it is not abstract but profoundly empirical, charged with the task of discovering the innermost connections of things below the surface of mere appearance. Reason in the authentic sense is not the reverse of intuition but its self-conscious illumination. It is not in principle hostile to the traditional and the venerable; rather, the ultimate rationality of many long-established institutions and practices can be amply illustrated. Like Hegel, Burke thought that reason unfolds itself in history, although by no means everything that happens in history is in accord with the law of reason.

Reason vs. "Metaphysics" in Politics

It is in this context that Burke's frequent condemnation of "theoretical" politicians and abstract "metaphysicians" needs to be understood. Burke stated his position on this matter quite clearly in a speech on electoral reform in 1782:

A prescriptive government, such as ours, never was the work of any legislator, never was made upon any foreign theory. It seems to me a preposterous way of reasoning, and a perfect confusion of ideas, to

---

1. Burleigh Wilkins has ably surveyed and adjudicated this reinterpretation in his *The Problem of Burke's Political Philosophy* (New York: Oxford University Press, 1967). See also Peter J. Stanlis, *Edmund Burke and the Natural Law* (Ann Arbor: University of Michigan Press, 1958), and Francis P. Canavan, S. J., *The Political Reason of Edmund Burke* (Durham, N.C.: Duke University Press, 1960).

take the theories which learned and speculative men have made from that government, and then, supposing it made on those theories which were made from it, to accuse the government as not corresponding with them. I do not vilify theory and speculation: no, because that would be to vilify reason itself. . . . No—whenever I speak against theory, I mean always a weak, erroneous, fallacious, unfounded, or imperfect theory; and one of the ways of discovering that it is a false theory is by comparing it with practice. This is the true touchstone of all theories which regard man and the affairs of men—Does it suit his nature in general?—does it suit his nature as modified by his habits?[2]

This passage brilliantly represents Burke's conservatism: the desire to pursue the "intimations" of a tradition rather than to plan a course of action on the basis of abstract, *a priori* principles. With reference to what he called the "metaphysical" approach to politics, Burke had this to say in a piece of highly impassioned rhetoric written during the year before his death:

Nothing can be conceived more hard than the heart of a thorough-bred metaphysician. It comes nearer to the cold malignity of a wicked spirit than to the frailty and passion of a man. It is like the principle of evil himself, incorporeal, pure, unmixed, dephlegmated, defecated evil. It is no easy operation to eradicate humanity from the human breast. What Shakespeare calls the "compunctious visitings of nature," will sometimes knock at their hearts, and protect against their murderous speculations.[3]

Burke's feelings about the effects of what he judged to be a disastrously faulty conception of political reason were clearly intense. The almost hysterical passion of his prose in parts of the "Reflections on the Revolution in France" (1789) and the "Letter to a Noble Lord" is due to his extreme reaction to the French Revolution and especially its Jacobin elements. His hatred for the work of the revolution led him to caricature its aims, to impugn the motives of all of its leaders, and to idealize the old regime. He was not content to attack the excesses of the Jacobins, but insisted that these excesses were unavoidable, given the principles espoused by the revolution. He was always a man of strongly held views, and the judiciousness that he demonstrated even in the heat of argument as he dealt with controversial issues in the British parliament

---

2. Edmund Burke, "Speech on the Representation of Commons in Parliament" (1782), in *Edmund Burke: Selected Writings and Speeches,* ed. Peter J. Stanlis (New York: Anchor Books, Doubleday, 1963), p. 332.

3. Burke, "Letter to a Noble Lord" (1796), in *The Works of the Right Honourable Edmund Burke,* 8 vols. (London: F. & C. Rivington, 1801), vol. 7, p. 426.

deserted him where the French Revolution was concerned. But to inquire into Burke's extreme reaction to the revolution is not my purpose here; rather I wish to search out the general orientation that we find so brilliantly argued in his speeches and letters. That orientation is conservatism, a conservatism that was for the most part generous and humane and which remains today as a kind of model for cosmopolitan conservative political thought.

Reason and Tradition

Burke is often said to have overthrown reason entirely in favor of tradition and "prejudice" or habit. This interpretation is most certainly wide of the mark. Burke did not indiscriminately defend any and every tradition or any and every policy that, out of long usage, had come to be accepted as "traditional." He valued the British constitutional tradition not only because it was his own, but more importantly because he found it to be reasonable. Thus the same man who could denounce abstract "metaphysical" politics could observe in the same work:

> I have ever abhorred, since the first dawn of my understanding to this obscure twilight, all the operations of opinion, fancy, inclination, and will, in the affairs of government, where only a sovereign reason, paramount to all forms of legislation and administration, should dictate. Government is made for the very purpose of opposing that reason to will and caprice, in the reforms or in the reformed, in the governors or in the governed, in king, in senates, or in people.[4]

Political Reason

What sort of reason was it, then, that Burke opposed to the allegedly abstract "rationalism" of the French radicals? Burke was not a philosopher, but a learned man of affairs, and so we should not expect from him the kind of conceptual clarity and sophistication that a philosopher can provide. Nonetheless, it seems possible to extract from his writings a fairly precise notion of what he meant by political reason.[5]

For Burke, reason in politics is predominantly practical or prudential rather than speculative or theoretical in nature. It takes into account the life situations of real men in specific historical milieus. Authentic reason in politics, then, begins with an awareness of the inevitable discrepancy between theory and practice. Rather than beginning with a paradigm of right order grounded on the experience of a theorist or philosopher claiming to be representative of man and then proceed-

---

4. Ibid., pp. 393–94.

5. Although I have worked independently of it, Father Canavan's *Political Reason of Edmund Burke* is a valuable extended analysis of this subject.

ing to the "dilution" or downright adjustment of the paradigm to existing circumstances—as did Plato, for example—Burke the conservative
begins with a given political order that he finds to be reasonable in
principle and makes it the touchstone by which to test proposed policies
and theories.

> The science of constructing a commonwealth or renovating it, or
> reforming it, is, like every other experimental science, not to be
> taught *a priori*. Nor is it short experience that can instruct us in
> that practical science. . . . The science of government being there-
> fore so practical in itself, and intended for such practical purposes, is
> a matter which requires experience. . . . It is with infinite caution
> that any man ought to venture upon pulling down an edifice which
> has answered in any tolerable degree for ages the common purposes
> of society, or on building it up again, without having models and
> patterns of approved utility before his eyes.[6]

"Natural Rights."   Burke's view of the proper role of reason in
human affairs assumes that man's "natural" habitat is society and not
some hypothetical "state of nature." Indeed, he considered "unnatural"
the kind of abstract "natural rights" speculation that he held the Enlightenment to have produced, because these "metaphysick rights entering into common life, like rays of light which pierce into a dense
medium, are, by the laws of nature, refracted from their straight line."
To Burke, "natural rights" truly conceived are very different from the
"primitive rights" of precivilized men; these primitive rights "undergo
such a variety of refractions and reflections, that it becomes absurd to
talk of them as if they continued in the simplicity of their original direction."[7] This is because "art is man's nature": "For man is by nature
reasonable; and he is never perfectly in his natural state, but when he
is placed where reason may be best cultivated and most predominates.
Art is man's nature."[8]

Thus Burke appeals from the predominant modern view that society
is an artifact to the Aristotelian view that man fulfills his natural end
(*telos*) only in the political community. That community, furthermore,
must minister to a complicated and intricate variety of personality and
character types. True political rationality must recognize the enormous
diversity of circumstances encountered in actual political life, and must
reflect a self-aware and imaginative grasp of the complexity resulting

---

6. Burke, "Reflections on the Revolution in France" (1790), in *Works,* vol. 5,
pp. 174–75.

7. Ibid., pp. 175–76.

8. Burke, "An Appeal from the New to the Old Whigs" (1791), in *Selected
Writings,* ed. Stanlis, p. 593.

from such diversity. Suppleness rather than "logical rigidity" of mind is the distinguishing characteristic of the truly rational approach to politics. To paraphrase Burke, reason must be capable of detecting the hidden intimations as well as the surface manifestations of a political event or constellation of events.

BURKE'S CONSERVATISM

The specific character of his conservatism is nowhere more vividly revealed than in his brilliant work "An Appeal from the New to the Old Whigs" (1791). For Burke was no blind reactionary seeking to return to an illiberal past. What he sought to "conserve" was the achievement of the Glorious Revolution of 1688. Thus Burke the conservative is not the antithesis of Locke the liberal. With far greater accuracy he could be described as a conservative liberal, as a conservative interpreter of the events of 1688.

For Burke the glory of the Glorious Revolution consisted in the fact that it was not really a revolution at all. Instead, it *prevented* a revolution with respect to the basic principles of the British constitution; 1688 to Burke was "that period of our history . . . when the constitution was settled on its actual foundation."[9] Similarly, the American Revolution began as a movement to redress grievances inflicted upon Englishmen in violation of their constitutional rights and ended as a war for independence. Burke totally rejected the charge that he had been "inconsistent" in championing the cause of the Whigs in 1688 and the Americans in 1776 while condemning the French in 1789. For the French Revolution, unlike the events of 1688 and 1776, represented the complete triumph of abstract, *a priori*, "metaphysical" reasoning, which he had denounced throughout his career. Instead of seeking to vindicate and expand traditional and prescriptive "rights"—or better, achieved "privileges"—which had been proven by reason and utility to minister to the varied and legitimate interests of the citizenry, the French revolutionaries acted to destroy the old order, root and branch, and begin *de novo* on some artificial "geometric" principle.

The "Mixed Constitution"

As an "Old Whig," Burke put himself forward as a champion of "our mixed Constitution."

> The British Constitution has not been struck out at an heat by a
> set of presumptuous men, like the assembly of pettifoggers run mad

---

9. Stanlis, ed., *Selected Writings*, p. 518.

at Paris. . . . It is the result of the thoughts of many minds in many ages. It is no simple, no superficial thing, nor to be estimated by superficial understandings.[10]

The key term in Burke's constitutional conception is "balance." He therefore sought on appropriate occasions to "vindicate the three several parts on the several principles peculiarly belonging to them."[11] Monarchy (the crown), aristocracy (the House of Lords), and democracy (the House of Commons) were to be defended equally on the basis of the principles appropriate to them. Each constitutional element had its rightful powers, and the task of a wise and rational statesmanship was to preserve the balance between them by resisting the attempt of any one branch to encroach on the prerogatives of the other. Thus at various points in his long parliamentary career Burke could be found defending or attacking the crown, depending on the historical context. He was quite emphatic on this point: if he were preoccupied with "raising fences about popular privileges on one day," this did not mean that on another he "would concur with those who would pull down the throne." Similarly, if he had occasion to defend the throne on another day, "it ought not to be supposed that" he had "abandoned the rights of the people."[12]

Electoral Reform

Although Burke was bold in calling for reform of some practices and policies (discrimination against Roman Catholics, for example, and the abuse of British power in India), he was infinitely and overly cautious with respect to any attempts at electoral reform of the House of Commons. During the 1770s and 1780s he made several speeches against attempts to do away with "rotten boroughs" and to extend the suffrage. The Reform Bill of 1832 was to be the work of Bentham, ironically sponsored and administered by a Tory government. Burke the conservative, the advocate of gradual and necessary change, was untrue to his principles in opposing electoral reform.

The reason for his attitude toward electoral reform appears to have been a somewhat doctrinaire interpretation of the constitutional settlement of 1688, which Burke insisted left the British government quintessentially monarchical in form. To Burke "a monarchy is a thing perfectly susceptible of reform, perfectly susceptible of a balance of power," and "when reformed and balanced, for a great country it is the best of all

---

10. Burke, "An Appeal from the New to the Old Whigs," p. 545.
11. Ibid., p. 524.
12. Ibid., p. 525.

governments."[13] He also regarded a hereditary nobility as essential to any "rational plan of free government" because it enabled one to avoid the "spirit of levelling." As for the "democratic" element of the constitution, Burke rejected all thought of direct popular influence on government through the election of representatives bound by instructions or a "mandate." In his great speech to the electors of Bristol in 1774 he propounded a theory of representation that has come to bear his name and which presupposes the selection by an informed and restricted electorate of a representative qualified enough to vote his own judgment and morally sensitive enough to follow his conscience, rather than of a delegate who slavishly follows popular whim.

Like Hegel, Burke was not antidemocratic so much as predemocratic. We may assume that if they had lived in later times, both men would have been less convinced that monarchy was essential to a rational political order and would have taken a more positive view of later developments of liberal constitutional regimes, such as the shift of effective power to parliament and the expansion of the suffrage. As it is, their thoughts on these subjects appear today to be decidedly among the transitory aspects of their political teachings. The goal of both men to ensure that the "best men" enter politics is, on the other hand, surely a permanent preoccupation of all of us.

Natural and Civil Society

In his "Appeal from the New to the Old Whigs," Burke, looking back over his life, stated that if he could "venture to value himself on anything, it is on the virtue of consistency that he would value himself the most."[14] It would appear that he was amply justified in making this claim, for in his very first work, a parody of Bolingbroke's political teaching entitled "A Vindication of Natural Society," published in 1756, we can make out the contours of the conservatism he was to espouse with a surfeit of rhetoric in "Reflections on the Revolution in France," published in 1790.

The author of the "Vindication" repudiates "courtly philosophers" who serve only the powers that be, and calls for the vindication of the "natural rights of mankind" against all forms of despotism. No matter how structured—whether as a monarchy, aristocracy, democracy, or "mixed regime"—all political societies, including the one governed by the supposedly matchless British constitution, are in fact "tyrannies." The "Vindication" culminates in a vivid but very possibly accurate description of numerous horrors and injustices committed by governments, both

13. Ibid., p. 531.
14. Ibid., p. 524.

ancient and modern. By contrast, "natural society" is portrayed as the "reign of God."[15]

Burke's true teaching, of course, is, as we might expect from the author of the phrase "art is man's nature," the reverse of the argument expounded in the "Vindication of Natural Society." A single paragraph from the "Reflections" illustrates Burke's fundamental conviction that without the restraints and artifices of civil society, man would be degraded to the level of a beast. Then he speaks, in a remarkable phrase, of those "pleasing illusions" that "make gentle" and "beautify and soften private society." These are the social customs of deference, politeness, and chivalrous treatment of women, which together with religion and conventional morality comprise the "decent drapery of life." Now, Burke adds, the radicals and revolutionaries of his day propose "rudely" to tear off this salutary cover thrown over man's "natural" defects:

> All the decent drapery of life is to be rudely torn off. All the super-added ideas, furnished from the wardrobe of moral imagination, which the heart owns, and the understanding ratifies as necessary to cover the defects of our naked shivering nature, and to raise it to dignity in our own estimation, are to be exploded as a ridiculous, absurd, and antiquated fashion.[16]

Politics and Practical Reason

The dominant theme of Burke's political teaching, then, is that politics is an affair of practical reason. Furthermore, practical reason cannot function properly without prior attunement to an order of being that it did not make, but to which it must conform. Burke "takes it for granted" that we may

> assume that the awful Author of our being is the Author of our place in the order of existence—and that, having disposed and marshalled us by a divine tactic, not according to our will, but according to His, He has . . . virtually subjected us to act the part . . . assigned us. We have obligations to mankind at large which are not in consequence of any special voluntary pact.[17]

Burke did not hold that any and every political tradition was good. As we have seen, he was capable of scathing criticism against specific practices that had acquired the sanction of tradition. He "did not commend prejudices indiscriminately" and did not "defer to all historic

15. Burke, "A Vindication of Natural Society," in *Works*, vol. 1, pp. 37, 39, 40, 48, 50–54, 59, 66.

16. Burke, "Reflections on the Revolution in France," p. 201.

17. Burke, "An Appeal from the New to the Old Whigs," p. 538.

rights."[18] Nonetheless, Burke's pronounced conservative inclination led him, in contrast to Bentham, to give a long-established institution the benefit of the doubt and to regard the task of political reason ordinarily to be the elucidation of the implications of a tradition and the application of the principles thus discovered to the particular concrete situation. As he expressed it, "When ancient opinions and rules of life are taken away, the loss cannot possibly be estimated. From that moment we have no compass to govern us; nor can we know distinctly to what port we steer."[19]

Tradition. Burke thought of tradition on two levels: that of a nation and that of a civilization. One of the principal reasons he was so alarmed by the French Revolution was that to him it constituted a direct threat to the basic principles of civilization itself:

> Nothing is more certain, than that our manners, our civilization, and all the good things . . . connected [thereto] . . . have, in this European world of ours, depended for ages upon two principles; and were indeed the result of both combined: I mean the spirit of a gentleman, and the spirit of religion.[20]

The English national society, then, participated in a common civilizational ethos, or cultural whole, which was the result of the interpenetration of the Judeo-Christian culture with a complex of manners and customs emanating from the late Middle Ages, loosely known as "chivalry." This ethos of European civilization is absorbed by a kind of cultural osmosis, and becomes so inextricably a part of the minds of people that they are unable to distinguish between what they learn from others and what they learn from their "own meditation."[21] Man is no solipsist, then; his individual reason develops in the context of a collective reason that has been developed over the centuries and transmitted as a cultural legacy from generation to generation. To neglect or destroy this legacy—as Burke believed the French revolutionaries and Enlightenment or "Parisian" philosophers in general had set out to do—is to destroy the very environment in which the practical reason of individual men takes root and flourishes.

National Society

Burke's concept of a national society was similarly organic, if you will. Monarch, clergy, hereditary nobility, "natural aristocracy," and decent, obedient common folk of his generation were knitted together into a

---

18. Wilkins, *Burke's Political Philosophy*, p. 251.
19. Burke, "Reflections on the Revolution in France," p. 203.
20. Ibid., p. 204.
21. Ibid., p. 238.

single body politic, at once temporal and spiritual. The religious establishment (the Church of England) gave visible evidence of the vital role
of religion in national life, respecting all the while the rights of Roman
Catholics and Protestant dissenters. Although nominally a Whig, and
therefore a follower of Locke's contractual polities, Burke originated
what was to become the Tory conception of society. It is "wise Prejudice," he avowed, to venerate and to demonstrate loyalty to the nation;
one should "approach to the faults of the state as to the wounds of a
father, with pious awe and trembling solicitude."[22]

> Society is indeed a contract [he wrote in one of the most famous
> and eloquent passages of the "Reflections"]. Subordinate contracts
> for objects of mere occasional interest may be dissolved at pleasure—
> but the state ought not to be considered as nothing better than a
> partnership agreement in a trade of pepper and coffee, calico or
> tobacco, or some other such low concern. . . . It is to be looked on
> with other reverence; because it is not a partnership in things sub-
> servient only to gross animal existence of a temporary and perishable
> nature. [Here Burke draws on Hooker far more than on Locke.]
> It is a partnership in all science; a partnership in every virtue, and
> in all perfection. As the ends of such a partnership cannot be ob-
> tained in many generations, it becomes a partnership not only be-
> tween those who are living, but between those who are living, those
> who are dead, and those who are to be born. Each contract of each
> particular state is but a clause in the great primeval contract of
> eternal society, linking the lower with the higher nature, connecting
> the visible and invisible world, according to a fixed compact sanc-
> tioned by the inviolable oath which holds all physical and all moral
> natures, each in their appointed place. . . .[23]

In this eloquent page Burke sums up his opposition to the spirit of
radical innovation and to any conception that the present generation has
any right fundamentally to alter the political inheritance of the past. Just
as Locke appeared to emphasize the universal aspects of the revolution
of 1688, Burke tried to traditionalize that revolution and to regard it
simply as designed to preserve—and enlarge—the "prescriptive" rights of
Englishmen. Three key words in Burke's political vocabulary were
prescription, presumption, and prejudice. "Prescription" had to do with
rights—or privileges—which are long-established and recognized by the
state. (Burke tended to use the terms "rights" and "privileges" interchangeably to mean a reasonable claim by a segment of the society that
is established and vindicated in history.) "Presumption" referred to the

22. Ibid., p. 233.
23. Ibid., pp. 233–34.

disposition to view any long-existing practice or institution as rightful and beneficial to society. Burke did not employ "prejudice" in the wholly pejorative way in which we tend to use it today, as when we speak of racial or religious prejudice; to him the word meant rather a settled inclination or habit of mind that prompts the individual to respond in a predictable and salutary manner to a given situation without taking the trouble to inquire into his reasons for doing so. Prejudice to Burke is virtuous habit; of all the prejudices of a free and rational society (for he did indeed believe that prejudice and reason were compatible), religion was "the grand prejudice, and that which holds all other prejudice together."

Tradition and Innovation. But what about those countries less fortunate than Great Britain in their inherited political institutions? Would Burke have replied with Horace, "If Sparta is your legacy, make the most of it"? Or would he have favored the decisive intervention of self-conscious, rational leadership to erect new foundations that in time would have the sanction of tradition? The whole drift of his thought is against the idea of an innovative leader or founder-legislator such as Machiavelli and Rousseau regarded as crucial to the formation of a free society. For Burke there is no single legislator: the legislator is rather a whole succession of generations of men who without being fully conscious of what they are doing manage to achieve an acceptable balance between the requirements of freedom and those of order. England had been fortunate in having a political tradition of freedom, and in each of its great constitutional crises its leaders could draw strength from the inherited predisposition to a balanced and mixed constitution to resolve the nation's problems. There is one passage in the "Reflections" where Burke does deal briefly with the problem of conscious political construction:

> To make a government requires no great prudence. Settle the seat of power; teach obedience; and the work is done. To give freedom is still more easy. It is not necessary to guide; it only requires to let go the rein. But to form a *free government;* that is, to temper together those opposite elements of liberty and restraint in one consistent work, requires much thought, deep reflection, a sagacious, powerful, and combining mind. *This I do not find in those who take the lead in the* [French] *national assembly.*[24]

As the last sentence indicates, although Burke did not have any confidence in the ability of the French revolutionary leaders to "form a free government," by implication he might conceivably have had con-

---

24. Ibid., p. 484 (emphasis added).

fidence in another set of legislators. Presumably, then, he was not opposed to all deliberate and conscious political innovation. Rather, where innovation is necessary because of the absence of a settled indigenous political tradition or because of the defectiveness (or despotic character) of that tradition, he looked for innovators who would be "rational" in the larger sense of the term as we have discovered him to employ it. They would be men of moderation who understood the need for ministering to a variety of customs and occupations in the specific society on behalf of which they worked. They would seek to combine freedom and order in the specific societal context concerned rather than to impose some arbitrary plan of abstract "reason." And they would draw on the intellectual and spiritual resources of their particular civilization. Despite the intensity of his patriotism, Burke had an inkling of the principle that Toynbee was to work out in his *Study of History*: that civilizations more than nations are the "intelligible units" of history. Even when a new state—to advert for a moment to contemporary conditions in our world of "newly emergent nations"—comes into being, apparently lacking a tradition for governing its own affairs, it can draw on the religious and cultural insights that it shares with numerous other political entities of the same civilization.

National Societies of Asia. Burke was not so parochial as to regard a concern for just and lawful government as the exclusive property of the West. He would have found curious Hegel's conception of the politics of the Orient as committed only to the untrammeled power of a single despotic ruler. In advocating the impeachment of Warren Hastings for his tyrannical oppression in India, Burke observed that "nothing is more false than that despotism is the constitution of any country in Asia...." He went on to cite the deep consciousness of the universe as an ordered whole and the insistence on a government according to legal codes and prescriptions in both the Moslem and Hindu religious traditions. "I challenge the whole race of man," he proclaimed, "to show me any of the Oriental governors claiming to themselves a right to act by arbitrary will." In its dedication to rule by law, "Asia is enlightened ... as well as Europe."[25]

The Conscience of a Conservative

Burke was a great and eloquent stylist whose fiercely polemical orientation at times interfered with his attempt to achieve a theoretical understanding of politics. He lacked what has been called the ironic quality of

---

25. Burke, "Speech on the Impeachment of Warren Hastings" (February 16, 1788), in *Selected Writings,* ed. Stanlis, pp. 399–440.

mind, and so it was only with great difficulty that he was able to attain a critical distance even from his own commitments. Other preintellectual qualities, however, enabled him not infrequently to remedy this defect. Although a staunch believer in and practitioner of partisan politics, Burke was at times disinterested in the best sense of that word. Of a fiercely independent spirit, he possessed the courage to attack his own party, country, or cause if he considered it to be violating his conceptions of the sound principles of a free and moderate government. He was rarely more eloquent than when, during one of his speeches concerning British misrule in India, he unequivocally exposed and denounced the blatant plunder and crass exploitation of the Indian economy which had been carried out by the British East India Company.[26] Nor did he hesitate to denounce as against all reason and justice the "Popery Laws" and other devices of discrimination against Roman Catholics.[27] Neither of these causes was likely to gain him any mileage in the House of Commons. Burke was not always right, but his basic humanity and generosity of temperament helped to ensure that on balance his political career and writings are of great benefit to all who study and are influenced by them. He was perhaps the greatest of the conservatives; many of those who today answer to that designation sorely need the basic preintellectual qualities that Burke exhibited with such distinction.

MAISTRE, BONALD, AND CUOCO

Although there were many thinkers across the Channel who opposed the type of political rationalism represented by the French Revolution, none of those who wrote in the immediate postrevolutionary period created an authentically conservative political style comparable to Burke's. If any continental thinker of the period resembles Burke, it is Hegel. And yet Hegel's dictum "The real is the rational and the rational the real" was for its author more than a tautology. As Pelczynski has pointed out in his introduction to a recent edition of Hegel's political writings,[28] Hegel was particularly preoccupied with the *reformation* of existing arbitrary and outmoded political practices; he was much more of a political reformer than Burke, and his attitude toward the French Revolution was, especially in his youth, far more positive than Burke's.

---

26. Burke, "Speech on the Affairs of India" (June 25, 1783), in ibid., pp. 356–59.

27. Burke, "Fragments of a Tract Relative to the Laws Against Popery in Ireland" (1765), pp. 211–27.

28. Z. A. Pelczynski, Introduction to *Hegel's Political Writings*, trans. T. M. Knox (New York: Oxford University Press, 1964).

Joseph de Maistre

The chief architects of the continental reaction to the French Revolution were two Frenchmen, Comte Joseph de Maistre and Viscomte Louis de Bonald. Maistre, an émigré who spent the years after the revolution in Italy and Russia, was a strange and moody man of considerable literary talent. His principal political works are his essays "On the Generative Principle of Political Constitutions," "Considerations on France," and "On the Pope." His approach is captured well in the opening paragraph to the first of these works:

> One of the greatest errors of a century which professed them all [i.e., the eighteenth century] was to believe that a political constitution could be created and written *a priori*, whereas reason and experience unite in proving that a constitution is a divine work and that precisely the most fundamental and essentially constitutional of a nation's laws could not possibly be written.[29]

It would be a mistake to call Maistre an original political thinker. In essence, what he did was to caricature the leading ideas of Enlightenment political thought and come up with a counterenlightenment. His approach is organic rather than contractual, communitarian rather than individualistic, hierarchical rather than egalitarian, traditionalist rather than revolutionary, religious rather than atheistic, emotional rather than logic-chopping, and aesthetic rather than utilitarian.

What is clear above all is that Maistre hated the French Revolution and all its works. He regarded it as an unprecedented act of impiety and rebellion by sinful and evil men. To him it proved conclusively that only God, through his providential work in history, could fashion a society and a people. When men attempt to challenge the providential design of God by leveling the social order, eliminating the established church, and executing the divinely sanctioned monarch, the result is scarcely the vindication of man against God; rather it demonstrates the *powerlessness* of man, alone and unaided by God, to create anything noble or lasting. Man has power, to be sure, but it is power to destroy, not to create. In France, according to Maistre, a kind of "philosophical frenzy" overtook men, which resulted in God's punishment of men through the destruction of the political order.

Maistre's thought is pervaded by a dour pessimism more appropriate to a caricature of Calvinism than to the ultramontane Catholicism he so militantly and intolerantly professed. He was a confused man who could

---

29. Joseph de Maistre, "On the Generative Principle of Political Constitutions," in *Joseph de Maistre: On God and Society*, ed. Elisha Greifer (Chicago: Regnery, 1959), p. 3.

never quite make up his mind whether he wanted to champion extreme nationalism under the French king or a political theocracy headed by the pope. Although we may assume that he was religiously sincere, the effect of his teaching was to reduce religion to an *instrumentum regni*. One could derive from Maistre the conclusion that religion was to be defended because it was traditional rather than because it was true—except that he saw little difference between the two. He was able to accept the most stupendous horrors of history as contributions to the divine plan for men. At times he seemed almost to exult in the repression and violence with which history is filled. He was in fact the supreme apologist for a repressive society. For Maistre, man in the mass is so evil and sinful that he must constantly be held at bay. In a famous parable he likened the executioner to the most exalted of mankind's benefactors. Maistre's commendation (in his "Soirées de St-Petersbourg") of horrible public executions was no doubt offered primarily for literary effect; nonetheless, the gory passage fits well with the general tenor of his beliefs. There is, then, an aspect of Orwell's *1984* pervading Maistre's thought; in part his thinking seems inspired by a cynical and misanthropic counsel to men to love their slavery or else. It is not surprising that his political teachings should have constituted one of the roots of the fascist antihumanism of Maurras and the *Action Française*.

Louis de Bonald

Bonald was a drier writer than Maistre, but he conveyed essentially the same message. *"Je n'ai rien pensé que vous ne l'ayez écrit; je n'ai rien écrit que vous ne l'ayez pensé"* (I have never thought anything that you have not written, nor written anything that you have not thought), wrote Bonald to Maistre. To this encomium Maistre wrote on the margin of the letter, "This flattering assertion admits of some exceptions."[30] (Presumably this refers to Maistre's relatively more absolutist tendencies, in regard to the powers of both the monarch and the pope.)

A characteristic of Bonald's political thought was his "ternary system," or penchant for perceiving events as part of a threefold system (cause-means-effect). Thus in regard to life, God is the cause, Christ the means, and the world the effect; to the family, man is the cause, woman the means, children the effect; to the political order, the king is the cause, the aristocracy the means, and the conservation and reproduction of the people the effect.[31] Bonald's teaching is one of the prime examples in the history of political thought of the abuse of metaphysics. The order

---

30. Cited in Émile Faguet, *Politiques et moralistes du dix-neuvième siècle* (Paris: Nouvelle Bibliothèque Littéraire, 1899), p. 69.

31. Ibid., pp. 76–77.

of being is invoked as justification for a particular set of political institutions. This is an ideological defense of the *ancien régime*—or rather of an idealized version of the *ancien régime* as a harmonious balance among monarchy, aristocracy, and the estates general, with monarchy taking the leading role.

For Bonald there were only two types of constitution: one good (corresponding to the "monarchical principle") and the other bad (all others). Thus there are "constituted peoples" (who live under a hereditary monarchy) and "unconstituted peoples." He agreed fully with Maistre that constitutions are not "made" or invented by men, but grow and evolve over centuries. It is true that they change, but only imperceptibly, once they are established according to the divine principle.

Bonald had an extraordinary interest in languages. Language is the gift of God, the vehicle for expressing ideas "natural" to man. Both Maistre and Bonald drew attention to the fact that man cannot invent a viable language but rather inherits one, provided by society, that has developed over the centuries. If our very language is derived from society, how "natural" that man should accept the other features of the God-created social order! Man to Bonald exists only in and through society. He has no separate personal existence. To destroy society, as it has been traditionally—and divinely—ordered, is for man to commit suicide. Thus political rebellion is a manifestation of the death wish. The more we pull away from the traditional order, the closer we approach death; the more we acknowledge our submission to and dependence on the existing order, the more we are enabled to live a truly "free" life.

Not all writers on the continent opposed to the French Revolution professed so rigid and wooden a conception of tradition as did Maistre and Bonald, nor did they all invoke religious piety to sanction the continuance of a social order that rested ultimately on inequality and hereditary privilege. The movement of history "from status to contract," as Sir Henry Maine put it, was not an unmixed blessing, but the difficulty with a society based primarily on status is that it ultimately makes sense only to those born at the top. The kind of romantic posturings and invocations of a vanished past found in the pages of Maistre and Bonald could not as such constitute a lasting contribution to the history of modern political thought.

Vincenzo Cuoco

Vincenzo Cuoco, born in Naples, a political writer of considerable acuity, has with some justice been called the "Italian Edmund Burke." We do not find any Maistrean tilting with windmills in Cuoco's thought, but rather a recognition of the need for a more broadly based empiricism in the implementation of political reforms than was exhibited by the French in the territories "liberated" by Napoleon's conquering armies. In the best known of Cuoco's works we encounter the following set of aphorisms:

> Constitutions are similar to garments: it is necessary that every individual, in every stage of his growth, have his own, which, if one should wish to give to others, would fit badly. It is impossible to fashion a single garment for all men. . . . The will to reform all is the same as the will to destroy all. . . . A constitution that is good for everyone is good for no one. . . . Men must be taken as they eternally are and will continue to be: full of vice and error. . . . Perfection is not the destiny of man. . . . Only someone like Condorcet could conceive of a finite being such as man to be capable of infinite perfectibility.[32]

Cuoco's "Letters to Russo" were probably written in 1796 or 1797. They were primarily concerned with refuting a proposal for constitutional reform put forward by another Neapolitan, Mario Pagano, who was deeply imbued with French Enlightenment liberalism. Cuoco made clear that he did not oppose reform, and in fact put forward his own proposals for political and administrative reform of the region. Rather, he insisted that one must not mechanically impose a constitution on a people, but must know its cultural substratum, the "basis" of any constitution. He held that no matter how corrupt a society might be, it surely possessed some customs worth preserving, as well as some glorious traditions. These customs and traditions should be emphasized and built upon.

By the "basis of a constitution" (*la base di una costituzione*) Cuoco meant the complex of mores and traditions that antedates any written constitution and which is therefore "more sacred" than the constitution. "Not even a despot is able to alter it," he observed. If a constitution is "too philosophical" it will be without a foundation because it is "too far from the senses and customs of the people." It is "very difficult to make a new constitution and very dangerous to change an old one." The French Declaration of the Rights of Man is too abstract to be of any use; better is Magna Charta or Roman law, in which the "rights" discussed are concrete and have already developed in history.[33]

Thus far Cuoco appears in accord with Burke, but it would be misleading to conclude that this is all there is to the Italian's political

---

32. Vincenzo Cuoco, "Lettere a Russo," in *Vincenzo Cuoco: Saggio storico sulla revoluzione napoletana del 1799*, ed. F. Nicolini (Bari: Laterza, 1913), pp. 219–20.

33. Ibid., pp. 245–46.

thought. Cuoco was more than an imitator of Burke; he possessed an exceptional ability to combine ideas from a number of sources and come up with a position that was at once realistic and innovative. Indeed, "realist" is probably a more accurate label for him than "conservative." His opposition to the French Revolution was not so thoroughgoing as Burke's, and he was no champion of feudal privileges. His political thought shows the influence of both Machiavelli and the great eighteenth-century Neapolitan historian Giambattista Vico. From Machiavelli he derived the idea of the legislator who can through dramatic means draw a people out of its lethargy and recover the *virtù* or public-spiritedness of the great times of antiquity. From Vico he absorbed the insight that seemingly irrational and haphazard customs possess their own rationality, and learned to think of history as a process of cyclical development. Cuoco was also influenced by the French school of *idéologues* headed by Destutt de Tracy, and he had ambitious thoughts about revolutionizing the educational methods of the Neapolitan schools. Although he was not a utopian, Cuoco did write a utopian book entitled *Plato in Italy*, which was widely interpreted during the *risorgimento* as a call to the creation of a unified and independent Italian nation-state.

With Cuoco we have definitely moved into the nineteenth century with its greater attention to history and to the process of development of institutions within history. His thought mirrors the tensions of a man who wishes to act on the basis of a sober appreciation of the political realities but who also sees the possibility of changing those realities in important ways. As one of the earliest intellectual figures in the movement to found an Italian nation and as an incisive political mind, Vincenzo Cuoco deserves to be rescued from the neglect he has suffered everywhere outside Italy.

9

Utilitarianism:
Bentham and Mill

Two terms that immediately come to mind in connection with Jeremy Bentham and John Stuart Mill are "utilitarianism" and "philosophic radicalism." James Mill (John Stuart's father), George Grote, Charles Butler, Sir William Molesworth, John Stuart Mill himself, and a number of other British intellectuals constituted "an intellectual coterie in the 1820s."[1] They all drew inspiration from Jeremy Bentham; their goal was through peaceful means basically to restructure British politics along more democratic and humanitarian lines. They were in favor of greatly expanding the suffrage, of frequent parliamentary elections, and of sweeping changes in the penal and legal systems.

I have chosen to concentrate on Bentham and J. S. Mill among this group because, despite James Mill's leading role, Bentham provided the original intellectual inspiration for the group and the younger Mill was the most critical and creative mind among the philosophic radicals. Actually, J. S. Mill's relationship to utilitarianism—which we might call the "philosophical" base of philosophical radicalism—was highly ambiguous. Although he never ceased to employ the language of utility, he ended by totally rejecting Bentham's thesis that no qualitative distinctions could be drawn between pleasures. In fact, as Himmelfarb and others have pointed out,[2] there are two sides to Mill's political thought, one oriented toward institutional reform and the other more concerned with the wider cultural dimensions of social life (Coleridge's influence is evident here). Practically speaking, Mill continued to work with the radicals for their political objectives, although he did not actually agree with the strictly rationalistic "one man, one vote" principle.

---

1. Joseph Hamburger, *Intellectuals in Politics: John Stuart Mill and the Philosophic Radicals* (New Haven: Yale University Press, 1965), p. 1.

2. In John Stuart Mill, *Essays on Politics and Culture,* ed. Gertrude Himmelfarb (New York: Doubleday, 1963).

JEREMY BENTHAM

Jeremy Bentham was born in 1748 and died in 1832, the year of the passage of the English Reform Bill, which brought the English electoral system into closer alignment with the "objective" principles he had espoused during his long and eventful life as a political writer and reformer. Bentham was a liberal and a humanitarian; he is one of the great followers in the tradition of Lockean political rationalism, even though he himself claimed David Hume as his principal intellectual progenitor.

Bentham has aroused fierce antagonism in all manner of men for both the style and the substance of his teaching. Some have accused him of the crassest philistinism (for example, his celebrated remark that "pushpin"—a popular game at the time—"is as good as poetry," if it affords the individual engaging in it an identical amount of pleasure). Others find his psychology hopelessly narrow and inhospitable to any sublime expression of genius. Goethe referred to Bentham as "that frightfully radical ass," while Marx described him as "the insipid leather-tongued oracle of the commonplace bourgeois intelligence... a genius in the way of bourgeois stupidity." One literary critic suggested, "His works have been translated into French—they ought to be translated into English."[3]

Bentham also had his admirers, however. The sage of Bloomsbury was widely hailed by contemporary legislators on several continents as a genius on legal reform and as one of the great champions of democratic thought. Perhaps it is as a legal reformer rather than as a political theorist that we ought principally to think of him. Sir Henry Maine once wrote, "I do not know a single law reform effected since Bentham's day which cannot be traced to his influence." Nonetheless, much of what he wrote was couched in the language of political theory, and in any event, however "antimetaphysical" Bentham was, there is an implicit philosophical anthropology at the base of his teaching which calls for critical scrutiny.

The Individual and Society

In a fundamental sense Bentham continues the individualist, nominalist approach introduced by Hobbes and revised by Locke. For him as for Hobbes, the individual is all and society only a fiction. Bentham defined community as a "fictitious *body*, composed of the individual persons who are considered as constituting... its members." The "interest of the com-

---

3. Mary Peter Mach, ed., *A Bentham Reader* (New York: Pegasus, 1969), Introduction, p. viii.

munity" was for him nothing but "the sum of the interests of the several members who compose it." We could not be further from Rousseau's idea of the general will.

Bentham also agreed with Hobbes that man is by definition a self-regarding animal. Men, he wrote, seek before all else to maximize pleasure and minimize pain. As he expressed the matter in the famous opening sentences of *An Introduction to the Principles of Morals and Legislation*:

> Nature has placed mankind under the governance of two sovereign masters, *pain* and *pleasure*. It is for them alone to point out what we ought to do, as well as to determine what we shall do. On the one hand the standard of right and wrong, on the other the chain of causes and effects, are fastened to their throne. They govern us in all we do, in all we say, in all we think: every effort we can make to throw off our subjection, will serve but to demonstrate and confirm it. In words a man may pretend to abjure their empire, but in reality he will remain subject to it all the while. The *principle* of *utility* recognizes this subjection, and assumes it for the foundation of that system, the object of which is to rear the fabric of felicity by the hands of reason and law. . . .[4]

Utility

Bentham proceeds further to define utility as

> that property in any object, whereby it tends to produce benefit, advantage, pleasure, good, or happiness (all this in the present case comes to the same thing) or (what comes again to the same thing) to prevent the happening of mischief, pain, evil, or unhappiness to the party whose interest is considered. . . .[5]

With his no-nonsense, antimetaphysical tone, Bentham advances a political teaching based on the utilitarian or "felicific" calculus. He was unambiguous and emphatic in asserting that (1) pleasure, happiness, goodness, benefit, advantage, and so on are interchangeable terms; (2) pleasure is quantifiable: it can be measured; (3) the guiding principle of action for both individuals and governments should be to maximize pleasure and minimize pain; and (4) "it is the greatest happiness of the greatest number that is the measure of right and wrong"[6] of human

---

4. Jeremy Bentham, *An Introduction to the Principles of Morals and Legislation*, in *A Fragment on Government, and An Introduction to the Principles of Morals and Legislation*, ed. W. Harrison (Oxford: Blackwell, 1948), chap. 1, p. 125.

5. Ibid., p. 126.

6. The "greatest happiness" principle is espoused in the Preface to Bentham's *Fragment on Government*, in ibid., p. 3.

action in every situation, and in particular when governmental action is called for.

Pleasure as the Summum Bonum. As mentioned earlier, it is precisely this insistence upon making pleasure as such the *summum bonum* and denying that there are qualitative distinctions between pleasures that led the younger Mill to reject the Benthamite system. Mill, as we shall see, in effect returned to Aristotelian ethics in this regard. Aristotle had insisted that not all objects valued as good by men are equally valuable; that the goods of the mind are qualitatively superior to the pleasures of the body, since they are more lasting and correspond to the distinctively higher capacities of man: that is, the mind (*nous*) and its faculty of reason (*logos*). The measure of right action for Aristotle is the *spoudaios*, or fully developed man, who has experienced the full range of pleasures available to man and so is competent to rank them. In Bentham's work the *spoudaios* is replaced by the *demos*; right action is not to be measured by its conformity with our better selves, but by its enhancement of the pleasure of the many. "Ethics," Bentham declared, ". . . may be defined [as] the art of directing men's actions to the production of the greatest possible quantity of happiness, on the part of those whose interest is in view."[7]

Bentham's basic assumptions, then, appear to lead us to a vulgar democratism wherein the lowest common denominator of mass belief and taste seems to call the tune in matters of social policy. For individuals as well, Benthamism would appear to justify the avoidance of exertion in the pursuit of excellence and settling instead for the self-indulgence of "pleasure," and a narrow, philistine, and pedestrian pleasure at that.

To interpret Bentham in this fashion, however, while legitimate up to a point—and it must be observed that he left himself open to such an interpretation through his incautious and apodictic pronouncements— would be to overlook the fact that he was above all a practical reformer rather than a political theorist or philosopher. It would also lead to the neglect of the authentic humanism at the root of his teaching.

Utility as a Democratic Principle. In his dry way, Bentham cared about man, the human person, and his dignity. In his well-known "greatest happiness" principle, Bentham attempted to give voice to his fundamental egalitarianism. He wished to extend such felicities as are afforded by this mortal life to greater and greater numbers of people, and to reform the laws so that both their benefits and their burdens would be more equitably distributed.

---

7. *Introduction to Principles of Morals and Legislation*, in ibid., chap. 17, p. 411.

There is good reason to call Bentham a democratized Hobbes. Both men shared an atomistic metaphysics from which they derived a radically individualist view of politics. Both are vulnerable to the charge of having been insensitive to the danger that uncautious application of their principles might well lead to tyranny, but they were united in their intention to widen the private space in which man might seek his own fulfillment, insofar as the limitations and instabilities of the human condition admit fulfillment. Both looked to utility as the ultimate foundation of government. Bentham, furthermore, was not always inclined to the view that the people themselves were the best judges and protectors of their own interests. Earlier in his career Bentham hoped to see his proposals for reforms in the legal system and penal code adopted by an enlightened parliament, and he spent large sums of money in connection with his Panopticon (or model prison) scheme with the understanding that parliament's support would be forthcoming. Only in 1809, after his hopes were dashed by parliament, did he turn resolutely to champion the cause of universal (male) suffrage and annual parliaments in his *Catechism of Parliamentary Reform.*

Utility and Natural Rights. Nonetheless, there are also important differences between Bentham and Hobbes. Bentham develops only one side, as it were, of Hobbes's thought. Hobbes, as we well know, attached immense importance to the hypothetical social contract in tracing the roots of political obligation. Bentham, on the other hand, followed Hume in denouncing the contract hypothesis as a useless fiction. The elements of "moral"—as opposed to expediential—obligation in Hobbes's teaching are ignored. Bentham would have nothing to do with the language of natural law or natural right; natural rights were rejected as "nonsense—nonsense upon stilts." Nonetheless, it is quite possible that Bentham was a natural-rights man in spite of himself. The deficiencies of a strict adherence to utilitarianism—a position that wholly forgoes any appeal to justice or moral norms, emphasizing only considerations of utility—have been so well chronicled that we need not preoccupy ourselves with them here.[8]

Liberalism and Reform

For all his deficiencies as a theorist—and he can hardly be ranked as a good one—Bentham deserves to be hailed as a friend of liberty and an archenemy of unjustified privilege. It is sometimes said that his passion

---

8. See, for example, the acute analysis of Bentham's felicific calculus in J. H. Hallowell, *Main Currents of Modern Political Thought* (New York: Holt, 1950), and of the difficulties inherent in J. S. Mill's partial adherence to utilitarianism in Robert Paul Wolff, *The Poverty of Liberalism* (Boston: Beacon Press, 1968), chap. 1.

for mathematical precision in the measurement of "amounts" of pleasure or pain smacked of social engineering and illiberal scientism.[9] To read him so is in my judgment to read him too dourly and literally. There is concern with the authentic art—instead of the pseudoscience—of politics in Bentham. Bentham, after all, was a great *liberal*. He eloquently defended the principles of representative government, free and periodic elections, the responsibility of the governors to the governed, the liberty of the press, the "liberty of public association," and the security of subjects from arbitrary action by government.[10]

Bentham was also a great reformer, inspired with zeal to remove irrational accretions to the English constitution as it had evolved over the centuries. His temperament could not have been more different from Burke's. Burke venerated tradition and wanted change to be gradual and slow. Bentham had an immediate suspicion that any institution that had been in existence for centuries needed reformation from the bottom up. Burke admired continuity and spoke of a contract between the living, the dead, and those yet to be born. Bentham wanted to wipe the slate clean of inherited abuses, to make a clean break with all those practices that had hindered the "greatest happiness of the greatest number." Like radicals of today, he was less impressed by the achievements of the past than by its errors, missed opportunities, toleration of intolerable abuses, and ignorance of what constitutes human happiness. He saw his generation as a watershed in the history of mankind: the age of "steam-intellect-improvement" would dramatically modify the human environment for the better, he overconfidently believed.

Despite his tendency to oversimplify, Bentham remains one of the great exponents of· what can be called the liberal-radical political style. His is a position not without merit, and one that may seem of particular relevance today, even though much of the substance of his political thought seems in need of thoroughgoing revision.

JOHN STUART MILL

John Stuart Mill received virtually his entire education under the strict supervision of his father, James Mill, the author of the well-known *Essay on Government* and a prominent "philosophical radical" and disciple of Bentham. Despite the enormous influence that his father's personality and

---

9. See, for example, the harsh judgment on Bentham's work in Shirley Robin Letwin, *The Pursuit of Certainty* (Cambridge: At the University Press, 1965), p. 188.

10. Bentham, *Fragment on Government*, pp. 94–95.

learning exercised on him, however, John Stuart Mill was a political writer of a fundamentally different sort. Where James Mill was simplistic, abstract, aprioristic, and narrow in his political speculations, John Stuart was eclectic, open, complex, and often empirical. And yet, although he left the rigid utilitarianism of both Bentham and his father behind, he always shared with them an interest in reform and continued to use the language if not the substance of utility. Gertrude Himmelfarb and others have claimed that there were two John Stuart Mills, one liberal-radical and the other conservative. The conservative is supposedly the Mill who was interested in culture and in elevating the intellectual and spiritual quality of existence. Actually, however, as C. L. Ten of the University of Singapore has demonstrated quite convincingly, such a dichotomy is forced. Even in the writings of the so-called liberal-radical or middle period of his life, one finds the same concern for excellence and quality that animates Mill's essays on Bentham and "The Spirit of the Times."[11]

Mill wrote upon a considerable variety of subjects, including himself, but his most important works for the historian of political thought are *Utilitarianism* and *On Liberty*. The former essay was published after the latter, but inasmuch as it succinctly illustrates the differences between the utilitarianism of Bentham and Mill, let us begin with it.

Utilitarianism

The opening paragraph of *Utilitarianism* is a vivid illustration of the continuity of the great "conversation of mankind." For here Mill deals with the age-old problem of the highest good or *summum bonum,* which, as we have seen, has been at the root of all political theory since its inception with Plato and Aristotle. According to Mill,

> From the dawn of philosophy, the question concerning the *summum bonum* . . . has been accounted the main problem in speculative thought, has occupied the most gifted intellects, and divided them into sects and schools, carrying on a vigorous warfare against one another. And after more than two thousand years the same discussions continue. . . .[12]

The Qualities of Pleasures. In choosing to enter the lists with so many other contenders in search of the fundamental principle of ethics, Mill is aware that the very variety of opinions about the nature of the

---

11. C. L. Ten, "Mill and Liberty," *Journal of the History of Ideas,* 30 (January–March 1969): 47–68.

12. John Stuart Mill, *Utilitarianism,* in *Utilitarianism, Liberty, and Representative Government* (New York: Everyman's Library, Dutton, 1950), p. 1.

summum bonum raises the problem of whether it is possible to judge among these opinions and if so whether all or only some persons are qualified to judge. Mill's answer is essentially the same as Aristotle's (in the *Nicomachaean Ethics*): Not all men are equally competent to judge between rival claimants for the role of highest good; only those "equally acquainted with, and equally capable of appreciating and enjoying," both physical and intellectual pleasures can judge their relative qualities.[13]

That Mill chose to distinguish between pleasures on the basis of *quality* as well as *quantity* meant, of course, the complete subversion of Bentham's elaborately contrived felicific calculus. For if pleasures differ in quality as well as in quantity, and if only those men who have experienced the entire range of pleasures and are capable of reflecting upon and coherently articulating their experience are capable of judging quality, then the legislator can no longer (if he ever could) determine governmental policy on the basis of "the greatest happiness of the greatest number." In fact, Mill replaces Bentham's "greatest happiness of the greatest number" with "greatest happiness" *per se*.[14] Utility or happiness continues to be defined as pleasure, but pleasures are qualitatively distinguishable:

> According to the Greatest Happiness Principle ... the ultimate end, with reference to and for the sake of which all other things are desirable (whether we are considering our own good or that of other people), is an existence exempt as far as possible from pain, and as rich as possible in enjoyments, both in point of quantity and quality; the test of quality, and the rule for measuring it against quantity, being the preference felt by those who in their opportunities of experience, to which must be added their habits of self-consciousness and self-observation, are best furnished with the means of comparison.[15]

Perhaps Mill's most pungent rejection of the leveling tendencies in Bentham's felicific calculus is his observation that

> It is better to be a human being dissatisfied than a pig satisfied; better to be Socrates dissatisfied than a fool satisfied. And if the fool, or the pig, are of a different opinion, it is because they only know their own side of the question. The other party to the comparison knows both sides.[16]

---

13. Ibid., p. 10. Aristotle had indicated that the "mature man" (*spoudaios*) is the "measure of right and wrong."

14. Ibid., pp. 10, 14.

15. Ibid., p. 14.

16. Ibid., p. 12.

Quality and the Common Man.   All of this sounds elitist to our contemporary democratic ears, and indeed some writers have interpreted the writings of the supposedly liberal and democratic Mill as an attack on the common man.[17] Mill himself, however, like his great contemporaries Acton and Tocqueville, did not conceive of the problem as one of democracy vs. excellence. He rather saw the supreme political task to be the fusion of quality and popular participation, or the dissemination of the experience of the noblest and most excellent pursuits of man to the widest possible circle of human beings. Indeed, Mill held that a level of "mental cultivation" sufficient to give its possessor an "intelligent interest" in the creative manifestations in art and thought of his civilization could and should "be the inheritance of every one born in a civilized country." The same was true of moral life; most men are capable of being drawn out of a petty and crippling egotism.

> In a world in which there is so much to interest, so much to enjoy, and so much also to correct and improve, every one who has this moderate amount of moral and intellectual requisites is capable of an existence which may be called enviable; and unless such a person, through bad laws, or subjection to the will of others, is denied the liberty to use the sources of happiness within his reach, he will not fail to find this enviable existence, if he escape the positive evils of life. . . .[18]

Mill is at pains to demonstrate in this essay that the "utilitarian standard" is very far removed from egotism and selfishness:

> . . . The happiness which forms the utilitarian standard of what is right in conduct, is not the agent's own happiness, but that of all concerned. As between his own happiness and that of others, utilitarianism requires him to be as strictly impartial as a disinterested and benevolent spectator. In the golden rule of Jesus of Nazareth, we read the complete spirit of the ethics of utility. To do as you would be done by, and to love your neighbour as yourself, constitute the ideal perfection of utilitarian morality.[19]

Education and opinion, Mill argues, should have an elevating influence on the development of human character through stressing the "indissoluble association" between the individual's own happiness and "the good of the whole."[20]

---

17. See Letwin, *Pursuit of Certainty*, p. 301. See also the judicious remarks on Letwin's book in Ten, "Mill and Liberty."

18. Mill, *Utilitarianism*, p. 18.

19. Ibid., p. 21.

20. Ibid.

On Liberty

On Liberty is Mill's political masterpiece; although written in 1859, it is still relevant to contemporary problems. The great themes of individual liberty, political obligation, the dangers of "mass society," the reconciliation of political equality and the pursuit of excellence, all are given eloquent treatment in *On Liberty*.

On Liberty is widely praised; it is, however, less widely read. Otherwise, so many misconceptions about its content could not have been so frequently disseminated. Far from being a plea for individual license, it is a sober and balanced presentation of its subject.

Although Mill was a staunch proponent of political democracy, his observations on the operation of democratic government are pronouncedly realistic. He was no naive exponent of democratic theory. Now that the "democratic republic" has spread over a large portion of the earth, he pointed out, "elective and responsible government" has become "subject to the observations and criticisms which wait upon existing fact." It is now apparent, Mill informs us, that

> such phrases as "self-government," and "the power of the people over themselves," do not express the true state of the case. The "people" who exercise the power are not always the same people with those over whom it is exercised; and the "self-government" spoken of is not the government of each by himself, but of each by all the rest. The will of the people, moreover, practically means the will of the most numerous or the most active *part* of the people; the majority, or those who succeed in making themselves accepted as the majority; the people, consequently, *may* desire to oppress a part of their number; and precautions are as much needed against this as against any other abuse of power. The limitation, therefore, of the power of government over individuals loses none of its importance when the holders of power are regularly accountable to the community, that is, to the strongest power therein.[21]

The Tyranny of the Majority. The danger of the "tyranny of the majority," then, is one of the leading themes of Mill's essay. This tyranny, however, as he is careful to point out, can assume many shapes, and its most dangerous form is not physically coercive political power but morally coercive social opinion. Society can practice "a social tyranny more formidable than many kinds of political oppression, since, though not usually upheld by such extreme penalties, it leaves fewer means of

---

21. Mill, *On Liberty,* in *Utilitarianism, Liberty, and Representative Government,* pp. 88–89.

escape, penetrating much more deeply into the details of life, and enslaving the soul itself."[22]

As highly as he values "individual independence," Mill does not in any way deny that man exists in society and is necessarily subject to both governmental and societal rules of conduct. Mill cannot be ranked among the anarchists or antinomians; he is concerned not to overthrow rules, but to discover the right kind of rules for the governing of men:

> All that makes existence valuable to anyone, depends on the enforcement of restraints upon the actions of other people. Some rules of conduct, therefore, must be imposed, by law in the first place, and by opinion on many things which are not fit subjects for the operation of law.[23]

Governmental Interference. On the question of whether social evils should be remedied by governmental action, Mill refuses to endorse either an extreme laissez-faire or extreme collectivist viewpoint. The "interference of government" to accomplish some good or prevent some evil "is, with about equal frequency, improperly invoked and improperly condemned."

Individual Interference. Mill then arrives at a statement of "one very simple principle" that constitutes his central thesis:

> The object of this Essay is to assert one very simple principle, as entitled to govern absolutely the dealings of society with the individual in the way of compulsion and control, whether the means used be physical force . . . or the moral coercion of public opinion. That principle is, that the sole end for which mankind are warranted, individually or collectively, in interfering with the liberty of action of any of their number, is self-protection. That the only purpose for which power can be rightfully exercised over any member of a civilised community, against his will, is to prevent harm to others. His own good, either physical or moral, is not a sufficient warrant.[24]

The Self and Society. Mill goes on to espouse what has come to be known as his distinction between "self-regarding" and "other-regarding" actions. "The only part of the conduct of any one, for which he is amenable to society, is that which concerns others. In the part which merely concerns himself, his independence is, of right, absolute. Over himself, over his own body and mind, the individual is sovereign."[25]

---

22. Ibid., p. 89.
23. Ibid., p. 90.
24. Ibid., pp. 95–96.
25. Ibid., p. 96.

The distinction between self- and other-regarding actions is often objected to because virtually every action by an individual affects others in some way. Mill was well aware of the problems posed by his distinction, however, and went on to say that it is only an action that *directly* affects others in such a manner as to bring them harm that is amenable to control by society.[26]

The Three Liberties. Within the inviolable domain of self-regarding activity Mill distinguished three types of liberty: (1) absolute liberty of thought, conscience, and speech; (2) liberty of tastes and pursuits; and (3) "freedom to unite, for any purpose not involving harm to others: the persons combining being supposed to be of full age, and not forced or deceived."[27] According to Mill, "no society in which these liberties are not, on the whole, respected, is free, whatever may be its form of government; and none is completely free in which they do not exist absolute and unqualified."

Liberalism and the Pursuit of Excellence. In view of Mill's emphatic defense of a sphere of absolute, inviolable liberty for all men, it is surprising that some writers have in recent years taken to questioning the authenticity of his liberalism. According to Shirley Letwin, for example, Mill

> marked the birth of the "liberal intellectual," so familiar today, who with one part of him genuinely values liberty and recognizes the equal right of all adults to decide their lives for themselves, but with another wants the government, under the direction of the superior few, to impose what he considers the good life on all his fellows.[28]

----

26. See C. L. Ten, "Mill on Self-Regarding Actions," *Philosophy,* January 1968, pp. 29–38, for an elaboration of this point.

27. Mill, *On Liberty,* p. 99. "This, then, is the appropriate region of human liberty. It comprises, first, the inward domain of consciousness; demanding liberty of conscience in the most comprehensive sense; liberty of thought and feeling; absolute freedom of opinion and sentiment on all subjects, practical or speculative, scientific, moral, or theological. The liberty of expressing and publishing opinions may seem to fall under a different principle, since it belongs to that part of the conduct of an individual which concerns other people; but, being almost of as much importance as the liberty of thought itself, and resting in great part on the same reasons, is practically inseparable from it. Secondly, the principle requires liberty of tastes and pursuits; of framing the plan of our life to suit our own character; of doing as we like, subject to such consequences as may follow: without impediment from our fellow-creatures, so long as what we do does not harm them, even though they should think our conduct foolish, perverse, or wrong. Thirdly, from this liberty of each individual, follows the liberty, within the same limits, of combination among individuals; freedom to unite, for any purpose not involving harm to others: the persons combining being supposed to be of full age, and not forced or deceived."

28. Letwin, *Pursuit of Certainty,* p. 8.

This is a surprising statement in view of Mill's unqualified rejection of "imposing" any pattern of life and his frequent allusions to the value of the individual's choosing his own mode of life simply because "it is his own mode."[29] As C. L. Ten has pointed out, a thinker does not cease to be a liberal simply because he is convinced of a certain hierarchy of values and is capable of making discriminating judgments with respect to the relative ranking of various patterns of existence:

> A liberal does not cease to believe in individual liberty just because he holds certain substantive doctrines or standards of human excellence, or because he attempts to propagate them by argument and persuasion. He is to be distinguished by his belief that these doctrines and standards should not be imposed on others who should be free to choose for themselves, and Mill clearly passes the test.[30]

> Mill's liberalism never led him to deny that some men are wiser and nobler than others. But he did not believe that these wiser and nobler men have the right to compel or coerce others.[31]

S. R. Letwin, Maurice Cowling, and others who have rebuked Mill for the "illiberal" side—or even core—of his thought misunderstand liberal "tolerance." The liberal welcomes diversity of view and a society in which strongly contending positions can coexist. Because of the polymorphic nature of human consciousness, it is to be expected that there will be a variety of perspectives on politics, culture, and every other activity of the human spirit. This does not mean that the individual liberal will cease to regard some ideas and artistic creations as superior to others or that he will of necessity refrain from regarding the demanding and difficult life of the spirit as superior to the life centered on the indulgence of physical appetite.

It is, then, Mill's commitment to excellence and to the intellectual and moral superiority of some men (such as Aristotle's *spoudaioi*) that have made him the target of accusations of illiberality. Mill, however, was confident that one could combine liberalism and the Socratic pursuit of intellectual and moral excellence. While his synthesis of the classical and liberal ideals is not effortlessly accomplished, it does seem to have been effectively achieved. Thus Mill explicitly repudiates the use of any form of coercion, whether by government or society, upon

---

29. It is not only "persons of decided mental superiority who have a just claim to carry on their lives in their own way. There is no reason that all human existence should be constructed on some one or some small number of patterns. If a person possesses any tolerable amount of common sense and experience, his own mode of laying out his existence is the best . . ." (Mill, *On Liberty*, p. 167).

30. Ten, "Mill and Liberty," p. 50.

31. Ibid., p. 51.

men who prefer to live at a level far beneath their potential development as human beings, as measured by the *spoudaioi*. He was clearly contemptuous of a passive and merely imitative existence—perhaps excessively so, for there may be inner richness in the lives of many ordinary men not easily visible to the active and articulate intellectual. But there can be no doubt that he rejected on principle, as a violation of liberty, any attempt to impose a "higher" pattern on these men. As he wrote in *On Liberty*, an individual cannot rightfully be compelled to live in a certain way

> because it will be better for him to do so, because it will make him happier, because, in the opinions of others, to do so would be wise, or even right. These are good reasons for remonstrating with him, or reasoning with him, or persuading him, or entreating him, but not for compelling him, or visiting him with any evil in case he do otherwise.[32]

Freedom of Thought and Speech.   Mill's unswerving commitment to untrammeled freedom of thought is expressed most emphatically in Chapter 2 of his essay, which contains his eloquent and memorable statement that if "all mankind minus one were of one opinion, and only one person were of the contrary opinion, mankind would be no more justified in silencing that one person, than he, if he had the power, would be justified in silencing mankind."[33] Freedom of thought and freedom of speech, then, are inseparable to Mill. This being so, there are no grounds whatsoever for limiting free discussion, even if in the opinion of governments or majorities such discussion is "pushed to an extreme." Unless the reasons for protecting freedom of speech "hold for an extreme case, they are not good for any case,"[34] wrote Mill. Constantly recurring to the example of Socrates, he notes how the subsequent intellectual and spiritual history of mankind has vindicated Socrates against the majority that persecuted him.[35]

Restrictions on Free Speech.   Although Mill objected to restrictions on free speech, he recognized the necessity of taking into account those situations that constituted what Justice Holmes later called "clear and present danger." "No one pretends that actions should be as free as opinions," he wrote.

> On the contrary, even opinions lose their immunity when the circumstances in which they are expressed are such as to constitute their

32. Mill, *On Liberty*, p. 96.
33. Ibid., p. 104.
34. Ibid., p. 110.
35. Ibid., p. 113.

expressing a positive instigation to some mischievous act. An opinion that corn-dealers are starvers of the poor, or that private property is robbery, ought to be unmolested when simply circulated through the press, but may justly incur punishment when delivered orally to an excited mob assembled before the house of a corn-dealer, or when handed about among the same mob in the form of a placard. Acts, of whatever kind, which, without justifiable cause, do harm to others, may be, and in the more important cases absolutely require to be, controlled by the unfavourable sentiments, and, when needful, by the active interference of mankind. The liberty of the individual must be thus far limited; he must not make himself a nuisance to other people.[36]

It is true that Mill did not elaborate on this distinction between absolute freedom of opinion on principle and limited freedom of expression in certain circumstances. Certainly the concept of "instigation to some mischievous act" is vague and ill defined. It is apparent, however, that accusations of naiveté on Mill's part with respect to the potential danger of subversion by forces inimical to a regime of liberty and intent on using civil liberties to destroy its foundations are ill founded. Mill did not live to confront the totalitarian challenge to representative democracy, so we cannot be certain what position he would have taken in the face of attempts to deny speech or political participation to "extremists" of right or left, or how he would have evaluated the charge that communism is an "international conspiracy" and as such is to be denied the protection of free speech. One suspects, however, that he would have decided these questions in favor of the greatest possible freedom of expression, thus reserving the "clear and present danger" doctrine for the most extreme situations of immediately impending violence and destruction.

Safeguards for Dissent. What impresses one about Mill's treatment of political problems and principles is its balance, common sense, and realism. He was, for example, in no way so naive as to believe that truth would always triumph. The "dictum that truth always triumphs over persecution is one of those pleasant falsehoods which men repeat after one another till they pass into commonplaces, but which all experience refutes," he wrote. "History teems with instances of truth put down by persecution. If not suppressed forever, it may be thrown back for centuries."[37] After recounting instances of successful persecutions, he con-

---

36. Ibid., pp. 152–53. If taken literally, this prohibition against "making oneself a nuisance" could, of course, severely curb creative dissent and therefore violate Mill's apparent aims.

37. Ibid., p. 118.

cluded that it is a "piece of idle sentimentality that truth, merely as truth, has any inherent power denied to error of prevailing against the dungeon and the stake."[38] It is therefore imperative that legal safeguards be enacted for the peaceful expression of dissent. Those who adopt the view that innovators should be willing to risk martyrdom or otherwise suffer for the advancement of truth in all probability "think that new truths may have been desirable once, but that we have had enough of them now."[39]

The One-Sidedness of Human Views.   Mill appears to have anticipated J. L. Lonergen's conclusion regarding the "polymorphous shape" of the human mind.[40] To Mill it was extremely unlikely that any human perspective could avoid being one-sided or entirely free from error. In the human mind, he wrote, "one-sidedness has always been the rule, and many-sidedness the exception." This means that

> even in revolutions of opinion, one part of the truth usually sets while another rises. Even progress, which ought to superadd, for the most part only substitutes, one partial and incomplete truth for another; improvement consisting chiefly in this, that the new fragment of truth is more wanted, more adapted to the needs of the time, than that which it displaces.[41]

Significantly enough, Mill praises Rousseau's dissent from the Enlightenment thesis that the advance of modern civilization means an unmitigated gain for the human race. By extolling the "superior worth of simplicity of life" and condemning the "enervating and demoralising effect of the trammels and hypocrisies of artificial society," Rousseau offered a needed corrective to the major thrust of Enlightenment thought.[42]

The Open Society.   In *On Liberty,* clear and away his greatest political work, Mill emerges as a champion of a diverse and open society. Although he did not use the precise term "open society"—this was to be the contribution of Henri Bergson—he did invoke the idea of a society committed to hearing both sides of the "open questions" perennially confronting mankind. To use a phrase that is now quite common, Mill fa-

---

38. Ibid., p. 119.

39. Ibid., p. 118. As Herbert Marcuse and others have pointed out, however, in contemporary society, where access to the expression of unpopular views in the mass media is severely limited, the simple guarantee of free speech to radical dissenters is insufficient to give them a true hearing. Hence the resort to street demonstrations, sit-ins, etc., as attention-getting devices.

40. J. L. Lonergen, *Insight* (London: Longmans, 1957).

41. Mill, *On Liberty,* pp. 140–41.

42. Ibid., pp. 141–42.

vored a "society of dialogue." Unless opinions favorable to democracy and to aristocracy, to property and to equality, to cooperation and to competition, to luxury and to abstinence, to society and to the individual, to liberty and to discipline, and all other standing antagonisms of practical life are expressed with equal freedom, and enforced and defended with equal talent and energy, there is no chance that society will recognize the degree of truth contained in any of its members' conceptions.[43]

In proclaiming his doctrine of "open questions," Mill advocated the practice of *inverse tolerance* toward the *minority opinion* as essential to maintaining society's critical freedom and perspective on great issues of substance. "On any of the great open questions just enumerated," he wrote, "if either of the two opinions has a better claim than the other, not merely to be tolerated, *but to be encouraged and countenanced,* it is the one which happens at the particular time and place to be in a minority."[44]

The Open Personality. Mill's basic and generous liberal humanism is nowhere more amply revealed than in his exposition of the open personality as the paradigmatic human type. We have already learned enough of his thought—and especially of his dedication to excellence in the cultivation of the human mind and spirit—to know that by openness he did not mean a formless existence without any rational principles of judgment and action. Mill meant by openness a basic generosity of mind and temperament, a certain preintellectual disposition to new perspectives and fresh insights.

> Many persons no doubt sincerely think that human beings . . . [who have been] cramped and dwarfed are as their Maker designed them to be; just as many have thought that trees are a much finer thing when clipped into pollards, or cut into figures of animals, than as nature made them. But if it be any part of religion to believe that man was made by a Good Being, it is more consistent with that faith to believe that this Being gave all human faculties that they might be cultivated and unfolded, not rooted out and consumed, and that he takes delight in every nearer approach made by his creatures to the ideal conception embodied in them, every increase in any of their capabilities of comprehension, of action, or of enjoyment.[45]

Comprehension, action, enjoyment: here Mill builds on the Aristotelian conception of the three types of life (contemplation, action,

---

43. Ibid., pp. 142–43.

44. Ibid., p. 143 (italics added). This insight could go a long way toward meeting the difficulty discussed in n. 39.

45. Ibid., pp. 160–61.

pleasure) expounded in the *Nicomachaean Ethics*. More successfully than Aristotle, however, Mill succeeds in eliminating artificial demarcations of the three "lives" by seeing each as a component of a single fully developed life. Even so, he retains the Aristotelian hierarchy; on principle he held mental activity or contemplation to yield greater happiness and fulfillment than either action or sensual pleasure.

Self-realization. Thus Mill's concept of self-realization or the fully developed human existence, for all its flexibility, is rich and specific in substance. Self-realization for Mill is not a vague, rhetorical phrase but a concrete human goal. His concept of the "developed" human existence could with profit be closely attended to at the present time, when the term "political development" rolls easily off the tongues of many scholars and activists. To Mill, "it is only the cultivation of individuality which produces, or can produce, well-developed human beings." A developed political and social existence is one that "brings human beings themselves nearer to the best things they can be. . . ."[46]

Mill had no illusion that a "developed society" would be one in which all or even the majority of individuals led a developed existence. Rather, such a society is on principle one in which "developed human beings" are encouraged and afforded a congenial environment. Further, it is a society in which "undeveloped" individuals—"those who do not desire liberty, and would not avail themselves of it"—profit indirectly from the presence of a creative and unhindered minority. "There is always need of persons not only to discover new truths, and point out when what were once truths are true no longer, but also to commence new practices, and set the example of more enlightened conduct, and better taste and sense in human life." Without this creative minority, the "salt of the earth," human life would become a "stagnant pool."[47] Nonetheless, it is with extreme difficulty that the mass of men can be persuaded to esteem originality and to allow genius to "breathe freely in an *atmosphere* of freedom," because originality "is the one thing which unoriginal minds cannot feel the use of."[48]

The Exceptional Individual. Surprising as it may appear to those accustomed to the conventional impressions of Machiavelli and Mill, the two are rather close together in their political teaching in a number of important respects. Machiavelli sought to humanize politics. His ultimate purpose in cataloguing the nefarious practices of men in their attempts to exploit and manipulate one another was to point the way to a more self-conscious and open politics. To indicate this process of develop-

---

46. Ibid., pp. 162–63.
47. Ibid., p. 163.
48. Ibid., pp. 164–65.

ment toward a new politics Machiavelli invoked the need for a founder of new modes and orders. What could sound more Machiavellian (in the authentic sense) than the following passage from *On Liberty:*

> The initiation of all wise and noble things comes and must come from individuals; generally at first from some one individual. The honor and glory of the average man is that he is capable of following that initiative; that he can respond internally to wise and noble things, and be led to them with his eyes open.[49]

Mill goes on to add, far more explicitly than Machiavelli did, that the founding individual must not employ compulsion to achieve the new politics:

> I am not countenancing the sort of "hero-worship" which applauds the strong man of genius for forcibly seizing on the government of the world and making it do his bidding in spite of itself. All he can claim is freedom to point out the way. The power of compelling others into it is not only inconsistent with freedom and development of all the rest, but corrupting to the strong man himself.[50]

The method that Mill proposes for those who "start on the higher eminences of thought" is deliberately and consciously to resist the tyranny of majority opinion. Exceptional individuals, "instead of being deterred, should be encouraged in acting differently from the mass."

The "Greatest Happiness" Principle. By now it should be abundantly clear why John Stuart Mill did not base his political teaching on the utilitarian principle of the "greatest happiness of the greatest number." Quite simply, for Mill happiness (or "pleasure," in the utilitarian vocabulary) is *not* the highest goal for men. That highest goal is rather the fulfillment of the best that is in man under conditions of liberty (that is, conditions that are noncoercive and which encourage spontaneity). It of course occurred to Mill that it was possible for the majority in a society actually to enjoy *greater* "happiness" where there is *less* liberty! This being the case, he could not subscribe to the "greatest happiness of the greatest number" principle because it might result in the sacrifice of liberty and excellence. This does not mean that he disapproved of Bentham's goal of improving the living conditions (and therefore enhancing the capacity for authentic choice) of the average man. Far from it. What it does mean is that he was far more alive to the drawbacks and ambiguities of the "greatest happiness" principle than either his father or Bentham. We can best describe John Stuart Mill as a humanist working out of (and to some extent away from) the tra-

---

49. Ibid., p. 166. Note the last three words.
50. Ibid., p. 166.

dition of utilitarian liberalism, rather than as a utilitarian in the precise sense of the word.

The Individual and Society. In Chapter 4 of *On Liberty* Mill attempts to answer several questions: "What . . . is the rightful limit to the sovereignty of the individual over himself? Where does the authority of society begin? How much of human life should be assigned to individuality, and how much to society?"

Mill strongly believes that the individual possesses obligations to the society from which he receives protection.

> Everyone who receives the protection of society owes a return for the benefit, and the fact of living in society renders it indispensable that each should be bound to observe a certain line of conduct towards the rest. This conduct consists, first, in not injuring the interests of one another . . . and secondly, in each person's bearing his share (to be fixed on some equitable principle) of the labours and sacrifices incurred for defending the society or its members from injury or molestation. These conditions society is justified in enforcing, at all costs to those who endeavor to withhold fulfillment.[51]

Mill proceeds to advocate the widest possible latitude to individuals and communities in determining for themselves the kind of existence they will lead. Insofar as enforceable sanctions are concerned, he is opposed to enjoining a particular moral or intellectual code or doctrine upon men. Mill, then, sets high value on "individual spontaneity"; in fact, he regards it as the necessary precondition for the good life. This does not mean, however, that he considers all individual determinations of equal value. Individuals may choose foolishly; however, if they neither harm others in their essential legal "rights" nor neglect their essential duties to society (such as paying taxes), then the only way open to those who regard such choices as erroneous or defective is persuasion. Mill, then, defends liberty in part as the indispensable prerequisite of human moral and intellectual development. Forced or imposed development is to him not true development. Liberty is necessary to the cultivation of excellence, to the full unfolding of a human being's distinctive higher qualities. At the same time, he also defends liberty on the grounds that it is a denial of the dignity of the person for society or government to control him except with regard to his essential duties to others. Liberty is a necessary attribute of human personality.

This, then, is Mill's position: although he is fully convinced that there is a hierarchy of faculties and ends proper to man's nature (he

---

51. Ibid., p. 177. In the light of contemporary experience of protest movements, this statement would require careful elaboration.

speaks of the "ideal perfection of human nature"),[52] he rejects on principle any attempt to impose such a pattern on individuals or communities, because any such attempt would violate individuals' legitimate interests or "rights" (he rejects any appeal to natural rights) and would inevitably lead to a uniform and stifling society. Although in principle he holds truth to be one, he believes that it inevitably is expressed in a variety of ways, depending on the distinctive perspective and talents of each human being. Liberty is necessary also, then, to permit and encourage the diverse contributions of gifted men to society. Liberty entails risk, however. It can be abused. There are customs and practices that Mill unequivocally condemns as irrational, retrogressive, or irresponsible on the basis of his carefully elaborated political anthropology.

Liberty in Principle and Practice. In Chapter 5, entitled "Applications," Mill restates his main thesis. The "one very simple principle" of the Introduction turns in Chapter 5 into the "two maxims which together form the entire doctrine of this Essay":

(1) the individual is not accountable to society for his actions, in so far as these concern the interests of no person but himself....
(2) for such actions as are prejudicial to the interests of others, the individual is accountable, and may be subjected either to social or to legal punishment, if society is of the opinion that the one or the other is requisite for its protection.[53]

Expressed so sparcely, Mill's principles seem rather vague and difficult to apply. In a sense, all principles of action elucidated by political theorists are open to this objection. The theorist cannot foresee the specific practical problems that will arise, and the precise implementation of their principles will depend on the context in which they are to be applied.

For this reason, Mill devoted considerable attention to concrete examples of ways in which his distinction between self-regarding and other-regarding actions could be applied. He defended the Mormons' practice of polygamy,[54] opposed "Sabbatarian legislation,"[55] supported the idea of compulsory education for children up to a certain age,[56] and

52. Ibid., p. 179.
53. Ibid., p. 201.
54. Ibid., pp. 199–200.
55. Ibid., p. 196.
56. Mill objected to the state's undertaking "the whole or any large part of the education of the people," however. It should assist parents in need to finance their children's education, but not run the schools themselves. He held a "general state education" to be a "mere contrivance for moulding people to be exactly like one another" (ibid., p. 217).

rejected a monopoly of the means of production, distribution, and exchange by the state as a danger to liberty, even it it coexisted with a free press and periodic competitive elections.[57]

What emerges clearly is Mill's commitment to a society admitting of and thriving on diversity, compatible with genius and excellence, actively striving for improvement in all areas of life but tolerant of human frailty and imperfection. Although some passages of On Liberty may imply a narrower perspective than others,[58] On Liberty has a rightfully prominent place in the history of liberalism. Its author is committed to the open society in the dual sense of appreciation of the advantages of diversity and commitment to the fullest possible development of the human person in all his range and depth. Mill's defense of the widest possible freedom of thought and speech for political dissenters and his insistence upon toleration of practices and life styles for which some people or the majority have a profound distaste constitute one of the major blows struck in defense of freedom of the individual. Today, as personal liberty and the right to privacy are threatened on many fronts, there is need to relearn the important lessons set forth in On Liberty.[59]

---

57. Ibid., p. 223.

58. As, for example, in the unflattering remarks on China and nonwestern cultures generally.

59. Justice William O. Douglas has indicated some of the threats to individual liberty and the right of dissent in Points of Rebellion (New York: Random House, 1970). For a more detailed argument, see Charles Reich, The Greening of America (New York: Random House, 1970), especially the chapter on the "corporate state."

10

Dilemmas of Liberalism: Spencer and Green

HERBERT SPENCER

In an essay written in 1864 entitled "Reasons for Dissenting from the Philosophy of M. Comte," Herbert Spencer summarized in the following mammoth sentence his conception of the kind of society toward which mankind was (happily) advancing:

> That form of society towards which we are progressing, I hold to be one in which *government* will be reduced to the smallest amount possible, and *freedom* increased to the greatest amount possible—one in which human nature will have become so molded by social discipline into fitness for the social state, that it will need little external restraint but will be self-restrained—one in which the citizen will tolerate no interference with his freedom, save that which maintains the equal freedom of others—one in which the spontaneous cooperation which has developed our industrial system . . . will produce agencies for the discharge of nearly all social functions, and will leave to the primary governmental agency nothing beyond the function of maintaining those conditions to free action, which make such spontaneous cooperation possible . . . and in which social life will have no other end than to maintain the completest sphere for individual life.[1]

Spencer contrasts his laissez-faire liberal political doctrine with the collectivist views of Comte, whose "ideal of society is one in which *government* is developed to the greatest extent" and in which "the individual life shall be subordinated in the greatest degree to the social life."[2] Although Spencer admired Comte's attempt to model the "social sci-

---

1. Herbert Spencer, *The Classification of the Sciences, to Which Are Added Reasons for Dissenting from the Philosophy of M. Comte* (New York: D. Appleton & Century, 1864), pp. 40–41 (emphasis in the original).
2. Ibid., p. 40.

ences" along the lines of the physical or "hard" sciences, as a good liberal he completely rejected the collectivist implications of Comte's teaching. Spencer wrote that the aim of his own teaching "is not the increase of authoritative control over citizens, but the decrease of it. A more pronounced individualism, instead of a more pronounced nationalism, is its ideal."[3] He held Comte's approach to be altogether too doctrinaire and intellectualist: society cannot be reorganized by philosophy; on the contrary, "society is to be re-organized by the accumulated effects of habit on character."[4]

Crane Brinton has said that just as John Stuart Mill "humanized" the utilitarian creed, Spencer "barbarized" it. While there is a good deal of truth in this statement, Spencer was not so narrow and insensitive as Brinton implies. His conception of scientific inquiry was more sophisticated than Comte's, for example, and for all his attraction to grandiose system construction (a not uncommon predilection of nineteenth-century intellectuals), he stressed the ineluctable limits to human knowledge. Nor did he follow Comte in advocating a new "religion of Humanity." Instead, Spencer posited an essentially unknowable "universal causal agent" as the only worthy object of religious contemplation and worship:

> Beginning with causal agents conceived as imperfectly known; progressing to causal agents conceived as less known and less knowable; and coming at last to a universal causal agent posited as not to be known at all; the religious sentiment must ever continue to occupy itself with this universal causal agent. Having in the course of evolution, come to have for its object of contemplation, the Infinite Unknowable, the religious sentiment can never again (unless by retrogression) take a Finite Knowable, like Humanity, for its object of contemplation.[5]

Although he continued the tradition of liberal individualism that had commenced with Hobbes and reached a certain culmination in Bentham, Spencer invoked new arguments for the defense of that tradition. He was neither a Lockean "natural rights" man nor a utilitarian. Of Bentham's "greatest happiness of the greatest number" principle, he wrote in the Introduction to his most important political work, *Social Statics* (1850):

> That is no rule at all . . . but rather an enunciation of the problem to be solved. It is your "greatest happiness" of which we have been

---

3. Ibid., p. 45.
4. Ibid.
5. Ibid., p. 41.

so long and so fruitlessly in search. . . . You tell us nothing new; you merely give words to our want. . . .

Every futile scheme for the general good has been based on opinion. . . . We demur to your action because it is not what we wanted—a guide . . . because it puts no veto on mistaken policy; because it permits all actions—bad, as readily as good—provided only the actors *believe* them conducive to the prescribed end. . . . We seek a system that can return a definite answer when we ask—"Is this act good?" and not like yours, reply—"Yes, if it will benefit you."[6]

Evolution, Politics, and Morality

Spencer took as his standard of moral and political right not the "human nature" of Bentham with its predictable and measurable quotient of pleasures and pains, but the evolutionary process. Man has no constant human nature, according to Spencer: peoples of different ages in the same locality and of different localities in the same age exhibit enormous variations in all aspects of their collective lives. Their psychological reactions, moral norms, and aesthetic standards are different—inevitably so, because every creature must adapt himself to his environment or die. The various political and cultural systems of men are simply examples of differing efforts at adaptation to the requirements of survival.

God and Nature. For all his ability and acuteness of mind, Spencer had a way of mixing theology and biology to the detriment of both. Thus the evolutionary process is invoked to explain the origin and development of the human species in a strictly "naturalistic" fashion and at the same time is regarded as the manifestation of the "Divine Will." To Spencer, evolution was at once a natural and a providential process governed by inexorable laws and unquestionably working for the eventual benefit of the human species. It was this process, rather than utility or natural rights, that provided the objective basis for morality so ardently sought by Spencer. Despite his disagreements with Bentham, Spencer strongly concurred in Bentham's belief that a "science" of morals and legislation is not only possible but mandatory. In his thought, therefore, we witness the hypostasizing of liberal individualism: it ceases to be a merely human creed—or better, a series of deductions from Lockean self-evident principles—and becomes transfigured into the plan of God and Nature (used interchangeably) for the universe.

The strange thing is that Spencer should have known better than

---

6. Herbert Spencer, *Social Statics, or the Conditions Essential to Human Happiness Specified and the First of Them Developed* (London: Chapman, 1851), pp. 1–2. Spencer specifically criticizes Bentham in ibid., pp. 15, 22–23.

to seek to reinforce his political opinions with such extravagant claims. Had he not said that the divine is ultimately unknowable? If God is unknowable, how can mere man know of the details of an alleged divine plan? From Spencer's illicit transference of theologico-scientific justifications into an immediate political creed all students of political thought can learn a lesson: that it is a bogus enterprise to claim ultimate, infallible justification for a set of proximate, all too human political judgments. In his condition man appears to be thrown back upon himself; the external world of nature will yield no answer to questions properly explored in the depths of the psyche.

Evolution and Individualism. Spencer's obsession with discovering a scientific and "objective" basis for legislation and morality led him to adopt what to my knowledge is the most simplistic and extreme version of laissez-faire individualism ever propagated. The tragedy is that Spencer was not lacking in benevolence for his fellows; much of his work exhibits an authentic concern for human freedom. He opposed unnecessary compulsion and regimentation, whether in the family or in other aspects of social life, and he defended freedom of speech and thought with an eloquence sometimes approximating that of John Stuart Mill. He was, initially at least—for toward the end of his life, beginning with the publication of *Man versus the State* in 1884, he tended to become dour and depressed by the tendencies of an age not proceeding according to his plan—in favor of many liberal political and humanitarian reforms such as expansion of the suffrage and penal and prison reform. He was a staunch opponent of slavery and of British imperialism.

Spencer's downfall as a thinker came in his adherence to what Ralph Waldo Emerson called a "foolish consistency," which belied all appeal to common sense. In aspects of his teaching—unfortunately those that had the greatest immediate practical influence—he exhibited the qualities of the perfect ideologue, proceeding from one abstract premise to another with a ruthless disregard for the real, existing human beings in our midst.

From his biological studies and his moral reflections on them Spencer concluded that, like all else in nature, the human species was inexorably and providentially slated to go through a series of evolutionary stages, beginning with simplicity and homogeneity and culminating in complexity and heterogeneity. In human affairs this process entailed the development from (1) "primitive anarchy" to the (2) "militant" or regimented society, with authoritarian, political, economic, and religious institutions, and finally to (3) "industrial" society, in which individualism reigns and men are restrained by internal instead of external discipline. In this third and final evolutionary stage, upon which mankind was then supposedly embarking, the "moral law of equal freedom" would everywhere prevail for the first time. Thus for Spencer the first principle of a developed political and social morality is that "every man has the freedom to do all that he wills, provided he infringes not the equal freedom of any other man."[7]

Social Darwinism

Spencer is often described as the first in a long line of "social Darwinists" —men who attempted to apply Darwin's evolutionary theories, and in particular the principle of the "survival of the fittest," to human society. Actually, he nowhere mentions Darwin in the *Social Statics*, nor does he list him as one of the great scientific precursors in his essay on Comte. It was not necessary for him to have been specifically influenced by Darwin; evolutionary ideas were in the air during the latter half of the nineteenth century. In any event, Spencer went far beyond what any careful natural scientist would admit in applying the "survival of the fittest" doctrine to human affairs. For however much he contended that his purpose was to promote "human happiness" (as the subtitle to *Social Statics* indicates), the policies he advocated on the basis of his dubious biologism could only promote human misery.

The most bizarre and extreme of all the passages in Spencer's works is probably the following:

> Pervading all nature we may see at work a stern discipline, which is a little cruel [a *little* cruel!] that it may be very kind. That state of universal warfare maintained throughout the lower creation . . . is at bottom the most merciful provision which the circumstances admit of. It is much better that the ruminant animal, when deprived by age of the vigour which made its existence a pleasure, should be killed by some beast of prey. . . .
>
> The development of the higher creation is a progress towards a form of being capable of a happiness undiminished by these drawbacks. It is in the human race that the consummation is to be accomplished. . . . And the ideal man is the man in whom all the conditions of that accomplishment are fulfilled. Meanwhile the well-being of existing humanity, and the unfolding of it into this ultimate perfection . . . are both secured by that same beneficent, though severe discipline, to which animate creation at large is subject. . . . The poverty of the incapable . . . starvation of the idle, and shoulderings aside of the weak by the strong . . . are the decrees of a large far-seeing benevolence. It seems hard that an unskilfulness which with all his efforts he cannot overcome, should entail hunger upon the

---

7. Ibid., p. 103.

artizan. . . . It seems hard that widows and orphans should be left to struggle for life and death. Nevertheless, when regarded . . . in connection with the interests of universal humanity, these harsh fatalities are seen to be full of the highest beneficence—the same beneficence that brings to early graves the children of diseased parents, and singles out the low-spirited, the intemperate, and the debilitated as the victims of an epidemic.

 . . . We must call those spurious philanthropists, who, to prevent present misery, would entail greater misery upon future generations. All defenders of a poor-law must . . . be classed amongst such. . . . Blind to the fact that under the natural order of things society is constantly excreting its unhealthy, imbecile, slow, vacillating, father-less members, these unthinking though well-meaning men advocate an interference which not only stops the purifying process, but even increases the vitiation—absolutely encourages the reckless and in-competent by offering them an unfailing provision and *dis*courages the multiplication of the competent and provident by heightening the prospective difficulty of maintaining a family. . . .[8]

The Flaw in the Liberal Ethos

For all his talk of the individual and of humanity, therefore, Spencer ends by endorsing a course of action—or rather of inaction—by society which is profoundly inimical to both. Humanity emerges not as the totality of persons, each of whom possesses inherent dignity, existing in diverse historical and cultural contexts, but as some kind of abstractly conceived phalanx of hideously efficient supermen who will tomorrow lord it over the globe. (One wonders, however, whether this "ideal man" would not resemble the prudent time-serving bourgeois more than the Nietzschean superman.) Although Spencer speaks frequently of freedom and individuality, what he really has in mind is only freedom to develop into the mold that he has set for humanity through his arrogant assumption of the role of superlegislator.

When we confront liberal extremists like Spencer we become more vividly aware than ever of a tragic flaw in liberalism, of the ease with which its often generous concept of liberty may be vitiated by a harsh and narrow rationalism and by an unthinking commitment to the pro-ductivist ethos. It is becoming clear that this attitude survives in much of contemporary liberal thought, and that as a result the liberal imagina-tion is often utterly unable to respond creatively to the demands of the more thoughtful and sensitive among us for a more compassionate and aesthetically alive society. For to these critics, the productivist-liberal-"rational" ethos does not mean freedom: it means spiritual death.

---

8. Ibid., pp. 322–24 (chapter entitled "Poor-laws").

The Functions of Government

In a way it could be argued that Spencer came close to an anarchist position, although anarchist thought stresses community and spontaneous solidarity in a way that Spencer never did. Spencer objected vehemently to the assumption that "government must necessarily last for ever."

> The institution of government marks a certain stage of civilization—is natural to a particular phase of human development. It is not essential but incidental. As amongst the Bushmen we find a state antecedent to government; so also there be one in which it shall have become extinct. Already has it lost something of its importance.[9]

Spencer's very definition of the state as a group of men "voluntarily associated for their mutual protection"[10] gives further indication of his extremely low estimation of the state. In advanced industrial society—the highest phase of man's development—it was to Spencer completely illegitimate for the state to take on any functions not related to the protection of the lives and property of its citizens. He was therefore opposed to all of the following types of governmental activity:

1. Factory laws
2. Sanitary laws
3. Legislation to license physicians
4. Pure food and drug laws
5. Monopoly of coinage by the state
6. A state postal system
7. Compulsory, state-supported education
8. Provision by the state of relief for the poor

Spencer anticipated that with the operation of the "salutary suffering" imposed by nature in the competition for the survival of the fittest, antisocial and criminal elements would gradually die out so that eventually there would be no need for an external agency such as the state to guarantee protection of lives and property. (Why he was so certain that the "virtuous" rather than the criminal elements would win out in such a raw struggle was never made clear.) At that happy moment the state would literally wither away and the entire monstrous process of suffering would be retrospectively justified.

When we consider this body of thought as a whole, we can scarcely classify Spencer with the anarchists despite certain surface affinities with them. And they would scarcely welcome him to their group, be-

---

9. Ibid., p. 13.
10. Ibid., p. 275.

cause they rejected his crude biological justification of present suffering and his enthronement of private property as an eternal and legitimate institution. Most decisively of all, the anarchists' view of what constitutes the authentic liberation of man contrasts fundamentally with that of Spencer. For Spencer's man—the superior man who survives—is above all characterized by his abstemiousness and his "faculty of self-control."[11] To those in the anarchist tradition, such a man is not free, but rather constitutes a prime example of the repression of present-day bourgeois society.

Spencerian Thought in America

Spencer is particularly important in the American context. His work greatly influenced William Graham Sumner, the Yale professor of sociology and crusader for rugged individualism. In 1916 Henry Cabot Lodge, Sr., Elihu Root, and other prominent conservative politicians brought out an American edition of Spencer's *Man versus the State*. Spencerianism has been a strand of America's public life from the time of Mr. Justice Field, whom Oliver Wendell Holmes accused of incorporating Spencer's *Social Statics* into the Fourteenth Amendment to the Constitution, to former Governor Pyle, who while serving the Eisenhower administration proclaimed the "right to suffer" as "one of the joys of a free economy."

T. H. GREEN

Whether or not we agree with John R. Rodman's conclusion that T. H. Green was "the most important political thinker between John Stuart Mill and the present,"[12] there is no question that the meticulous Oxford don is one of the most interesting figures in the history of liberalism. Green was a man who combined to an unusual degree rare gifts for philosophical speculation and creative insights into the practical politics of his day. He played a key role in the history of liberalism in that his concept of "positive freedom" provided intellectual support for the newly

---

11. Ibid., p. 185.

12. John R. Rodman, ed., *The Political Theory of T. H. Green* (New York: Appleton-Century-Crofts, 1964), Introduction, p. 1. It is unfortunate that Rodman used the term "political thinker" rather than "political theorist." It is highly doubtful that there has been no more important political *thinker* since Mill (who died in 1873) than Green, particularly if one moves beyond the confines of Western civilization. This observation is not meant to detract from the overall excellence of Rodman's introduction, however. The best full-length treatment of Green's political thought is Melvin Richter, *The Politics of Conscience: T. H. Green and His Age* (London: Weidenfeld & Nicolson, 1964).

emerging welfare-state proposals whose adoption helped immeasurably to secure a kind of stabilization of conditions under an advanced industrial and capitalist society.

One can see many of the tensions of present-day liberal thought mirrored in Green's teaching. Profound humanistic concerns and insights mingle with exceedingly timid suggestions for political change. One notices an ambiguity in his concept of freedom which reflects insensitivity to the importance of spontaneity and authentic freedom of decision. Green showed a tendency to hold out his own ideal of freedom as the only one worth attaining. Finally, despite his passionate interest in reforms to improve the lot of the working class, there is in Green more than a touch of a conservative spirit of accommodation to "the system." His constant talk of duty, self-sacrifice, work, and moral self-improvement grows tiresome at times and does not always square well with his reputation as a great liberal-democratic reformer.

Nonetheless, for all his limitations, Green did bring new philosophical and practical dimensions to Western liberalism in general and English liberalism in particular. In philosophy he was an exponent of what came to be called "English idealism"; the center of this movement was at Oxford, where he was a fellow of Balliol College. Green looked to Kant and Hegel rather than to Locke and the utilitarians for his metaphysics and ontology. Although highly sympathetic to Hegel's work, he was not above criticizing it, as he did in the following observations on a book by a disciple of the German philosopher:

> From the distance at which most readers will consider our criticism of Dr. Caird, if they consider it at all, the difference between author and reviewer will no doubt appear insignificant. It comes to this, that in his method, though not in his conclusion, we think he has been too much overpowered by Hegel. We suspect that all along Hegel's method has stood in the way of an acceptance of his conclusion, because he, at any rate, seemed to arrive at his conclusion as to the spirituality of the world, not by interrogating the world, but by interrogating his own thoughts. A well-grounded conviction has made men refuse to believe that any dialectic of the discursive intelligence would instruct them in the reality of the world, or that this reality could consist in thought in any sense in which thought can be identified with such an intellectual process. It may not, indeed, have been of the essence of Hegel, but an accident explicable from his philosophical antecedents, that his doctrine was presented in a form which affronted this conviction. That there is one spiritual self-conscious being, of which all that is real is the activity or expression; that we are related to this spiritual being, not merely as parts of the world which is its expression, but as partakers in some inchoate measure

of the self-consciousness through which it at once constitutes and distinguishes itself from the world; that this participation is the source of morality and religion; this we take to be the vital truth which Hegel had to teach. It still remains to be presented in a form which will command some general acceptance among serious and scientific men. Whoever would so present it, though he cannot drink too deep of Hegel, should sit rather looser to the "dialectical" method than Dr. Caird has done.[13]

Green and Herbert Spencer were, of course, contemporaries. Inasmuch as they held sharply contrasting views on the proper role of government in economic and social life, one would have expected the two men to clash head-on in fierce polemic. Green did write in 1877 a long article on Spencer, but the subject was Spencer's psychology and epistemology, not his politics. Green clearly regarded Spencer's philosophical position as naive and sought to expose the deficiencies of any kind of biologism or sensationalist epistemology, but he was by no means lacking in respect for Spencer's intellectual powers.[14]

Positive Freedom

The crux of the difference between the teachings of Green and Spencer lies in their conflicting notions of freedom. Spencer is surely the most relentlessly consistent apostle of negative freedom (freedom *from* government interference in people's lives) in the history of Western liberalism; Green, following in the footsteps of Hegel, gives a coherent and carefully reasoned argument for positive freedom—a notion that became the touchstone of all arguments in support of welfare-state as opposed to laissez-faire liberalism. Over a quarter of a century before its enactment into law, Green provided the theoretical justification for the welfare-state program adopted under the Asquith–Lloyd George cabinet.

The most succinct expression of Green's concept of positive freedom is contained in his lecture "Liberal Legislation and Freedom of Contract," originally delivered to the Liberal Association of Leicester in 1881. Near the beginning of the lecture he remarks:

We shall probably all agree that freedom, rightly understood, is the greatest of blessings; that its attainment is the true end of all our effort as citizens. But when we thus speak of freedom, we should

13. T. H. Green, review of J. Caird, *Introduction to the Philosophy of Religion,* in *Works of Thomas Hill Green,* ed. R. L. Nettleship, 3 vols. (London: Longmans, 1966), vol. 3, p. 146.

14. Green, "Mr. Spencer on Subject and Object," in *Works,* vol. 3, pp. 374–441. See also "An Answer to Mr. Hodgson," in ibid., pp. 521–41.

consider carefully what we mean by it. We do not mean merely freedom from restraint or compulsion. We do not mean merely freedom to do as we like irrespectively of what it is we like. We do not mean a freedom that can be enjoyed by one man or one set of men at the cost of a loss of freedom to others. *When we speak of freedom . . . we mean a positive power or capacity of doing or enjoying something worth doing or enjoying,* and that, too, something that we do or enjoy in common with others.[15]

Freedom for Green, then, is not equivalent to the absence of compulsion or restraint by society. A society's growth in freedom is not measured by the diminution of the powers exercised by its government, but rather by the "greater power on the part of the citizens as a body to make the most and best of themselves." An active government, concerned with the welfare of *all* citizens, will promote rather than hinder freedom as it is properly understood—that is, as the effective capacity to lead the good life.

Lest we conclude, however, that Green is a Plato *redivivus,* it must be emphasized that he strongly endorses the liberal principle that "there can be no freedom among men who act not willingly but under compulsion." The point Green is chiefly interested in making is that "the mere removal of compulsion, the mere enabling a man to do as he likes, is in itself no contribution to true freedom." His example, somewhat unfortunately chosen perhaps, is that of the "noble savage," who while "not a slave to man" is a "slave to nature," and whose "actual powers . . . do not admit of comparison with those of the humblest citizen of a law-abiding state."[16] This example rings false to many inhabitants of today's industrial society, who scarcely experience the growth in "positive freedom" that Green thought would accompany the extension of collective control over the environment and increased general affluence. Instead of experiencing an expansion of his "power," a man of our time may more often reel in horror at the way forces beyond his control mar his surroundings with ugliness, waste, and utter disregard for ecological and social necessities. Therefore, when Green asserts that "to submit" to the restraints demanded by society is the "first step in true freedom," because it is the "first step towards the full exercise of the faculties with which man is endowed," discerning contemporary readers are left with the feeling that there is something profoundly awry with his analysis of freedom.

---

15. Green, "Liberal Legislation and the Freedom of Contract," in *Political Theory of T. H. Green,* ed. Rodman, pp. 51–52 (italics added).

16. Ibid., p. 52.

Freedom and Self-Discipline

Although the gulf in *practical* politics between Green and Spencer is vast, at the substantive level their conceptions of freedom are not so far apart as one might at first think. Perhaps this is scarcely surprising, since they are both widely—and accurately—denominated "liberals." Let us compare two passages, the first from Spencer's *Social Statics* and the second from Green's *Lectures on the Principles of Political Obligation*:

> What . . . is the most important attribute of man as a moral being? . . . May we not answer—the faculty of self-control? [Are not] civilized races . . . superior to the savage [precisely in this quality]?[17]

> . . . The nature of . . . freedom . . . differs . . . according to the nature of the object which the man makes his own. . . . It is one thing when the object in which self-satisfaction is sought is such as to prevent that self-satisfaction being found, because interfering with the realisation of the seeker's possibilities or his progress towards perfection: it is another thing when it contributes to this end. . . . From . . . bondage [to a condition in which self-satisfaction is not to be found] he emerges into real freedom, not by overcoming the law of his being, not by getting the better of its necessity,—every fancied effort to do so is but a new exhibition of its necessity,—but by making its fulfillment the object of his will; by seeking the satisfaction of himself in objects in which he believes it *should be* found, and seeking it in them *because* he believes it should be found in them. . . . [The] law of our being [enjoins that we] gladly do and suffer what we must.[18]

Spencer, we will recall, had in his 1864 article on Comte looked hopefully to a future age in which "human nature will have been so molded by social discipline into fitness for the social state, that it will need little external restraint but will be self-restrained. . . ."[19] What is so striking about the above passages is that their authors took themselves—and have been taken by others—to be expounding a *liberal* interpretation of freedom. Liberalism supposedly sets great store by such values as individuality, spontaneity, and self-determination; in the concept of freedom put forward by Spencer and Green, however, there is more than a trace of an illiberal rigidity and a love-your-servitude mentality quite inconsistent with these values. Both for Spencer and for Green, man is and should be free, but only apparently to conform to their programmed conceptions of moral "perfection" and "self-control." The living, breath-

---

17. Spencer, *Social Statics*, p. 185.

18. Green, *Lectures on the Principles of Political Obligation* (London: Longmans, 1941), pp. 2–3.

19. Spencer, *Classification of the Sciences*, p. 40.

ing individual is eagerly sacrificed to social (Green) or natural (Spencer) "necessity," for this same "necessity" is reinterpreted to be supportive of the individual's "self-satisfaction." Thus neither Green nor Spencer leaves much room for the development of man's substantive, inner freedom. Spencer's man is so "molded by social discipline" (the image of a robot comes to mind) that society scarcely needs government at all. Man can be trusted with his "freedom" precisely because he will not use it, having been conditioned to forget it. In Green's case, the various prohibitions and injunctions of an active state are all alike to be borne without complaint; indeed, they are to be embraced as if we had willed them ourselves. Because Green does not clearly distinguish—as Rousseau and Hegel had done, for example—between the paradigmatic society and the existing social order, he comes at times closer to teaching a civil religion of conformism than a critical theory of politics. It is indicative of his general tendency toward conformism that Green nowhere admits the possibility of any general right to resist unjust acts of government or other organs of society.

Liberalism vs. the Radical Tradition

Whatever the case that can be made for the proposition that true freedom can be found only in the voluntary acceptance—indeed, self-imposition—of restraints, one thing is clear: this is not at all what is understood by freedom in the anarchist and radical currents of political thought. The perspective of political radicalism—as distinct from Communist orthodoxy—has been neglected in histories of political thought; it is deserving of greater attention both because of its intellectual merit and because it seems to point to a vital dimension of the problem of freedom generally overlooked by liberalism. If we today can better understand how repressive the liberal concept of freedom appears to those in the radical tradition, the existence of sizable movements of radical protest in our midst will at least seem less mysterious and incomprehensible. It seems clear to me, at least, that the time is long overdue for replacing the ritualistic celebration of the virtues of modern liberalism frequently offered in histories of political thought by a disciplined analysis of both the limitations and achievements of the liberal tradition.

It also needs to be observed that what we may for the moment call the premodern concept of freedom as attunement with a higher law, with the *agathon*, with the world-transcendent God, differs from the concept of freedom as service to one's better self, for attunement is not the same as submission to a repressive domination. There is, in principle at least, a certain gaiety and suppleness to life which is possible in an imperfect obedience to the *agathon* but which is lost in the struggle to whip the immanent self into line. Perhaps the problem with Green is his strong dose of Puritanism and austerity, but it must be observed that this makes him no surprising exception among the ranks of liberal thinkers. There is something flat and cheerless about the liberal political tradition in general, whether one is talking of Locke or the physiocrats or Adam Smith or Bentham. John Stuart Mill stands virtually alone among liberals in his genuine enthusiasm for diversity and respect for the polymorphous perspectives of individual consciousnesses.

Governmental Regulatory Powers

Green's practical program contrasted sharply with Spencer's in his refusal to concede that the right of "freedom of contract" between employer and employee was absolute, and he rightly detected that in actuality such a "freedom" allowed unlimited exploitation of the mass of workingmen (then unorganized and weak) by the owners of the means of production. Freedom of contract—that is, "freedom in all forms of doing what one will with one's own"—is valuable only as a "means to an end," he wrote.[20] Green justified the use of the state's regulatory power to safeguard the health and well-being of the oppressed working classes. Specifically, he approved of factory acts regulating hours and conditions of work, public health measures setting minimum conditions for housing to be provided the workers, and vastly increased expenditures for compulsory education. He was also (and here the gulf between Mill and Green is at its widest) in favor of "temperance legislation"—prohibition of the sale of alcohol to workers. Green's advocacy of prohibition may be more than simply an individual eccentricity attributable to his brand of evangelical religiosity; it appears to be a further confirmation of the narrowness of his concept of freedom and his tendency to enforce a rigid pattern of life on others.

State Regulation and Positive Freedom. Green's justification for increased state activity to promote improvements in working conditions, housing, and educational opportunities for the masses was based on his concept of positive freedom. If freedom is viewed as a "positive capacity of doing something worth doing or enjoying," then no one can complain of a diminution of freedom if the state *restrains* some men who are preventing great numbers of people from living at a level above that of mere survival, Green observed. Only if freedom is viewed negatively, as the absence of external restraint, can government regulation to correct

---

20. Green, "Freedom of Contract," in *Political Theory of T. H. Green,* ed. Rodman, p. 53.

social "nuisances" be regarded as adverse to mankind's interests. As he puts it:

> Our modern legislation . . . with reference to labour, and education, and health, involving as it does manifold interference with freedom of contract, is justified on the ground that it is the business of the state, not indeed directly to promote moral goodness, for that, from the very nature of moral goodness, it cannot do, but to maintain the conditions without which a free exercise of the human faculties is impossible.[21]

The Individual and the Social Self

Despite the strong dose of Hegel he had imbibed, and despite his philosophical criticism of the earlier foundations of English liberalism— whether of the natural-law, utilitarian, or Spencerian biologistic variety— Green never really amended in any fundamental way the individualistic presuppositions common to all liberal writers. Although there was much talk of the "social self," and an apparent recognition of the role society plays in the shaping of the psyche, Green's ultimate paradigm of the good society remained that of a collection of autonomous individuals capable of regulating their own affairs without any interference of external authority. Again, for all their divergencies, one is struck by certain fundamental affinities in the concepts of Green and Spencer regarding the final desirable social condition of mankind:

> Now, we shall probably all agree that a society in which the public health was duly protected, and necessary education duly provided for, by the spontaneous action of individuals, was in a higher condition than one in which the compulsion of law was needed to secure these ends. But we must take men as we find them. Until such a condition is reached, it is the business of the state to take the best security it can for the young citizens' growing up in such health and with so much knowledge as is necessary for their real freedom. In so doing it need not at all interfere with the independence and self-reliance of those whom it requires to do what they would otherwise do for themselves.[22]

"Independence," "self-reliance," absence of the "compulsion of law"— here we have the core of Green's political commitment. Green was undoubtedly sincere in all of his talk of obligation to others and involvement in the community, but it is doubtful that he possessed any real

---

21. Ibid., p. 56.
22. Ibid., pp. 57–58.

concept of community at all. His "independent," self-governing man is ultimately too absorbed in his own personal problems and possessions[23] to become fully involved with those of others.

Civil Disobedience

One of the topics with which Green inevitably dealt in his *Lectures on the Principles of Political Obligation* was civil disobedience against laws held to be unjust. Judged by today's standards, at least, he is extraordinarily timid in his conclusions:

> As a general rule, no doubt, even bad laws, laws representing the interests of classes or individuals as opposed to those of the community, should be obeyed. There can be no right to disobey them, even while their repeal is urged on the ground that they violate rights, because the public interest, on which all rights are founded, is more concerned in the general obedience to law than in the exercise of those powers by individuals or classes which the objectionable laws withhold.[24]

Through this analysis, Green has already loaded the dice in favor of "law and order." Once one declares that "the public interest," on which "all rights are founded" (why *all* rights—are there not rights of the person in his capacity as a unique being?), is "more concerned" with "general obedience to law" than with social justice, it is clear where Green would have stood on contemporary questions involving sit-ins and other acts of civil disobedience in protest against racial injustice, archaic institutional structures, and an intolerable war. Here we see the tragedy of liberalism: so long as such presuppositions are maintained, liberalism is wholly incapable of assimilating any of the valid and creative insights of the radical perspective.

Green, to give him credit, although denying any "right of revolution" by either majority or minority, does speak of a "duty to resist" in "extreme cases." But these cases, he makes clear,[25] do not apply under a liberal parliamentary government, or what he calls a "popular government and settled methods of enacting and repealing laws."[26] He will thus not admit that even in societies where formally free debate has been institutionalized, along with mechanisms for peaceful political change, majorities may become insensitive to the requirements of social justice

---

23. Green wanted everyone to own property as a "condition of moral well-being"; even so, he refused to advocate any restrictions on the "freedom of bequest." The "amount which children may inherit may not be limited" (*Lectures on Political Obligation*, par. 224, p. 272).

24. Ibid., in *Political Theory of T. H. Green*, par. 144, p. 136.

25. Ibid., pars. 101–12, pp. 111–20.

26. Ibid.

and so prompt more emphatic acts of dissent than the registering of a negative vote in an election in which none of the principal candidates may address themselves in any way to the issues arousing the concern of a creative minority. Despite his liberalism, Green really has no sympathy for the gadfly or the social critic who may dissent in important fundamental respects from the liberal vision of society. Throughout, his emphasis is on "good citizenship" and "intelligent patriotism," on piety and conformity.

Green does recognize the possibility that even in a society with a liberal or "popular" government, on rare occasions the "public interest" might best be served "by a violation of some actual law." The public interest is not to be interpreted "according to some remote philosopher's view of it," however; a Socrates would presumably not be listened to in Green's society. Thus he permits his "good citizens" to resist compliance with laws promoting slavery "when [and presumably only when] the public conscience has come to recognize a capacity for right . . . in a body of men to whom legal rights have hitherto been refused, but when some powerful class in its own interest resists the alteration of the law."[27] Yet even the right to disobey laws maintaining slavery is not unqualified:

> Under certain conditions the right of helping the slave may be cancelled by the duty of obeying the prohibitory law. It would do so if the violation of law in the interest of the slave were liable to result in general anarchy. . . . [S]uch a destruction of the state would mean a general loss of freedom, a general substitution of force for mutual good-will in men's dealings with each other, that would outweigh the evil of any slavery under such limitations and regulations as an organised state imposes on it.[28]

Thus the "destruction of the state" is to Green a greater evil than the continuance of slavery; the slave, it would appear from a close reading of the passage, is not fully a man, for the elimination of slavery is not worth the cost of disturbing the "mutual good-will in men's dealings with each other." That the human being in a condition of slavery might not experience much of that "mutual good-will" seems not to have crossed Green's mind. One cannot escape the conclusion that when the chips are down, timidity and bourgeois punctiliousness prevail over the person and social justice in Green's liberalism.

The Achievements and Failures of a Liberal

If I have been—as I freely admit I have been—harder on Green than on some others, it is precisely because Green had the ability, perspective,

27. Ibid., par. 144, p. 137.
28. Ibid., par. 147, p. 138.

and perspicacity to do much better than he did. History rightfully accords him an important place in the evolution of liberalism, which he revised in an important respect. His doctrine of positive freedom was developed and broadened by Leonard T. Hobhouse[29] at the London School of Economics and by the political practitioners in the first Liberal government in Britain in the twentieth century. The concept of government's "hindering the hindrances" to individual self-realization, of the state's responsibility to take an active role in creating minimal conditions for the realization of freedom in the positive sense, remains an important intellectual achievement. The liberal capitalist industrial system, both in Europe and in the United States, has undoubtedly been made more livable for many by the enactment of laws providing for minimum wages and maximum hours, progressive taxation, and social security and welfare benefits.

Nonetheless, Green did not fulfill the humanistic promise latent in the liberal idea. His notion of freedom, as I have tried to show, was restrictive and timid. Furthermore, he was excessively—even naively—optimistic in his belief that liberal ideas and institutions constituted the wave of the future. With the elimination of the rule of a privileged class (apparently the rural gentry), the great conflicts agitating modern industrial society both within and without would diminish, he believed. There would be prosperity at home and peace in the world (under a world court organized according to liberal principles, which would adjudicate disputes between sovereign states). Thus the Enlightenment idea of progress continued to be advanced by Green: mankind was undergoing a steady political evolution toward peace and freedom; all that liberal humanists need do was patiently to assist this evolutionary process.

Green's liberal politics essentially entailed gradualism and conformity within the system. As a political theorist, he should have known better than to neglect even to ask whether the system as such might develop in an antihumanist direction, and whether conflict and direct challenges to unjust conditions might not be required before any reversal of this downward trend might be hoped for. Many of us, at least, would today conclude that Green's assumption of an automatic upward evolution or "political development" of mankind toward a bright liberal future has been proved a chimera by our everyday experience. Liberalism badly needs a sense of both tragedy and gaiety to supplement its restricted analysis of and prescription for man's political condition.

---

29. See Leonard T. Hobhouse, *Liberalism* (London: Home University Library, 1911). Hobhouse was directly influenced by Green.

11

Scientism:
Saint-Simon and Comte

Claude Henri de Saint-Simon and Auguste Comte, two of the most striking figures of nineteenth-century political thought, for a time shared a close personal relationship as well as pronounced similarities of thought. Each man believed himself to be the inspired prophet of a new age for mankind. Each held an unshakable faith in the power and beneficence of the "sciences of observation" and called for the application of these sciences to human affairs. Each believed that mankind was in need of a new religious dispensation, in harmony with the findings of science, which would serve as the basis of a society that was both organically integrated and productively efficient. Both men appropriated insights from the thinkers of the Romantic Reaction against the French Revolution, and yet their commitment to science, progress, and the amelioration of the condition of the "most numerous and poorest" class links them to some degree with socialist and radical critics. Saint-Simon in particular is often hailed as one of the founding fathers of modern socialism.

For all their similarity in outlook and temperament, however, there are important differences between them. Auguste Comte was relatively more thoroughgoing in his collectivism and more rigid in the temporal and spiritual controls he proposed to institute over men. There was a pronounced repressive and ascetic streak in Comte, while Saint-Simon's disciples, at least, made one of their principal objectives the revolutionizing of sexual attitudes and practices. Comte was the more disciplined writer and was more knowledgeable than Saint-Simon in the physical sciences. Although he was far more than a mere disciple, he learned much from the inventive Saint-Simon. We need not enter into the sterile debate over which writer made the more significant and original contribution to political thought. Both have been influential and both are worth studying, for their errors and fixations as well as for their insights.

SAINT-SIMON

Saint-Simon was forever inventing projects for the collective regeneration and redemption of mankind. His first published work, *Letters of an Inhabitant of Geneva*, was a proposal (addressed to Napoleon as "the only one of my contemporaries capable of judging it"[1]) to establish a Council of Newton, composed of twenty-one men of genius, for the governance of all mankind. Council members would be elected by all persons who had subscribed financially to the project. The list of candidates, which would be composed of an equal number of mathematicians, physicists, chemists, physiologists, writers, artists, and musicians, would be drawn up by Saint-Simon himself after consultation with experts in the respective fields. The council would be chaired by the mathematician receiving the greatest number of votes. Below the Grand Council, which would meet at the tomb of Newton, there would be four divisional councils, corresponding to the four divisions of "humanity," the English, French, German, and Italian. Asian and African peoples were to be kept under the tutelage of Europeans; it was not clear what the status of the peoples of the Western Hemisphere would be. The Europeans, once united, were to embark on a crusade, under the direction of the founder of the new religion revealed by God to Saint-Simon, to "deliver their Greek brothers" from the Turks and to force the "children of Cain" (the Africans and Asians) to submit to the new religion.[2]

The New Religion

Although the *Letters of an Inhabitant of Geneva* is a rather brief document, it is replete with details about the reorganization of the world. Part of this remarkable essay is in the form of an exchange of letters between Saint-Simon (the "inhabitant of Geneva") and a friend; the other part purports to be an account of a dream in which God appeared to Saint-Simon and delivered to him a set of specific instructions about the new religion and about the establishment and operation of the Council of Newton. Thus Saint-Simon claimed to be a prophet articulating the new "divine science."[3] The will of God and the progress of the natural sciences (and their application to the moral and political spheres) were proclaimed to be identical.

It is not completely clear whether Saint-Simon was serious in claiming

---

1. Claude Henri de Saint-Simon, *Lettres d'un habitant de Genève a ses contemporains* (1803), in *Oeuvres de Claude Henri de Saint-Simon*, 6 vols. (Paris: Éditions Anthropos, 1966), vol. 1, p. 9. This edition is a reprint of the 1868 edition published by E. Dentu.

2. Ibid., p. 56.

3. Ibid., p. 49.

to have been directly inspired by God, whether he believed that a claim to such inspiration was indispensable to the successful propagation of the new doctrine, or whether the dream was a mere *jeu d'esprit*. Perhaps there was a mixture of all three elements. The work itself lacks coherence, as do all of his writings. The "First Letter"—the opening of the work proper—states that he (Saint-Simon—God is not mentioned until later) has conceived of a "useful" project for "humanity."[4] It is only toward the end of the *Letters* that the dream is brought in.[5] Perhaps at the time the dream was only a literary device designed to attract attention to his proposals, but it is significant that his last work, *New Christianity*, was also devoted to the problem of founding a new religion.[6] Indeed, Saint-Simon returned to this matter constantly.

The Social Order

Despite the strangeness of Saint-Simon's first work and its lack of literary elegance, it contained in seminal form most of the leading ideas that its author was to develop and repeat endlessly throughout his lifetime. Thus we find included in the *Letters* Saint-Simon's class analysis and his demand for rule by the scientists and intellectuals (*savants*) and the artists in cooperation with the productive members of the propertied classes. The *savants* are described as the "party of humanity." They stand for innovation, progress, and the control of the environment through scientific and technological advance. They comprise a kind of intellectual aristocracy above the two competing "temporal" classes, the owners of property and the "remainder of humanity."[7] Only under an arrangement whereby the first class (*savants* and artists) gives intellectual and spiritual direction to the productive members of the second class (property owners), whose managerial and entrepreneurial skill will be harnessed to increase society's total wealth many times, will the lot of the masses be substantially improved. Under the new rational and scientifically managed society, class conflict will disappear. There will be no reward for idleness ("all men will work"[8]) and no privileged social

---

4. Ibid., p. 11.

5. A defect of the otherwise useful selection and translation of Saint-Simon's works edited by F. M. H. Markham (*Henri Comte de Saint-Simon: Selected Writings* [Oxford: Blackwell, 1952]) is that it omits this section of the *Lettres* and so gives an inaccurate impression of the nature of the work.

6. Frank Manuel, the foremost contemporary interpreter of Saint-Simon, is of the view that up until the final period of his life Saint-Simon's "religious posturings" were essentially "literary artifices." By the time he composed his *New Christianity*, however, he had "truly come to believe . . . that he was the messiah of the new creed" (*The Prophets of Paris* [Cambridge: Harvard University Press, 1962], p. 142).

7. Saint-Simon, *Lettres,* vol. 1, p. 26.

8. Ibid., p. 55.

orders. Instead of envy and competition, there will be cooperation among all classes for the subjugation of nature. Everyone will recognize that those differentials in prestige and material reward that do exist among the three classes are based on merit and the quality of contribution to the common effort. (Saint-Simon was not an egalitarian in any sense: he held that there were natural and irremediable differences between men in intellect and creativity.)

The Redemptive Role of Science

Saint-Simon's faith in the redemptive mission of science and scientists is evident throughout the pages of the *Letters*. A majority of the Council of Newton was to be made up of mathematicians and physical or life scientists. Saint-Simon was greatly impressed by the precision and predictive power of the sciences, and already in this first work we have the germ of an idea that both he and Comte were to develop at length—the necessity for applying the methods and procedures of the physical and life sciences to the study of man's moral and political life. Comte came to call this endeavor "positivism," and although he developed his own positivist program at length and refined and deepened many of Saint-Simon's concepts, the original idea of establishing a science of society on the model of the natural—and specifically the life—sciences must be attributed to Saint-Simon. The seed of Comte's famous dictum *Savoir pour prévoir* ("To know in order to predict") may be found in Saint-Simon's pronouncement that "a scientist, my friends, is a man who predicts; it is because science gives us the means to predict that it is useful and that scientists [*les savants*] are superior to all other men."[9]

Saint-Simon's faith in the methods and results of the "hard" sciences implies a hostility to all "metaphysical" speculation. The new science of society must be modeled on physiology, and it is necessary that the physiologists "expel from their company the *philosophers, moralists, and metaphysicians,* as the astronomers have excluded the astrologers, as the chemists have excluded the alchemists."[10] He thus revolted against political philosophy as it had been known from Plato to Rousseau. In his

---

9. Ibid., p. 36. It should be noted that, at least in this essay, Saint-Simon is far more modest than Comte ever was about the scope of scientific knowledge. "Do not believe that I wish to give you the idea that scientists can predict everything," he writes in ibid., p. 37. In his *Mémoire sur la science de l'homme* of 1813, however, he was far bolder in his claims for the new science, which was to comprise natural sciences, politics, philosophy, and religion under a single "positive" principle. See the lengthy quotation from this work in Frank Manuel, *The New World of Henri Saint-Simon* (Cambridge: Harvard University Press, 1956), pp. 135–36.

10. Saint-Simon, *Lettres,* pp. 39–40.

enmity toward the "unscientific" and "metaphysical" approach of political philosophy, Saint-Simon continued and developed a theme central to the teaching of his immediate precursors, the ideologues of the postrevolutionary period. However, his conception of a social science resting on empirical "laws" comparable to those discovered by the natural sciences went beyond anything advocated by the ideologues. The roots of the positivist idea of a predictive political science modeled on the natural sciences are to be found in these lines written by Saint-Simon in 1814:

> Until now, the method of the sciences of observation has not been introduced into political questions; each individual has employed his own point of view and manner of reasoning and judging, and so it happens that there has yet been neither precision in the solutions proposed nor universality in the results proclaimed.
>
> The time has come when this infancy of the sciences should cease, and it is certainly desirable that it cease, for the troubles of the social order emerge from obscurities in political studies [la politique].[11]

The Structure of the New Order

Saint-Simon proceeded in the *Letters* to develop a plan according to which all classes, now transformed into functional groups, could participate in the activity and governance of the society. To the scientists he reserved the "spiritual power." This idea was to be embroidered at length in later writings. The scientists would replace the priests of the old religion and would serve as secular priests of the new. The temporal power would remain in the hands of the property owners. Saint-Simon was later to devise a name for the productive and progressive businessmen and industrialists of the new order: *les industriels*. The rulers of the new temporal order would be the present propertied classes (a concession, presumably, to win the support of these classes for his scheme), purged of parasitical elements. There would be no room in the society of the future for the idle rich (*les oisifs*) or for hereditary privileges (Saint-Simon himself had voluntarily given up his own title during the French Revolution). Finally, to the "largest and most numerous class," the manual workers of factory and farm, he gave the power to elect the "great leaders of humanity," the members of the Council of Newton, from among those nominated by experts. In order that the masses would be content with this largely symbolic power, Saint-Simon envisaged that

---

11. Saint-Simon, *De la réorganisation de la société européenne*, in *Oeuvres*, vol. 1, p. 183. For a discussion of Destutt de Tracy and the ideologues, see Dante Germino, *Beyond Ideology: The Revival of Political Theory* (New York: Harper & Row, 1967), pp. 48–51.

they would be thoroughly educated in the advantages of leaving to the more intelligent and active elements of society their spiritual and temporal governance.[12]

Saint-Simon quite clearly was sincerely convinced that without a fundamental reorganization of the world along these lines chaos was inevitable. There was no middle way: either the adoption of his scheme, which would "make of the earth a paradise,"[13] or total disorder. Yet the conviction that in a moment of divine illumination he had found the perfect answer to man's predicament did not prevent him from revising the details of his scheme frequently throughout his life. In 1819 he published a revised plan, this time with the collaboration of Comte, who had by then become his disciple and amanuensis, under the title of *L'Organisateur,* calling for all producers to be represented by three bodies:

1. The *Chambre d'invention,* made up of 200 engineers and artists, with the task of drawing up plans for public undertakings.
2. The *Chambre d'examination,* composed of 100 biologists and 100 physicists and mathematicians, whose function was to scrutinize and approve the plans.
3. The *Chambre d'exécution,* containing the most successful bankers, industrialists, and entrepreneurs, who would see to it that approved projects were expeditiously implemented.

Critiques of Technocracy. Saint-Simon and Comte's call for a government run principally by scientific and technocratic "experts" has been echoed by a number of people, most prominently by the Americans Lester Frank Ward at the end of the nineteenth century and, in our own day, Harold Lasswell, one of the most eminent of our contemporary political scientists. Many writers then and now, however, have been unconvinced of the merits and feasibility of such proposals. They fail to see how politics can be equated with administration, and they regard as philosophically untenable the attempt to reduce political and moral judgments, which are inherently concerned with qualitative and intangible questions, to precise measurement and quantification. Finally, they regard with skepticism the simplistic assumption that rule by self-appointed experts in "social physics" or "social engineering" would really be benevolent in practice, and doubt that even if it were, it would really redound to the dignity and well-being of man.

These and other objections to rule by experts in the new science of man either were not considered or were given short shrift by Saint-

---

12. Saint-Simon, *Lettres,* p. 47.
13. Ibid., p. 48.

Simon and Comte. They were not interested in the critical debate of first principles; absolutely certain of the correctness of their position, they were chiefly concerned with elaborating practical programs of reform and reconstruction.

Politics as the Science of Production

For Saint-Simon, the root of his inability to see that in practice politics is a competitive process concerned with the provisional establishment and continuous revision of priorities to meet changing societal conditions lay in his conviction that the question of priorities had already been settled and needed never to be debated again. For him, "the only reasonable and positive end politics can set for itself" was the "production of useful things." Politics, in fact, was nothing else than the "science of production." Society thus came to be regarded as similar to a factory. All problems were technical and administrative. The end itself, maximum productivity of "useful things"—useful for what and for whom?—was never questioned.

The Role of Religion in the Scientific Polity. It is true that Saint-Simon's interests and concerns were actually broader than many of his pungent aphorisms and catechismic conclusions would indicate. He was also interested in the inner life of man, and his disciples—men like Barthélemy Prosper Enfantin and Benjamin Olinde Rodrigues—wrote, sometimes sensitively, of the impoverishment of the human spirit that often accompanies the material advances of modern industrial society. For Saint-Simon, however, religion could not be understood on its own terms any more than practical politics could be. The new phenomenal science of man was a science of collective enrichment and increased material productivity. The function of religion was to serve as therapy to that end. Religion was made wholly subservient to worldly activity; its task was to instruct and move men to more faithful fulfillment of their social duties, to prod them to more efficacious activity on behalf of humanity. As Saint-Simon wrote:

> Nowadays the form of worship should be regarded only as a means of reminding men, on the day of rest, of philanthropic feelings and ideas, and dogma should be conceived only as a collection of commentaries aimed at the general application of these ideas and feelings to political developments, or encouraging the faithful to apply moral principles in their daily relationships.[14]

Saint-Simon possessed in full measure the apocalyptic vision and simplistic frame of mind characteristic of the most extreme of the po-

14. Saint-Simon, *New Christianity,* in *Selected Writings,* ed. Markham.

litical prophets and messiahs that have appeared in Western history to offer total redemption here and now—or at least in the proximate future. To this psychological disposition we must add a mania for system construction characteristic of the nineteenth century in particular. As his *Mémoire sur la science de l'homme* of 1813 illustrates, he was obsessed with the urge to reduce all explanations, all principles to a single overarching formula. There could be only *one* science, *one* government, *one* religion, *one* organization of social classes. Absolute and certain knowledge of the only correct way to organize and direct man's social existence had now, in the fullness of time, been revealed to an inspired hero of the human race, Claude Henri de Saint-Simon.

Progress Through Peace

In all of this there are many signposts pointing the way to totalitarianism. Saint-Simon was saved from embarking on this road by his consistent refusal to endorse violence as the means of establishing his new order. Despite their repeated failures to do so, he appears never to have doubted that the propertied classes (and the scientists themselves, many of whom, after all, might not wish to have such vast responsibilities thrust upon them) could be peacefully persuaded to adopt his project for universal salvation. The masses would go along as a matter of course.

Saint-Simon's philosophy of history was of a strongly progressivist variety. His optimistic view that history was moving in escalator-like fashion to ever higher plateaus of progress was reminiscent of Condorcet, but the similarity stops short at Saint-Simon's scientism. For Saint-Simon the future need not be left to random and unplanned progress; man's active intelligence, informed by the new all-encompassing science of man and society, could now rationally and centrally plan the future down to the smallest detail.

History and the Law of Alternativity

Saint-Simon viewed history, up until the presumably final dispensation of the new science, as having alternated between "organic" and "critical" periods. The "law of alternativity"[15] of the two periods operated in man's institutional life as well as in his scientific and intellectual development. An organic period was characterized by stability, synthesis, and consensus; a critical period was marked by instability, negative criticism, and a chaos of conflicting opinions. Critical periods were es-

---

15. See Manuel, *New World of Henri Saint-Simon*, chap. 11, pp. 139–40, for an elaboration of Saint-Simon's "law of alternativity."

sentially epochs of transition between the dissolution of one organic period and the emergence of another. In one of his works, *L'Industrie* (1816–1818), Saint-Simon

> divided universal history at two crucial points, the first sometime around the third and fourth centuries A.D., the second around the eleventh and twelfth, breaks or cut-off dates which resulted in three major divisions. The first had a polytheist ideology and a societal order based on slavery; the second, an ideology called "theological" and a feudal system; the ideology of the third, which had not yet attained fullness, was scientific or positive and its social system was industrial.[16]

What Comte was later with characteristically greater precision and rigor to call the "law of the three stages" of history was clearly present in Saint-Simon's writings. (The idea of conceiving of history triadically was not original with either man, however; it has a long history, going back at least to Joachim of Fiore in the twelfth century.) What is interesting about the conceptualizations of both Saint-Simon and Comte is the specific vocabulary they brought to the subject and their vision of the third age as one based on science. It is also noteworthy that certain variations in terminology are to be found in their works, perhaps in part at least as a result of Comte's desire to distinguish his doctrine from that of his former master after the break that occurred between them.

The Scientific Stage. To Saint-Simon, the periods did not succeed each other in any neat fashion; there was rather extensive overlapping of stages. Thus it was only at the present moment (that is, the nineteenth century) that the third or scientific stage was about to reach fruition, after an extensive period of preparation that began in the high Middle Ages. Saint-Simon saw the French Revolution, with all of its abstract, destructive, and "metaphysical" thinking, as the final watershed between the second and third periods. The third age would be organic in the full sense. In his *Du système industriel* of 1821, Saint-Simon proposed "measures finally to terminate the Revolution." Although it was necessary to pass through the disorder of the revolution in order to give the final death blow to feudalism and the theological ethos and thus prepare the way for the new scientific age, the liberal principles of the revolution in and of themselves could produce nothing lasting and constructive. He opposed most of the cardinal principles of liberalism: individualism, the rights of man, the parliamentary system, free competition in the intellectual, political, economic, and religious realms. In place of liberalism

---

16. Ibid., pp. 219–20.

he offered a doctrine of consensus in scientific, political, economic, and religious matters, centralized planning, administration by experts, and integration of each individual into the community.

The Four Criteria of Progress. Saint-Simon held that progress in history was measurable by means of four criteria. These criteria are perhaps of some interest today in view of the quantity of literature on "political development," a term that has come to be a kind of euphemism for progress. Saint-Simon's first criterion of advance in "social organization" was the extent to which a particular political and social form made the majority of men happy "by procuring for them the greatest means and faculties for the satisfaction of their elementary needs." The second criterion was the degree to which advancement in society was based upon ability rather than traditional privilege. The third was an increase in population. (An increase was taken as an index of the prosperity of a society. This criterion would be drastically revised by most contemporary students of political development, in view of the population crisis.) Saint-Simon's fourth standard for measuring political and social progress was the degree to which a society valued scientific and technological achievement and research.[17]

The New Christianity

Saint-Simon's last work, *New Christianity,* is in a sense simply a continuation and elaboration of the religious teaching of his first work. Written in the year of his death, it exercised a prodigious influence over his disciples. The leading themes are scarcely surprising, since they develop logically out of the propositions he expounded earlier. The only novelty is his decision to call his new unitary religion a form of Christianity, and one may only speculate as to why he did so.

In the *Letters* he had announced that God had removed the mantle of authority from the pope; now in *New Christianity* he dons the mantle himself. He is at once the new prophet and the new pope.[18] Both Protestantism and Catholicism are branded as "heretical" because each in its own way has betrayed the "single principle" on which God has determined to base his religion. That "single principle" is that "men should treat each other as brothers." It "comprises all that is divine in the Christian religion."[19]

For all of its talk of religion, *New Christianity* is singularly devoid

---

17 See ibid., pp. 227–28.

18. Saint-Simon, *New Christianity,* in *Selected Writings,* ed. Markham, p. 86: "The best theologian is the real Pope, God's deputy on earth. If the deductions I have made are correct . . . I shall have spoken in the name of God."

19. Ibid., p. 83.

of any indication of religious experience. The entire approach is utilitarian: the new religion will reinforce, especially for the masses, the ethical aspect of the Saint-Simonian teaching, which has itself been discovered independently by the new science. In defining brotherly love as the essence of the Christian religion, Saint-Simon transforms Christianity into a purely immanent social religion,[20] severing it from its grounding in the revelation of the world-transcendent God. Furthermore, in beclouding the authenticity of the initial revelatory event, in failing to mention the Incarnation, and in proclaiming himself as the new, presumably final, interpreter of the divine instructions, Saint-Simon cut himself off from any conceivably Christian position, and indeed from any religious position whatever as rigorously defined. What he did in a somewhat blurred fashion Comte was to do radically and systematically —that is, eliminate God and substitute humanity as the ultimate object of worship.

Social Welfare: Concerns and Contradictions

In his last years Saint-Simon became increasingly concerned about improving the welfare of "the most numerous and poorest class." This concern was also central to the political thought of his disciples and constitutes the link between his doctrine and that of continental European socialism. Indeed, the Saint-Simonians were among the first to use the term "socialist," which entered the Western political vocabulary in the late 1820s. Saint-Simon's "socialism," however, was quite foreign to the thinking of such men as Fourier and Proudhon, to say nothing of the later English and continental socialist reformers, because of its emphasis on detailed centralized planning, even of the spiritual life of the masses, and its neglect of or even contempt for spontaneity as a value. Fourier, Owen, Proudhon, and Marx, whatever the extensive differences among them, all rejected the paternalism and omnipresent centralized supervision characteristic of Saint-Simon's utopian social order. Instead of fabricating a substitute religion of humanity, all of these writers with the exception of Fourier were atheists of one form or another.

Saint-Simon's doctrine, particularly as it is put forward in *New Christianity*, is a strange combination of humanism and antihumanism. He seems to have been disingenuously ignorant of the antihumanistic implications of his counsels for manipulating the psychic conditions and behavior of men by deftly arousing in them both fear and hope—fear of the "terrible evils in store for them if they depart from the rules laid

---

20. Ibid., p. 104: "The happiness which comes from the esteem of one's fellow men is greater than any other form of happiness."

down" and hope that they will enjoy "the delights which will follow their efforts along the paths put before them."[21] And he seems to have been blissfully unaware of the contradiction between centering his teaching on love and "perpetual peace" and calling for the "mobilization" of all reconstituted societies against any "nation which tries to gain its own advantage at the expense of the good of the whole human race."[22] Such a nation would *ipso facto* be one that did not accept his principles, declared to be the only true ones. And yet Saint-Simon's emphatic and consistent rejection of violence as a means for winning converts to the new system,[23] as well as the evident sincerity of his concern for improving the "moral and physical existence" of the poor, reveals a constant core of humanistic commitment that prevents him from going over the abyss in the direction of what was to be known as totalitarianism. All the same, it must be concluded that he lacked the critical awareness and feel for the complexity of political reality characteristic of the political philosopher. He was blind to the ironic fact that a militant and messianic humanism[24] may in the actual world of the old Adam be derailed into a fanatical antihumanistic ideology that knows no limits.

THE SAINT-SIMONIANS

The Religious Movement

After Saint-Simon's death, a group of followers headed by Barthélemy Prosper Enfantin launched a movement aimed at developing the "mystical" aspects of the Master's teaching. The "scientific" content was not entirely neglected, but it formed only a minor part of their concern. The movement was constantly in difficulty with the authorities, and in assessing the accusations brought against them by the police it is perhaps impossible today to unravel fact from fiction. They preached a message of full psychic and physical liberation that anticipated in many respects the attack of contemporary radical thought on the "repressive society." Inevitably they were accused of advocating sexual promiscuity, but

21. Ibid., p. 103. In the language of a more contemporary doctrine of the political uses of psychology, these are forms of positive and negative reinforcement.

22. Ibid., p. 105.

23. Ibid., pp. 110–11. The New Christians, like the early Christians, "should use nothing but their intelligence to spread their doctrine. It is by persuasion and demonstration only that they should work...." New Christians should suffer any acts of violence and unjust condemnations that might be used against them; "but in no circumstances whatever, would they use physical force against their opponents, or act as judges or executioners."

24. For the messianic ingredient in Saint-Simon's thinking, see especially the passage in ibid., pp. 85–86, anticipating the spiritual and temporal unification of all men in one messianic "great age."

their intentions appear to have been rather to advocate purer and more authentic love relationships between human beings. When Enfantin spoke of free love, he seems quite clearly to have meant the freedom of each man to love in the way that would fulfill his own psychic needs; but it was perhaps inevitable that his words would be interpreted as a call for total promiscuity and the abandonment of all moral standards.[25]

In organizing themselves into a religious cult, the Saint-Simonians continued in the spirit of Saint-Simon's *New Christianity*, although not in its letter, for the cult muted the claim that its doctrine was based on Christianity and instead announced the need to find a female messiah for mankind. Enfantin, the father of the cult, claimed only to be the forerunner, the John the Baptist of the new messiah, who in fully emancipating her own sex would complete the emancipation of mankind. He led expeditions to Africa and the Near East in search of the Great Mother, but she was nowhere to be found.

Despite the strange and often comic aspects and trappings of this movement, a good deal of the social and political thought it produced was of a serious nature and deserves more study than it has generally received. The group's call for passional liberation, also sounded by Fourier, has been taken up today by such radical writers as Herbert Marcuse and Norman O. Brown, as well as in more measured terms by a whole host of neo-Freudians. As Frank Manuel has written in his able study *The Prophets of Paris*, the Saint-Simonians sought to achieve a "future world where the passions were free, where both jealousy and indifference had been extirpated, where each man loved and worked according to his capacity, where the flesh was not mortified, where monogamy was not imposed but was practiced spontaneously—though only by the monogamous."[26]

The Economic Movement

The economic ideas of the Saint-Simonians were also radicalized versions of tendencies in the Master's writings. Despite their constant adherence to their faith in spontaneity, they endorsed an economic system based on thoroughgoing centralization and control by a single governing board of financial experts. The nation was conceived as a single "workshop," in which presumably all mankind would eventually be included. In the "new world" individual owners and managers of firms "whose habits are alien to industrial labors" will no longer "control the

---

25. See Manuel, *Prophets of Paris*, p. 155. The entirety of chap. 5 of this work deals with the Saint-Simon school.

26. Ibid., p. 154.

choice of enterprises and the destiny of the workers." A "social institution" would be invested "with these functions that are so badly filled today." The unitary directing bank, whose governors would be able to "comprehend all parts of the workshop at the same time," would allocate resources, control investment, and "preside over all exploitation of materials."[27]

Although the Saint-Simonians were for thoroughgoing centralized control over the economy, they did not propose the elimination of private ownership of the means of production, and they were eager to distinguish their economic views from those of "communism." Nor did they advocate equality of rewards even as a distant goal. Income would be geared to productivity. With man's inner psychic conversion to the new morality, however, he would cease to place any importance on differentials in material wealth and type of occupation. He would lose the "possessive" mentality altogether and feel at one with all other human beings.

The Conflicting Demands of Freedom and Discipline

The Saint-Simonians made no explicit attempt to reconcile the conflicting demands for increased spontaneity and passional freedom on the one hand and the requirements of discipline, hard work, and increased productivity on the other. How could the psychology of the new man, liberated from all repression and free to follow the inclinations of his "psychic nature," fit in with the remorseless demands of an industrial and technological society?

One response to the dilemma could have been that of Fourier and Proudhon: to scrap industrial efficiency as the foremost aim of organized society and divide mankind into small groups of nearly self-sufficient producers in immediate relationship to their work, whether as farmers or as artisans. The Saint-Simonians chose instead to make the goals of passional liberation and spontaneity only a part of their total program for man's redemption. In the course of working out their objectives they claimed to have discovered in man a "tripartite nature"; the whole man was "at once a rational scientist, a practical industrial activist, and a man of feeling and moral drives, a creature of emotion."[28] To the disciples of Saint-Simon, these three principal inclinations—the scientific, the activist, and the emotional—were present in all men and were capable of endless development, and the problem of priorities was

---

27. Cited in ibid., p. 177.
28. Ibid., p. 165.

thus swept under the rug. It is indeed difficult to see how a total commitment to sexual liberation as they understood it would not come into sharp conflict with the relatively "repressive" demands of arduous and sustained mental and practical activity.

The Saint-Simonians: Forerunners of Totalitarianism?

At one point in his perceptive study, Frank Manuel considers whether the Saint-Simonians were precursors of twentieth-century totalitarian politics. He cites their collectivism ("association" was extolled at the expense of the individual), their amorphous concept of punishable moral "crimes" against science and society, their irrationalism, and their stress on hierarchy and the elite as the bases for accusations advanced by various writers that the Saint-Simonians were indeed champions of totalitarian politics—or better, antipolitics. Manuel perhaps goes too far in charitably relieving them of the burden of these accusations. And yet there is much truth to his contention that there is something "far-fetched" in the attempt to "relate the Saint-Simonians ... to the monster states of Hitler and Stalin." Manuel emphasizes their reliance on preaching and persuasion alone to win converts, the tremendous emphasis they placed on love, and their naive faith, inherited from Saint-Simon, that with the victory of their teaching men would certainly become more loving. "There was something unique about the German experience under the Third Reich. Remembrance of it should not be diluted by the discovery of antecedents that are of a qualitatively different character," Manuel observes.[29]

Manuel is unquestionably correct in rejecting any attempt to establish a direct link between political messianists such as the Saint-Simonians and the totalitarian regimes of Hitler and Stalin, with their systematic mass murders. There is a humanistic core to the thinking of the Saint-Simonians which separates them from these cold-blooded organizers of brutality. What he does not mention are the antihumanistic implications of many aspects of the Saint-Simonian teaching; in its simplistic antipoliticism, compulsive communitarianism, and eagerness for total solutions, Saint-Simonian doctrine tended to endorse the benevolent tyranny of the closed society over the individual. In this respect, Saint-Simon was a forerunner of B. F. Skinner and his "behaviorist" utopia. What was a strong tendency in the political thought of the school became the principal obsession of Saint-Simon's most gifted pupil, Auguste Comte, the disciple who "betrayed" his master.

---

29. Ibid., p. 184.

AUGUSTE COMTE

Comte first met Saint-Simon in 1817, when he was nineteen and Saint-Simon was in his late fifties. Saint-Simon was looking for a secretary and was impressed with the young man's scientific training (he had just been graduated from the famous École Polytechnique). Saint-Simon not only hired Comte as his secretary but regarded him as his intimate collaborator, almost an adopted son. Inevitably, since the two men had widely differing temperaments, they quarreled after a few years. Comte was too independent a thinker to serve as a disciple for long, and in his first pamphlets, written from 1819 to 1822, he demonstrated disagreement with Saint-Simon over the priority to be given the elaboration of an all-encompassing science of man. Saint-Simon had sketched the bare outline for such a science in his *Mémoire sur la science de l'homme* in 1817, and Comte was convinced that its completion was essential as the first step toward thoroughgoing political and social reconstruction of human affairs. The activist phase could come later. In 1824 the two men quarreled fiercely and severed their relationship. The occasion for their break was a dispute over whether Comte's essay, *Le système de politique positive*, should be included as part of Saint-Simon's own *Catéchisme des industriels*. Comte insisted on being given credit for the essay, and Saint-Simon finally consented, but only after informing Comte that this marked the end of their association. Comte was convinced that Saint-Simon was jealous of his ability, and declared he would never forgive his former mentor for having tried to claim credit for his work, and for ending the relationship when Comte would not submit.[30]

Positivism and the Universal Religion

Comte published voluminously throughout his lifetime. He himself came to distinguish two phases in his thought, the "Aristotelian" and the "Platonic." His first phase, down to the publication of his *Discours sur l'ensemble du positivisme* (*Treatise on the General View of Positivism*) of 1848, tended to be relatively more analytical, and emphasized the meaning of "positivist" methodology—for he was the true inventor of the term "positivism," even if he must share with Saint-Simon the honor of having introduced the concept. It was during this first phase that he attracted the support of John Stuart Mill, who had been impressed by the methodological principles set forth in Comte's six-volume *Cours de philosophie positive* (1830–1842). In his later phase Comte turned increasingly to practical problems of organizing, down to the last detail,

---

30. See ibid., pp. 251–54.

the "positive polity" on the basis of the new "positivist philosophy." The new religion of Humanity (always capitalized) became ever more central to his concerns, and he himself became increasingly obsessed with his role as "Founder of the Universal Religion" and "High Priest of Humanity," titles he conferred upon himself and with which, in the last year of his life, he signed his letters. Inasmuch as he came to regard himself as identical with the Great Being (that is, with his God-substitute, Humanity), he insisted that his own person was sacred—far more sacred than that of the Catholic pontiff. Not surprisingly, many of his earlier supporters, including Mill, fell by the wayside when confronted with these developments. To them, Comte had at the very least betrayed the scientific principles that he had originally claimed to be the basis of his "mystical" and "religious" sentiment, and had transformed them into despotic schemes for total control of the lives of individuals by the new society.[31]

Although there does appear to have been some break in Comte's intellectual and spiritual development, it would be an exaggeration to assume that there was any abrupt reversal of his earlier views. His conception of the "positive polity" as flowing ineluctably from the positivist science or "philosophy" was expressed as early as 1844, in his *Discours sur l'esprit positif*,[32] and his conception of the new religion of Humanity, together with its ritual, was expounded in detail in the last chapter of the *Discours sur l'ensemble du positivisme* of 1848.[33] Of all his many works, this one provides us with his most succinct and coherent account of positivism as at once a scientific, political, and religious doctrine.

The General View of Positivism

After Comte's death, Paul Littré, a former disciple, together with Comte's widow, attempted to have a good part of Comte's later works on his religion of Humanity suppressed on the grounds that they were the products of a mental aberration brought on by a physical illness in the latter part of his life. Those of Comte's disciples who remained faithful fought this attempt in court and were successful, after many years of litigation, in preventing the mutilation of the Comtean *corpus*. Comte

---

31. See ibid., p. 265.

32. For a discussion of the *Discours sur l'esprit positif*, originally published in Paris in 1844, see Germino, *Beyond Ideology*, pp. 53–55.

33. Translated into English as *A General View of Positivism, or Summary Exposition of the System of Thought and Life Adapted to the Great Western Republic* (London, 1865). It is true, however, that Comte's apotheosis of Clothilde de Vaux, whom he ardently pursued in life but worshiped as the virgin mother after her death, did add a new element to his religious views in his last few years. See Manuel, *Prophets of Paris*, p. 268.

himself provided the rebuttal against any claim that his positivist methodology could be severed from his politico-religious teaching in the Introduction to the *Discours sur l'ensemble du positivisme*, in which he defined positivism as

> essentially . . . a Philosophy and a Polity. These can never be dis-
> severed; the former being the basis, and the latter the end of one
> comprehensive system, in which our intellectual faculties and our
> social sympathies are brought into close correlation with each other.
> For . . . the science of society, besides being more important than any
> other, supplies the only logical and scientific link by which all our
> varied observations of phenomena can be brought into one consistent
> whole.[34]

For Comte, positivism was a "regenerating doctrine" that, when it
had sufficiently permeated contemporary European and eventually world
society, would redeem man from his present condition of corruption,
near-anarchy, and ignorance. Positivism, then, was not only an epistemology or scientific doctrine; it was an all-embracing creed to be propagated
(and Comte apparently invented the word "propaganda" with the term
"positivism") throughout society.

The Initial Converts. Initially, Comte held, few converts to the new
creed could be expected from the upper classes. Members of these classes
were all in bondage to the outmoded "metaphysical theories" of the
previous age and were chiefly concerned with the preservation of their
privileges. It was rather to the workers (the "proletariat") and the
women that he looked for support. These two groups, comprising the
vast majority of society, in cooperation with a small vanguard of philosophers, would initiate the final decisive revolution in human history.
It would be, Comte believed, a peaceful revolution. Women were particularly appropriate as agents for universal redemption because in
the female psyche we witness the "subordination of intellect to social
feeling."[35]

The Laws of Man and Nature. For Comte, "the object of all true
Philosophy is to frame a system which shall comprehend life under every
aspect, social as well as individual. It embraces, therefore, the three kinds
of phenomena of which our life consists, Thoughts, Feelings, and
Actions."[36] As a science based on the observation of phenomena, positive

---

34. Comte, *General View of Positivism*, p. 1. Frank Manuel incorrectly attributes
the opening sentence and the first part of the second sentence (from "Positivism" to
"dissevered") in this quotation to Comte's English disciple Dr. J. H. Bridges. See
Prophets of Paris, p. 267.

35. Comte, *General View of Positivism*, pp. 3–4.

36. Ibid., p. 8.

philosophy aimed to discover the "definite and invariable laws" that govern human behavior and development. For Comte, however, positivism was not only or even chiefly a contemplative science; it was also operational and active. It sought to employ the knowledge gained of the laws governing the development of humanity in such a way that mankind, which had hitherto progressed passively, borne along by the process itself, could actively intervene in and accelerate the process so as to realize its full potential for well-being and happiness. The "system" of reality, he held, was in part capable of modification; science did not teach the dominion of nature over man but of man over nature in accordance with nature's laws:

> We are . . . able to modify this process systematically; and the importance of this is extreme, since we can thereby greatly diminish the partial deviations, the disastrous delays, and the grave inconsistencies to which so complex a growth would be liable were it left entirely to itself. To effect this necessary intervention is the proper sphere of politics.[37]

Human Intellect. Only now, in Comte's own time, had man reached the stage where he was capable of applying positive science, hitherto confined to "the study of the inorganic world," to the totality of his life, including the moral and social spheres. But although Comte called for the greatest possible extension of scientific intelligence to the analysis of human existence, he was careful to point out that he did not mean thereby to enthrone the intellect as the highest human faculty. Rather paradoxically, the new science of man showed man's intellect to be inherently weak; properly, it was the servant of the passions and above all of the most sublime and necessary passion, social feeling. It was a manifestation of unpardonable pride for man to place his own individual intellect above the demands of society: this was the error of "metaphysical" thinking, with its conceptions of individualism and natural rights. "The intellect is intended for service, not for empire; when it imagines itself supreme, it is really only obeying the personal instead of the social instincts."[38] It was a "fundamental doctrine" of positivism that "the Heart preponderates over the Intellect."[39]

The Law of Human Development. It is in the first chapter of the *General View* that Comte gives perhaps his most succinct formulation of his famous "law of the three stages," which he held to be "the general

---

37. Ibid.
38. Ibid., p. 17.
39. Ibid., p. 18.

law of human development, social as well as intellectual." According to this law,

> our speculations upon all subjects whatsoever, pass necessarily through three successive stages: the Theological stage, in which free play is given to spontaneous fictions, admitting of no proof; the Metaphysical stage, characterised by the prevalence of personified abstractions or entities; lastly, the Positive stage, based upon an exact view of the facts of the case. The first, though purely provisional, is invariably the point from which we start; the third is the only permanent or normal state; the second has but a modifying or rather a solvent influence, which qualifies it for regulating the transition from the first stage to the third. We begin with theological Imagination, thence we pass through metaphysical Discussion, and we end at last with positive Demonstration. Thus by means of this one general law we are enabled to take a comprehensive and simultaneous view of the past, present, and future of Humanity.[40]

The Laws of Scientific Classification and Political Development. To this law of human development Comte added two others wholly consistent with the first: the law of classification of the sciences and the law of political development. (The latter has a very contemporary ring indeed.) Each of the sciences passed through three comparable stages or developments. The six sciences, or rather the six divisions of the single science of Humanity—mathematics, astronomy, physics, chemistry, biology, and (the last to appear) sociology—evolved from simple and general to complex and specific conceptions.

Inasmuch as Comte held that there was an "unbroken connection between the development of Activity and that of Speculation," on the "combined influence" of which "depends the development of Affection," he saw a parallel three-stage pattern emerging with respect to "active, that is to say, of political development. Human activity . . . passes suc-

---

40. Ibid., pp. 34–35. Comte's terminology was somewhat confusing: he regarded the medieval theologians as representatives of the beginning of the "metaphysical" rather than the "theological" stage. The "positive" stage had its incipient beginnings with Galileo and Bacon, but was only fully coming into its own with Comte himself, just as the metaphysical stage, with its abstractions of "natural rights," etc., had come to a decisive end with the French Revolution. Clearly there was a good deal of overlapping among the three stages. Comte considered the theological stage in all its manifestations from polytheism to monotheism and its rituals of "fetishistic" worship to have been preserved and definitively superseded by positivism. "Metaphysicism," however, was a negative, provisional, and "critical" stage of no inherent value save as a necessary period of transition between the two "organic" periods—the initial "theological" and the final "positive" stage. See Manuel, *Prophets of Paris,* pp. 277–83, for a discussion of the complexities of Comte's terminology of the three stages.

cessively through the stages of Offensive warfare, Defensive warfare, and Industry."[41]

For Comte, if one viewed man's intellectual and social development in terms of the three stages—theological, metaphysical, and positive—one possessed "a complete explanation of history." In all its manifestations the law of the three stages "reproduces in systematic form the only historical conception which has become adopted by universal consent"; that is, the division of history into ancient, medieval, and modern periods.[42]

The Closed Society of the Positive Age

Comte participated fully in a tendency of much of nineteenth-century thought—the passion for grandiose system construction. To him, as for Saint-Simon, all knowledge had to rest on a single principle, and no loose ends could be left lying around after the scientist-philosopher had done his work. In order that this system could be achieved, the universe with which thought was to deal had to be closed to the consideration of "metaphysical questions." Inevitably this meant that the social and political aspects of Comte's teaching would be based on a conception of a closed society. The Metaphysical Age—one of disputes and questioning about the origin and end of existence, the basis of political obligation, natural rights and natural law, and all the rest—was to be "permanently" and "finally" superseded by the Positive Age, which was only just beginning and which would be characterized by consensus and agreement in intellectual matters. Positive science, based on exact, certain knowledge, would banish doubt, anxiety, and dispute from the scene. Such a felicitous result was to be effected not by coercion but by irrefutable "demonstration" of the validity of the "laws" uncovered by the positivist scientist. All would be led to accept the truth of these laws as completely as they had accepted Newton's law of gravity.

Comte was clearly convinced that his doctrine was the inevitable wave of the future, and so he never clearly faced up to the problem of dissent. What would happen to those individuals who stubbornly persisted in asking metaphysical questions, who refused to confine their studies only to areas that "social feeling" had declared to be "legitimate" and "useful"? What fate would await those who refused to acknowledge that with positivism a "firm objective basis" had been laid down for the "complete coordination of human existence"?[43] Although Comte clearly

---

41. Comte, *General View of Positivism*, pp. 34–35.
42. Ibid.
43. Ibid., pp. 37–38.

did not anticipate that dissent would be a serious problem, his later writings do acknowledge the probability of certain "social misfits," who would have to be either rehabilitated or punished. But even if corporal punishment or imprisonment were kept to a minimum in Comte's society, it is clear that the social pressures to conform would be enormous. It is small wonder that John Stuart Mill found Comte's "positive polity" the most despotic system ever conceived. Although it would be misleading to label Comte's system totalitarian, there is no doubt that it is an extreme example of the closed society and, as such, wholly inimical to the freedom of the human spirit. It is equally clear that a totalitarian society such as those that have developed in the twentieth century was far from Comte's intentions, which were to extol, serve, and minister to the well-being of all humanity. Again we encounter the irony of the professed militant humanist whose teaching, if adopted, would lead inexorably to antihumanistic conclusions.

Provisional Freedom. It is quite true that Comte was in favor of freedom of speech and inquiry so long as the "provisional," prepositivist order, or what he liked to call the "spiritual interregnum," lasted. "Positivism," he declared, "is now the only consistent advocate of free speech and free inquiry. Schools of opinion which do not rest on demonstration . . . can never be sincere in their wish for Liberty, in the extended sense here given to it."[44] Comte therefore called for the abandonment by the state of its monopoly of education. However, one cannot overlook the fact that he endorsed free speech and inquiry only during the period of transition between the Metaphysical Age and the Positive Age. Freedom of inquiry as such was anathema to him, as it was to Saint-Simon. It was appropriate to an age of criticism and social anarchy. Under positivism all would acknowledge the truth of a single doctrine and ritual.

It might also be said in Comte's defense that he insisted on the separation of spiritual and temporal powers in the new society. He applauded certain aspects of the medieval system, among them the distinction between the spiritual and temporal realms.[45] However, the influence he expected the positivist "clergy"—scientists and women—to

---

44. Ibid., p. 128.

45. Ibid., pp. 92–94. By separating the moral from the temporal sphere, Comte expected to preserve both positivist science and religion from corruption. Temporal affairs would continue to be managed by bankers and industrialists. Inequality of rewards and the system of private property would be retained, although the great majority of men would have achieved both material sufficiency and spiritual happiness and so would not be envious of those who possessed greater power and wealth (i.e., the managers of the temporal power). For Comte's discussion of property and his condemnation of all systems of communism, which he regarded as "subversive," see ibid., pp. 172f. Comte held that "capitalists" would be the "political leaders of modern society" (ibid., p. 394).

exert over the entire social order was so vast as to minimize the significance of the distinction.[46] Still, this aspect of his teaching is of some importance with respect to the question of whether he was a precursor of totalitarianism. As I have already indicated, I believe the answer given for Saint-Simon and his followers must in principle apply also to Comte, even though Comte's system was more rigid than Saint-Simon's and he devoted much more attention to the control of human behavior. Comte advocated a closed society but not, in principle at least, a terroristic one. He clearly conceived both the process of take-over and the eventual rule by the positivists to be based on persuasion and the freely accepted authority of the new science. It would have been an exceedingly unfree society and it might well have degenerated into totalitarian terrorism after the anticipated mass conversion to positivism failed to take place; but both charity and accuracy compel us to note that Comte's political program was not totalitarian in intention, and that a certain humanism is implicit in the entire approach, even if the human person is often lost sight of in the idolatry of Humanity.

The Nonexistence of the Individual. I have described Comte's endorsement of a closed society. We might go one step further and call it a smothering society. "Social feeling," "love for others," the benevolence of the new society—these are the themes that he constantly stresses.[47] Indeed, he goes so far toward submerging the individual in the collectivity that at one point he even denies that the individual exists! "Man indeed, as an individual, cannot properly be said to exist, except in the exaggerated abstractions of modern metaphysicians," he informs us. "Existence in the true sense can only be predicated of Humanity...."[48]

The Religion of Humanity

Comte's "religion of Humanity" was the capstone of his system. He held his discovery of this religion to be on a par with his scientific discoveries;

---

46. See for example, Comte's comment at the very end of the *General View,* where he observes that the "priests of Humanity," who are the systematic organs of the moderating power, will always find themselves supported, in their attempts to modify the governing power, by women and by the people—i.e., by the "workers" or "proletariat" (ibid., p. 423). "Modify" in this context is more likely to mean "control." Comte never faced up to the problem of restraints on the "priests" themselves; the fact that they did not possess temporal power was supposedly sufficient. Readers will note a parallel with Plato's *Republic;* but for Plato the best regime was in principle a paradigm that would not be actualized in history, barring a miracle. The difference between a paradigm and a utopia is fundamental.

47. See, for example, his statement that positivism "sets forth social feeling as the first principle of morality.... To live for others it holds to be the highest happiness. To become incorporate with Humanity... is the constant aim of life... self-love... is the greatest infirmity of our nature..." (ibid., p. 374).

48. Ibid., p. 354.

indeed, the former was the completion of the latter. The "unity of Positivism as a system of life" could be established only if it were "condensed round one single principle.... There should be a central point in the system, towards which Feeling, Reason, and Activity alike converge."[49]

Such a central point for the positivist system, he wrote,

> we find in the great conception of Humanity, towards which every aspect of Positivism naturally converges. By it the conception of God will be entirely superseded, and a synthesis be formed, more complete and permanent than that provisionally established by the old religions.... Towards Humanity, who is for us the only true Great Being, we, the conscious elements of whom she is composed, shall henceforth direct every aspect of our life, individual or collective. Our thoughts will be devoted to the knowledge of Humanity, our affections to her love, our actions to her service.[50]

In subsequent years Comte was to develop further the "theology" of the religion of Humanity, adding, perhaps in conscious or unconscious imitation of the Christian Trinity, two other objects of worship besides the Great Being: the Grand Fetish (the earth) and the Grand Medium (space). He also developed in detail some other ideas only briefly mentioned in the *General View of Positivism*. He invented a new thirteen-month calendar, with each day and month named for a great scientist or artist. He anticipated group therapy when he elaborated a system of group worship designed to reinforce social feeling and reduce unproductive and hostile impulses. He also devised ceremonies and "sacraments" to mark each stage of one's life, from birth to "incorporation" or "transformation" in the Great Being.[51] (Comte's denial of the existence of the individual as such enabled him to deal with the awkward subject of death with a certain familiar ease: Since Humanity itself was presumably immortal, death could come only to those who failed to do their duty to Humanity. These were to be buried in the "field of the forgotten"; the faithful would be "transformed," the occasion celebrated with fitting ceremony.) Comte even devised positivist marriage ceremonies, over which he officiated. It was only logical that he should finally confer upon himself the title of High Priest of Humanity. And it is scarcely to be wondered at that, as his conviction of his sacred character

---

49. Ibid., p. 348.

50. Ibid., pp. 349–50.

51. The positivist "sacraments" were: presentation of the infant, initiation at fourteen, admission at twenty-one, destination at twenty-eight, marriage before thirty-five, maturity at forty-two, retirement at sixty-two, and finally the sacrament of transformation.

grew, Comte became increasingly intolerant of those who failed to recognize it, and consigned his opponents to the positivist equivalent of hell.

The Positivist World

From the very beginning, Comte had demonstrated his fondness not only
for sweeping generalizations and historical "laws," but also for minute
legislative details to be carried out by the future society. The latter impulse became progressively stronger with age, as he grew increasingly
convinced that he was the supreme legislator of mankind, and indeed one
who had become virtually identical with the Great Being himself. Thus,
for example, in the *General View* we find Comte giving quite extraordinarily detailed instructions about the two positivist flags (one
religious and the other political) that would be used in the new society:

> To speak first of the banner to be used in religious services. It should
> be painted on canvass. On one side the ground would be white; on
> it would be be the symbol of Humanity, personified by a woman of
> thirty years of age, bearing her son in her arms. The other side would
> bear the religious formula of the Positivists: *Love is our Principle,
> Order is our Basis, Progress our End,* upon a ground of green, the
> colour of hope, and therefore most suitable for emblems of the future.
>   Green, too, would be the colour of the political flag, common
> to the whole West. . . . The principal motto of Positivism will, in this
> case, be divided into two, both alike significant. One side of the flag
> will have the political and scientific motto, Order and Progress; the
> other, the moral and esthetic motto, Live for Others. The first will
> be preferred by men; the other is more specifically adapted to
> women, who are thus invited to participate in these public mani-
> festations of social feelings.[52]

For the purpose of the worldwide propagation of the positivist faith,
Comte called for the establishment of a Positive Council (needless to say,
chaired by himself), initially composed of forty-eight members. The
majority of the membership would be drawn from the countries of
western Europe; membership from countries outside Europe would be
gradually increased in accordance with the social development of the
various countries and the spread of positivist ideas within them. France
would be the hegemonic nation, and Paris, where Comte would establish
his headquarters, would be a spiritual world capital—a new Rome.

Colonization. Comte's benevolent attention to the psychological
management of the lives of individual European positivists was to be

---

52. Comte, *General View of Positivism,* pp. 413–14. Interestingly enough,
Comte's motto "Order and Progress" was emblazoned by some of his followers on
the flag of Brazil, where it remains to this day.

extended to nonwestern peoples, who were to be blessed by the advantages of spiritual colonization by the future positivist Europe. "Wise and generous intervention of the West on behalf of our sister nations who are less advanced, will form a noble field for Social Art, when based on sound scientific principles." Comte predicted that this type of "intervention," designed to convert the "retarded" peoples of Asia, Africa, and elsewhere to the religious and political systems of positivism, "will form a system of moral and political action far nobler than the proselytism of theology or the extension of military empire." He was clearly blind to the fact that what he proposed was simply another form of Western imperialism, just as he was blind to the fact that, from an internal point of view, his system of positive polity was based on a stifling paternalism— not to say despotism—toward the populace for whose benefit he constructed it.

That Comte advocated a new style of Western cultural and intellectual imperialism is not at all surprising, given his premises. What is surprising, in view of his insistence on the oneness of Humanity and the universalism of his doctrine, was his apparent advocacy, in one place at least, of the doctrine of white supremacy. "The first [after Europe] to join the Western movement will necessarily be the remaining portion of the White race: which in all its branches is superior to the other two races,"[53] he wrote in the concluding pages of The General View of Positivism. Yet this statement, however regrettable, apparently referred to the cultural rather than the biological "superiority" of the "White race." He does not appear to have believed in the permanent inferiority of nonwhite peoples; presumably such nations would in time "catch up" with the "advanced" countries of Europe. In this decisive respect, Comte's "racism" must be distinguished from the pseudo-science and corrupt biologism of such notorious racist intellectuals as the Comte de Gobineau in France, Richard Wagner in Germany, and Houston Stewart Chamberlain in Britain.

Positivism in Retrospect

We have seen that to Comte himself, no separation of the intellectual, social, and religious aspects of positivism was conceivable, and that indeed the foundations of his entire doctrine had been erected in his earlier writings. Those former disciples, like Littré, who saw a logical contradiction between his positivist methodology and his detailed system of legislation for the future positive polity were certainly correct, however. In the Discours sur l'esprit positif of 1844, Comte wrote that positivism

53. Ibid., p. 417.

acknowledged as a fundamental methodological principle that "every proposition which is not strictly reducible to the enunciation of a fact ... is unable to offer any real and intelligible sense."[54] He thereby anticipated the "verification principle" adopted by the "logical positivists" of the Vienna Circle in the 1920s. Comte was at one with twentieth-century positivists in rejecting "metaphysical" propositions as incapable of empirical verification. And he enunciated a cardinal tenet of behavioral social science, which (at least until recently, when changed conceptions of the natural sciences have begun to have their impact) has aspired to the prediction and control of human behavior through the articulation of tested operational propositions that uncover behavioral regularities with a precision comparable to that of the "hard" sciences. Comte's famous motto, *Savoir pour prévoir* ("To know in order to predict") could well serve as a summation of the aspirations of a contemporary behavioralist writer such as Harold Lasswell.

It is difficult to imagine how anyone could more flagrantly violate the positivist injunction against claiming scientific status for nonempirical or—in the language of later positivism—"value" propositions than did Comte himself. His political and religious utopia is a reflection of his own tormented emotional experience and his own desperate search for absolutes to fill the void left by the uprooting of the traditional religions and the philosophies of both the classical and the modern ages. He believed that he had shown that all previous political and religious speculation had been definitively superseded and "outmoded" by the advance of "positive" science. It is perhaps instructive, however, that even a man who sought salvation through science, who yearned to extend to all areas of life and thought the certainty and rigor he believed scientific knowledge to possess, could not escape constructing what amounts to a parody of the metaphysical and religious world views he opposed and despised. Those who seek a critical and authentically empirical social and political science based on the multidimensional human experience may eventually find the drama of Comte's emotional struggle, which gave rise to the fantastic, bizarre, and oppressive political and religious system he concocted, more instructive than the restrictive positivist methodology he so freely violated. For Comte was in many respects an intelligent and sensitive man struggling to make sense out of the human predicament. We can learn much from his errors, derailments, and enthusiasms.

---

54. Comte, *Discours sur l'esprit positif* (1844; reprinted, with a German translation, Hamburg, 1956), p. 26.

12

Messianic Nationalism:
Fichte and Mazzini

Nationalism, like socialism and democracy, has many meanings, each depending on the context in which the term is used. Nationalism is easily praised and easily condemned; understanding it is rather more difficult.

The type of nationalism that may properly be described as messianic has become the subject of a growing body of literature, among which one of the more useful volumes is Elie Kedourie's study, which despite its fundamental lack of sympathy with this sort of movement ranks as a major critical analysis of it.[1] According to Kedourie, the word "nation" was not used in a way that would make it amenable to a messianic interpretation until the French Revolution. For the Romans, *natio* was a group of men, larger than the family but smaller than the "people" (*populus*), who shared common customs and a common place of birth. During the Middle Ages *natio* was used in vague and imprecise ways, sometimes to designate various linguistic groupings within the larger *respublica christiana*. Machiavelli also employed it in an imprecise way. When he spoke of his *patria* (country) he ordinarily meant Florence, and when he referred to France, Spain, or some other area, he often used *provincia* (province). He sometimes even used *nazione* (nation) as a term of abuse when he spoke of a faction or clique; thus he referred to the Ghibellines as a "nation."

Subsequently in the modern period "nation" acquired a specifically political meaning, indicating a body of persons that could represent or choose representatives for a particular territory (the *pays legal*); this body, generally composed in Europe of the aristocracy, clergy, and non-titled property owners, constituted only a very small portion of the total population. With the French Revolution, "nation" took on the connotation of popular sovereignty. The nation was here conceived as more than a part of the people; the people as a whole were held to possess sovereignty

---

1. Elie Kedourie, *Nationalism* (London: Hutchinson, 1960).

when they came together to decide on a scheme for their government and to elect a legislature to act in their name. The democratic idea thus became an essential ingredient of the concept of the nation; states that did not rest on the will of the people were not viewed as nations in the true sense.

During the nineteenth century the idea of the nation underwent further evolution; for the first time the definition of the nation came to include a common language and a common ethnic (or "racial") origin. It was at this time that the idea of self-determination of a people defined as a "natural" division of the human race made its way into the political vocabulary of the West. Each "nation" or "people" was held to be entitled to its own independent "state"; societies that included more than one linguistic-ethnic group or nation, such as the Austro-Hungarian Empire, were regarded as historical anomalies or anachronisms, doomed to be replaced by as many nation-states as the number of peoples they currently incorporated.[2]

Kedourie sharply distinguishes nationalism from patriotism, and he deems it erroneous to date the history of nationalism from any point in time earlier than the French Revolution. He takes issue with historians who date the rise of nationalism from the sixteenth century, and denies that the leaders of the English and American Revolutions can be regarded as "nationalists" in the strict sense.

> Patriotism, affection for one's country or one's group, loyalty to its institutions, and zeal for its defence, is a sentiment known among all kinds of men; so is xenophobia, which is dislike of the stranger. ... Neither sentiment depends on a particular [racial-linguistic] anthropology and neither asserts a particular doctrine of the state or of the individual's relation to it. Nationalism does both; it is a comprehensive doctrine which leads to a distinctive style of politics. But far from being a universal phenomenon, it is the product of the last 150 years.[3]

My only quarrel with Kedourie's interpretation is that he tends to equate nationalism as such with messianic nationalism (a term he does not employ but which would have lent clarity to his analysis). Later in the book he does distinguish between "Whig" (or Anglo-American) and "continental" nationalism, but this distinction ignores significant divergencies within both Anglo-American and continental nationalist thought. The tenor of his argument tends to condemn most of the nationalist movements that have secured the political independence of their countries in

---

2. Ibid., pp. 13–19 and *passim.*
3. Ibid., p. 74.

our own time. While these sweeping conclusions and negative judgments are unacceptable to all but the most conservative students of politics, they should not blind us to the value of Kedourie's insights into one particular strand of nationalism which is of relatively recent origin and which constitutes an ingredient (although ordinarily only one of many) in contemporary nationalist movements and "new" nations around the world. As the example of current nations such as India, Singapore, Canada, and the Philippines indicates, it is possible for nationalism based on linguistic, cultural, and ethnic diversity to be open to universal values and a cosmopolitan outlook. This kind of nationalism may be called "moderate" as distinct from "messianic."

JOHANN GOTTLIEB FICHTE

Fichte (1762–1814) is one of the more interesting and influential exponents of a kind of political attitude prevalent among many nineteenth-century intellectuals who called for fulfillment of man in a world-immanent collectivity. He was a strenuous activist who insisted that the world be reshaped in accordance with the demands of reason; a rational society for him was one that acknowledged man's rights to equal recognition in society and his need for communal participation with his fellows.

Fichte looked upon the nation as the proper mechanism by which man's self-realization might be achieved. Although he was perhaps not entirely impervious to specious biologism, on the whole he regarded the nation as a cultural entity, and, like Mazzini after him, saw nationalism and cosmopolitanism as complementary rather than contradictory. At a late point in his career, presumably under the influence of the Napoleonic invasion and its subsequent repulsion, he came to emphasize the crucial role of force in international relations; in this important respect he was quite unlike Mazzini, who never wavered in his conviction that a world-wide association of free and equal nations to ensure world peace was the way of the future.

It is scarcely surprising that Fichte should have found aspects of Machiavelli's political teaching attractive; like his famous Florentine predecessor, he dreamed of some kind of political unification of his divided homeland and its liberation from foreign domination. It was not only the final chapter of *The Prince*, with its fiery call for the liberation of Italy, that appealed to him in Machiavelli, however; it was also Machiavelli's apparent insistence that force rather than the moral law calls the tune in international relations. (As we saw in Chapter 2, Machiavelli's teaching was more complex than this; there is a moral

dimension to his comprehensive political thought that Fichte missed.)
Yet Fichte did not entirely approve of the "amoral" approach he believed
Machiavelli had adopted; on the whole, his own turgid prose is
characterized by a fervent and often tedious moral earnestness. But in the
final years of his life, after witnessing the turbulent events of the period
and the conquest of his homeland by the French, he came to adopt the
view that the right of the strongest was the ultimate governing factor in
relations between nations, at least in the stage of historical development
through which men were just then passing.[4]

Because of this teaching and other excesses, Fichte has often been
portrayed as one of the principal forerunners of Hitler's National Socialism. It would appear that this designation has in general been applied far
too loosely to German thinkers prior to the Hitler regime and that it is
often wide of the mark. One cannot deduce the main strands of Nazi
ideology from Fichte's thought, even though it is true that some Nazi
propagandists purported to find inspiration in his teachings.[5]

Both Kant and Rousseau had a profound influence on Fichte's intellectual development. Fichte saw himself as carrying forward and per-
fecting Kant's philosophical idealism, although he threw Kant's caution
to the wind by failing to observe the limits he had assigned to reason.
Specifically, Fichte could not tolerate the notion that the Kantian *Ding
an Sich* (thing-in-itself) remain in essence unknowable and beyond the
reach of consciousness.[6] Like so many nineteenth-century intellectuals, he
possessed an absolute mania for philosophical system construction, but
unlike Hegel, he did not possess the philosophical gifts to overcome the
deadening effect of his system and make a major contribution to the
history of philosophy.

The *Ich*: From Autonomy to Submission

Fichte's emphasis upon the ego, or the *Ich*, led him in the direction of
an extreme subjectivism, and he clearly revealed what Nietzsche was to

4. See Reinhold Aris, *History of Political Thought in Germany from 1789 to
1815* (London: Allen & Unwin, 1936), p. 357. The title of Fichte's interesting essay
on Machiavelli, written in 1807, is "Ueber Machiavell, als Schriftsteller, und Stellen
aus seinen Schriften."

5. The NSDAP publishing house put out a selection of Fichte's writings entitled *Rufe an die deutsche Nation* (Berlin: Zentralverlag der NSDAP, 1943), edited by
Hans Schmoldt. The only remarkable thing about this edition was the negligible
amount of assistance it was able to contribute to the spread of Nazi ideology, even
when an effort was made to bend Fichte's thought into the appropriate categories.

6. See the excellent discussion of Fichte's idealist metaphysics in Frederick
Copleston, S. J., *A History of Philosophy*, vol. 7: *Modern Philosophy: Fichte to
Nietzsche* (London: Burns & Oates, 1963), chaps. 2–4.

describe as an intellectualized will to power. Everything external to consciousness, Fichte held, must be made over and transformed by it.[7] He called insistently for the "unity of thought and deed," and wrote on one occasion: "As for myself, I haven't the slightest inclination to become a professional scholar. I want not only to think, I want to act.... I have only one desire ... to act on my surroundings."[8]

Emphasis upon the *Ich* also led to an extreme valuation of autonomy; the only law that man was morally obligated to obey was that which he gave himself. Fichte's stress on autonomy and on the good will as the free will was derived from Kant. But unlike Kant, who drew liberal implications from his philosophical position (Kant's political views were similar to those we have earlier described as "Enlightenment liberalism"), Fichte ultimately deduced from the concept of the autonomous will a doctrine calling for the unconditional subservience of the individual to the nation. Although he meant by the "nation" an idealized ethical community that had little relation to reality, he did not clearly distinguish between the idea of the state and its imperfect realization at a given point in time. Fichte was fond of speaking of the "general will," a term he admittedly—and carelessly—adopted from Rousseau. Rousseau's concept of the general will was the result of a prolonged philosophical analysis of the grounds of political obligation, and he set it forth in greatest detail in his treatise on the paradigmatic society (*The Social Contract*). Fichte, on the other hand, having taken the term ready-made from Rousseau, used it for essentially practical purposes, as a concept to inspire loyalty to the German nation that was in the process of creation.

Fichte appears to be an example of an increasingly numerous and significant breed: the ideologue. Ideas to him were weapons, of little value unless they were put into use in action. There is little balance and sobriety in his teaching, which is remorselessly deduced from a single *a priori* principle. The result was his endorsement, with quite the best of intentions, of a collectivism centered around national *élan* and fellow-feeling. Only by unconditionally willing what the (actual) nation wills does the individual become "free." As so often happens, extreme devotion to autonomy ends in courting the danger of unqualified submission in heteronomy (or submission to an alien force).

---

7. The desire to conquer the world by the power of philosophic thought, which Robert Tucker finds the essence of Hegel's teaching, would with considerably greater accuracy be applied to that of Fichte. See Tucker's *Philosophy and Myth in Karl Marx* (Cambridge: At the University Press, 1965), chaps. 1–3.

8. Cited in George Armstrong Kelly's preface to Fichte's *Addresses to the German Nation*, ed. Kelly (New York: Harper & Row, 1968), p. ix.

The Closed Commercial State

In 1800 Fichte published a work entitled *Der geschlossene Handelsstaat* (*The Closed Commercial State*), which vividly illustrates his manner of deducing an extreme collectivist conclusion from an atomistic individualist premise. The "closed commercial state," which would rest on the wholehearted and voluntary allegiance of its citizens, would guarantee to each member a minimal level of economic well-being. A carefully planned and self-sufficient economy would ensure the prosperity of all. It was only through the closed nation-state that each individual could achieve his full development. In the new social order that Fichte conceived,

> travel abroad will be allowed only when the journey is really necessary, and then on government allowances, since no relations with foreign countries will be maintained, and so no foreign currency will be available to any private person. The citizens will be very happy. The government will levy few taxes, as it will not need much to spend. It may have more numerous tasks than the existing governments, such as surveying and holding the balance between the various economic factors, but it is hardly likely to need a more overstaffed civil service than is the case elsewhere. . . . The state of the future will have little occasion to prosecute or punish people. Nobody will be driven to rebellion, no one will be animated by greed—"the load of misery, the fear of want eliminated . . . to what on earth could they turn their increased possessions?"[9]

Reason and Religion: The Fulfillment of History

Fichte rejected much of the teaching of the French Enlightenment, which he regarded as a near-anarchic intellectual phase that had led to the reign of egotism and greed. In at least one respect, however, he was very much its heir: he was an ardent believer in historical progress, and from his earliest writings he displayed the conviction that "reason" would triumph in the world. Yet in contrast to Condorcet, for example, who never held out the promise of an all-fulfilling "end" to history, Fichte, like many other messianists of his day, saw history as affording an end to the "alienation" of man from himself, from nature, and from his fellow human beings.

There is also an explicitly religious element in Fichte's thought.

---

9. J. L. Talmon, *Political Messianism* (London: Secker & Warburg, 1960), pp. 189–90. This entire section (pp. 177–201) is highly recommended for those who wish to read more about Fichte's political thought.

Again one notes a parallel with Mazzini. Fichte was at one point accused of atheism by conservative professors of theology at Jena; he defended himself vigorously against the charge and was able to continue his successful academic career elsewhere, ultimately being called to Berlin. (Upon his death, Hegel was named to succeed him.)

Fichte has also been called a pantheist, and this label, while not entirely satisfactory, fits him much more adequately than atheist. His "theology" was radically immanentistic. God, as absolute Ego, manifests himself in history through the operation of individual egos, which have no independent status but exist only as parts of the whole. In Fichte's religious views, as in other aspects of his thought, there is a tension between subjectivity and objectivity, particularism and universality, which in a sense is reminiscent of Hegel. His theological views are less profound and interesting than Hegel's, however, and contain none of the pronounced strain of resigned submission to the Absolute which we find in Hegel. It is not difficult to understand why Fichte's critics have accused him of in effect equating the human species with God. Fichte assumed that the divinization of the world through the immanent activity of mankind organized into distinct national collectivities was to be the end result of history.

Two of Fichte's works are particularly revelatory of his view of history: *The Characteristics of the Present Age*, written in 1804–1805, and the *Addresses to the German Nation* of 1807. The *Characteristics* divides history into five epochs, representing the advance of the collective moral consciousness from an instinctual to a heteronomous and finally to an autonomous grasp of the rule of reason in human affairs. The fifth epoch will witness the ordering of all human relations in accordance with reason in act as well as in thought. The nature of this ordering is spelled out in the *Addresses*.

The Messianic People. The *Addresses* is devoted to two main themes: the distinctiveness of the German nation vis-à-vis all others and the messianic role of that nation in leading mankind to its fulfillment in reason and freedom. The idea of a messianic people that will lead the world to salvation is central to the thought of all messianic nationalists, and it serves to resolve the dual commitment to universalism and nationalism. Problems arise, of course, when a number of peoples simultaneously advance conflicting claims to this role, and when other peoples demonstrate reluctance to be saved—or liberated, as we say today—by any of them. In the nineteenth century Fichte, Mazzini, Michelet, and Mickiewicz staked out claims to this role for Germany, Italy, France, and Poland. Conceivably there could be as many messianic peoples as there are nations, or, at any rate, "true" nations. Lacking any clear sign from the Providence invoked by all of them, such a situation could usher in a nightmare of "wars of principle" rather than a reign of universal reason and peace. Of all the problems with which messianic nationalism must contend, this one is clearly its Achilles' heel.

For Fichte, the German nation was the vehicle of man's worldly salvation by virtue of its cultural superiority, and this superiority in turn rested above all on the "originality" of the German language. (Like the great majority of Western writers, Fichte assumed that the cultural advance of the West over all other civilizations was beyond debate.) Unlike the "neo-Latin" languages, which were degenerate imitations of the language of a past culture and as a result did not encourage serious and creative thought, the German language lent itself to bold and mighty conquests in the realms of thought and action. As Fichte expressed the matter in his "Fifth Address":

> So we may say that genius in foreign lands will strew with flowers the well-trodden roads of antiquity, and weave a becoming robe for the wisdom of life which it will easily take for philosophy. The German spirit, on the other hand, will open up new shafts and bring the light of day into their abysses, and hurl up rocky masses of thoughts, out of which ages to come will build their dwellings. . . . The German spirit is an eagle, whose mighty body thrusts itself on high and soars on strong and well-practiced wings into the empyrean, that it may rise nearer to the sun whereon it delights to gaze.[10]

The Earthly Paradise, Now and Forever. It is a leading characteristic of messianic humanists to assume that time and eternity can in a sense be fused, and that ultimate fulfillment of all human needs and aspirations need not wait for perfection beyond time. Here and now man can construct a social world that will appear a paradise in comparison with what he has experienced before. Also typical of this school of thought is the prophecy that the reign of worldly bliss will be achieved in the imminent future. Both of these themes—the fusion of time and eternity and the prophecy of a new messianic age—are expressed in the *Addresses to the German Nation*:

> The natural impulse of man, which should be abandoned only in case of real necessity, is to find heaven on earth, and to endow his daily work on earth with permanence and eternity; to plant and to cultivate the eternal in the temporal—not merely in an incomprehensible fashion or in a connection with the eternal that seems to the mortal eye an impenetrable gulf, but in a fashion visible to the mortal eye itself.[11]

---

10. Fichte, *Addresses*, pp. 73–74.
11. Ibid., p. 113.

The dawn of the new world is already past its breaking; already it gilds the mountain tops, and heralds the coming day. I wish, so far as in me lies, to catch the rays of this dawn and weave them into a mirror, in which our grief-stricken age may see itself; so that it may believe in its own existence, may perceive its real self, and, as in prophetic vision, may see its own development, its coming forms pass by. In the contemplation of this, the picture of its former life will doubtless sink and vanish; and the dead body may be borne to its resting place without undue lamenting.[12]

Fichte, it is true, did not literally claim to abolish the distinction between time and eternity. Although he urged men to achieve a sense of immortality through immersion of the self in the national collectivity—in an "eternal people"—his vision did not obliterate the common-sense awareness that neither men nor nations are immortal. Political messianism is not a literal substitute for salvation by grace beyond time. But by deliberately obfuscating the insight of both theocentric and anthropocentric humanism that sheer temporality can afford only finite and limited fulfillment, it enables men to avoid facing the problem of the relation of finite existence to the ground of being. There is a nobility in the earnestness of the messianic humanists' attempt to heighten the quality of human existence in society, but in promising more than existence can bear they run the grave danger of inducing a disillusionment that can turn men away from the pursuit of more attainable goals.

GIUSEPPE MAZZINI

Mazzini (1805–1872) was one of those individuals who seem born to man the revolutionary barricades. Far more than Marx, who was actually very cautious about engaging in revolutionary activity and spent most of his time in the library and the study, Mazzini was involved in countless plots, projects, and secret machinations. As a young man he joined what was at that time the most avant-garde activist group in Italy, the *Carbonari* ("Charcoal Burners"), and participated in the uprisings of 1831. He soon left the *Carbonari*, however, impatient at their failure to develop a revolutionary program. Never one to be content without working actively in some cause, he immediately founded a new revolutionary organization, Young Italy, committed to achieving Italian unity, independence, and egalitarian social reforms. The remainder of his life was essentially one long conspiracy against established authority; most of the time he lived in exile from his beloved Italy, returning sporadically

12. Ibid., p. 15.

to "plan or lead armed insurrections"[13] and being forced to flee again when they failed. In 1834 he founded another movement, Young Europe, in the hope of extending his influence beyond Italy.

In 1849 he emerged as a member of the ruling triumvirate of the short-lived "Roman Republic." His dreams of leading the Italian people in general and the working class in particular to create an independent nation organized in accordance with his principles of egalitarian republicanism were dashed as more moderate and pragmatic heads prevailed under the leadership of Cavour. He resented bitterly the fact that Italian independence was gained under the Piedmontese monarchy and that Italy was organized as a monarchy rather than a republic. Had he lived longer he would have been equally distressed by the perpetuation of economic and social inequalities in the nation and by the severe limitations placed on the right to vote, which persisted into the twentieth century. Not until 1948 did Italy become a republic, as he had dreamed it would be; but again he would have been bitterly disappointed, for he was strongly anticlerical, and Italy's largest political party, which has headed every postwar government up to the present, is the Christian Democratic party, dedicated to moderate social reform in accordance with Catholic principles. Mazzini had prophesied the end of the papacy, and indeed of all organized Christianity, which he hoped to see replaced by a new religion of his own founding, based on "God and the People."

The Third Rome

Though Mazzini's literary output was prodigious, he was a political activist rather than a theorist or scholar. Everything he wrote resounds with apocalyptic pronouncements and eloquent exhortations. His leading political ideas were few and simple: the redemption of mankind was at hand, and Mazzini was its prophet. The individualism and egotism of the eighteenth century, which had culminated in the French Revolution, were to be replaced by a new doctrine emphasizing duty, association, nationalism, and the moral law of God. Italy would lead the world to its redemption: the Rome of the people would replace the Rome of the papacy, just as the papacy had filled the void left by the collapse of the empire. In his invocation of a third age of history—*Roma terza*, the third Rome—Mazzini employed a symbolism that had great appeal to messianic humanists in the nineteenth century. As we have seen, both Saint-Simon and Comte looked to the advent of a new "third age" of mankind, which would qualitatively transfigure the individual and collective existence of

---

13. Hans Kohn, *Prophets and Peoples* (New York: Macmillan, 1946), p. 83. Kohn's chapter on Mazzini is well worth consulting by the student of political messianism.

mankind on this planet. And there were many others who shared this dream.

Idealism and Dogmatism

Mazzini displayed to an exceptional degree a tendency to oversimplify issues and to view the political world in the dualistic terms characteristic of ideological thinking. (This same either/or attitude can be found to underlie Fichte's teaching, although he presented the dichotomy in speculative rather than practical terms, as the philosophical conflict between "dogmatism" and "idealism." As so often happens when an opposing position is denounced as "dogmatism," Fichte was often more dogmatic than the targets of his denunciation. He is hardly an example of the open, inquiring philosopher.) The following passage from the Introduction to Mazzini's famous essay *The Duties of Man* reflects the "he who is not with me is against me" mentality, which is always fatal to a genuinely political resolution of problems:

> If you would withdraw yourselves from beneath the arbitrary rule and tyranny of men, you must adore God. And in the war which is being fought in the world between Good and Evil, you must enroll yourselves under the Banner of Good and combat Evil without truce, rejecting every dubious course, every cowardly dealing, and every hypocrisy of leaders who seek to compromise between the two. On the path of the first you will have me for a comrade as long as I live.[14]

God and the Revolutionary

Much more explicitly than Fichte, Mazzini may be described as a "religious" thinker, and yet his theology, however seriously he intended it to be otherwise, is no more successful than Fichte's in meeting the objections of those who insist that to speak meaningfully of God there must be a recognition of his inviolable transcendence as well as his immanent presence. The confusion of the eternal and temporal which was evident in Fichte's thought is also present in Mazzini's, if somewhat less obviously:

> To the others who speak to you of *heaven*, separating it from the *earth*, you will say that heaven and earth, like the way and the end of the way, are one thing only. Do not tell us that the earth is clay. The earth is God's; God created it that we might climb by it to Him. The earth is not a sojourn of expiation and temptation; it is the place appointed for our labour of self-improvement, and of development towards a higher state of existence. God created us not for

---

14. Giuseppe Mazzini, *The Duties of Man and Other Essays*, ed. T. Jones (London: Dent, 1907), p. 3.

contemplation, but for action; He created us in His own image, and He is Thought and Action—nay, in Him there is no thought which is not simultaneous action.[15]

Mazzini's theistic position, like Marx's atheism, was rooted in a preconceived demand of revolutionary action. Marx arrived at the conclusion that belief in a world-transcendent God made man psychologically incapable of grasping the fact that he alone is the agent of change, and that if revolutionary change is to be brought about, man can and must initiate it. Mazzini, on the other hand, held that the only secure basis for a transformation of the world of brute "fact" into a condition of equality, peace, and social justice was a belief in a higher moral law authorized by God.

> If there be not a holy and inviolable law, not created by men, what rule have we by which to judge whether an act is just or unjust? In the name of whom, in the name of what, shall we protest against oppression and inequality? Without God there is no other sovereign than Fact; Fact before which the materialists ever bow themselves, whether its name be Revolution or Buonaparte; Fact, which the materialists of today also, in Italy and everywhere, use as a justification for inactivity even when they agree in theory with our principles. Now, how shall we demand of them self-sacrifice, martyrdom, in the name of individual opinions? . . . As long as we speak as individuals in the name of whatever theory our individual intellect suggests to us, we shall have what we have today, adherence in words, not in deeds. The cry which rang out in all the great revolutions—the cry of the Crusades, *God wills it! God wills it!*—alone can rouse the inert to action, give courage to the fearful, enthusiasm of self-sacrifice to the calculating, faith to those who reject with distrust all merely human ideas. . . .[16]

Mazzini's repeated reference to the tyranny of "fact" is fascinating, as is his attempt to use the idea of God to support a specific political revolution. God and the moral law are brought in to justify a specific institutional blueprint and project for the future of mankind, in order to overcome the charge of subjectivism. Marx, of course, discovered his realm of unshakable values in the historical process itself—embedded, as it were, in the realm of "facts," and requiring only future action to be made explicit. In any case, both thinkers sought to justify a given political program by claiming to have deduced it from that which is most basic in reality. Speculation on the nature of being is the basis

---

15. Ibid., p. 25.
16. Ibid., p. 29.

of every valid attempt to set forth a theory of moral duty—or, as scholars who delight in word play might put it, no deontology without ontology —but moral principles of action are not the same as a specific political program; nor does even the most philosophically grounded ethical analysis qualify men to instruct the world as to what in particular should and will be its future course. There are limits to what theory can do for practice, and perhaps the most valuable function of theory is to indicate that practice can claim a certain legitimate autonomy, which it must retain if it is to remain open to the unpredictable possibilities of the world of contingency.

Mazzini's Nationalism

Like Fichte, Mazzini is a nationalist with a difference: he sought not only the political independence and welfare of his own country, but also the salvation of humanity by means of that country's leadership and influence. Messianic nationalism is a position in political thought which maintains that (1) nations are the historically most advanced human associations, the basic units into which men organize themselves and within which they fulfill themselves; (2) once men have articulated themselves into their proper national entities as determined by "nature" or "providence," the stage will be set for a new epoch in mankind's development that marks a qualitative moral advance over previous ages; (3) one nation (typically the writer's own) has been singled out among all others to lead the way to this new era, in which peace, prosperity, and freedom will abound in a world of coexisting equal and sovereign nations; and (4) violence may well mark the transition from the old era to the new as forces hostile to progress attempt to halt the inevitable and salutary liberation of the world's peoples through the formation of new nations and the reordering of social relations on a more egalitarian basis within all nations, both emerging and established; but such violence is justified by the final outcome, which serves the good of humanity.

There is thus only an apparent tension in the thinking of the messianic nationalist between his commitment to his nation and his dedication to humanity at large; there is no reason to doubt that men who share this orientation are convinced that nationalism and humanism are fully compatible, and that they intend to work to achieve the welfare of both the particular and the universal communities. Indeed, in *The Duties of Man* Mazzini discusses the "duties to humanity" before "the duties to country [*patria*]." It remains open to question whether this ordering represents a clearly conceived hierarchy of duties, so that conflicting obligations might require men's loyalty to the nation to give way to their loyalty to mankind, or whether the distinction is merely a verbal device rather than an ethically existential commitment.

National Boundaries: The Design of God. To Mazzini it was impossible to speak of humanity without also affirming the sacredness of the nation. Thus he discovered a convenient identity of goals, established by providence, between the nations—and above all the "initiator people" —and humanity: "In laboring for our country on the right principle we labor for humanity. . . . Before men can associate with the nations of which humanity is composed, they must have a national existence."[17] Humanity is so vast that the individual can relate to it only through the instrumentality of the nation. God in his wisdom "divided Humanity into distinct groups upon the face of our globe, and thus planted the seeds of nations."[18] By God's "design" the boundaries of nations had been clearly established, but the irrational actions of men and the lust for conquest had altered them beyond recognition in many places. Through the coming revolution of the peoples, this iniquitous interference with God's design would be nullified, the map of Europe would be redrawn, and peoples would once again occupy the territories established for them by God:

> Bad governments have disfigured the design of God, which you may see clearly marked out, as far, at least, as regards Europe, by the courses of the great rivers, by the lines of the lofty mountains, and by other geographical conditions; they have disfigured it by conquest, by greed, by jealousy of the just sovereignty of others; disfigured it so much that today there is perhaps no nation except England and France whose confines correspond to this design. They did not, and do not, recognize any country except their own families and dynasties, the egoism of caste. But the divine design will be infallibly fulfilled. Natural divisions, the innate spontaneous tendencies of the peoples will replace the arbitrary divisions sanctioned by bad governments. The map of Europe will be remade. The Countries of the People will rise . . . upon the ruins of the Countries of Kings and privileged castes.[19]

The Messianic Mission of Italy. Mazzini believed Italy to be "especially favored" by God to lead humanity to a new age of happiness and fulfillment in which all the progressive tendencies hitherto manifested in history would be gathered together and, with future advances, used to consummate the earthly Kingdom of God. The messiah of humanity

---

17. Cited in Talmon, *Political Messianism*, p. 265.
18. Mazzini, *Duties of Man*, p. 52.
19. Ibid.

this time would not be a single man, but a "whole people, free, great and bound together by a single thought and a single love."

Mazzini's conception of the messianic mission of the "initiator people" was quite remarkable:

> When the time is ripe, God inspires in the people that has suffered most and has kept its own faith intact, the will and the courage to conquer or die for all the rest. This is the initiator people. It takes up arms and fights; whether it triumphs or dies, from its ashes or its crown of victory the Word of the Epoch will be evolved and the world will be saved.[20]

Italy was the country chosen by Providence to lead the nations to the new age of equality, peace, and brotherhood, not only because it had "suffered the most and kept its own faith intact," but because its geographical location made it the only logical one to overthrow the last, most powerful center of opposition to the emergence of this age—the papacy.

Like Dante and Cola di Rienzo before him, Mazzini was mesmerized by the idea of Rome. Rome was the center of the world, the hub of the political universe. Twice before the world had been united under the aegis of Rome. But the new third Rome, *Roma terza*, would put an end to the opposition of man by man. The first Rome, the Rome of the emperors, had given way to the Rome of the popes when its mission had been fulfilled. Now the second Rome, the Rome of the papacy, was destined to extinction, for the papacy was the "matrix . . . of all arbitrary power in Europe, which holds the human soul in bondage, and prohibits all future religious development"; it was an enemy to all human progress. The third Rome, the "Rome of the people," would be the source of a new religion of humanity that would bring about a new political, spiritual, and cultural unity among the sovereign, free, and equal peoples of the earth. It was only from Italy that this new unifying spiritual force of the future could proceed: "From Rome alone can the word of modern unity go forth, because from Rome alone can issue the absolute destruction of the old unity. . . . The crux then of the whole European question lies in Italy. To Italy belongs the high office of solemnly proclaiming European emancipation."[21]

In a manner similar to the populists of Russia, Mazzini embraced the faith that the great majority of men are by nature good and that it is evil institutions that corrupt them. He saw God as working and speaking through the people, and frequently wrote of "God and the people"

---

20. Cited in Talmon, *Political Messianism*, p. 265.
21. Ibid., p. 266.

almost as if they were synonymous. To him, however, the people were thus linked to God only when they expressed their "true" will, not when they were deprived of an occasion to discover it by the deceptions of false prophets (such as "Marxist materialism") and the self-serving teachings of their corrupt governments.

Unity. Mazzini typically thought in monistic terms. The universe was a single system governed by a single law, and humanity had only one aim: to discover and implement this law. Mazzini always regarded the appearance of numerous conflicting political doctrines as indicative of chaos and anarchy in a society. In the third age there would be only one doctrine and one religion—that of Humanity—fully subscribed to by all. But he believed that the achievement of this objective required a preparatory period of dictatorship, during which a new system of national education could propagate the new creed, which was at once religious, political, and social.

Mazzini's passion for unity was so strong that he subscribed to what Michael Oakeshott has termed the "ethic of the anti-individual." "Association" was his key word, and he vehemently rejected all forms of liberal individualism. "Do not say I; say we"[22] was his motto, and it is no accident that the title of his most famous essay is *The Duties of Man.* He meant the title to underscore his view that the liberal doctrine of natural rights was faulty in theory, and in practice had led only to egotism and materialism.

Mazzini equally rejected most of the socialist systems that were being advanced in his day, on the grounds of their materialism and failure to recognize the primacy of the nation over class or party. His philosophical reflections are considerably less sophisticated than Fichte's, since he lacked the German's background in speculative philosophy, but he embraced a form of activist idealism similar to Fichte's, and there are other affinities between them. Both men celebrated the triumph of spirit and will over the natural and historical world and assumed the identity of the divine and human spirit at work in the world. Both tended to think in monistic terms, of wholes rather than parts, and both advocated a collectivism centered on the nation. And both of them conceived of a nationalism that was ethnic and populistic rather than dynastic and political; a nation might have had a long history under a single dynasty, but if its boundaries did not coincide with the "natural" ethnic-linguistic divisions of mankind, it lacked legitimacy. To both Mazzini and Fichte the nation was a homogeneous people politically organized under one government in a single sovereign state. To men such as these, the "di-

---

22. Mazzini, *Duties of Man,* p. 55.

vine" laws of "unity" and "association" demanded the creation of all-embracing, all-fulfilling homogeneous national communities, all of which, for reasons not fully explained, would at the end of days lie down in peace together like the proverbial lion and lamb.

The Populist Dilemma: The "Democratic Dictatorship." Mazzini was too much of a humanitarian and egalitarian to be legitimately regarded as a precursor of fascism, although the Italian Fascists inevitably attempted to claim him as their own. Yet there were disturbing resonances of his thought in Fascist ideological rhetoric. The "third Rome" mystique was at the center of the Fascist operational program,[23] and even Mussolini's sordid adventure in Ethiopia was foreshadowed by Mazzini's call for Italian expansion in the Mediterranean area and establishment of colonies (or missions, as he preferred to think of them) in Asia and Africa. Beyond this, we cannot ignore Mazzini's advocacy of a dictatorship until the new age had become firmly established.

Mazzini's embracing of dictatorship despite his commitment to populist democracy brings to the fore a profound paradox that haunts all thinkers of populist inclinations. On the one hand they affirm boundless confidence in the goodness and judgment of the common people and dedicate themselves to eradicating all traces of social hierarchy and privilege. On the other hand they are confronted with the empirical fact that the real living human beings with whom they must deal do not correspond to the idealized beings they have conceived. In fact, the majority of people may prove to be apathetic or even positively opposed to the new messianic ideas. What is to be done? The logic of messianic ideology inevitably points in the direction of "temporary" dictatorship or "guidance" by an inspired cadre that knows the people's real interests and aspirations better than they do themselves. This vanguard assumes for itself the task of "guidance" and "education" until the people have acquired an awareness of their potentialities; that the majority presently lacks such an awareness is attributed to the crippling effect of current unjust and exploitive institutions, which have warped the minds of the masses. When the doctrine of the necessity of a provisional dictatorship is joined with the assumption that only through total war against the established order can the goals of the revolution be accomplished, the seeds of totalitarianism are sown, however far this result may lie from the intention of a compassionate and sincere man like Mazzini. Here we witness the tragedy of merely good intentions in politics; as Max Weber was later to argue so cogently in "Politics as a

---

23. For elaboration of this point, see Dante Germino, "Italian Fascism in the History of Political Thought," *Midwest Journal of Political Science,* May 1964.

Vocation," failure to recognize the need to measure the probable consequences of a policy in the world as it is often leads to results far removed from the better world envisioned by well-intentioned messianic
humanists.

Mazzini's views on dictatorship have been well summarized by Hans
Kohn:

> Mazzini thought much about insurrection and revolution and he
> developed the theory of the leadership of [a] dictatorial elite which
> a century later was applied so successfully. He stressed the need
> for a small and homogeneous minority, determined to armed action,
> highly disciplined and ranged in the hour of need as a compact
> phalanx, which in a combative spirit of "energetic initiative" would
> foment insurrection which "forms the military education of the
> people, and consecrates every foot of the native soil by the memory
> of some warlike deed." The movement would become a crusade
> teaching the people "that war is inevitable—desperate and deter-
> mined war that knows no truce save in victory or the grave. The
> secret of raising the masses lies in the hands of those who show
> themselves ready to fight and conquer at their head." The struggle
> may be long and the goal distant; therefore until it is fully attained
> Italy must be governed by "a provisional dictatorial power, concen-
> trated in the hands of a small number of men." Only when total
> victory has been achieved and the foundations securely laid, will the
> dictatorship give way to the perfect democracy of a nation united in
> liberty and equality by a common faith.[24]

Who would know when "total victory" had been achieved (if indeed
it is achievable at all) and when "provisional" dictatorship could give
way to "perfect democracy"? "Total" victory would apparently mean the
triumph of "humanity" over all its "foes"; victory in Italy alone or even
in all of Europe would not be total. When its practical consequences are
considered, Mazzini's exhortation for the victory of humanity becomes
a call for the victory of Mazzini's own messianic nationalist movement,
centered in Italy, *over* humanity.

Imperialism.   In his advocacy of an expansionist imperial foreign
policy for Italy, Mazzini demonstrated how the most sublimely idealistic
rhetoric can become a mask for the same raw struggle for power that
it condemns. Writing in his newspaper, *Roma del Popolo*, in 1871, Mazzini proposed that Italy extend its "civilizing mission" to Asia and
Africa. Italy should lay open "every pathway leading to the Asiatic
world," and "fulfill at the same time the mission of civilization pointed
out by the times, through the systematic augmentation of Italian in-

---

24. Kohn, *Prophets and Peoples*, p. 84.

fluence at Suez and Alexandria, and by seizing the earliest opportunities of sending a colonizing expedition to Tunis."[25] In an article written in 1872, only a few months before his death, Mazzini returned to the theme of European penetration of Asia:

> Europe is pressing upon Asia, and invading her various regions on every side: through the English conquests of India, through the slow advance of Russia on the north, through the concessions periodically wrung from China . . . through colonization, and through contraband. Shall Italy, the earliest and most potent colonizing power in the world, remain the last in this splendid movement?[26]

Messianic nationalism thus leads easily to "manifest destiny"—and woe to those peoples regarded as "undestined" or "played out." They may value and wish to preserve their cultural heritage, but must submit to being "civilized" and "emancipated" by the West. Mazzini failed to recognize the parochialism and ethnocentrism behind what he fervently believed to be the ways of universal Providence. He was not the last messianically inclined nationalist to do so.

Mazzini as Ideologue

Mazzini is a perfect example of the ideologue: he was utterly impatient of empirical realities that stood in the way of his vision of man and the world, and affirmed as an act of faith that it was the law of history that his vision be realized in its totality, without compromise or accommodation. Theory and practice, thought and action were one; the spiritual life of the individual was to be totally absorbed in the collective life of the nation and, ultimately, of "humanity." There were to be no autonomous spheres of activity in the new age. Education, religion, philosophy, the arts—all were to combine into a unity directed by the collectivity itself. The new immanentist religion of nationalism and association was to replace the now happily defunct "individualist" philosophies of Christianity and liberalism.

Although Mazzini stressed that the true messiah of the coming age would be the "initiator people," in time his premises led inescapably to their logical conclusion, and he himself assumed the messianic role. Less extravagantly than Comte but in a basically similar manner he came to identify humanity's voice with his own. He died neglected and in exile, but there is no reason to believe that he ever wavered in his conviction that he was the prophet of the new age come to lead first Italy and then all mankind to peace, freedom, and equality. The multi-

---

25. Cited in ibid., p. 95.
26. Ibid.

plicity of neither prophets nor nations claiming the messianic role ever constituted a problem to him. The prophet entertained no doubts that he and his people had been sent by Providence to redeem mankind.

CONCLUSION

Adam Mickiewicz in Poland, Jules Michelet in France, and Nikolai Danilevsky and other Slavophile intellectuals in Russia shared the messianic nationalism of Mazzini and Fichte.[27] All saw mankind in desperate need of social reintegration and fulfillment, and all promised salvation of the world through the leadership of their respective peoples. They all had an apocalyptic conception of history and viewed themselves as harbingers of a totally new era. Before the terrestrial paradise could be entered, however, a terrible purgatory of violence and holy warfare had to be endured. These men were so certain that their cause was the only one compatible with the good of humanity that they never stopped to ask whether the living human person was being sacrificed in the process. Some recent American leaders have spoken of "policing the world" and exporting the "Great Society" to Asia. It is difficult not to see the war in Indochina as in part a tragic reflection of messianic nationalist ideas, however distasteful this conclusion may be to the fabricators of these policies.

---

27. For a discussion of Mickiewicz, Michelet, and Danilevsky see the relevant portions of Talmon and Kohn, cited above.

13

Hegel

The Philosophy of Right is the definitive expression of Hegel's political teaching. Other important elements of that teaching may be found in his *Phenomenology of the Spirit* and *Lectures on the Philosophy of History*, and in minor political writings such as *The German Constitution, The Proceedings of the Estates Assembly in Württemberg,* and *The English Reform Bill.*[1] While these writings provide striking confirmation of Hegel's keen attention to "empirical" detail in political and historical analysis, they add nothing of decisive significance to what is treated in *The Philosophy of Right.*

The problem with *The Philosophy of Right* is that, in the English-speaking world at least, it is so rarely read, and when read, is rarely taken seriously enough—a fate attributable in part to the author's predilection for system construction and his fondness for needlessly ponderous jargon. Hegel's political thought, however, even in its definitive expression, can be understood without constant reference to his total metaphysical system.[2] In fact, I am convinced that excessive preoccupation with Hegel's system and with the not inconsiderable obscurity of the dialectic hinders rather than advances our appreciation of his contribution to political theory.

---

1. For the political essays, see T. M. Knox, trans., *Hegel's Political Writings* (New York: Oxford University Press, 1964), and C. J. Friedrich, ed., *The Philosophy of Hegel* (New York: Modern Library, Random House, 1953). The most relevant sections of the *Phenomenology* for the student of Hegel's political thought are those on the master-servant relationship and the objective spirit. See pp. 228–40 and 462–506 of the only complete English translation, *The Phenomenology of Mind,* trans. J. B. Baillie (New York: Macmillan, 1931). Walter Kaufmann has translated the famous Preface to the *Phenomenology,* with a commentary on facing pages, in *Hegel: Texts and Commentary* (Garden City, N.Y.: Anchor Books, Doubleday, 1965).

2. See Z. A. Pelczynski, Introduction to *Hegel's Political Writings,* trans. Knox: "Hegel's political thought can be read, understood, and appreciated without having to come to terms with his metaphysics" (p. 136). This statement is somewhat extreme, but I am in basic agreement with it. I have deliberately chosen here to concentrate upon the results of Hegel's political theory in the *Philosophy of Right* rather than on his use of the "dialectic" in its exposition, on the grounds that preoccupation with Hegel's dialectical method tends to obscure the fact that Hegel was above all a man of insight and vision rather than the prisoner of a method.

THE STATE AS THE ETHICAL UNIVERSE

The Philosophy of Right is an immensely "conversable" work: it continues the philosophical inquiry regarding man's political existence begun over two millennia ago by the Greeks. In fact, the three principal topics of the original Platonic-Aristotelian *epistēmē politikē*—ethics, the good society, and the problem of meaning in history—comprise almost exactly the divisions of subject matter in the book.

Hegel's treatment of the three *topoi* is preceded by a preface and an introduction. The Preface sets forth the author's theoretical intention to "apprehend and portray [literally to "grasp and represent"] the state as something inherently rational," or to "show how the state, the ethical universe, is to be understood."[3] Hegel declares in the same place that political philosophy "cannot consist in teaching the state what it ought to be." This remark must be understood in context, for in a sense this is precisely what Hegel, as a true political philosopher, proceeds to do. He is here arguing against a narrow and abstract political "rationalism" which erects an institutional blueprint to which existing regimes are expected to conform, irrespective of the specific historical situation. This is the attitude of mere understanding (*Verstand*) rather than of true reason (*Vernunft*). Hegel is intent on portraying the essence or idea of the state as grasped from within. For him, the answer to the question regarding the *essence* of the state will also contain the answer to the question regarding the nature of a *good* state. To Hegel, "is" and "ought" are convertible. There is nothing to which he would have objected so strenuously as the "fact-value" dichotomy that has acquired so massive an influence in the social sciences since its employment by the neo-Kantians in the late nineteenth century.[4]

---

3. T. M. Knox, ed. and trans., *Hegel's Philosophy of Right* (London: Oxford University Press, 1967; first published by Clarendon Press, 1952), p. ii (hereinafter cited as *Philosophy of Right*). This is the first complete translation into English of the *Philosophie des Rechts*. It also contains the "Additions" (taken from notes made at Hegel's lectures and included by Gans in his 1833 edition of the work) to the original text and helpful notes and comments by the translator. Readers will also wish to consult Friedrich's own translation of pars. 257–340 in his edition of *The Philosophy of Hegel* cited above, as well as the valuable comments in his Introduction.

4. Hegel's position on the "is-ought" problem is ably discussed by Nikolaus Lobkowicz in his essay on Hegel in *Die Revolution des Geistes*, ed. Jürgen Gebhardt (Munich: List, 1968), 103–10. Lobkowicz comments in particular on the famous dictum in the Preface to the *Philosophy of Right*, "*Was vernünftig ist, das ist wirklich; und was wirklich ist, das ist vernünftig*" ("What is rational is real, and what is real is rational"). In the second edition of his *Encyclopedia*, published in 1827, Hegel protested against those who had misinterpreted this sentence to mean that whatever *exists* is rational. *Wirklich* is sometimes translated as "actual." By *wirklich*, Hegel meant something that has perfectly realized its potentiality and has developed without a flaw. Under this conception, no existing state is *wirklich*, for to exist on earth means to be in the sphere of caprice, error, etc.

The Idea of Right

The introduction informs us that Hegel intends to deal with the idea of right, meaning by "idea" the concept (*Begriff*) together with its actualization (*Verwirklichung*).[5] The concept cannot be apprehended abstractly—i.e., independently of the "shapes" it "assumes in the course of its actualization." Hegel's teaching that the idea of right develops "dialectically" in history should not be permitted to obscure his conclusion that institutions such as slavery and serfdom, which were "actual" in the flat empirical sense at a given point in time (when virtually whole societies accepted them), are against right, philosophically considered. The world spirit (*Weltgeist*) works itself out at the depth dimension of history, and phenomena at the level of historical appearance must be judged in the light of the spirit's full unfolding. Although the obscurities of the dialectic and the looseness of his argument in places have left him open to the charge of "historicism," Hegel does not fully merit this accusation. He takes history seriously but does not regard that which is historically existent as normative.

For Hegel, a "genuinely philosophical" as opposed to a "merely historical" viewpoint recognizes that existing positive laws may be against right, philosophically considered—i.e., against natural right (*das Naturrecht oder das philosophische Recht*).[6] Thus, in the very introduction to his major political work, he distinguishes his own position from the vulgar positivism or historicism that he is so often accused of representing.[7]

---

5. Hegel understood the "concept" dialectically. As C. J. Friedrich has expressed the matter: "The central experience with which dialectic struggles is the inadequacy of all concepts. Hence Hegel insists that such concepts must be made to correspond to the fluidity and richness of what is being seen. . . . Besides first the object with which the conception is concerned and second the conceiver, one other persistent core of so fluid a conception remains: its various aspects form a unique system, and through this interrelationship all the conceptions in turn form a system" ("The Power of Negation: Hegel's Dialectic and Totalitarian Ideology," in *A Hegel Symposium*, ed. D. C. Travis [Austin: University of Texas Press, 1962], pp. 21–22). Friedrich prefers "conception" to "concept" as a translation of *Begriff*.

6. *Philosophy of Right*, pp. 16–17 (par. 3, Remarks); Hegel, *Grundlinien der Philosophie des Rechts*, ed. J. Hoffmeister, 4th ed. (Hamburg: Meiner, 1955), p. 22. Knox here translates *Naturrecht* as "natural law." *Recht* may mean either "right" or "law" according to the context (hence C. J. Friedrich's preference for *The Philosophy of Right and Law* as the best translation of Hegel's title). The context here seems to call for "right." It should also be noted that Hegel uses *Naturrecht* in the alternative title to the *Philosophie des Rechts* (*Naturrecht und Staatswissenschaft im Grundrisse—Natural Right and the Science of the State in Outline*).

7. For example, W. T. Blackstone, in a paper entitled "Civil Disobedience: Is It Justified?" asserts that for Hegel "there are no moral standards or set [sic] of moral obligations over and above those of the state" (paper presented at the meeting of the Southern Political Science Association, Gatlinburg, Tennessee, November 1968, p. 18). And he cites *The Philosophy of Right* as the reference for this! Hegel's great

HEGEL'S THEORY OF THE PERSON

Man to Hegel is a being of reason and will, potentially capable of grasping in his consciousness the principles and structures of reality and of articulating his experiences in philosophically valid symbols. The audacity of Hegel's philosophy stems from his supreme confidence in the capacity of human thought to comprehend and portray the reality in which man finds himself.

Hegel deserves to be described as a humanist. He respects and reveres the dignity of man. In the process of history man is the being who increasingly expands in depth of personality to the point where he can consciously grasp the end of his existence, which is to be "a person and respect others as persons."[8] Personality itself is "inherently infinite and universal."[9] As a person man is free. Freedom for man as such, and not only for one or a few, is the goal of world history. History is at its deepest level nothing other than the actualization of freedom through the instrumentality of the modern state.

As a person, man is set off from the world of things. It is "unjustifiable and unethical" to view and treat persons as things; legal provisions that contribute to such reification violate the idea of right.[10] With respect to things, man possesses "the absolute right of appropriation."[11]

Rights and Obligations

Personality realizes itself through the possession of rights and the subjective recognition of moral obligations. Rights and duties go together; the enjoyment of rights is impossible without the corresponding recognition of duties, for rights are claims that other human beings must acknowledge and respect if they are to be effective.[12] A man who pressed only his rights or claims and acknowledged no duties would be living at the level of an empty egoist and would deny his capacity for full development as a person. A man who was assigned only duties and was not seen as the bearer of rights would be a slave. Slavery is contrary to the dignity of human personality. Men are equal "in respect of their personality."

Private Property. Personality manifests itself as particularity. Each

---

admiration for Sophocles' Antigone, the heroine *par excellence* of "civil disobedience," should be cited in this context.

8. *Philosophy of Right*, p. 37 (par. 36).

9. Ibid., p. 38 (par. 38).

10. Ibid., p. 41 (par. 43, Remarks).

11. Ibid. (par. 44).

12. Ibid., pp. 109–10 (par. 155).

man has a right to what is his own. This means that the institution of private property is justified. Property is the external embodiment of personality, for man in the act of thought has the capacity to "appropriate" things as his own. Any doctrine, such as that of Plato in the *Republic*, that forbids the holding of private property "violates the right of personality."[13]

The fact that men are equal as persons does not mean that justice demands that they should have equal property; justice "requires only that everyone shall own property." "The truth is that particularity is just the sphere where there is room for inequality and where equality would be wrong."[14] The modern state recognizes the rights of individuality, and these include variation in property and wealth. It ought to be only in "exceptional cases" that the state cancels private ownership.[15] A grave problem for modern society is created, however, when "disproportionate wealth" is concentrated in a few hands at one end of the scale, while at the other "a large mass of people" falls below the subsistence level necessary to live in dignity as members of society.[16] If a "rabble of paupers" exists, this means that a wrong has been done by one class to another. "The important question of how poverty is to be abolished is one of the most disturbing problems which agitate modern society."[17]

Man may alienate his property, may abandon it to another, insofar as it is a thing external in nature. He may not, however, legitimately alienate "those goods, or rather substantive characteristics that constitute his own private personality and the universal essence of his self-consciousness"; these are "inalienable" and one's right to them is "imprescriptible." The individual as person remains inviolable with respect to his ethical life, religion, and "universal freedom of will."[18]

Duty. Man is not only the possessor of rights but the agent who seeks responsibility to fulfill his duties, who freely takes upon himself obligations to others and does not regard these obligations as burdens. In acting, the person must be animated by the right intention *and* must look to the consequences of his action. It is erroneous to view either the intention or the consequences as exclusively important. We cannot ignore the consequences of an act in evaluating its moral quality, but

---

13. Ibid., p. 42 (par. 46, Remarks).

14. Ibid., p. 237 (Addition to par. 49).

15. Ibid., p. 236 (Addition to par. 46).

16. Ibid., p. 150 (par. 244).

17. Ibid., pp. 277–78 (Addition to par. 244).

18. Ibid., pp. 52–53 (par. 66). This passage is, of course, altogether antithetical to any form of totalitarianism.

contingent circumstances may interfere to distort the effect of the action, and for those the individual is not responsible.[19]

Hegel rejects any hairshirt concept of duty. Morality is something other than a "bitter, unending struggle against self-satisfaction." In his view the "subjective satisfaction of the individual himself"—including the "recognition which he receives by way of honor and fame"—properly accompanies the "achievement of ends of absolute worth." He proclaims the "right of the subject's particularity" to be the "pivot and center of the difference between antiquity and modern times."[20]

The Individual and the Community

The good life is achieved not in isolation but in community with others. The individual is initiated into the very concept of the moral life in the community. It is possible that a clash may occur between the community's demands and those of the individual conscience. There have been occasions when the good man has had no alternative to inner emigration, or withdrawal from active and committed participation in the society. [21] In principle, however, there should be no conflict between the moral aims of the individual and those of the state. The end of man and of the political community (which is after all not something alien to the life of its citizens) is the same: the realization of freedom in the world.[22]

The individual conscience may err, and man must guard against the temptation arrogantly to set up his merely private judgment in opposition to what may be the universal interest. It is also true, however, that the moral judgment of the "better men" may be superior to that of the "actual world of freedom"; if that world becomes "faithless to the will of better men" (i.e., the moral *virtuosi*), then these men will seek in "the ideal world of the inner life alone the harmony which actuality has lost."[23]

Duty as Freedom. It is in ethical life, i.e., the good life in the context of the family, civil society, and the state, that true freedom is realized and the harmonious integration of the claims and obligations of the person occurs. Within the political order it is possible for man to

---

19. Ibid., p. 80 (par. 118, Remarks).

20. Ibid., p. 84 (par. 124 and Remarks).

21. Ibid., p. 255 (Addition to par. 138).

22. Ibid., p. 86 (par. 129). See pp. 90 and 254 (par. 135 and Addition) for Hegel's discussion of Kant's categorical imperative as of only partial validity: it would be "admirable if we already had determinate principles of conduct" (ibid., p. 254).

23. Ibid., p. 92 (par. 138, Remarks).

become aware that duty, far from constituting a restriction or hindrance to man, is the essence of freedom. If one were to outline a doctrine of man's duties, it would consist of nothing except the "serial exposition of the relationships which are necessitated by the idea of freedom and are therefore actual in their entirety in the state."[24] It is "in duty that the individual finds his liberation."[25]

If freedom is viewed negatively and abstractly, then every institution of society and state is seen as a restriction. Duty, however, is "not a restriction on freedom, but only on freedom in the abstract, i.e., on unfreedom. Duty is the attainment of our essence, the winning of positive freedom."[26]

HEGEL'S THEORY OF THE GOOD SOCIETY

Hegel's teaching about the state in *The Philosophy of Right* is regarded by some interpreters as containing the seeds of totalitarianism. As we shall see, it is quite true that some of the passages concerning the state are at variance with the personalism and humanism of the first two sections. In some instances, however, Hegel has been seriously misunderstood by later critics who fail to take into account the way he employs the term "state" in the specific context of the argument.

At least some of the misconceptions regarding his meaning and intention result from the failure to recognize that when Hegel writes about the state, he generally means the state in its rational essence or idea and not a particular existing state. In other words, he is concerned with elaborating his own theory of the paradigmatic society. He is writing political theory in the grand manner of Plato, Aristotle, and Rousseau. The theory of the state is not a justification of the status quo. The idea of the state serves as a model in terms of which the political communities that actually emerge in history may be measured. Only to the extent that they approximate the model or idea of the state do these communities deserve the name of state. In this sense his theory of the state is a target or a goal.

If one keeps in mind that when Hegel speaks of the state he generally means the "idea of the state," and that this idea is at best imperfectly realized at a given point in time by an existing state, then his utterances, admittedly extravagant, about the state as the "march of God

---

24. Ibid., p. 107 (par. 148, Remarks).

25. Ibid. (par. 149).

26. Ibid., pp. 259–60 (Addition to par. 149). The term "positive freedom" plays a key role in T. H. Green's political thought.

in the world"[27] and as "something divine on earth"[28] appear in proper perspective.

The state for Hegel is not an institution that is in any sense optional; only in the state can men achieve the full development of their potentialities. All so-called social contract theories must be rejected for their failure to emphasize this point.[29] Where a state is lacking, reason demands that one be founded. The state is the essential condition for the full development of the human personality. It is therefore not something to be avoided or circumvented if possible. It is the vehicle for the actualization of reason and justice.

Hegel's conception of the role of the state is an elevated one. The state is not a mere contract for convenience and expediency; neither is it essentially an engine of repression and coercion. Hegel expounds at length upon the ideas of a contemporary reactionary writer, von Haller, who had written that might is right and that force is the basis of the state and its sufficient title to obedience.[30] The state, as the "actuality of the ethical idea," can scarcely rest on such a foundation without completely corrupting itself. In general, when one reads Hegel on the state, one is reminded of the reverence of the ancient Greeks for the *polis* or, more recently, of Burke's veneration of the political community.

The *polis* analogy is misleading in part because Hegel sought to distinguish the modern state from the *polis*, but there is no question that for him the term "state" had a more concrete and immediate connotation than it is generally accorded. The state to him is the all-embracing political unit, which encompasses a complicated network of institutions intermediary between the atomistic individual and the highest governing power. The state is not a whole apart from society; it is society and all its diversity *plus* the regulative and unifying structure of government— not an arbitrary government, but a government of laws.

The Family and Civil Society

Prior to discussing the state in its completeness, Hegel discusses the family and civil society. Here we have an example of a context in which his "dialectical" method can be illuminating, for both the family and civil society are at once "preserved and transcended" (*aufgehoben*) in the state. Of particular importance is his distinction between civil society (*bürgerliche Gesellschaft*) and the state. Civil society is described as a

27. Ibid., p. 279 (Addition to par. 258).
28. Ibid., p. 285 (Addition to par. 272).
29. Ibid., pp. 58–59 and 242 (par. 75 and Addition).
30. Ibid., pp. 157–60 (par. 258, Remarks and note).

"battlefield" where selfish interests clash. It is essentially a collection of isolated individual atoms; in this sense it is the "negation" of the family. In contrast to the family, civil society is impersonal (contractual relations prevail between the members) and lacking in any shared sense of purpose. It is at this point that the corporate group or "corporation" appears as a mediating link between civil society and the organs of the state.

The Corporation

The corporation, which is, after the family, the second "ethical root"[31] of the state, helps to rationalize the otherwise anarchic competition between the members of civil society by incorporating them into organs that facilitate the pursuit of their occupations. Membership in the corporations is freely chosen—for it is a signal achievement of the modern state that it guarantees every citizen the right of choosing his own occupation—and they are self-governing. Corporations are not controlled by the state, but they share the state's concern with the universal interest. Corporations serve at once to mitigate the acerbity of the struggle between individuals in civil society through their recognition of the need to set bounds to the pursuit of particular interests and to defend the legitimate particular interests of their members.[32]

Corporations were regarded by Hegel as modern substitutes for the medieval guilds and feudal institutions. The modern corporations preserve the distinctive identity and particularity of plural groups while at the same time being themselves under the general supervision of the public authority. The modern corporation, situated within the state at the boundary between civil society (which provides "free play for every idiosyncrasy, every talent, every accident of birth and fortune") and the public authority (the mission of which is to minister to the universal interest), was ideally suited to be the organ of mediation between particular and universal demands.

The state, then, was not to Hegel a ruthlessly centralizing force that subjugated the aspirations of individuals and lesser groups within

31. Ibid., p. 154 (par. 255). Hegel uses "corporation" in the sense of corporate body or group. He has a distinctive place in the history of corporativist political thought; in essence he calls for a marriage of corporativism and liberalism, and his teaching on this subject should not be confused with romantic attempts to revive the medieval pattern.

32. Hegel's teaching regarding the corporation has been falsely equated with Italian Fascist "corporativism" by some interpreters. The Fascist corporations were merely façades—another instrument for the control of the citizenry by the regime. See Herbert Marcuse, *Reason and Revolution: Hegel and the Rise of Social Theory* (New York: Oxford University Press, 1941), on the speciousness of confusing Hegel's political thought with Fascist ideology, as well as for an illuminating general discussion of aspects of his political thought.

the society. The state was a unity of universality and particularity: it included, without annulling, the entire sphere of the family and civil society now organized into corporations. The corporation is the individual's "second family."[33] Hegel went so far as to say that the "primary purpose" of government with respect to its "police" (*polizei*) functions of providing for the health, safety, and well-being of its citizens, was to "actualize and maintain the universal contained within the particularity of civil society." The control exercised by the public authorities over the corporations "takes the form of an external system and organization for the protection and security of particular ends and interests." The universal interest was "immanent in the interests of particularity." Ultimately, therefore, through the rational organization and mediating activity of the corporations, the demands of particular interests and the common good of the society would be brought into harmony rather than being in conflict with each other.[34] To Hegel, however, this was to be a genuine reconciliation that took into account the initiatives and activities of individuals and groups within society, not an imposed "harmony" from the top down.

The Synthesis of Individuality and Universality

In one particularly striking passage, Hegel has summarized his view that the underlying principle or essence of the modern state is the synthesis of individuality and universality. Indeed, if one passage were selected from *The Philosophy of Right* to illustrate his balanced approach and his concern to avoid the extreme of either atomistic individualism or coercive collectivism, this would perhaps be the most appropriate:

> The state is the actuality of concrete freedom. But concrete freedom consists in this, that personal individuality and its particular interests not only achieve their complete development and gain explicit recognition for their right (as they do in the sphere of the family and civil society) but, for one thing, they also pass over of their own accord into the interest of the universal. . . . The principle of modern states has prodigious strength and depth because it allows the principle of subjectivity to progress to its culmination in the extreme of self-subsistent personal particularity, and yet at the same time brings it back to the substantive unity and so maintains this unity in the principle of subjectivity itself.[35]

---

33. *Philosophy of Right,* p. 153 (par. 252).

34. Ibid., p. 152 (par. 249).

35. Ibid., pp. 160–61 (par. 260). See also p. 280 (Addition to par. 260). Here we have a particularly striking example of Hegel's dialectical "transcending" of antinomies (in this instance the opposition between the particular and universal interest).

Church and State

Hegel's theory of the modern state can be further elucidated through his treatment of the problem of the relations between church and state. He did not favor compulsion by the state to establish religious uniformity. On the contrary, he strongly endorsed the principle of freedom of conscience. Religious belief or doctrine as such "has its domain in the conscience and falls within the right of the subjective freedom of self-consciousness, the sphere of inner life, which as such is not the domain of the state."[36] On the other hand, as we might expect from his general philosophical orientation and temperament, Hegel does not conceive of this separation as implying hostility or even indifference of the one toward the other. Religion is an "integrating factor in the state," and the state is obliged to render churches "every assistance and protection" in the pursuit of their "religious ends." Insofar as their external organization and activity are concerned, however, churches may be considered as subject to "the general control and oversight" of the public authorities.[37]

Hegel regarded the union of church and state as a characteristic of "oriental despotism" rather than of a true state. (His use of the term "oriental despotism" in this context reveals his ethnocentrism. Although Hegel was learned in the history and thought of Asia and possessed a certain appreciation for it, he could not transcend the limitation of his philosophy of history, which held that the world spirit "moved from east to west.")

THE CONSTITUTION OF THE STATE

Hegel defines the internal constitution of the state as the "organization of the state and the self-related processes of its organic life, a process whereby it differentiates its moments within itself and develops them to self-subsistence."[38] It is in the section on the political constitution that he discusses the separation of powers.

Hegel regarded the division of powers as essential to any rational constitution of the state. This is because the concept contains within itself the three "moments" of universality, particularity and individuality.[39] The three powers or divisions of the "political state" are:

---

36. Ibid., pp. 169–70 (par. 270, Remarks).
37. Ibid., p. 169.
38. Ibid., p. 174 (par. 271).
39. Ibid., p. 175 (par. 272, Remarks).

1. The power to determine and establish the universal—the legislature.
2. The power to subsume single cases and the spheres of particularity under the universal—the executive.
3. The power of subjectivity, as the will with the power of ultimate decision—the crown. In the crown the different powers are bound into an individual unity, which is thus at once the apex and basis of the whole, i.e., of constitutional monarchy.[40]

Constitutional Monarchy

For Hegel, constitutional or limited monarchy based upon the division of powers is "the achievement of the modern world."[41] From the perspective of constitutional monarchy the premodern division of constitutions into democracies, aristocracies, or monarchies is seen as inadequate. Constitutional monarchy may possess elements of each of these forms, and yet in it they are welded into a new unity.

In his discussion of monarchy, Hegel does indeed leave himself open to the accusation of being an apologist for a specific institution then in existence. It would appear that in this discussion he veers sharply away from his role of philosophical theorist and that his work is in danger of assuming a publicistic and thoroughly time-bound character. His justification of monarchy in terms of the dialectic seems artificial and forced. On closer inspection, however, even the section on monarchy can be considered as a theoretical treatment of the problem of the advantages of a ceremonial as well as a political executive for the modern state. This is especially evident if we take into account the Additions to the pertinent paragraphs (273–81). His rejection of elective monarchy is based in part on his fear of the emergence of a plebiscitary regime, democratic in form but dictatorial in content.[42]

In no sense did Hegel envisage the monarch as invested with absolute or arbitrary power. He was to be a limited monarch and not a dictator. His services were needed as the holder of an office, as the official who could perform the final legitimating function that made a law or administrative edict an act of the state. This formal "power of decision" needed to be invested in a man, because it thereby confirmed

---

40. Ibid., p. 176 (par. 273). The German terms are *gesetzgebenden Gewalt* (literally, "law-giving power"), *Regierungsgewalt* ("governmental power"), and *fürstlichen Gewalt* ("princely power") (*Grundlinien der Philosophie des Rechts*, ed. Hoffmeister, p. 235).

41. *Philosophy of Right,* Remarks.

42. Ibid., p. 186 (par. 281, Remarks).

the deepest ethical principle of the modern, as distinct from the feudal or ancient, state. That principle is that it is man himself and not some power beyond him who acts in history and is responsible for his action.[43]

It is in this context that we can most fruitfully consider Hegel's treatment of sovereignty. Not surprisingly, in view of his attachment to a balanced view and his conviction that extreme positions betray a superficial or inadequate grasp of the matter at hand, Hegel rejects any absolutist concept of sovereignty, either of the monarch or of the people. The state as a whole possesses sovereignty, both internally with respect to its parts and externally with respect to other states. But Hegel emphatically rejects any view that equates sovereignty and despotic power.[44]

The Executive Power

The executive power of government is concerned with "subsuming the particular under the universal," i.e., with the application of laws and policies to the specific situations for which they were intended. Hegel meant in the main to include the administrative machinery as divided into specialized departments under this heading. He also deals with the judiciary as an aspect of the executive, rather than as a separate power.

Hegel's conclusions regarding the organization of the executive apparatus according to the principles of reason and freedom involved the blending of centralization and devolution of power at the local level. As T. M. Knox has pointed out, Hegel saw the modern state as combining (1) administrative efficiency with (2) private freedom.[45]

Throughout Hegel's discussion of administrative organization, there is stress upon the advantages of devotion of power upon corporations and local governments where particular interests are concerned. Hegel deplored the emphasis in Montesquieu and much of the classical liberal thought upon limiting and restricting government power as if it were something basically hostile to man. In his view the state, as organized into an administrative structure, was in principle a positive force for good in human life and rendered invaluable services in promoting human freedom. Still, he recognized that in practice the state's civil servants might well be prone to act arbitrarily and that the power of local bodies

---

43. Ibid., p. 184 (par. 279). It is in passages like this that what we may term Hegel's anthropocentric humanism is most strikingly revealed. He argued that even Socrates had failed to "look within [his] own being" for the "last word" on "great events" or "important affairs of state." Instead he sought to derive the "last word" from a "divine sign" (his daemonion). See also ibid., pp. 288–89 (Additions to pars. 279 and 280), for elaborations on the theme of the monarch as assuming responsibility for the society with his "I will."

44. Ibid., p. 180 (par. 278, Remarks).

45. Ibid., p. 371 (Knox's note to par. 290).

or other entities intermediate between the individual and the central government could serve as a "counterpoise" to such arbitrariness. There is, then, a strong element of constitutional pluralism in Hegel's political thought, although in no sense could it be interpreted as sanctioning the view that plural groups are in some logical sense antecedent to the state and enjoy a kind of absolute autonomy by right. They are only "relatively independent" of the state, and their legitimate actions on behalf of particular interests must take place within the framework of common interest supplied by the state. The state is needed to regulate the competition among particular interests.

Hegel utterly rejected the laissez-faire theories of the physiocrats, Adam Smith and others, which posited a natural harmony of interests. Unregulated competition leads not to universal benefit but to chaos. To Hegel laissez-faire doctrines were the result of confusing the state with civil society. Civil society is the "battlefield where everyone's individual private interest meets everyone else's."[46] The public authorities of the state, manned by civil servants dedicated to safeguarding the universal needs and interests of the community,[47] have the task of regulating the activities of individuals as members of civil society, not to the end of subjugating those activities but of curbing excesses damaging to the public good and of raising these activities to the level where they meet with and contribute to the universal interest. The officials of the corporations, whose elections he apparently held to be subject to ratification by public authority (par. 288), also were charged with moderating the demands of their particular organizations in the light of the public interest.

The Legislative Power: Hegel's View of Democracy

Hegel saw the modern state as including among its basic institutions a legislative assembly representative of the major socioeconomic interests in the society. Unlike Rousseau, Hegel held the idea of representation to be thoroughly compatible with freedom and a free society. Also unlike Rousseau, he favored a large state rather than a small community as the optimal framework for the realization of freedom. This was because a large community, which contains many and varied interests, is more likely to foster attitudes of impartiality and objectivity in its citi-

---

46. Ibid., p. 189 (par. 289, Remarks).

47. Ibid., pp. 190–91 (pars. 291 and 294, Remarks). The civil service shall be open to all and appointment shall be on the basis of merit. As servants of the crown, civil servants were to forgo the "selfish and capricious satisfaction of their subjective ends." They should find fulfillment only in the "dutiful discharge of their public functions" (ibid., p. 191). Hegel frequently refers to civil servants as members of the "universal class."

zens when they deal with public questions than is a small society, in which personal interests and family ties are apt to gain the upper hand.[48]

Hegel did not hold in high regard the ultrademocratic views current since the French Revolution about the sovereignty of the people and the mandate theory of representation. On these points he is close to Burke and the position of conservative liberalism generally. He rejected the conception of "the people" as a mass of atomic individuals whose opinion should be binding on the legislators or deputies. "The people" so considered is an abstraction that exists only in the minds of those who do not comprehend political reality. Individuals do not exist in isolation but in relation to others, and people act in society and politics through organized groups. "The people" as such, then, does not exist, and has no opinion to be consulted.

Representation, he thought, should be based on the divisions within civil society known as the "estates." Society is not a formless mass but an articulated whole composed of various economic and cultural units. In Hegel's view, the "estates" in Prussia constituted the basis for the model parliament, although he did not consider them institutions to be copied mechanically and dressed with the garb of theory. The estates had developed historically within the modern state itself and were capable of rational explication and elaboration.

The Upper House.   The estates were comprised chiefly of two sections. The first was the landed aristocracy (the equivalent of a house of lords); membership in this section of the legislature was determined by birth. The landed estate represented stability, permanence, and tradition. Hegel held the view—of doubtful validity—that the landed aristocracy would exercise greater impartiality of judgment by virtue of its financial independence (both in absolute terms and in relation to the fluctuations of the market). Hegel defended the law of primogeniture, which guaranteed the existence of a hereditary landed aristocracy, as making possible this source of stability in the state.

The Lower House.   In contrast to the upper chamber, members of the lower house represented the common people and were to be chosen by election. The deputies of the "second section of the estates" were to be chosen by society primarily in accordance with the corporate principle of representation. The territorial basis for the representation would not be entirely discarded, provided that territorial lines were not drawn mechanically on some merely numerical principle, but encompassed regions or localities that existed authentically as communities with common interests and cultural traditions. Any scheme of representation

---

48. Ibid., p. 193 (par. 296).

grounded on the division of the citizenry in an abstract, merely numerical fashion was unacceptable. This is so, Hegel remarks, because
civil society, whose representatives these deputies are, is not a collection of "atomic units," but is a society "articulated into associations,
communities, and corporations." These associations, "although constituted
for other purposes," acquire "a connection with politics"[49] through serving
as the basis for representation in the lower house of the legislature.

   Direct vs. Representative Democracy.   In the elaboration of his
theory of the paradigmatic society, Hegel is fundamentally opposed to
Rousseau's theory of direct democracy as the norm for a free society.
The people in Hegel's political theory are not present in person for the
law-making task, but are represented by deputies chosen by corporations
and associations to which they belong. Far from being the enemy of freedom, the representative principle of government was to Hegel a key
element in the realization of freedom.

   Hegel has often been characterized as an antidemocratic thinker.
This is true only if one considers that the populistic ideal of direct democracy has a monopoly on the meaning of the term "democracy." It
would be more accurate to say that he was a proponent of moderated
or tempered democracy; he was certainly at least as democratic as either
Aristotle or Locke. Some of his teaching has clearly been bypassed by
subsequent events, at least with respect to the evolution of competitive
democracies in the West and elsewhere. In other respects, however, his
observations are a rich mine of insight for any serious discussion of contemporary democracy and its problems.

   The Representative.   Hegel's view of the duties and role of the representative closely approximates that expressed by Edmund Burke in his
speech to the electors of Bristol. A representative in the true sense of
the term is an individual who has the confidence of the electorate and
who has a "better understanding" of public affairs than do the electors
themselves. He should also be a man who is attentive to the universal interest and who does not put the narrowly defined interest of the con-
stituency or corporation he represents ahead of that interest. Hence, the
relation of representatives to their electors "is not that of agents with a
commission or specific instructions." Parliament is meant to be an assembly "in which all members deliberate in common and reciprocally

---

49. Ibid., p. 200 (par. 208). On p. 202 (par. 311), however, Hegel seems to
state that the corporations are the only constituencies for the election of representatives to the lower house. See also ibid., pp. 202–3 (par. 311, Remarks), for Hegel's
view that direct popular election achieves "the opposite of what was intended;
election actually falls into the power of a few, of a caucus. . . ." Here he seems to
anticipate the observations of Michels and others on the oligarchical tendencies of
even the most "democratic" institutions.

instruct and convince each other."[50] While independent means and the possession of landed wealth are the tests for membership in the upper house, knowledge, character, and political and managerial skill are the criteria for election to the lower house, which represents the "fluctuating and changeable element in civil society."[51] Representative assemblies serve as training grounds for the full development of the skills of men with political ability, and when their sessions are public—a most desirable practice—the debates in parliament serve as an excellent means for the political education of the public.[52]

Representatives, then, are to seek the universal interest, which is not contrary to particular interests, but contains and preserves them. Grounding representation in the corporation means that each major interest in society (trade, manufacture, agriculture, etc.) will have spokesmen in parliament. Deputies are "representatives in an organic, rational sense only if they are representatives not of individuals or a conglomeration of them, but of one of the essential spheres of society and its large-scale interests."[53] All of this sounds quite contemporary, as if it might have been taken from the current literature on interest groups and the need for interest-group representation. This more recent literature, however, often fails to place its conclusion within the framework of a comprehensive political theory as Hegel has done. Some writers on interest groups, influenced by Arthur Fisher Bentley, also seriously neglect the concept of the public interest. Hegel would never have regarded the public universal interest as something fictitious or as merely the result of the interplay of competing particular interests. Hegel was neither an advocate of laissez faire nor a nominalist who regarded the community as only the sum of the individuals and groups within it. As on other questions, Hegel demonstrated here his great instinct for balance. He eschewed both extreme individualist and extreme collectivist views. Both the parts as parts and the whole as an authentic whole are present in his profound analysis of society.

Public Opinion. This characteristic sense of balance is also present in his discussion of public opinion. In one respect Hegel places a high value on public opinion as the "repository of the genuine needs and correct tendencies of common life, but also, in the form of common sense [i.e., all-pervasive fundamental ethical principles disguised as prejudices], of the eternal, substantive principles of justice, the true content and

---

50. Ibid., p. 201 (par. 309).
51. Ibid. (par. 310).
52. Ibid. p. 294 (Addition to par. 315).
53. Ibid., p. 202 (par. 311, Remarks).

result of legislation, the whole constitution and the general position of the state."[54] On the other hand, he saw that there is much chaff mixed with wheat. Public opinion also "becomes infected by all the accidents of opinion, by its ignorance and perversity, by its mistakes and falsity of judgment." Thus, both the proverb "*Vox populi, vox dei*" and Ariosto's lines that "the ignorant mob [*il volgare ignorante*] rebukes everyone and speaks most of that which it understands least" are equally true.[55]

Freedom of Communication. Hegel regarded the "freedom of public communication" (*die Freiheit der öffentlichen Mitteilung*) as essential in a fully developed state. It was to be "directly assured by the laws and by-laws which control or punish its excesses." He thought that the "rationality of the constitution, the stability of government, and . . . the publicity of Estates Assemblies" would ensure that this freedom would be exercised responsibly.[56] He does not anticipate John Stuart Mill in arguing for absolute freedom of speech, but he does emphasize the advantages of relatively untrammeled public communications for a society that realizes ordered freedom. Censorship or "enforced silence" can have harmful results. It is in conformity with the "principle of the modern world" that citizens have their "share in discussion and deliberation" so that they come to accept laws and policies not as something alien or enforced from above, but something in which they have a voice and which they regard as "entitled to recognition."[57] The public debates of the representatives in the legislature can play an important role in broadcasting the views and grievances of various sectors of society, and these views are to be taken into account by the representatives and the executive (or cabinet), whose principal members also have seats in the legislature.[58]

THE STATE AS ACTOR IN WORLD HISTORY

If Hegel had ended his *Philosophy of Right* at this point (par. 320), there could be little dispute that, far from serving as a precursor of totalitarianism, he deserves to be listed among the leading proponents of liberalism, albeit of a revised version that incorporates some of the objections of Burke and anticipates some of the ideas of T. H. Green

---

54. Ibid., p. 204 (par. 317).

55. See ibid., p. 205 (par. 318 and Remarks).

56. Ibid. (par. 319).

57. Ibid., p. 294 (Addition to par. 317).

58. Ibid., p. 292 (Addition to par. 300). Hegel agreed with the basic principle of a parliamentary system such as England's—that government ministers should be members of parliament—but he would not have regarded with favor the shift of power to parliament that was in the process of occurring. Ministers were to be responsible to the crown and not to parliament.

and welfare-state liberalism. He speaks of "the rule of law, representative government, the importance of plural groups, separation of church and state, trial by jury, the distinction between the spheres of civil society and government, division of powers, freedom of the press, the equality of citizens before the law, and the responsibility of the state to protect rather than suppress legitimate particular interests.

However, in the concluding (very brief) portions of the work, where he considers the role of the state vis-à-vis other states in world history, Hegel places the personalism and political liberalism of the earlier part of the work in grave jeopardy. Here he seems to allow his system and his fascination with the dialectic to get the better of the person whose fulfillment and development it had been his purpose to affirm.

In relation to other states, the state itself seems to acquire personality and absolute worth, with the members who comprise it serving as mere means to its own higher end. Thus Hegel declares that the state, considered in its "moment" of negative opposition to other states, acquires "absolute power against everything individual and particular, against life, property, their rights, even against societies and associations."[59]

In keeping with his dialectical method, which he worked out in his *Logic* and which discovers truth to inhere in the underlying unity of opposites, Hegel proclaims that the utter and complete sacrifice of individual interests on behalf of the state at a time of war or extreme crisis is not the destruction but the apotheosis of individuality and personality. This is because personal development can occur only in and through the state, not apart from it. The survival of the state thus becomes the *conditio sine qua non* of individual self-realization and the preservation and enhancement of particular interests.[60]

War

These considerations lead Hegel to some remarks that reveal a certain insensitivity to the moral aspects of war. In his concern to show the rationality of the historical process as such, he makes judgments that, although qualified in other places, appear to justify war as something essentially good and moral. At any rate, he is led to regard war as virtually inevitable by his assumption that the sovereign nation-state is the final form of political community to appear in history. Hegel holds up to scorn Kant's vision of "perpetual peace." War is, then, not something intrinsically evil, nor is it an accident attributable to the passions,

---

59. Ibid., p. 209 (par. 323).
60. Ibid. (par. 324). See also ibid., p. 211 (par. 328).

ambitions, or ignorance of the actors involved. It is an absolutely necessary phenomenon in the course of the world spirit's unfolding in history.

It has been argued in Hegel's defense that when he spoke of war he could scarcely have contemplated its being waged on the scale of destructiveness known to the twentieth century. He thought of war as a limited conflict between rival professional armies of states that were allied at least by common conceptions of "civilized" warfare and in general were conscious of being part of a larger European or Western civilization. The civilian population and the domestic institutions of a state would be spared in the conflict. There are passages in *The Philosophy of Right* to support this view.[61] It needs to be recalled, however, that Hegel lived after the French Revolution and its citizens' armies. He was aware of the possibility that war might involve whole populations instead of only relatively small groups of professional soldiers. Thus at one point he writes that "if the state as such, if its autonomy, is in jeopardy, all its citizens are in duty bound to answer the summons of its defence. If in such circumstances the entire state is under arms and is torn from its domestic life at home to fight abroad, the war of defence turns into a war of conquest."[62]

He also speaks of selected peoples as being carriers of the world spirit at different epochs in history; in comparison with them, other peoples are "without right" (*rechtlos*) and "count no longer in world history."[63] In another place he condemns those who regard politics and morality as opposed to each other and who refuse to understand that "the welfare of the state has claims to recognition totally different from those of the individual."[64] All of this could be interpreted as a justification of unlimited aggression and conquest.

We must consider, however, that Hegel keeps returning to the idea that "world history is not the verdict of mere might,"[65] but rather the unfolding of reason and the freedom of the spirit. If we read the unfortunate passages seeming to glorify war and deify the state in context, recalling especially his constant search for balanced judgments and the

---

61. E.g., ibid., p. 215 (par. 338); also pp. 213 (first sentence of par. 333) and 297 (Additions to pars. 338 and 339).

62. Ibid., pp. 210–11 (par. 326).

63. Ibid., pp. 217–18 (par. 347). Cf. the German text in Hoffmeister, *Philosophie des Rechts*, p. 291. Knox translates *rechtlos* as "without rights." The difference between the singular and plural is important here. Hegel seems to mean that the idea of right advances to a new stage of development through the activity of a particular people (*Volk*). However, he later speaks of "rights" of "barbarians" being "unequal" to those of a "civilized nation" (*Philosophy of Right*, p. 219 [par. 351]).

64. Ibid., p. 215 (par. 337, Remarks).

65. Ibid., p. 216 (par. 342).

reconciliation of opposite views, Hegel does not emerge as a blatant militarist and warmonger. His long section attacking the views of the arch-reactionary von Haller should be recalled,[66] as well as his argument, expounded in the final few paragraphs devoted to "world history," that not the national but the world spirit is the final judge of history. From this vantage point, the nation-state is only in a provisional sense an end in itself. It is worthy of complete devotion and sacrifice only insofar as it lives up to its potentiality to be a true state and to serve as a carrier of the world spirit, which means to promote the reason and freedom of all mankind.

Hegel devoted only a few pages explicitly to the subject of world history in *The Philosophy of Right,* and yet they conclude the work and were presumably intended by its author as its culmination. Although this section gives his philosophy of history only in outline form, it is important because it is in full conformity with the philosophy of history contained in the *Lectures on the Philosophy of History,* never published in his lifetime.

Hegel's philosophy of history partakes of the three-stage symbolism so prevalent in nineteenth-century political thought. It also contains the Enlightenment idea of progress, although in a more sophisticated form. The leading philosophical idea is clear: history is the unfolding of freedom in the world and moves by stages from the Oriental world (in which only one is free—the despot) to the Greco-Roman world (in which some are free—the citizens but not the slaves) to the Germanic-Christian world (in which all are free as citizens of the state). This schematic division hardly does justice to Hegel's prodigious knowledge of historical detail, but it does state the essential philosophical message about history that he sought to convey. As he expressed the matter in his *Lectures on the Philosophy of History:*

> The East knew and to the present day knows only that One is free; the Greek and Roman world, that some are free; the German world knows that All are free. The first political form therefore which we observe in History, is Despotism, the second Democracy and Aristocracy, the third Monarchy.[67]

Basically the same division of history is found in *The Philosophy of Right.*[68] In both works Hegel defends the thesis that history has a meaning discoverable by the human mind and that it is a rational process un-

---

66. Ibid., pp. 157–59 (par. 258, Remarks and Note on von Haller's *Restauration der Staatswissenschaft*).

67. C. J. Friedrich, ed., *Hegel: The Philosophy of History,* trans. J. Sibree (New York: Dover, 1956), p. 104. Unfortunately, the Sibree translation renders *germanisch* "German" instead of "Germanic."

68. *Philosophy of Right,* pp. 219–20 (par. 353).

folding dialectically.[69] He saw himself as living in a sense at the "end" of history. By this he did not mean that history had achieved its absolute culmination. The dialectic would continue its unfolding. Rather, he meant that for the first time it had become possible for man's consciousness to discover the dialectical principle at the foundation of reality and thus to survey in retrospect the course of the development of the world spirit through time.

Hegel concludes *The Philosophy of Right* by speaking of the modern world as in principle having overcome the "opposition" between the temporal and spiritual realms of the medieval period. Through the principle of the modern state, temporal existence becomes spiritualized, while spiritual reality abandons the "world of beyond" and actualizes itself in history. The essential state, "the image and actuality of reason," is the arena for the full flowering of the highest activities of the consciousness, *activities that themselves transcend the state:* i.e., art, religion, and philosophy.[70]

HEGEL: PRECURSOR OF "FASCIST TOTALITARIANISM"?

The following statement, taken from a leading text-anthology, is representative of much of the interpretive writing on Hegel that has been published during the past several decades: "Though garbed in high-sounding philosophical terms, Hegel's political theory thus contains all essential elements of fascism: racialism, nationalism, the leadership principle, government by authority rather than consent, and, above all, the idolization of power as the supreme test of human values."[71]

This charge will have to be rejected as false. Its fallacy becomes clear if one examines the supposedly "fascist" elements one by one. Hegel was not a racist. One will find in his writings no advocacy of innate biological racial superiority. His categories of analysis are cultural,

---

69. Ibid., pp. 216 and 220–23 (pars. 342 and 355–59). See also Friedrich, ed., *Philosophy of History*, p. 9.

70. Ibid., pp. 222–23 (par. 360).

71. William Ebenstein, *Great Political Thinkers: Plato to the Present*, 3rd ed. (New York: Rinehart, 1966), p. 595. See also Karl Popper, *The Open Society and Its Enemies*, 2 vols. (New York: Harper & Row, 1962). *Contra*, see in particular Friedrich, *Philosophy of Hegel*, Introduction, and Eric Weil, *Hegel et l'état* (Paris: J. Vrin, 1950). Friedrich has also more recently discussed the problem of Hegel and totalitarian modes of thought from a different perspective (that of the dialectic and its notion of "negation") in his previously cited "The Power of Negation: Hegel's Dialectic and Totalitarian Ideology." Friedrich's brilliant and subtle analysis does turn up a possible connection between aspects of the dialectic and totalitarian thought, while specifically excepting Hegel's substantive political theory from any such linkage. To my mind, this constitutes an additional justification for dwelling on the substantive achievements of Hegel's political theory rather than on his often obscure and amorphous dialectic.

and he thinks of history in terms of civilizations that are themselves spiritual and intellectual products. It would be a gross distortion of his philosophy, which stressed the activity of spirit and mind, to link him with the crude and pernicious biologism of Nazi race thinking. Furthermore, Hegel was vociferous and explicit in his condemnation of anti-Semitism. "To exclude the Jews from civil rights," he wrote, "would be blamable and reproachable" and "the silliest folly." The "fierce outcry against the Jews ... ignores the fact that they are, above all, *men*."[72] In another passage of *The Philosophy of Right* he eloquently proclaimed the essential equality of men as persons by virtue of their humanity: "A man counts as a man in virtue of his manhood alone, not because he is a Jew, Catholic, Protestant, German, Italian, etc."[73]

Nor are the other points in the indictment valid. To accuse Hegel of endorsing the "leadership principle" would make a mockery of his elaborate attempt to institutionalize and limit the power of the crown in the modern state. The "leader" in his construct of the paradigmatic society is a constitutional monarch, not a *Führer*. As for basing government on authority rather than consent, it may be concluded that the whole point of Hegel's political theory was to show that authority and consent are not opposites but are bound up with each other, and that the distinguishing characteristic of the "mature" modern state is its enjoyment of the fully conscious and willing allegiance and consent of its citizens. Authority is not brute force but voluntarily elicited consent to the laws and acts of a government representative of an organized people. With regard to the charge that he was a nationalist, that is correct, but not in an ethnic or biological sense: he did not demand that every ethnic or linguistic group comprise an exclusive nation with its own sovereign political organization. He did not even advocate political unification and independence for the German-speaking areas of Europe. His focus was on the state, the political form, not on the nation as a fixed ethnic unit. The state was above all a product of culture and loyalty to a common idea; in principle it could contain a multiplicity of ethnic and linguistic groups.[74] To the charge that he worshiped power, he is, as we have seen, vulnerable because of certain extravagant and unfortunate passages. If these passages are taken in the context of the whole work—and especially together with the passages that explicitly reject the view that might and brute force call the tune in world history and that right is a function of military conquest—then his position on this

---

72. *Philosophy of Right*, pp. 168–69 (par. 270, note to Remarks).

73. Ibid., p. 134 (par. 209, Remarks).

74. See Shlomo Avineri, "Hegel and Nationalism," *Review of Politics*, 24 (October 1962): 475f.

question, although defective, is certainly not comparable to the vulgar power worship of a Hitler or a Mussolini.

CONCLUSION

Hegel is in need of reinterpretation, especially with respect to his political thought. At the very least, we are entitled to ask that critics cease the all too common practice of making him a favorite whipping boy through a fundamental distortion of his teaching as illiberal and "authoritarian" in the extreme. Beyond that, we might consider whether all of us who today seek to forward the critical science of politics might not learn much from both the substance and the spirit of his inquiry into political matters.

This does not mean that we shall become Hegelians—any more than the careful study of Plato and Aristotle makes us Platonists and Aristotelians. There are limitations and serious defects in Hegel's teaching. His system weighs heavily on him, and however much we may admire his enormous capacity for synthesis—and even envisage a time when philosophy will again need this gift—we shall not wish to follow him in believing that the construction of an all-encompassing system is the task of philosophy, or of any other discipline. His philosophy of history will seem unconvincing and subject to grave misinterpretation to most of us, however much we may applaud his determination to take history seriously. The mystery of being remains even after reason has done its work. At the present time, Camus speaks to many of us more directly than Hegel.

Despite his system, his dialectical excesses, his ethnocentrism, his inability to see beyond a world organized into competing states, and his consequent failure fully to draw out the universalism implicit in his philosophy, even despite his overemphasis on authority, Hegel today richly repays reading by those who seek to continue the great conversation of political theory. For in his reflections on the person and his existence in society in reason and freedom, Hegel managed to say much that was not vitiated by his system. In this we can take heart, for it confirms that the person—in this instance the man we know as Hegel— is greater than any system.[75]

---

75. For further discussion of Hegel's theory of the state, especially as it is elaborated in the *Lectures on the Philosophy of History*, see my article "Hegel's Theory of the State: Humanist or Totalitarian?" in *Statsvetenskaplig Tidskrift* (*Swedish Journal of Political Science*), December 1970, pp. 293–313, and the literature cited therein. I argue that if one takes Hegel's theory of the person and philosophy of history seriously, a world-state capable of maintaining peace without threatening or destroying diversity is a demand of reason.

14

Nineteenth-Century
Radical Thought:
Fourier, Proudhon, Marx

The modern period has witnessed the development of a number of distinctive political styles, the three most significant of which are liberalism, conservatism, and radicalism. The liberal and conservative political styles are dealt with in other chapters;[1] radicalism is a perspective shared in varying degrees by a number of major modern political thinkers. Rousseau has a radical side, particularly evident in the *Second Discourse* (*On the Origins of Inequality*), but the many tensions and ambiguities in his thought keep him on the fringes of radicalism. Karl Marx was perhaps the most brilliant and perceptive—and has certainly been the most influential—spokesman for political radicalism; but other intellectuals among Marx's contemporaries who are today far less well known than he also provided eloquent and incisive statements of the radical position. Among them were the so-called utopian socialists, such as Charles Fourier, Pierre-Joseph Proudhon, and Robert Owen. These men did not see themselves as utopian in the negative sense, naturally; they saw radical change as resulting from new advances in our knowledge of man and his condition.

All of the great upheavals of the modern age have been accompanied by schools of thought and political protest that have some affinities with recent expressions of radicalism. The Reformation had its "communist" sectarians and "free spirits"; the English Revolution of the 1640s produced the Levellers and Fifth Monarchy men; and the French Revolution brought forth Gracchus Babeuf and his vision of "the last revolution," which would be permanently in process and would usher in a qualitatively different type of society.

It was not until the nineteenth century, however, that the radical

---

1. On liberalism, see in particular chaps. 5, 6, 9, and 10; on conservatism, see chap. 8. Many observers also would find elements of conservatism in Richard Hooker (pp. 74–88) and in Hegel (chap. 13).

vision of society received full and detailed elaboration at the hands of theoretically gifted and articulate spokesmen. Because of the very nature of the radical vision, which is suspicious of all structures, systems, and "objectifications" of the existential situation, radicals are typically disinclined to offer treatises in political theory. The radical genius is in a sense antipolitical, and the most appropriate outlet for its expression is in music and art rather than in political tomes. It is no accident, therefore, that the radicalism of youth in the United States and elsewhere today has characteristically expressed itself in rock music, poetry, underground newspapers, "happenings," festivals, and other theatrical innovations. Nonetheless, there have been radical spokesmen who wrote serious and substantial political works. Fourier, Proudhon, and Marx were among the principal exponents of this perspective in the nineteenth century, just as Herbert Marcuse is today.

Alan Ritter, an authority on Proudhon, has written that "a critic qualifies as radical" if he carries his "assault on the status quo beyond its surface defects to their hidden sources. He grabs matters by the root, as Marx said, while others are content to prune their leaves and branches."[2] This is a good beginning of a definition, reflecting the etymology of the term from *radix* (root).

Radicalism is often portrayed by hostile critics as if it were wholly negative or destructive. The radical is *ipso facto* supposedly an apostle of violence and terrorism. Such a characterization does little to enhance our understanding of radicalism as a phenomenon of major importance in our political past and present. There are numerous varieties of radical thought, some wholly nonviolent, some advocating recourse to violence under strictly defined conditions, and a relatively small minority seeming to exult in violence in a kind of nihilistic frenzy, as if destruction of life and the works of man were a pure and ennobling act. One thinks of the mad Russian Nechaev, who in 1869 published the blood-curdling *Catechism of a Revolutionary*,[3] as exemplifying this type of nihilistic radicalism.

---

2. Alan Ritter, *The Political Thought of Pierre-Joseph Proudhon* (Princeton: Princeton University Press, 1969). This able study deserves to be read by all serious students of nineteenth-century political thought.

3. Until recently it was thought that the Russian anarchist Mikhail Bakunin (1814–1876) had co-authored the *Catechism*, but research has now indicated that it was the work of Nechaev alone. See the reference by James Joll to the researches of Michael Confino in *Government and Opposition*, 5 (Autumn 1970): 544. Joll carefully concludes that, despite the fact that Bakunin dissociated himself from Nechaev's extreme praise of violence and cruelty, his "belief in direct action . . . has much in common with the assumptions of the contemporary apostles of direct action." For the full text of the *Catechism*, see Franco Venturi, *The Roots of Revolution* (New York: Knopf, 1960), pp. 365–66.

All serious radicalism (as distinct from nihilistic adventurism) is at once an affirmation and a negation. It is an *affirmation* of the value of each unique human being and of his rightful claim to express his uniqueness creatively and in community with his fellows. It is a *negation* of the existing social order, which is seen as a denial of that uniqueness. Radical humanism contends that the age-old triumph of the system over the person can now be decisively reversed: in Marx's dialectical language, the economic and technological conditions now exist for the "negation of the negation" of the human in man. Radicalism proclaims that fundamental, *qualitative* change in man's condition is now not just a utopian dream but an objective possibility.

CHARLES FOURIER

Both Fourier and Proudhon were born in the small French provincial town of Besançon, Fourier in 1772 and Proudhon in 1809. Fourier never married and lived a lonely life, holding down a menial job by day and devoting himself to his writings during all his available spare time. He did manage to attain a modest reputation and to acquire a few disciples: Victor Considérant was his most well-known French disciple, while Albert Brisbane expounded his doctrine in America. Brook Farm, established near Boston in 1841 as a communal venture of intellectuals, farmers, and artisans, was reorganized along the Fourierist lines in 1845, but survived only two years after that. A number of other Fourierist colonies (or "phalanxes") sprang up in the United States during this period and were disbanded almost as quickly; the longest-lived of them, the North American Phalanx in New Jersey, lasted twelve years. Yet Marx mentioned Fourier more favorably than he did any other "utopian socialist" (Engels' derogatory term for socialists whose views differed from Marxist or "scientific" socialism).

Fourier was given to flights of fantasy bordering on lunacy, as his contemporaries would have termed the dissociation of ideas that he frequently demonstrated; yet as Frank Manuel[4] and others have shown, he possessed an original and creative mind, and much that he wrote deserves to be taken seriously. Contemporary social critics like Erich Fromm continue to draw inspiration from him, as Fromm's book *The Sane Society* (1956) amply demonstrates.

Universal Harmony: The New Morality

Fourier's radicalism is evident from his first work, *Theory of the Four Movements*, published in 1808. In this book he defiantly announced his

---

4. I am indebted to Manuel's excellent chapter on Fourier in his *The Prophets of Paris* (Cambridge: Harvard University Press, 1962).

rejection of existing "civilized incoherence" and offered his own plan of "societal order."[5] Although Fourier was a creative explorer of the human psyche, one generally thinks of him as a dreamer or visionary rather than a hard-nosed "scientist of society." This was not, however, the way in which he saw himself. He denounced the "authors of uncertain sciences—political writers, moralists, economists, and others, whose theories are incompatible with experience and which are derived only from the fantasy of their authors."[6] He was referring to the *philosophes*, whom he accused of having made false claims about progress in human knowledge and the arts of civilization.

Fourier, then, was eager to dissociate himself from the liberalism of the Enlightenment. To him all "civilized" knowledge was a fraud. He regarded himself as the Newton of the moral world: he had discovered in the "law of passionate attraction" an explanation for human affairs equivalent in importance to the law of gravity for the physical world, and it remained to him alone to usher in an age of true progress and happiness for mankind:

> I alone will have refuted twenty centuries of political imbecility, and it is to myself alone that the present and future generations will owe their immense well-being. Before me, humanity lost several thousand years in struggling senselessly against nature. . . . Possessed of the Book of Destiny, I have come to dissipate political and moral shadows and on the ruins of the uncertain sciences I am raising the Theory of Universal Harmony.[7]

Sexual Liberation. More than any other nineteenth-century author or school—with the possible exception of the Marquis de Sade and the disciples of Saint-Simon—Fourier defended the proposition that human passions were good and that society should be organized around their expression rather than their repression. Fourier was in particular a champion of "sexual liberation"; all prohibitions, whether of law or of social pressure, on sexual behavior of any sort whatever were to be eliminated in the new, healthy society. His manuscript on sexual liberation, *The New World of Love*[8]—published for the first time only in 1967—comprises some five hundred printed pages of detailed analyses of practices officially regarded in pre-Fourierist society as perverse or immoral. In the Fourierist phalanx every sexual inclination would find satisfaction, for men and women of all of the 810 purported character

5. Charles Fourier, *Théorie des quatre mouvements et des destinées générales*, in *Oeuvres complètes de Charles Fourier*, 9 vols. (Paris: Éditions Anthropos, 1966–1967), vol. 1, p. 9.

6. Ibid., p. 2.

7. Ibid., p. ii.

8. Fourier, *Le nouveau monde amoureux*, in *Oeuvres complètes*, vol. 7.

types would find suitable partners. To our post-Freudian age of extensive sexual permissiveness and frank public discussion of sexual behavior, Fourier's manuscript seems less revolutionary than it was at the time he wrote it (during the 1820s and 1830s). Even so, it is a remarkable and revolutionary document. It is interesting that Fourier's socialist disciples played down this side of his teaching and chose instead to stress his attacks on the liberal capitalist economic system.

The Law of Passionate Attraction. Fourier claimed to have discovered the "law of passionate attraction," which governed the social world just as the law of gravity governed the rotation of the planets. The difficulty with society, he found, was that instead of conforming institutions to human beings and their needs, it forced human beings to conform to the requirements of repressive institutions. The resulting widespread frustration of men's desires fostered aggression, violence, inefficiency and misery.

The Fulfillment of Human Nature. Fourier insisted that he was the only social reformer to accept human nature as it was and pronounce it good. It is interesting to compare his teaching with that of his English contemporary Robert Owen, who proclaimed human nature to be infinitely malleable and argued for the creation of an environment in which the "desired" human nature might be produced. Fourier maintained that man was fundamentally an emotional, desiring animal; that all desires were good and "according to nature"; and that evil was the result of repressive social and political institutions that combined to produce antagonism and conflict rather than "harmony" and "association."

Each personality type had the potentiality for individual happiness and constructive contributions to the common good; if some types seemed destructive in existing society, it was because their passions had been denied the opportunity to express themselves. Thus a man of a "sadistic" personality type would play a constructive role in society if he were employed as a butcher. Similarly, those children who liked to play in the dirt would enjoy collecting garbage. There was no reason why destructive impulses had to be directed against other people or against oneself. In the Fourierist new world, wars and unproductive human conflicts and rivalries would cease. Mankind would work efficiently because each person would find joy in his work, and all would have leisure to enjoy the delights of this life, including food (Fourier thought of himself as a gourmet), sex, and artistic creativity.

The Phalanx

Fourier combined the words *phalange,* phalanx, and *monastère,* monastery, into the term *phalanstère* (translated into English simply as "phalanx") to designate the community governed according to the law of passionate attraction. Each phalanx was to have between 1,100 and 1,800 persons and was to cultivate about 5,000 acres of land. (The number of inhabitants decided upon was large enough to ensure that all personality types would be represented and would find compatible associates and sexual partners, yet small enough to ensure an intimate, face-to-face society.) Within the phalanx there would be smaller units, composed of people spontaneously attracted to each other. The basic unit was the "group" of seven persons; five groups constituted a "series." Productive work would be carried out on a group basis; individuals would not have to remain with a single group, but could "flit" from one to another as their inclinations led them. No one would do work he did not enjoy.

The central building or "palace" of the phalanx was to contain both living and working quarters for the inhabitants, as well as ample facilities for recreation, so that it would be unnecessary to go outside during inclement weather. Living quarters were to be private and were to differ in luxuriousness, at least initially, in accordance with the financial contributions brought to the phalanx by individual members. (Fourier was opposed to communal property and the abolition of inheritance; he regarded the equalization of property as "unnatural.") Meals were to be taken in common, so that the richer and poorer members of the community would have an opportunity to mingle and learn from one another. The family as it had hitherto been known would not exist in the phalanx. Children were to be cared for in a communal nursery by women who chose the work of child care, so that those who found other tasks more interesting would be free to perform them. Permanent monogamous alliances would of course continue to exist for those character types disposed to maintain them; other members were free to seek sexual partners wherever they wished for as long as they wished.

In order to attract additional investors, Fourier included in his plan a provision to set aside an enormous share of the profits of the phalanx for capital (one-third, in contrast to five-twelfths for laborers and one-fourth for "managers"). There was to be an upper limit to capital accumulation for any member of the phalanx, however. The managers were to be elected by universal suffrage.[9]

Stages on the Road to Harmony. Fourier apparently had a touching faith in the willingness of existing political and social elites to attend to his proposals and to be persuaded of their worth. He was confident that

_____

9. For the detailed presentation of Fourier's plan for the phalanx, see in particular his *Le nouveau monde industriel et sociétaire* in *Oeuvres complètes,* vol. 6.

if only a few phalanxes could be started, the contrast between the peacefulness and happiness of their inhabitants and the frustrations and misery of the outside world would be so stark that everyone would soon be clamoring at the gate of the nearest phalanx, pleading for admission. Nonetheless, he did not expect that the transition from the present so-called civilized stage to "harmony"—or the first historical stage—would occur overnight, even under optimal conditions. There would be two intermediate stages, which he termed *garantisme* (guaranteeism) and *sociantisme* (associationism), on the way to the promised land of *harmonisme* (harmony). During these intermediate phases in man's progress toward true happiness, people would be educated to the advantages of the phalanx system and the impoverished masses would be afforded a basic minimum of subsistence and comfort to prepare them for cooperative living. Thus even the "utopian" Fourier was "realistic" enough to recognize the need for a possibly rather lengthy transition period between the alienated society and the "harmonious" society. No one was to be coerced into entering a phalanx; for such a community to succeed, its membership had to be entirely voluntary.

Fourier as Socialist

Fourier was not an anarchist. If any label can be pinned to him, "associationist socialist" will perhaps do as well as any, although it falls short of indicating the depth of his interest in the erotic dimension of human life, an area that was on the whole little explored by nineteenth-century socialists. Nonetheless, it does appear that the word "socialism" was first used among the followers of Saint-Simon, Owen, and Fourier during the 1820s and 1830s, and that it stood for an interest in the "social question"—that is, the lot of the "poorest and most numerous class"—as well as an emphasis on cooperation and association rather than competition and individualism.

World Government and Technology

Fourier put forward a scheme for world government based on a loose confederation of phalanxes to be headed by an "omniarch" (or "universal ruler"), and he offered the job of first omniarch to Napoleon. Even for Fourier's own intentions, however, it was fortunate that the emperor failed to accept the offer, for Fourier had always advocated decentralization and devolution of power. He disagreed completely with Saint-Simon's proposal for a centralized, unitary Europe and world, just as he rejected Saint-Simon's program of extensive industrialization. Fourier was an agrarian reformer, but not only or even primarily out of a romantic attraction to the land. Rather he saw industrialization as unnecessarily multiplying the wants of men and inevitably requiring centralized planning. To him industrialization would spell the death of human freedom, and his plan for the phalanxes provided that they would confine themselves to farming, arts, and crafts on a scale that has come to be known as "cottage industry"; inhabitants would be content with only a few clothes, implements, and other articles appropriate to a simple life.

Fourier did not reject technology and its uses, however. The central task of the world union (or government) of phalanxes was to undertake gigantic public works that in time would transform the face of the earth. Men would even learn to control the weather, so that the deserts and the polar regions would become habitable. "Harmonious armies," drawn from 2 to 3 percent of the population of all phalanxes, would carry out these projects. At the "international" level there would be mock wars to provide harmless outlets for aggressive impulses in some elements of the population.

This radical political thinker envisaged an organizational pyramid with thousands of phalanxes at the base and proceeding upwards via the "caesarates" (regional groupings of phalanxes), "empires" (nations or blocs of nations), and "caliphates" (civilizations or cultures) to the omniarch at the apex. Constantinople was to be the capital of the New World of Harmony.[10] (Fourier developed a hatred of Paris and so took some pleasure in depriving it of this honor.)

Fourier's Relevance to Contemporary Radicalism

While some of Fourier's predictions are clearly fantastic and even demented (he predicted, for example, that the seas would turn to lemonade and the planets copulate), many of his prophecies and proposals today appear quite feasible. More interesting to the student of political thought than his Jules Verne–like imaginitiveness in foreseeing many technological developments is the uncannily contemporary sound of his diagnosis of the ills of industrial society. The themes of the alienation of labor, sexual restraint, the exploitation of women, and the repression of spontaneity and authentic individuality, all of which were central to his thought, loom large in the literature of today's radical protest. To the extent that today's radical youth becomes more interested in the history of ideas, Fourier will be rescued from the semi-obscurity to which he has thus far been consigned. He would no doubt sympathize completely with the young radicals' demands for a more loving, compassionate society in which invidious competition—to say nothing of war—is a thing of the past and where delight in the pleasures of the body can be ex-

---

10. See the discussion in Manuel, *Prophets of Paris*, pp. 238f.

perienced without guilt and fear. The practices and ideals of communal living espoused by contemporary radical youth in America and elsewhere are very much in the spirit of Fourier's vision for a new world based on cooperation and compassion. The failure of all the earlier communal experiments, with the sole exceptions of those that reorganized along capitalist lines (such as the Oneida Community) and those demanding strict conformity to rules based on religious principles (such as the Hutterite communities), is also worth pondering.

The "Design of God"

Unlike such revolutionaries as Marx and Bakunin, Fourier was not an atheist. In fact, he developed an elaborate, if highly idiosyncratic, theology.[11] The whole purpose of his teaching was to prove that all human passions were the work of God and would have beneficial results if they were allowed to express themselves freely and spontaneously. His law of passionate attraction demonstrated that all men's passions, like all planetary bodies, were in orderly relationship to one another, according to the "design of God." It remained for man to establish a social solar system and all would be well. The phalanx plan conformed fully to this law, and so was the only natural and God-ordained social system.

Fourier completely rejected "civilization" as it was presently constituted. He believed that it was incapable of change and eventually would be destroyed. Fourier saw society as a prison; while the reformers were trying to improve conditions within it, he could think only of escape. Although he never developed a theory of historical change comparable to the Marxian dialectic, he had faith that mankind's ascent to a period of "association" and "harmony" as he described it was inevitable. But the fruits of progress were not to be enjoyed forever. Eros was to be succeeded by Thanatos. After a period of erotic and sensual fulfillment and enjoyment (which he called "harmony"), mankind would "disappear in a general dissolution of the earth." The pleasures of the phalanx were to end in destruction. This fate did not appear to disturb Fourier. His new men, having led full lives, would not fear death.

Fourier's Contribution to Political Thought

It is easy—too easy—to dismiss Fourier as a mere dreamer who allowed his fantasies full reign and who finally lost all contact with reality. Yet embedded in his works one finds extensive and disciplined analyses of one side of human experience which has been neglected in political and

---

11. See in particular the concluding chapters of *Nouveau monde industriel*, pp. 445–58, dealing with the "plan of God" for human destiny, the problem of the immortality of the soul, etc.

social thought until comparatively recently: the reality of the unconscious. Contemporary students of Freud might find much that is valuable
in Fourier's writings. There is a "clinical" side to his vast work.

Fourier cared passionately about human freedom, understood as the
unconstrained expression of individual uniqueness. Whatever the limitations of his perspective, he raised an eloquent voice against the tendency
of even liberal thought in the West to fit man into a Procrustean bed of
"true" or "disciplined" freedom. Although liberalism talks—it seems endlessly—about spontaneity, individuality, the dignity of the individual,
and so on, it appears that the expression of real eccentricity and radical
difference in perspective or life style is too easily branded "license" or
"deviance." The liberal imagination has been stunted in its conception
of the variety of possibilities for human development; an infusion of
radical perspectives such as Fourier's may well serve to enrich it. In
practice it should be possible to approximate more closely than we have
yet done his aim of having the system fit the person rather than the
person the system. Contemporary society in all its aspects must make
more room for the free play of unconstrained and undirected individuality. This insight may turn out to have been Fourier's lasting contribution.

PIERRE-JOSEPH PROUDHON

Proudhon has more in common with Fourier than the coincidence of
having been born in the same town. Like Fourier, he was self-educated,
was radical in his political thought, and spent most of his life in poverty.
(He earned his living as a proofreader.) Proudhon was more famous
during his day and was more of a political activist than his fellow towns-
man, however. He took a leading role in the Revolution of 1848 in Paris,
and he was active in the early development of the European socialist
movement. His best-known works were (and are) *Property* (1840), *The
Revolution of the Nineteenth Century* (1851), and *Federalism* (1863).

Proudhon agreed with Fourier that liberty involved an irreducible
element of spontaneity and that it resisted all efforts to impose a rigid
pattern upon it:

> Liberty recognizes no law . . . no cause, no limit, no end, except
> itself. . . . Placing itself above everything else, it waits for a chance
> to escape . . . all laws but its own . . . to make the world serve its
> fancies and the natural order its whims. To the universe that sur-
> rounds it it says: no; to the laws of nature and logic . . .: no. . . . It
> is the eternal adversary that opposes any idea and any force that
> aims to dominate it; the indomitable revolutionary that has faith in

nothing but itself, respect and esteem for nothing but itself, that will not abide even the idea of God except insofar as it recognizes itself in God as its own antithesis.[12]

Evil in God and Man

Proudhon differed from Fourier in his estimate of human nature and in his "theology" (or antitheology). For him the social problem was much more intractable than for Fourier, and, as Alan Ritter has indicated in his able study, there is a strong element of realism in his political writings. Proudhon had a rather pessimistic view of man and thought him to have been "wrongly made" (*malfait*).[13] It was necessary for man to re-create himself in his own image if he were to have an end to his misery. God to Proudhon was not a beneficent force but an evil one, the source of all that is irrational, cruel, and destructive in man's instinctual makeup. Man's liberation, Proudhon wrote with passion, was conditional on the defeat of God, who must be "hurled down upon the ground." One attains to progress and happiness "despite God."

For Proudhon, then, God was a symbol of the presence of evil in man and the world. As one of Proudhon's biographers has observed, his phrase "God is evil" was as startling and provocative to his contemporaries as his other famous dictum, "Property is theft."[14] Of all his works, *The Philosophy of Poverty*, which appeared in 1846, is the most vociferous in its expression of an antitheistic (as opposed to an atheistic) position. God is there declared to be "a being who is essentially anti-civilized, antiliberal, antihuman." "We reach knowledge in spite of him, we reach well-being in spite of him, we reach society in spite of him. Every step forward is a victory in which we overcome the Divine."[15]

In view of his conclusion that man was "wrongly made," it is not surprising that Proudhon lacked Fourier's faith in the beneficence of

12. Pierre-Joseph Proudhon, "Hymn to Liberty," from *Justice* (1858), cited in Ritter, *Political Thought of Proudhon*, p. 21.

13. See the excellent discussion in James Joll, *The Anarchists* (Boston: Little, Brown, 1964), chap. 3. Proudhon himself defined anarchy as "the government of each man by each man," or "self-government" (*Du principe fédératif*, ed. C. Brun [Paris: Éditions Bossard, 1921], p. 52). Anarchy is therefore not in principle hostile to government *as such*. Elsewhere Proudhon defines anarchy as "the absence of a master" or the "government of man over man," thus distinguishing anarchy from "absence of rule" or of "principle." Knowledge, rather than arbitrary will, is apparently to govern in "the good society." See Proudhon, *What Is Property?*, trans. B. R. Tucker (New York: Howard Fertig, 1966), pp. 277, 286. The first "memoir" of *Property* was published in 1840.

14. George Woodcock, *Pierre-Joseph Proudhon* (London: Routledge & Kegan Paul, 1956), p. 99.

15. Cited in ibid., p. 98.

all human passions. In fact, on the question of "sexual liberation," Proudhon was an extreme puritan, and he eulogized the family and monogamous marriage. Despite his general radical approach, his thought has a traditionalist side that later appealed to Charles Maurras and the *Action Française*. Proudhon never forgot the rural surroundings of his youth, and he always extolled the virtues of the agrarian life. A conservative with regard to marriage and the family, he was also conservative in his attitude toward the role of women. He was opposed to the feminist movements of his day, and he would surely have objected to the "women's lib" groups of today, with their demands for full equality of the sexes in jobs, wages, working conditions, life styles, and all the rest. The many sides to Proudhon's thought provide an excellent indication of the danger of a loose and thoughtless application of labels—in themselves indispensable and unavoidable—such as "liberal," "conservative," and "radical." No more than liberalism and conservatism—and perhaps less so, given its inveterate antipathy to rigid categorization—can radicalism be treated as a monolithic entity.

The Anarchist Society

Like Fourier, Proudhon was an advocate of nonviolent revolution. He "wanted no St. Bartholomew's massacre of landlords," he observed on one occasion. The "redeemed society" could be achieved by persuading the existing ruling classes of the superiority of his doctrine. In the new society of anarchism,[16] industrial organization would replace government, contracts between citizens and communes would replace laws voted by legislatures, and all standing armies and police units would be done away with. Centralized political power—the "state" as such—would not exist; functional economic groups (agricultural, industrial, commercial, etc.) would interact harmoniously with each other for the good of the whole. All men, regardless of differences, would "unite in an ineffable fraternity."

Federalism. Toward the end of his life, Proudhon published a remarkable little work on federalism, obviously inspired by recent events in the Italian peninsula.[17] In it he foresaw a time when the "whole of Europe will become a federation of federations," each with authority as decentralized as possible. He hoped that Italy would recognize the regional aspirations of Naples, Sicily, and other areas, and not impose a centralized, uniform administration on the entire country. In this hope he was, as we know, disappointed. It is not clear whether Proudhon regarded federalism as an intermediary stage on the way to the final

16. James Joll has called Proudhon the "first and most important anarchist philosopher" (*The Anarchists*, p. 79).

17. Proudhon, *Du principe fédératif*. The work was originally published in 1863.

historical phase of anarchism or whether federalism was itself another name for the organizational structure of the new world united in accordance with anarchist principles. Probably he regarded federalism as something of both. The constant thrust of his teaching was against the centralization of political power, and federalism seemed to him consistent with this objective. As the federal systems of America, Canada, and other countries have amply demonstrated, however, federalism need not be incompatible with a national government far stronger than Proudhon would have dreamed of countenancing. It seems that "federation" to him was virtually equivalent to "confederation," and that he envisaged a Europe that would no longer consist of nations, but would be a single federation of "communes" loosely bound together by voluntary contracts.[18]

Economic Arrangements. Proudhon's economic theories, which he summed up under the label of "mutualism," are shot through with contradictions and need not detain us here. As Ritter has pointed out, he seemed to espouse in principle the equal distribution of social wealth, but actually he allowed for the very real possibility of inequality of rewards because of greater efficiency in producing the goods for which credits would be given in a kind of barter system of exchange.[19] Presumably he believed that as the "redeemed society" became more and more firmly established, all men's economic performances would tend toward equality, although he never gave any convincing arguments to support such an assumption. The important thing to notice about Proudhon's economic teaching is his conviction that the "abolition of the whole existing structure of credit and exchange" was the essential precondition for restoring "the direct relationship between the producer and the consumer."[20] The money economy itself would need to be eliminated.

Proudhon in Retrospect

Proudhon was a diffuse and often inconsistent writer. His contribution to our common stock of political ideas is uneven in quality. While much of his analysis was subtle, complex, and imaginative, there was also a narrow and simplistic streak in his personality which frequently warred with his more generous and sophisticated side. His deplorable anti-Semitism, which is not mentioned by some of his admirers, later helped

---

18. These contracts would "always reserve a greater part of sovereignty of action" for the smaller units than they "abandon" to the larger ones (ibid., p. 112). Even so, this concept of federalism seems to move rather sharply away from anarchism, unless we view federalism as an intermediary stage.

19. Ritter, *Political Thought of Proudhon,* pp. 137–38.

20. Joll, *The Anarchists,* p. 64.

fan the fanaticism of Maurras and the *Action Française*. Beyond that his early writings exhibited a simplistic faith that all human problems are capable of resolution through an objective "science" of politics. As he observed in *What Is Property?*, in the new redeemed society

> every question of domestic politics must be decided by departmental statistics; every question of foreign politics is an affair of international statistics. The science of government rightly belongs to one of the sections of the Academy of Sciences, whose permanent secretary is necessarily prime minister; and, since every citizen may address a memoir to the Academy, every citizen is a legislator. But, as the opinion of no one is of any value until its truth has been proven, no one can substitute his will for reason—nobody is king.
>
> All questions of legislation and politics are matters of science, not of opinion. The legislative power belongs only to reason, methodically recognized and demonstrated.[21]

Proudhon here seems naively optimistic in his dream of a society where objective and mathematically demonstrable reason decides every question. Toward the end of his life, however, having witnessed the failure of a number of revolutions and having become wiser in the ways of the world, he worked out a richer and more subtle psychology. His work *Justice* contains a sophisticated criticism of the kind of ethical naturalism on which depends the view that policy can be made "scientifically."

Proudhon began to relegate the dawn of a new era to an ever more distant future. In his last days he became overwhelmed by pessimism, and a desperate fear becomes apparent in his writings. Before mankind could enter the promised land, he wrote, there would be a tumultuous time of troubles. He predicted an age of utter darkness, of mass killings and blood baths. It was a prediction that has proved all too accurate as we survey the results of world politics in the first two-thirds of the twentieth century.

KARL MARX

A balanced appraisal of Karl Marx's political thought is exceedingly difficult to obtain because his work has become confused with the later vulgarization of his thought known as "Marxism." Marx himself once commented that there could not be any "Marxists," and a reading of his complex teaching, especially in the light of his creative early writings, leads us to suspect that with him we are in the presence of one of the great and

---

21. Proudhon, *What Is Property?*, p. 278.

seminal minds of the modern period in Western political thought. Marx deserves to be ranked with Machiavelli, Hobbes, Locke, Rousseau, and Hegel for the range, depth, originality and influence of his political writings.

Materials for an interpretation of Marx's political thought are more fully available today than ever before. Marx's early writings, such as his "Critique of Hegel's *Philosophy of Right*," his *German Ideology* (in its full text), and the vitally important *Philosophical-Economic Manuscripts* (discovered only in 1932), have now been published and translated into English. In addition, valuable analyses of his thought have been recently published.[22] The author of one of these works, Shlomo Avineri of the University of Jerusalem, has argued impressively for the necessity to "emancipate Marx from both his disciples and his enemies and to conduct the discussion with an eye towards restoring the inner balance of Marx's thought as a political theory."[23] Avineri concludes that Marx was one of the leading critical and humanistic writers in the history of Western political thought.

Some interpreters of Marx, such as Daniel Bell, have drawn a sharp distinction between an "early" and a "late" Marx, contending that in his youthful writings he was humanistic and democratic, while his mature works reflect a determinism and materialism that seriously jeopardize these values. Avineri, on the other hand, contends that there was only one Marx, and that the distinction between his early and late teachings has "no foundation whatsoever in the Marxian texts themselves." Beginning with his earliest attempts at political and social analysis in the early 1840s and continuing until the end of his life, Avineri observes, Marx offered a coherent vision of the political and social world. Where a contrast seems to occur between the early and late writings, it is due to Engels' oversimplifications of these writings. Engels adopted a mechanistic determinism closer to positions Marx had emphatically rejected than to Marx's own position. Finally, Lenin was able to combine the "Jacobin subjectivist view of political revolution with a

---

22. Extensive portions of the early writings have been translated in Erich Fromm, *Marx's Concept of Man* (New York: Ungar, 1961); Karl Marx, *Early Writings*, trans. and ed. T. B. Bottomore (New York: McGraw-Hill, 1964); and Loyd D. Easton and Kurt H. Guddat, trans. and eds., *Writings of the Young Marx on Philosophy and Society* (Garden City, N. Y.: Doubleday, 1967). The most useful edition of the texts in German may be found in S. Landshut, ed., *Karl Marx: Die Frühschriften* (Stuttgart, 1953). Two particularly valuable works about Marx recently published are Robert Tucker, *Philosophy and Myth in Karl Marx* (Cambridge: At the University Press, 1961), and Shlomo Avineri, *The Social and Political Thought of Karl Marx* (Cambridge: At the University Press, 1968).

23. Avineri, *Social and Political Thought*, p. vii.

somewhat mechanistic interpretation of history derived from Marx through Engels. That the outcome may have been similar to what Marx calls in the *Manuscripts* 'crude communism' should not be surprising."[24]

The Problem and the Solution of the Modern State

Avineri views Marx as having fruitfully engaged in a dialogue with Hegel. Marx concluded that although Hegel's method (the dialectic) had revolutionary potential, his employment of it in *The Philosophy of Right* only served to confirm the status quo. Hegel presented the monarchy and the bureaucracy as ministering to the universal interest, while the estates were held to be mediating organs between the requirements of the universal interest and the demands of particular interests in civil society. Actually, Marx held, the modern state as idealized by Hegel does not and cannot exist; Hegel only described what the state *claimed* to accomplish. The division between civil society and the state is an artificial one, which succeeds only in compounding the alienation between man and himself, between man and his fellows, and between man and nature. The state (monarch, legislature, and bureaucracy taken together) is not separated from the clash of material interests prevalent in civil society, but reflects this clash in its own composition. Whether the state is a monarchy or a republic is all ultimately the same, according to Marx, because existing economic arrangements (which he later identified as "capitalism") dominate and control human life. Even the property "owners" are in fact owned by property. Man is subjected to an alien force that makes inhuman or dehumanizing demands. The solution to the problem of the existing state lies in its dialectical transcendence. It must not be rationalized in the manner of Hegel; the state, along with civil society, must be abolished and transcended (*aufgehoben*). On the ruins of the old order a new society must be created, one that will enable man to regain his human essence, which itself is a societal essence. This new society, which is not a utopia but rather the observable trend and outcome of human history, can be called "true democracy," or communism. This "democracy," however, is not a particular kind of political constitution (based on universal suffrage, representative government, and so on); rather, it represents the abolition of all political constitutions. Under communism, which is the true humanism, man will destroy the multiple tyrannies that have ruled over him and will organize a world in which he will be free to create his own destiny.

These thoughts, found in Marx's "Critique of Hegel's *Philosophy of the State*" of 1843, are deepened and confirmed in his later works, which

---

24. Ibid., p. 258.

also deal more fully with other problems, such as the relationship of consciousness to society, the universal mission of the proletariat, the specific forms of capitalist alienation, and the various stages on the road to final liberation (including the phase of "raw" or "crude" communism). Avineri concludes that throughout his works Marx displays a flexible, open, and inquiring spirit, that he repudiates adventurism and Jacobin-style terror,[25] and that in general he adopts the perspective of humanity as a whole rather than that of a merely partisan cause. Communism itself is to be transcended in the final phase of social development, so that Marx's vision of the good society is inconsistent with a narrow and reductionist ideology.

I have cited Avineri's important recent study at length because I am in basic agreement with its general conclusions about the nature and development of Marx's political thought. Let us now turn to an analysis of Marx's *Philosophical-Economic Manuscripts*, written in 1844 when their author was twenty-six years old;[26] for the *Manuscripts* contain the key to the understanding of the basic orientation of all of Marx's writings.

The *Philosophical-Economic Manuscripts* of 1844: Alienation, Private Property, and Communism

The Alienation of Man. In present society, according to Marx, the "*increase in value* of the world of things is directly proportional to the *decrease in value* of the human world. Labor not only produces commodities. It also produces itself and the work as a *commodity*, and indeed in the same proportion as it produces commodities in general." The worker stands in relation to the product of his work as if it were an "alien *thing*," a "*power* independent of the producer."[27] The worker is diminished and impoverished, both externally and internally, as a result of the process.

---

25. See especially Avineri's helpful analysis of Marx's views on the French Revolution and Jacobin-style terror in ibid., pp. 185f.

26. Tucker adds the view that Marx systematically distorted the insights in this work by subsequently transposing self-alienation into societal alienation (the struggle between the capitalists and the working class). Although a shift of emphasis might be said to occur, I find the class-struggle idea quite central in the *Manuscripts* themselves. For example, Marx speaks of the "whole society" dividing into "two classes of *proprietors and propertyless workers.*" (From *Writings of the Young Marx on Philosophy and Society,* ed. and trans. Loyd D. Easton and Kurt H. Guddat, p. 287. Copyright © 1967 by Loyd D. Easton and Kurt H. Guddat. Reprinted by permission of Doubleday & Company, Inc.) Also: "The nonworker does everything against the worker which the worker does against himself, but he does not do against his own self what he does against the worker" (ibid., p. 300). And again: "That the product of labor does not belong to the worker and an alien power confronts him is possible only because this product belongs *to a man other than the worker*" (ibid., p. 296).

27. Ibid., p. 289.

The more the worker exerts himself, the more powerful becomes the alien objective world which he fashions against himself, the poorer he and his inner world become, the less there is that belongs to him. It is the same in religion. The more man attributes to God, the less he retains in himself.[28]

What should be the most human activity in which man engages— work, the fabrication of his world according to his own creative insights and impulses—becomes a profoundly dehumanizing force.

The worker does not affirm himself in his work but denies himself, feels miserable and unhappy, develops no free physical and mental energy but mortifies his flesh and ruins his mind. . . . His work, therefore, is not voluntary but coerced, *forced* labor. . . . It is not his own spontaneous activity. It belongs to another. It is the loss of his own self.[29]

As a result, "man (the worker) feels that he is acting freely only in his animal functions—eating, drinking, and procreating, or at most in his shelter and finery—while in his human functions he feels only like an animal. The animalistic becomes the human and the human the animalistic."[30] In alienating himself from nature (the external world) and his human nature, man also alienates himself from his fellow men. When he is authentically himself man is also a member of society—of the human society, the human *species*. Man is a "species-being." He participates in the adventure of existence with his fellow human beings, and together with them consciously alters the material environment to make it a human rather than a merely animal one.

In a striking phrase, Marx observes that unlike animals, which respond only to physical need, man "creates also according to the laws of beauty."[31] Alienation—alienated labor—deprives him of this possibility, the possibility of fulfilling his truly human essence. "In taking from man the object of his production, alienated labor takes from his *species-life*, his actual and objective existence as a species. It changes his superiority to the animal to inferiority, since he is deprived of nature, his organic body."[32] Free spontaneous activity becomes a "means" of man's "physical existence."

The Source of Man's Alienation. If, then, current societal existence is grounded on alienation and specifically on the alienation of labor, what

28. Ibid., pp. 289–90.
29. Ibid., p. 292.
30. Ibid.
31. Ibid., p. 295.
32. Ibid.

is the nature of the alien power that dominates man? Who or what is it that keeps man in bondage? Man's alien master is neither God (an abstraction of an alienated imagination) nor nature, but man himself. More specifically, it is a special type of man, the nonworker (later to be called the "capitalist"). "That the product of labor does not belong to the worker and an alien power confronts him is possible only because this product belongs to *a man other than the worker*. . . . Not gods, not nature, but only man himself can be this alien power over man."[33] Contemporary man thus exists in a state of exploitation, and human society is divided between the exploiter and the exploited. Even the exploiters are not truly free, however, for they are impelled by subhuman urges, above all by greed. They are also in the very process of their activity preparing the conditions for their own overthrow.

The Development of Communism. The process of overcoming the condition of alienation of labor and the exploitation of man by man will, we are told, be lengthy and tortuous, beginning with "raw" communism, or communism considered as the "negation of the negation." As the mere negation of alienated labor, exploitation, and the domination of man by property and money, "raw" communism only universalizes the inhuman features of the preceding society. It is a regime of force, greed, envy, and human degradation. "Immediate, physical *possession* is for it the sole aim of life and existence. The condition of the laborer is not overcome but extended to all men." This frightening state, Marx says, implies the overthrow of all standards, or better, the adoption of the least common denominator as the measure of everything. Yet it would appear, according to his analysis, necessary for mankind to pass through this dreadful purgatory before it could begin to ascend the heavenly heights and at last attain paradise.

Communism then proceeds through two further stages of development: (1) political communism, in which the state persists in some form, and (2) communism in which the state is transcended (*aufgehoben*), but in an incomplete and imperfect way, so that it is still "influenced by private property, that is, by the alienation of man." In both forms,

> communism already knows itself as the reintegration or return of man to himself, as the overcoming of human self-alienation, but since it has not yet understood the positive essence of private property and . . . the *human* nature of needs, it still remains captive to and infected by private property.[34]

---

33. Ibid., p. 297.

34. Ibid., pp. 303–4. In a subsequent manuscript, Marx criticizes Hegel's dialectic for claiming the "negation of the negation" to be something "absolutely

After these transitional phases we arrive at a completed communism. This fully developed communism is described as the

> *positive* overcoming of *private property* as *human self-alienation*, and thus as the actual *appropriation of the human* essence through and for man; therefore as the complete and conscious restoration of man to himself within the total wealth of previous development, the restoration of man as a *social*, that is, human being. This communism as completed naturalism is humanism, as completed humanism it is naturalism. It is the *genuine* resolution of the antagonism between man and nature and between man and man; it is the true resolution of the conflict between existence and essence, objectification and self-affirmation, freedom and necessity, individual and species. It is the riddle of history solved and knows itself as this solution.[35]

Private Property. The private ownership of property—by which Marx understands the entire social world of alienated man—leads to the production of objects, both intellectual and material, which dominate man. Man becomes restricted and distorted in his inner life. Instead of being able to attend to the world with all of his senses and to create according to the "laws of beauty," man suffers a serious imbalance in his inner life and looks at the world only as something to be *possessed*. The social system based on private property produces a man dominated by greed. "Private property has made us so stupid and one-sided that an object is *ours* only if we have it, if it exists for us as capital or is immediately possessed by us, eaten, drunk, worn, lived in, etc., in short *used*." As a result, "*all* the physical and spiritual senses have been replaced by the simple alienation of them all, the sense of *having*."[36]

The "positive overcoming of *private property* as the appropriation of *human* life" permits the "positive overcoming of all alienation and the return of man from religion, family, state, etc. to his *human*, that is, *social* existence. Religious alienation as such occurs only in the sphere of inner human *consciousness*, but economic alienation belongs to *actual life*—its overcoming thus includes both aspects.[37]

In a world grounded on the activity of man as a many-sided creator, society will not be established as "an abstraction over against the individual." There will be a real and actual unity of the universal and the particular. There is a reciprocal relationship between man and

positive" (ibid., p. 317). This critique of Hegel's *Phenomenology* is another indication of Marx's profound interest in Hegel, especially during the early period.

35. Ibid., p. 304.
36. Ibid., p. 308.
37. Ibid., p. 305.

society; man both fashions and is fashioned by society. The "immediate actuality" of man's individuality

> is at the same time his own existence for other men. . . . [The] *human* essence of nature primarily exists only for *social* man, because only here is nature a *link* with *man*, as his existence for others and their existence for him, as the life-element of human actuality— only here is nature the *foundation* of man's own *human* existence. Only here has the *natural* existence of man become his *human* existence and nature become human. Thus *society* is the completed, essential unity of man with nature, the true resurrection of nature, the fulfilled naturalism of man and humanism of nature.[38]

Man, then, is at once "a *particular* individual" and the "*totality*, the ideal totality, the subjective existence of society explicitly thought and experienced."[39]

Social Man. The "overcoming of private property" will usher in the "complete emancipation of all human senses and aptitudes. . . ."[40] In fact, it will result in the appearance of a new type of human being: "social" man. The "senses of social man differ from those of the unsocial" [*darum sind die Sinne des gesellschaftlichen Menschen andere Sinne, wie die des ungesellschaftlichen*].[41] Social man is able to cultivate not only his five senses but also the "so-called spiritual senses" and "practical senses," such as "willing, loving, etc."[42]

In a particularly eloquent passage Marx describes the dehumanization of man as the result of the atrophy of his sensual life:

> *Sense* subordinated to crude, practical need has only a *narrow* meaning. For the starving man food does not exist in its human form but only in its abstract character as food. It could be available in its crudest form and one could not say wherein the starving man's eating differs from that of *animals*. The care-laden, needy man has no mind for the most beautiful play. The dealer in minerals sees only

---

38. Ibid., pp. 305–6.

39. Ibid., p. 307.

40. Ibid., p. 308.

41. Ibid., p. 309. (German text in Landshut, ed., *Marx: Die Frühschriften*, p. 242.)

42. Ibid. I have changed Easton and Guddat's translation, which reads "also the so-called spiritual and moral senses (will, love, etc.) . . ." The German text reads "*sondern auch die sogennanten geistigen Sinne, die praktischen Sinne (Wollen, Lieben, etc.*)." The text is not clear as to whether willing and loving are included among the practical or intellectual-spiritual senses, or whether Marx meant to portray them as identical (a position perhaps compatible with his stress on the dialectical unity of theory and practice). It seems arbitrary, however, to translate *praktischen* as "moral."

their market value but not their beauty and special nature; he has no mineralogical sensitivity.[43]

The Science of Man. The fully constituted society (*die gewordene Gesellschaft*) "produces man in this entire wealth of his being, produces the rich, deep, and *entirely sensitive* man as its enduring actuality."[44] It thus becomes clear that the resolution of the antitheses between "subjectivism and objectivism, spiritualism and materialism, activity and passivity," can occur only in society and only through practical activity. Philosophy could not resolve them because it "grasped the problem as *only* theoretical."[45] In the developed society, natural science and its application in industry and technology will be merged with humanistic studies to form one science of man, which will be at once natural and social. The separation of philosophy and the natural sciences will be overcome. Then it will be possible to employ industry and technology as humanizing rather than dehumanizing forces. Natural science "has penetrated and transformed human life all the more *practically* through industry, preparing for human emancipation however much it immediately had to accentuate dehumanization." In the future society it will "lose its abstract . . . tendency and become the basis of *human* science as it has already become, though in an alienated form, the basis of actual human life. One basis for life and *another* for *science* is in itself a lie."[46] "Natural science will in time include the science of man as the science of man will include natural science. There will be *one* science."[47]

Beyond Communism. Marx's analysis has focused on (1) modern industrial society as productive of man's degradation and alienation and (2) a humanistic social order that will eventually be achieved after society has passed through several stages of "communism." It is important to note that in one passage, he holds that the final "developed" society would itself be "beyond communism." This is presumably the meaning of Marx's otherwise puzzling remark that "*communism* is the necessary form and dynamic principle of the immediate future but not as such the goal of human development—the form of society."[48]

---

43. Ibid., pp. 309–10.
44. Ibid., p. 310.
45. Ibid.
46. Ibid., p. 311.
47. Ibid., p. 312.
48. Ibid., p. 314. It is easy to understand from this comment alone why the authorities in the Soviet Union were so slow to acknowledge the existence of the *Manuscripts* and to permit them to be published. The German text reads: *"Der Kommunismus ist die notwendige Gestalt und das energische Prinzip der nächsten*

Creation. Marx concludes the core section of his *Philosophical-Economic Manuscripts* with a highly significant passage on the philosophical problem of creation. This passage must under no circumstances be overlooked, for it is essential to an understanding of his implicit metaphysics (or countermetaphysics). He here reveals himself to be in open revolt against all previous philosophical speculation, from Plato to Hegel, which was based on the experience (Marx would say the false assumption) of a ground of being independent of man himself. He proclaims the necessity of eliminating the idea that man owes his creation to a source beyond himself:

> A *being* only regards himself as independent when he stands on his own feet, and he stands on his own feet only when he owes his *existence* to himself. A man who lives by the favor of another considers himself dependent. But I live entirely by the favor of another if I owe him not only the maintenance of my life but also its *creation, its source.* My life necessarily has such an external ground if it is not my own creation. The notion of *creation* is thus very difficult to expel from popular consciousness. For such consciousness the self-subsistence of nature and man is *inconceivable* because it contradicts all the *palpable facts* of practical life.[49]

Marx then addresses himself to the problems of the ground of existence as such. That is, how are we to deal with the metaphysical question regarding the origin of existence—of man and the world? To the question "Who created the first man and nature as a whole?" Marx answers impatiently, "Your question is itself a product of abstraction." He continues:

> Ask yourself how you arrive at that question, whether it does not arise from a standpoint to which I cannot reply because it is

---

Zukunft, aber der Kommunismus ist nicht also solcher das Ziel der menschlichen Entwicklung,—die Gestalt der menschlichen Gesellschaft" (Landshut, ed., *Marx: Die Frühschriften,* p. 248). This passage has been interpreted as referring only to "raw" communism, but this interpretation is not convincing. On the other hand, Marx's earlier references to a fully developed communism that is the "solved riddle of history" leaves one puzzled as to how it is possible for man to go beyond this state. It should also be observed that Marx always speaks affirmatively of socialism in the *Manuscripts;* in a sense it can be said that his view here is that communism is an intermediary stage between capitalism and socialism! This amounts to a reversal of the usual order attributed to Marx (i.e., that socialism is a preparatory stage for communism). My interpretation of this text—that here Marx emphasizes socialism rather than communism as the end of history—is supported by Shlomo Avineri, who adds (in a personal communication) that so far as he is aware, this is an oddity that no other interpreter of Marx has noticed. But the work was only a draft, so it would be unwise to read too much into what may be only a lapse.

49. Ibid., pp. 312–13.

twisted. Ask yourself whether that progression exists as such for rational thought. If you ask about the creation of nature and man, you thus abstract from man and nature. You assert them as *nonexistent* and yet want me to prove them to you as *existing*. I say to you: Give up your abstraction and you will also give up your question. Or if you want to maintain your abstraction, be consistent and if you think of man and nature as non-existent, think of yourself as non-existent as you too are nature and man. Do not think, do not question me, for as soon as you think and question, your *abstraction* from the existence of nature and man makes no sense.[50]

To the metaphysical conception of a ground of being, Marx juxtaposes the notion of man's self-creation. Here we have the link between Marx and radical thought in general, for this passage is essentially a proclamation of a radical humanism that exalts man alone as the fabricator of his world and the author of his existence, in opposition to all theological or metaphysical modes of experiencing and conceptualizing the problem:

> Since for socialist man, however, the *entire so-called world history* is only the creation of man through human labor and the development of nature for man, he has evident and incontrovertible proof of his *self-creation*, his own *formation process*. Since the *essential dependence* of man in nature—man for man as the existence of man—has become practical, sensuous and perceptible, the question about an *alien* being beyond man and nature (a question which implies the unreality of nature and man) has become impossible in practice. *Atheism* as a denial of this unreality no longer makes sense because it is a *negation of God* and through this negation asserts the *existence of man*.[51]

Having now before us the argument of what is perhaps the most creative single segment of the extensive and rather diffuse Marxian *corpus*, the *Manuscripts* of 1844, we are in a position to examine leading themes of Marx's political teaching as a whole.

Marx's Epistemology: The Role of Human Consciousness in the Making of History

One example of the oversimplification that mars many commentaries on Marx is the tendency to attribute to him a simplistic "copy" theory of knowledge. It is alleged that for Marx the human mind or consciousness is simply the reflection of prevailing material conditions—

---

50. Ibid., p. 313.
51. Ibid., p. 314.

ultimately of the productive forces that in turn determine the economic relations characterizing a given society at a particular stage of historical development. Thus Marx is held further to have been a "materialist" and a "determinist." If we add the dialectic, then we have him reducing man to a pawn at the mercy of some remorseless material process working independently of man's own consciousness to engineer first his enslavement and then his liberation.

Marx himself is in part to blame for such distortions and oversimplifications of his teaching. He did not always fully explain and qualify what he wrote, especially in the heat of controversy (and he frequently engaged in vigorous controversy, both with enemies and with would-be allies). As we know, he is not the only great political writer at whom this criticism may be leveled: Machiavelli and Rousseau, for example, also frequently left themselves open to misinterpretation.

One key source of the common interpretation of Marx as a mechanistic materialist and determinist is his famous Preface to his *Critique of Political Economy of* 1859. There he writes:

> The mode of production of the material means of existence conditions the whole process of social, political, and intellectual life. It is not the consciousness of men that determines their existence, but, on the contrary, it is their social existence that determines their consciousness.[52]

If read with sufficient care, even the Preface to the *Critique of Political Economy*, which Marx himself declares to contain but a "brief summation" of the position he first advanced in his "Critique of Hegel's *Philosophy of Right*" (1844)—and therefore highly condensed and requiring consultation of his early works—will not sustain the interpretation of Marx as a simple "economic determinist." First of all, we must note the difference between "conditions" and "determines" in the above passage. Marx's use of both words may well have been intended to serve as a warning against interpreting the text insensitively or in a gross fashion. Even had he not employed the verb "conditions" in the first sentence, however, the qualifying adjective "social" in the second sentence prevents such a reading. For to say that men's "social existence . . . determines their consciousness" opens the door wide to a consideration of the prior problem of the manner in which that social existence itself comes to be created. The answer to this question, which is already implicit in the *Manuscripts*, is contained in the "Critique of Hegel's

---

52. Karl Marx and Friedrich Engels, *Basic Writings on Politics and Philosophy*, ed. Lewis S. Feuer (New York: Anchor Books, Doubleday, 1959), p. 43.

Philosophy of Right" and *The German Ideology* (1846) in particular. As we shall see, these texts firmly establish Marx's belief that, as a "species-being," man always exists in the context of society and that society does not spring like Minerva fully formed from the head of Zeus, but is the creation of man.

Philosophy and the Proletariat. The thesis of Marx's "Critique of Hegel's *Philosophy of Right"*—which, as Marx himself admits, does not specifically deal with Hegel's political treatise, but with Germany and the need for a truly "radical revolution"—is that German (post-Hegelian) philosophy must proceed from its successful criticism and unmasking (through Feuerbach, David Strauss, etc.) of religious alienation to a criticism and unmasking of the society that has produced the "perverted" religious consciousness. Philosophy will then be fulfilled by transforming itself into a tool of action on behalf of the proletariat, the universal class. Theory

> becomes a material force once it has gripped the masses. . . . To be radical is to grasp things by the root. But for man the root is man himself. . . . The criticism of religion ends with the doctrine that *man* is the *highest being for man,* hence with the *categorical imperative to* overthrow all conditions in which man is a degraded, enslaved, neglected, contemptible being . . .[53]

In the "Critique" of 1843 Marx stated implicitly the proposition that he was to develop in *The German Ideology:* that man is both product and producer of society. He also stated a corollary to this proposition: in modern industrial society, as in the ancient slave and medieval feudal orders, men become enslaved by conditions that deny them the fruits of their humanity. However, the objective possibilities for man's complete and radical liberation had been prepared in the very process of his enslavement by virtue of the simplification of class antagonisms in modern industrial society and the emergence of the proletariat as the universal class.

Thus the "deterministic" side of Marx's teaching pertains to the antihuman conditions prevailing in class society, which by definition is a system of oppression, in the first instance of the ruling class over the working class but in a second sense of the property system and its fetishism of commodities over all of society, both rulers and ruled. Man in class society is unfree. His consciousness is a reflection of an alienated and "inverted" social order:

---

53. From "Toward the Critique of Hegel's *Philosophy of Law:* Introduction," pp. 257–58, in *Writings of the Young Marx on Philosophy and Society,* ed. and trans. Loyd D. Easton and Kurt H. Guddat. Copyright © 1967 by Loyd D. Easton and Kurt H. Guddat. Reprinted by permission of Doubleday & Company, Inc.

The basis of irreligious criticism is: *Man makes religion,* religion
does not make man. . . . But *man* is not an abstract being squatting
outside the world. Man is *the world of men,* the state, society. This
state and this society produce religion, which is an inverted consciousness of the world because they are an *inverted world.*[54]

How can man, who throughout recorded history has been the
prisoner of a social order that systematically denies his human essence
and leaves him spiritually and materially impoverished, break his
chains and secure liberation? How can he manage to transcend his
situation long enough to see it as a situation of unfreedom and oppression? How can man, whose consciousness is inverted because it is the
product of an inverted society, come to acquire the kind of consciousness
that is radical, critical, and free, and which is the necessary precondition
for his liberation?

Marx's reply is interesting, even if not entirely adequate. Obviously
we here encounter a key *aporia* in his thought, for, having defined consciousness as a product of the social milieu, and the social milieu as
based on unfreedom and exploitation, how can Marx produce a free
and unalienated consciousness? Certainly he cannot appeal to some
Archimedean point outside of history, for even as early as his doctoral
dissertation at the University of Bonn he had rejected all philosophies
that presupposed the possibility that the philosopher might attain to
some such timeless or transcendent position.[55] He nowhere satisfactorily
explains how it happens that he himself is able to take a self-consciously
radical and critical stand vis-à-vis contemporary society: how is he
himself able to break the chains of ideology that bind men in class society? This is what Karl Mannheim was later to identify as the problem
of the "free-floating intellectual."[56] This failure on Marx's part is in all
probability due to his rejection on principle of the very idea of a free-
floating intellectual or philosopher. Marx held that philosophy is drawn
by its very nature toward the world of action, where it serves as the
animating spirit of world-historical developments. The task of philosophy, and specifically German philosophy (as the most "advanced"
thought of the contemporary world), is to ally itself with the proletariat
and achieve its fulfillment in the transformation of an unphilosophical
and irrational world into a world of reason and freedom. The philosophy

54. Ibid., p. 250.
55. "Notes to the Doctoral Dissertation" (1839–1841), in ibid., pp. 63–64.
Aporia stands in Greek philosophy for a difficulty or an impasse in the argument.
56. Karl Mannheim, *Essays on the Sociology of Knowledge,* ed. Paul Kecskemeti,
2nd ed. (New York: Oxford University Press, 1952).

that serves as the "head" of the general emancipation of mankind develops and actualizes itself only with the appearance of and in alliance with the proletariat, or the oppressed workers who comprise a class in but not of civil society.

The Place of the Proletariat in History. For Marx, "philosophy" stands for alienated man's self-aware, articulated conception of himself and of his possibilities for liberation within history; it is, more precisely, the "subjective" consciousness of the liberating sector of society, the proletariat, and its intellectual "vanguard." The proletariat itself, however, "objectively" exists only under conditions of advanced industrial society, and furthermore is capable of utilizing its potentiality on behalf of the radical revolution only if it acquires a fully developed consciousness of this potentiality. For Marx, then, man's liberation requires the congruence of both "objective" and "subjective" factors, of both the proletariat—which can emerge only under certain socioeconomic conditions—and (radical) philosophy, which has the task of imbuing the proletariat with self-consciousness but which itself emerges only after the appropriate "objective" conditions (under "mature" capitalism) have come into being.

In the place of belief in an Archimedean point outside of history, Marx substitutes a faith in the rationality of history and, specifically, of his own time as the axial time. In this respect, at least, he remains close to Hegel, whose works, more than those of any other philosopher, he read deeply and extensively. He agrees with Hegel that ultimately the historical process is rational, and that at a given point in its dialectical unfolding it becomes possible for men to grasp its rational essence. Like Hegel, Marx saw himself as living in the fullness of time.

The Dilemma of Marx's Epistemology. We have spoken of the congruence for Marx of "objective" and "subjective" factors and of his conception of the achievement of a new liberated world order as requiring both the maturation of certain "objective" economic conditions and the development of an accompanying "subjective" consciousness (philosophy), which will make explicit to men the possibilities of their liberation. In employing the subjective-objective dichotomy, however, we already distort Marx's epistemology, which is grounded on a denial of such distinctions. Yet in another sense—that is, in regard to his analysis of "inverted" society itself—Marx does preserve the traditional distinctions, because he regards class society as defective precisely in the sense that it lacks the wholeness and integration proper to reality itself. Shlomo Avineri has ably summarized Marx's epistemological doctrine and its dilemma:

Marx's epistemology occupies a middle position between classical materialism and classical idealism. Historically it draws on both traditions; and, since it synthesizes the two traditions, it transcends the classic dichotomy between subject and object. Indirectly this synthesis solves the Kantian antinomy between the cognitive and the moral spheres. But Marx thinks that present circumstances still make it impossible to practise this new, adequate epistemology: alienation indicates the continuing existence of the dichotomy between subject and object, as a result of the still distorted process of cognition.

Marx's epistemology thus conceals an internal tension. It tries to solve the traditional epistemological problems, but it tacitly holds that human consciousness could operate according to the new epistemology only if the obstacles in its way in present society were eliminated. Hence Marx's epistemology is sometimes divided against itself: it is both a description of consciousness and a vision of the future. Consequently Marx never fully denies the validity of traditional mechanistic materialist modes of consciousness as expressions of alienated life in existing society. These imperfect modes of consciousness will exist as long as bourgeois society continues to exist.[57]

Consciousness and Society.   Marx's fundamental teaching regarding the relationship of consciousness to society, then, is that the two are dialectically united. Consciousness is at once a social product *and* (because society itself is produced by men in interaction with each other) the producer of society. In his famous "Theses on Feuerbach," Marx dissociates himself from "all previous materialism" on the grounds that in all such simplistic views, "the object, actuality [or reality: *Wirklichkeit*], sensuousness" is conceived in a merely contemplative or "objective" manner, whereas reality must be grasped "subjectively"— that is, as "sensuous human activity," or "practice" (*Praxis*). For Marx, Feuerbach and other proponents of materialism made the mistake of conceiving of human consciousness as itself a mere object, acted upon by external circumstances. If material circumstances change men, it is equally true that "circumstances are changed by men." Once this truth is grasped, a merely passive or contemplative attitude toward the human condition becomes impossible, and one recognizes the significance of "revolutionary" or "practical-critical" activity. Hitherto "philosophers have only *interpreted* the world in various ways; the point is, to *change* it."[58]

---

57. Avineri, *Social and Political Thought,* p. 69.

58. "Theses on Feuerbach," Theses 1, 3, 11, pp. 400–2, in *Writings of the Young Marx on Philosophy and Society,* ed. and trans. Loyd D. Easton and Kurt H. Guddat. Copyright © 1967 by Loyd D. Easton and Kurt H. Guddat. Reprinted by permission of Doubleday & Company, Inc.

Marx's whole point is to transcend the dichotomy between theory and practice, subject and object, the individual and society. The fact that these distinctions are drawn in modern social thought reveals its ideological and alienated character; this thought is a reflection of alienated social conditions that must themselves be overcome by revolutionary praxis, a praxis that itself involves both thought and action, both a new consciousness and the fabrication of new external ("material") conditions.

The New Society: Man as the "Ensemble of Social Relationships"

To Marx, the "essence of man is no abstraction inhering in each single individual. In its actuality it is the ensemble of social relationships."[59] By arguing in this vein, he seems to deny the reality of any human nature or essence as such, for the essence of man is radically historicized and we can speak only of feudal man, bourgeois man, socialistic man, and so on, never simply of man. Again Marx calls history, which produces this dilemma, to the rescue. Man does have an authentic essence that is realizable at the end of history, for history is ultimately the story of man's liberation, of his attainment of reason and freedom in this world. All human types produced by all previous societies were one-sided, the members both of the ruling classes and of those classes that emerged from the society's womb and were themselves destined to replace the existing ruling classes and usher in a new epoch and beget a new class struggle resulting in their own overthrow. But with the appearance of the proletariat, Marx held, this process had changed, because the victory of the proletariat would not be a victory merely of another class, destined to rule in place of the bourgeoisie before being itself replaced by another emerging class, but the victory of humanity as a whole.

The Dialectical Unity of Opposites. When Marx writes that man is the "ensemble" of his societal relationships, he means to indicate both that man exists in history and cannot transcend his time and milieu and that conditions have developed to the point where man can finally exercise conscious control and domination over his social environment. The statement does *not* mean simply that as an individual, man is dominated by "society." To say this would be to regard the "ensemble of societal relationships" in a passive and contemplative manner—a manner that, as we have seen, Marx severely criticized in his "Theses on Feuerbach." We push beyond reflexive and ideological thinking and acting only by

---

59. Ibid., Thesis 6, p. 402.

grasping in both a theoretical and a practical fashion the real dialectical unity of "opposing" propositions, such as "Man makes society, society makes man," or "Man shapes circumstances, circumstances shape man."[60]

Man's Self-Fulfillment under Communism. The coming radical communist revolution will result in the victory of man over the tyranny of circumstances; it will bring forth a condition that truly and for the first time will deserve to be called "human." The new society will be the field for man's self-fulfillment and self-direction. No longer will the individual be opposed to "society" and its "laws," but will realize his own essence in and through the new network of societal relationships. In previous or so-called natural society, governed by the division of labor and the class struggle, man's own activity

> becomes an alien power opposed to him and enslaving him instead of being controlled by him. . . . For as soon as labor is distributed, each person has a particular, exclusive area of activity which is imposed on him and from which he cannot escape. He is a hunter, a fisherman, a herdsman, or a critic, and he must remain so if he does not want to lose his means of livelihood. In communist society, however, where nobody has an exclusive area of activity and each can train himself in any branch he wishes, society regulates the general production, making it possible for me to do one thing today and another tomorrow, to hunt in the morning, breed cattle in the evening, criticize after dinner, just as I like, without ever becoming a hunter, a fisherman, a herdsman, or a critic.[61]

"United Individuals." Communism, Marx informs us, "differs from all previous movements because it overturns the basis of all previous relations of production and interaction, and for the first time consciously treats all natural premises as creations of men, strips them of their national character, and subjects them to the power of united individuals."[62] However much one might object that Marx has glossed over the problem of the abuse of power in the new society and of the problem, analyzed by Mill, of the tyranny of social pressure demanding conformity to majority opinion, it was clearly his conviction that conditions were maturing for the emergence of a universal society that, far from repressing individual spontaneity and creativity, would be devoted to the maximal fulfillment of individual needs as determined by the individuals themselves. Only in the new society would the individual cease to regard himself as an atom isolated from society, or from the totality of "united individuals." The new man would cease to be bur-

---

60. *The German Ideology,* in ibid., p. 432.

61. Ibid., pp. 424–25.

62. Ibid., p. 461.

dened with the artificial and irrational divisions and tensions that characterized the psychology of alienated man. He would determine or "make" his own life—a life not separated from society but fully and healthily integrated with it—in cooperation with others. As Marx expressed the matter in *The Communist Manifesto:* "In place of the old bourgeois society, with its classes and class antagonisms, we shall have an association in which the free development of each is the condition for the free development of all."[63]

The State

Marx is often quoted as having postulated the eventual "withering away [*Absterbung*] of the state." Actually, this was Engels' phrase (in the *Anti-Dühring*). Marx himself referred to the "transcending" (*Aufhebung:* literally, both "annulment" and "preservation") of the state.[64] Whatever problems exist with reference to Marx's vision of the good society in the final phase of history, we may assume that he was aware of the problem of organization in a complex, technologically advanced society. In other words, his views on the transcending of the state cannot be dismissed as simply naive.

The State vs. Society. To Marx the state was a specifically historical phenomenon within alienated class society; it followed as a matter of course that the "state," in contradistinction to "society," would have no place in final communist society, any more than would the notion of the abstract individual in isolation from society. Insofar as the question of political control was concerned, Marx clearly foresaw the abolition of the police apparatus as it was known by bourgeois society. On the whole, he was silent about the need to deal with persistent antisocial behavior in an organized way. This silence can be attributed to his caution about predicting the details of future society. Since we are dealing with a writer of Marx's stature, we may assume that this caution involved more than a desire to avoid being proved wrong if events failed to conform to predictions. It was also related to his basic epistemological premises. He held man to be the maker of society and history; it was therefore impossible for anyone to prescribe in advance a blueprint of what man, finally come into his full heritage of freedom, would create.

Marx defined the state as "the form in which the individuals of a ruling class assert their common interests and the entire civil society of an epoch is epitomized." Under capitalism, through the "emancipation of private property from the community, the state has become a separate

---

63. *The Communist Manifesto,* in Marx and Engels, *Basic Writings,* p. 29.
64. See Avineri, *Social and Political Thought,* pp. 202–3.

entity beside and outside civil society." In the more "advanced" countries, the state has lost any semblance of independence from control by the bourgeoisie and exists "only for the sake of private property."[65]

The Transcendence of the State. It is the capitalist state that will be *aufgehoben* (abolished and transcended) in fully developed communist (or socialist) society.[66] This transcendence of the state, however, does not mean the disappearance of central direction and planning (which, one might add, necessitates forms of control, and of selection and control of the controllers), especially over the economy; thus, as Avineri has pointed out, for Marx "even in its higher stage, socialist society will require direction and planning . . . since socialism implies the subjection of man's creative powers to his conscious direction."[67] Furthermore, as Marx insisted with scarcely concealed impatience in one of his later works, *The Critique of the Gotha Program,* even the bourgeois or capitalist state would not immediately cease to exist on the morrow of the successful communist revolution, for at first the new society would bear the birthmarks of the old. Bourgeois attitudes toward property, inequality of rewards, and antisocial activity of various forms would continue to exist during the period of transition from capitalism to fully developed communism:

> Between capitalist and communist society lies the period of the revolutionary transformation of the one into the other. There corresponds to this also a political transition period in which the state can be nothing but the *revolutionary dictatorship of the proletariat.*[68]

It is only when communist society has become fully developed, after the individual is no longer enslaved by the division of labor and after classes and class conflict have vanished, that the transition from a repressive state to a society of fully equal human beings, each developing himself in and through the development of all, can be completed. That the state as such is inimical to man's full and total liberation and must in the end be superseded by an authentic community of free and equal

---

65. *German Ideology,* p. 470.

66. See n. 48 for a discussion of Marx's use of the terms "socialism" and "communism" in the *Philosophical-Economic Manuscripts.*

67. Avineri, *Social and Political Thought,* p. 202.

68. *The Critique of the Gotha Program,* in Marx and Engels, *Basic Writings,* p. 127. Neither here nor elsewhere does Marx repeat the *Manuscripts'* dire observations on the necessity of passing through a brutal form of "raw" communism before the achievement of final communism. We are thus left uncertain as to whether he modified his earlier views or thought it imprudent to publish them. "Raw" communism resembled the Stalinist regime in important respects, and it is understandable that Soviet "Marxists" have been uncomfortable about the *Manuscripts* ever since their discovery and publication in the 1930s.

human beings is one of Marx's cardinal tenets. The society presided over by a state is an "illusory" or sham community:

> Only in community do the means exist for every individual to culti-
> vate his talents in all directions. Only in the community is personal
> freedom possible. In previous substitutes for the community, in the
> state, etc., personal freedom has existed only for the individuals who
> developed within the ruling class and only insofar as they belonged
> to this class. But this was ... not only a completely illusory com-
> munity but also a new fetter because it was the combination of one
> class against another. In a real community individuals obtained their
> freedom in and through their association.[69]

"Democracy" and the Transition Period. In the *Communist Manifesto* of 1848, written in collaboration with Engels, Marx wrote fairly
extensively of the character that the state assumes during the transition
period. The "first step" in the working-class revolution is to "raise the
proletariat to the position of ruling class, to win the battle of democracy."
By "democracy" Marx did not mean what liberalism intends—universal
suffrage, parliamentary institutions, periodic direct elections, multiplicity
of parties, and so on. These were at best formal institutions of which the
proletariat might make use in its struggle to abolish the liberal order
itself. Liberal democracy to Marx was not a free society but a "democracy
of unfreedom." Democracy in the substantive sense—"true democracy"—
was for Marx neither liberalist nor Jacobin (or populist) democracy, but
a society in which the "free development of each is the condition for the
free development of all."

Transitional Measures. In the *Manifesto*, presumably Marx's most
explicitly revolutionary work, the transition period is seen as one of a
gradual wresting away of economic power from the bourgeoisie:

> The proletariat will use its political supremacy to wrest, by degrees,
> all capital from the bourgeoisie, to centralize all instruments of
> production in the hands of the state, i.e., of the proletariat organized
> as the ruling class, and to increase the total of productive forces as
> rapidly as possible.[70]

Marx proceeds to list ten measures, "generally applicable" in the
"most advanced countries," which the proletariat, newly come to power,

---

69. From *German Ideology*, pp. 457–58, in *Writings of the Young Marx on
Philosophy and Society*, ed. and trans. Loyd D. Easton and Kurt H. Guddat.
Copyright © 1967 by Loyd D. Easton and Kurt H. Guddat. Reprinted by permission
of Doubleday & Company, Inc.

70. *Communist Manifesto*, pp. 27–28.

will initially take to consolidate its victory over the bourgeoisie and to forward its aim of "entirely revolutionizing the mode of production":

1. Abolition of property in land and application of all rents of land to public purposes.
2. A heavy progressive or graduated income tax.
3. Abolition of all right of inheritance.
4. Confiscation of the property of all emigrants and rebels.
5. Centralization of credit in the hands of the state, by means of a national bank with state capital and an exclusive monopoly.
6. Centralization of the means of communication and transport in the hands of the state.
7. Extension of factories and instruments of production owned by the state; the bringing into cultivation of wastelands, and the improvement of the soil generally in accordance with a common plan.
8. Equal liability of all to labor. Establishment of industrial armies, especially for agriculture.
9. Combination of agriculture with manufacturing industries; gradual abolition of the distinction between town and country, by a more equable distribution of the population over the country.
10. Free education for all children in public schools. Abolition of children's factory labor in its present form. Combination of education with industrial production, etc.[71]

Public Power vs. Political Power.   "When, in the course of development, class distinctions have disappeared and all production has been concentrated in the hands of a vast association of the whole nation," Marx observes, "the public power will lose its political character." Thus the completion of the revolutionary process will bring about the abolition of politics and the state. "Political power, properly so called, is merely the organized power of one class for oppressing another." The proletariat, in the process of eliminating, by force if necessary, the "old conditions of production," will have prepared the way for the abolition of "the existence of class antagonisms and of classes generally, and will thereby have abolished its own supremacy as a class."[72]

Marx nowhere details how the "public power," having lost its "political character," will be organized, selected, and replenished. He is also silent on the future of the Communist party, which is described in the *Manifesto* as "the most advanced and resolute section of the working-class parties of every country" and as "that section which pushes forward all others." Clearly it is to have the leading role in initiating and carrying

71. Ibid., pp. 28–29.
72. Ibid., p. 29.

forward the revolutionary process. Inasmuch as Communists are declared to have "no interests separate and apart from those of the proletariat as a whole,"[73] presumably its own leading position will be abolished with the abolition of the proletariat's own "supremacy as a class."

Marx's Interpretation of History

The usual labels attached to Marx's theory of history ("economic determinism," "dialectical materialism," etc.) are not so much inaccurate as inadequate. As we have already established with reference to his epistemology, Marx cannot strictly be called a determinist or materialist, since he emphasizes man's active role in shaping his own history, opposes a merely mechanical and "objectivist" materialism, and conceives of theory and practice as a unity. Thus, for Marx, men's ideas are not simply the reflections or, in Lenin's vulgarization, the "copies" of prevailing material conditions; there is an input from "subjective" consciousness itself. It would be more accurate to say that for Marx there is an inter-action between consciousness and the material conditions in which man finds himself; the "real life" situation comprises both these factors, *plus* man's activity in responding to and shaping them. As he expresses the matter in *The German Ideology:* "Men are the producers of their con-ceptions, ideas, etc., but these are real, active men as they are con-ditioned by a definite development of their productive forces. . . . Consciousness can never be anything else except conscious existence, and the existence of men is their actual life process."[74]

Marx's appreciation of empirical detail and the complexity of the interaction between subjectivity and the external world did not deter him from making large-scale generalizations about the course of history. To arrive at these generalizations he inevitably had to abstract from the wealth of detail in history, and, like all synthesizers and system con-structors, he left himself open to severe criticism with regard to both his general scheme and some of his specific points. Thus his periodization of history into primitive, ancient, feudal, capitalist, and (future) commu-nist epochs is excessively neat and stylized, as is his often brilliant and profound but ultimately oversimplified and distorted analysis of the capitalist economy.

History and the Mode of Production and Exchange. Marx's interest in economics is scarcely a late development, even though his unfinished

---

73. Ibid., p. 20.

74. From *German Ideology*, p. 414, in *Writings of the Young Marx on Philosophy and Society*, ed. and trans. Loyd D. Easton and Kurt H. Guddat. Copyright © 1967 by Loyd D. Easton and Kurt H. Guddat. Reprinted by permission of Doubleday & Company, Inc.

work *Das Kapital* (*Capital*) was the major preoccupation of his mature years. His concern with economics dates from his earliest writings, and much of the argument of *Das Kapital* is prefigured in *The German Ideology*. This interest stemmed ineluctably from his interpretation of history, which stressed the key importance of the mode of production and exchange of the material goods necessary for life in conditioning the entire style and quality of life of men in a particular historical period.

In *The German Ideology*, Marx enumerated four premises of an adequate theory of history, which may be summarized as follows:

1. Men must be able to live in order to make history.
2. Once a given need is satisfied, new needs arise.
3. Men exist in relation to others for purposes of procreation (the family) and, with increased population and the rise of new needs, of production (society).
4. "The production of life . . . now appears as a double relationship: on the one hand as a natural relationship, on the other as a social one."[75]

Thus "a certain mode of production or industrial stage is always combined with a certain mode of cooperation or social stage and this mode of cooperation is itself a 'productive force.' "[76] (Marx here makes clear that the "productive force" he frequently cites in his works as "determining" the forms of property relations and, indirectly, the "higher" institutional forms such as government, religion, education, etc., is itself a form of human social cooperation and not a blind or mechanical material force.) He goes on to observe that "the multitude of productive forces accessible to men determines the nature of [a particular form of] society and that the 'history of mankind' must always be studied and treated in relation to the history of industry and exchange."[77]

Belief Systems and Socioeconomic Relations. Marx dates the beginning of the long process of man's progressively increasing alienation from his natural environment, his fellow human beings, and his own authentic self-knowledge from the appearance of the division between menial and mental labor. From that point elaborate rationalizations of existing socioeconomic relations are produced in the form of supposedly " 'pure' theory, theology, philosophy, ethics, etc." These ideological belief systems remain until they and the productive relations they serve to justify are replaced as a result of the emergence of a new stage in the

75. Ibid., pp. 419–21.
76. Ibid., p. 421.
77. Ibid.

development of productive forces. The new productive forces in time produce a new set of productive relations, together with new social-cultural-political institutions, and corresponding religious, philosophical, and political ideologies to justify them.

Marx depicts the dialectical process at work in history in the following way:

> [The] contradiction between the productive forces and the forms of commerce, which we observe occurring several times in past history without endangering the basis of history, had to burst out in a revolution each time, taking on at the same time various secondary forms, such as comprehensive collisions, collisions of various classes, contradictions of consciousness, battles of ideas, etc. . . .
>
> In our view all collisions in history have their origin in the contradiction between the productive forces and the form of interaction [*Verkehrsform*].[78]

Capitalism and the Emergence of the Proletariat. The capitalist mode of production has resulted in extreme specialization and division of labor, and with the emergence of manufacturing and international trade on an unprecedented scale, divisions and conflicts between social classes and between town and country have occurred in all of the "advanced" societies. Within capitalist society, which marks the fourth and final historical epoch prior to the communist revolution, the bourgeoisie itself eventually "splits into various fractions according to the division of labor . . . and finally absorbs all propertied classes," while developing "most of the previously propertied class into a new class, the proletariat. . . ."[79]

According to Marx's interpretation of history, under capitalist conditions the two essential, practical premises for overcoming this remorseless and complete subjugation of man to alien powers, seemingly beyond his control, have been realized: (1) the emergence of the proletariat as an oppressed and propertyless class and (2) the development of productive forces on a "*world-historical* rather than local scale." The existence of the proletariat, or the workers who possess nothing but who live off wages paid in return for their labor—wages that, Marx wrongly predicted, of necessity had to be kept at a minimum level as a result of the inner workings of capitalism—means that a class that will launch the truly radical revolution to end oppression and exploitation has come into being. Unlike previous classes that rose to power only to become exploiters themselves, the proletariat comprises—or will comprise—the

---

78. Ibid., p. 454.
79. Ibid., p. 456.

"great majority of all members of society." Advanced capitalist society simplifies class antagonisms to the point where humanity at large is reduced to the condition of oppressed paupers who have no stake in class society as such, but, imbued with a "consciousness of the necessity of fundamental revolution," possess the power and the will to overthrow the last and most oppressive of history's ruling classes.

With the overthrow of the small ruling class of monopoly capitalists and the establishment of the dictatorship of the proletariat, the way is open to harness the immensely productive technology developed under capitalism for the benefit and liberation of man rather than for his oppression and degradation. Capitalism creates the technological basis for the abolition of want. And because it is an international phenomenon, it prepares the way for the victory of communism on a global scale. The communist revolution will occur not only in one nation or region; it will be worldwide, for capitalism has fashioned an economically inter-dependent world in which a revolutionary transformation in one part will inevitably extend to all the others.

Marx's Analysis of Capitalism

An extensive and detailed analysis of Marx's writings on capitalism falls more properly within the scope of economic rather than political theory. Nonetheless, no account of his political teaching would be adequate without reference to the argument developed in his *Outline of the Critique of Political Economy* (1859) and *Capital* (Volume 1, 1867; Volume 2, 1885; and Volume 3, 1894). *Capital* was never completed by Marx himself, who published only Volume 1 in his lifetime. The subsequent two volumes were edited and supplemented by Engels. The whole work runs to over 2,200 pages.[80] All that I shall attempt to do here is to indicate some of the leading themes of the argument, especially as they bear on Marx's theory of history and politics.

According to Marx, the logic of capitalism's development led to two results: (1) the accumulation of capital in fewer and fewer hands and (2) the increasing impoverishment of the proletariat in relation to the total wealth produced. Marx designated these tendencies as the "law of capital accumulation" and the "law of the increasing misery of the proletariat."

The Accumulation of Capital. In order to survive competitively, the capitalist must produce more cheaply than his rival. To do this he must

---

80. I have consulted the edition of *Das Kapital* that forms vols. 23, 24, and 25 of Marx and Engels, *Werke* (Berlin: Dietz Verlag, 1962). Vol. 1 was published in the United States in 1936 by the Modern Library; a complete English translation was published in Moscow.

increase the productivity of labor (the source of all value, according to Marx). Inasmuch as large-scale, highly specialized and mechanized production is more efficient than small-scale industry, the smaller enterprises are pushed to the wall by the larger ones. In order to remain ahead in the race, more and more capital is required for the purchase of ever more sophisticated and expensive machinery.

The Exploitation of the Workers. As a result of the insatiable demand for greater and greater amounts of capital, the capitalist must expend a minimum amount in wages, and thus increasingly impoverish the workers. What this minimum is, Marx tries to explain by his theory of "surplus value." According to his labor theory of value, the value of a commodity is equivalent to the average number of hours of labor necessary for its production. The capitalist, who owns the means of production, is able to pay the worker less than the (labor) value of the thing produced. The difference between the full value of a commodity and the amount paid the worker is profit. The worker therefore spends part of the day working for himself and part for the capitalist. He is paid only as much as is necessary to keep him alive and productive. With increases in population and technological efficiency, fewer and fewer workers will be needed in proportion to the total available labor force. Inasmuch as there is always a reserve army of unemployed, the economic "law" of supply and demand determines that wages will always be in a depressed state under capitalism. The more the productivity of each individual is increased, the fewer hours he will spend working for himself and the more he will devote to creating surplus value for the capitalist. Therefore, capitalism is based on progressively increasing exploitation of the workers.

Money as an End in Itself. Capitalism is based upon a fetishism of money. From being a medium of exchange for the necessities and enjoyments of life, money becomes an end in itself. Capitalism is organized to make money rather than to satisfy human needs. It is rational and "progressive" only to the extent that it has developed the productive forces of mankind and achieved the *de facto* socialization of the means of production (labor is now cooperative and interdependent). This means that capitalism is necessary as a preparation for the victory of communism. It is irrational, however, in the way it uses the enormous wealth it engenders not for the enhancement of human life but for the creation of more wealth as an end in itself.

The Conversion of Capital into Common Property. Most of the leading themes of *Capital* were present from Marx's early writings. In particular, Parts 1 and 2 of *The Communist Manifesto* anticipate the analysis of *Capital*, which provides detailed documentation of his views.

In the *Manifesto* Marx promised an end to the system of exploitation prevailing under capitalism through the abolition "not of property generally," but of "bourgeois property." Communism, in converting capital into "common property . . . the property of all members of society," does not thereby transform personal property into social property. "It is only the social character of the property that is changed. It loses its class character."[81] Communism will guarantee, not deny, man's right to appropriate the products of his own labor (although under final communism one will think only of creating and producing, not of having; he will in any case have abundantly); all that it will abolish is the accumulation of property gained by living off the labor of others, by robbing them of much of the value they have produced by their labor. Capitalism from its very beginning has rested on force, robbery, and exploitation; "primitive" or "original" accumulation (*ursprüngliche Akkumulation*) of the initial capital to begin the entire process of capitalist development was achieved principally by "conquest, enslavement, robbery, murder—briefly, force."[82]

The Inevitable Collapse of Capitalism. Marx maintained that capitalism was beset with internal contradictions of such magnitude that it would inevitably collapse. Because of its irrational and antihuman dedication to the production of ever more capital as an end in itself, capitalist society would have to go through cycles of inflation and depression. If wages rise, new machinery that has previously been economically unfeasible will be employed. The increase in technological efficiency raises production per capita; workers are laid off. The result is a glut of material goods on the market, for the masses now lack the money to buy the goods produced. This leads to a decrease in production, further unemployment, and depression of wages. With the growth of the reserve army of the unemployed, willing to accept virtually starvation wages, production may now resume. The rise in employment leads to an increase in wages, which leads to the introduction of new machinery to replace workers, and the entire cycle repeats itself.

Marxian Economics in Retrospect. Marx's theory of capitalism—like all economic theories—is obviously a model abstracted from reality, and perhaps he should not be taxed so severely as he has been for having incorrectly predicted the collapse of capitalism. If the interventionist policies of the new Keynesian economics, social welfare legislation, guarantees of the right of workers to join unions and bargain collectively, and like developments had not occurred, it is possible that his model would not have been so wide of the mark. It is difficult to know what

---

81. *Communist Manifesto*, pp. 21–22.
82. *Capital*, vol. 1, chap. 26, in Marx and Engels, *Basic Writings*, p. 161.

adjustments and revisions Marx would have made in his theories had he lived through these developments; it seems quite certain that he would have revised them, for he had an impressive feel for the details of the empirical political and economic situation as well as a formidable capacity for theoretical generalization. Some contemporary noncommunist observers are convinced that, if Marxian economics was wrong with regard to the internal development of the advanced capitalist societies, it has been and continues to be considerably more relevant than liberal or Keynesian economics to the underdeveloped world as it faces the difficulties of economic competition with the developed world. Others would point out that "capitalism" itself no longer exists as such, but has been transformed into a mixed economy with an extensive and even controlling public sector. In any event, there is little doubt that Marx remains one of the towering figures in the history of both political and economic thought.

CONCLUSION: THE RELEVANCE AND LIMITATIONS OF RADICALISM

It is clear that in the conversation of mankind, radicalism is one of the voices that deserves a hearing. Many of us in the Western liberal democracies automatically close our minds to the radical position, and some troglodytic public figures have even called for its extirpation. But we need the leaven of radical insight in our lives.

Some thirty-five years ago one of the foremost exponents of American liberal and progressive thought, John Dewey, stated in a series of lectures at the University of Virginia:

> Liberalism must now become radical, meaning by "radical" perception of the necessity of thorough-going changes in the set-up of institutions and corresponding activity to bring this about. . . . If radicalism be defined as perception of the need for radical change, then today any liberalism which is not also radicalism is irrelevant and doomed.[83]

However, Dewey continues, radicalism

> also means in the minds of many, both supporters and opponents, dependence upon use of violence as the main method of effecting drastic changes. Here the liberal parts company. . . . Any frank discussion of the issue [however] must recognize the extent to which

---

83. John Dewey, *Liberalism and Social Action* (New York: Putnam, 1935), p. 62.

those who decry the use of any violence are themselves willing to resort to violence. . . . They do not need to advocate the use of force; they only need to employ it. Force, rather than intelligence, is built into the procedures of the existing social system, regularly as coercion, in times of crisis as overt violence. The legal system . . . rests upon coercion.[84]

Dewey's words of 1935 have an exceedingly contemporary ring, and provide much food for thought today. At a minimum, he demonstrates that violence is of concern not only to the radical, but also to the liberal and the conservative, and indeed to any man who seeks to act politically. A prime task for a creative radical humanism today would appear to be the elaboration of nonviolent theories of social change, for humanism is incompatible with terror of any variety. This is something that the ideological politics of the twentieth century should have taught us all too well. However good their intentions, men cannot save the world by destroying it.

It is, then, a sign of hope that in America today one detects the emergence of an important, indigenous radical movement that in its thought and life style reflects the possibilities of far-reaching nonviolent change through what Emmanuel Mounier once described as the "lateral revolution." Such a peaceful revolution at the level of culture and consciousness has been poetically called by one of its most eloquent and perceptive advocates "the greening of America."[85]

Charles Reich's book, which some reviewers have lightly judged to be of merely passing or journalistic interest, has the very great merit of completely overcoming the tendency of some radical thinkers to see the world in Manichean terms and to view those who disagree with them as "the enemy." Even Marx, who was not lacking in compassion, fell prey to this error and believed that radical change must come in large measure through direct action. The humanism of the radical vision is grounded on love and respect for man as such. Marx's emphasis on the "class struggle" can obscure the universalism of his larger goal—the liberation of all men for a fuller life. And this larger objective is shared by all men who call themselves humanists.

---

84. Ibid., p. 63.

85. Charles A. Reich, *The Greening of America* (New York: Random House, 1970).

EPILOGUE

All of you who have gone through the material in this book and have made a conscientious effort to grapple with some of the great treatises discussed here know that the determination of the goals a society should seek and the arrangement of priorities form the most important and most difficult problem of political theory. You know further that the problem cannot be solved without an understanding of man's condition and possibilities as a creature who lives in society. Finally, you will have learned that the debate over the configuration of man's social existence is never ending, and that the writers studied in these pages have contributed mightily to it.

It is perhaps appropriate that this book should end with a discussion of radicalism, because radicalism causes us to return again to the beginning, to the "roots," which in this case means to return to the question of the nature of political philosophy and political theory. There is in fact, as Plato showed so well when he inaugurated this activity, something essentially radical in the urge to engage in philosophizing. The radicalism of *philosophy,* however, is an arduous enterprise, involving the entire person in the search for truth and an end to illusion about his condition.

Philosophy, Plato tells us, originates in erotic passion (see Diotima's speech in the *Symposium*) and culminates in a "dying" to an inverted existence. Philosophy involves the "conversion" (*periagoge*) of the whole person to a new mode of existence. It is a "study in death and dying"—dying to the old attitudes of unreflective, passive acceptance of the world as it has been made to appear. To philosophize in earnest is to partake of a "liberated" existence, to be one's own man, think one's own thoughts, and stand on one's own ground, while at the same time being aware of one's participation in the community of man.

For all its achievements, the Platonic conception of philosophy had its limitations. Ultimately, it came down to an affair of the happy few and ended in a call for philosophically inclined men to withdraw into the cities of their own individual souls.

The great modern masters of political philosophy added an activist dimension to philosophy, stressing its relevance to the lives not only of a few, but of all. As Hegel viewed the matter in his *Lectures on the Philosophy of History*, it was the "goal of world history" to build a "world which is suitable for the spirit to inhabit." As such, history is the progressive unfolding of reason and freedom for the entire community of man. Philosophy brings to men a new self-consciousness of the possibilities for an unalienated existence. That which is "rational," Hegel taught, is also "real," and does not abide eternally in some heaven of pure contemplation, but calls out to be actualized in history. Hegel's conception of the relationship between philosophy and politics may be summarized in the words attributed to him by Heinrich Heine: "What is rational must be!"

There is risk in the relatively more activist orientation of modern political philosophy, to be sure; if philosophy gives herself wholly over to changing the world, she may cease to understand it (*contra* Marx). Perhaps we need both the Platonic, or premodern, *and* the modern perspectives on political philosophy. Without the Platonic stress on the demanding nature of life in openness to truth, philosophy may be in danger of losing its integrity. Without the modern emphasis upon building reason into the world, we run the risk of needlessly enfeebling philosophy and making it unresponsive to the challenges and opportunities of the present.

One thing seems clear (to me, at least) as a result of my labors on this volume: theory (or the disinterested observation and explanation of a given segment of reality) derives its nourishment from philosophy (or the attempt to see reality, insofar as a man can, as a meaningful whole). While theory can be analytically *distinguished* from philosophy, it is disastrous to *separate* these two activities. Thus one can have theories of political and social change, types of regime, the circulation of elites, voting behavior, and political development, for example, but if they are separated from the concerns that have perennially preoccupied political philosophy, their meaning will appear distorted or prove barren and irrelevant. For the intellectuality of theory must be leavened with the poetic vision of philosophy.

The six master philosopher-theorists of the modern period (Machiavelli, Hobbes, Locke, Rousseau, Hegel, and Marx) managed to combine in a remarkable way the passion of philosophy with the objectivity of theory. Each activity helps to complement the other and keep it in balance, for theory can tell philosophy where it is lost in its own enthusiasms, while philosophy is needed to remind theory that prose is not the only language of life.

Let us resolve to be worthy successors of those fallible but intrepid men who have engaged in the quest for political philosophy and theory. By following in their footsteps we shall no doubt complicate our lives. But through philosophy and theory we can escape being bound by the image of our social world produced by the conventional wisdom and find an alternative paradigm that may bring us new and needed understanding. From there to the reality of a world ruled by the *thought* of man—in all the richness of his being—is perhaps a smaller step than we might dare to hope.

INDEX

Alembert, Jean d', 152–54
Althusius, Johannes, 73
Anabaptists, 68
Anglicanism, 75
  See also Elizabethan settlement
Anthropocentric humanism. *See* Humanism, anthropocentric
Aquinas, Thomas:
  and fourfold division of law, 78–79
  on property, 131–32
  religious beliefs of, 80–81
Arendt, Hannah, 17
Aris, Reinhold, 303n
Avineri, Shlomo, 342n, 358–60, 366n, 371–72, 375, 376

Babeuf, Gracchus, 344
Bakunin, Mikhail, 345n, 352
Beccaria, Cesare, 158
Bell, Daniel, 358
Bentham, Jeremy, 158, 233–38
  compared with Burke, 220, 223
  compared with Hobbes, 237
  deficiencies of, as theorist, 237–38
  definition of community of, 234–35
  democratism of, 236–37
  egalitarianism of, 236–37
  as father of utilitarianism, 233
  individualism of, 234–36
  as liberal, 237–38
  life and times of, 234
  and Mill, 233, 236, 239, 240, 251
  on natural rights, 237
  and pleasure principle, 235–36
  as reformer, 234, 236–38
  on utility, 235–37
Bergson, Henri:
  on closed and open society, 212
  compared with Machiavelli, 53–54

compared with Mill, 248–49
compared with Rousseau, 212–13
Best regime. *See* Paradigm
Beza, Theodore, 73
Blackstone, W. T., 322n
Bockelson, Jan, 68, 69
Bodin, Jean, 57
  compared with Hobbes, 109, 111
Bonald, Louis de, 214, 229–30
Borghese, G. A., 44n
Brinton, Crane, 256
Brisbane, Albert, 346
Brown, Norman O., 61, 62, 285
Buchanan, George, 73
Burke, Edmund, 214–32
  compared with Hegel, 221
  conservatism of, 215–27
  on electoral reform, 220–21
  on innovation, 225–26
  on man as social animal, 218
  on mixed constitution, 219–20
  on "natural rights," 218
  on natural society, 221–22
  organic theory of society of, 223–24
  on representation, 221
  and role of reason, 215–19, 222–23
  on tradition, 216–17, 223, 225–26
Bury, J. B., 5, 166–67

Caird, J., 263–64
Calvin, John, 69–74
  on civil government, 72–74
  as founder of Reformed Church movement, 69
  on nationalism, 57
  on natural law, 71n
  theological views of, 69, 73–74
Calvinism, 56, 59, 72–74

PRINTED IN U.S.A.